D1476157

Capri
Owners
Workshop
Manual

by J H Haynes
Associate Member of the Guild of Motoring Writers
and B L Chalmers-Hunt
TEng (CEI), AMIMI, AMIRTE, AMVBRA

Models covered
Capri 2600 Coupe. V6 155 cu in (2550cc)
Capri 2800 Coupe. V6 171 cu in (2792cc)

ISBN 0 85696 205 8

Printed in England *(205-7M2)*

ABCDE
FGHIJ
KLM

THE BOOK

AUTOMOTIVE PARTS & ACCESSORIES ASSOCIATION MEMBER

Haynes Publishing Group
Sparkford Nr Yeovil
Somerset BA22 7JJ England

Haynes Publications, Inc
861 Lawrence Drive
Newbury Park
California 91320 USA

Introduction to this manual

Its aim

This is a manual for the 'do-it-yourself' owner of a Capri fitted with the V6 engine. It shows how to maintain these cars in first class condition and how to carry out repairs when components become worn or broken. By doing maintenance and repair work themselves owners will gain in three ways: they will know the job has been done properly; they will have had the satisfaction of doing the job themselves; and they will have saved some garage labour charges. Regular and careful maintenance is essential if maximum reliability and minimum wear are to be achieved.

All the major mechanical and electrical assemblies and most of the minor ones as well, have been investigated and dealt with in this manual. Only through thorough investigation can solutions be found for the sort of problems facing private owners. Other hints and tips are also given which have been obtained through practical experience.

The step-by-step instructions given in the text and supported with many illustrations should make all the work quite clear - even to the novice who has never previously attempted the more complex job.

Manufacturer's official manuals are usually splendid publications which contain a wealth of technical information. Because they are issued primarily to help authorised dealers they tend to be written in a technical language, and skip details of certain jobs which are common knowledge to garage mechanics. This workshop manual is different in that it is intended primarily to help the owner and therefore contains details of all sorts of jobs not normally found in official manuals.

Owners who intend to do their own maintenance and repairs should have a reasonably comprehensive tool kit. Some jobs require special service tools, but in many instances it is possible to get round their use with a little care and ingenuity.

A further function of this manual is to show the owner how to examine malfunctioning parts; determine what is wrong; and then how to make the repair.

Given the time, mechanical do-it-yourself aptitude, and a reasonable collection of tools, this manual will show the enthusiastic owner how to maintain and repair his car really economically with minimum recourse to professional assistance and expensive tools and equipment.

Using the manual

The book is divided into thirteen Chapters. Each Chapter is divided into numbered Sections which are headed in **bold type** between horizontal lines. Each Section consists of serially numbered paragraphs.

There are two types of illustration: (1) Figures which are numbered according to Chapter and sequence of occurrence in that Chapter. (2) Photographs which have a reference number on their caption. All photographs apply to the Chapter in which they occur so that the reference figure pinpoints the pertinent Section and paragraph number.

Procedures once described in the text, are not normally repeated. If it is necessary to refer to another Chapter the reference will be given in Chapter number and Section number thus: Chapter 1/16.

If it is considered necessary to refer to a particular paragraph in another Chapter the reference is given in this form: 1/5:5'. Cross-references given without use of the word 'Chapter' apply to Sections and/or paragraphs in the same Chapter (eg; 'see Section 8') means also 'in this Chapter'.

When the left or right side of the car is mentioned it is as if looking forward from the rear of the car.

Great effort has been made to ensure that this book is complete and up-to-date. The manufacturers continually modify their cars, even in retrospect.

Whilst every care is taken to ensure that the information in this manual is correct no liability can be accepted by the authors or publishers for loss, damage or injury caused by any errors in, or omissions from, the information given.

1973 Capri V6

Contents

Buying spare parts and vehicle identification numbers

Buying spare parts

Spare parts are available from many sources for example: Ford (Mercury) dealers, other dealers and accessory stores, and motor factors. Our advice regarding spare part sources is as follows:

Officially appointed Ford (Mercury) dealers - This is the best source of parts which are peculiar to your car and are otherwise not generally available (eg complete cylinder heads, internal gearbox components, badges, interior trim etc). It is also the only place at which you should buy parts if your car is still under warranty - non-Ford (Mercury) components may invalidate the warranty. To be sure of obtaining the correct parts it will always be necessary to give the storeman your car's vehicle identification number, and if possible, to take the 'old' part along for positive identification. Remember that many parts are available on a factory exchange scheme - any parts returned should always be clean! It obviously makes good sense to go straight to the specialists on your car for this type of part for they are best equipped to supply you.

Other dealers and accessory stores - These are often very good places to buy materials and components needed for the maintenance of your car (eg; oil filters, spark plugs, bulbs, fan belts, oils and greases, touch-up paint, filler paste etc). They also sell general accessories, usually have convenient opening hours, charge lower prices and can often be found not far from home.

Motor factors - Good factors will stock all of the more important components which wear out relatively quickly (eg; clutch components, pistons, valves, exhaust systems, brake cylinders/pipes/hoses/seals/shoes and pads etc). Motor factors will often provide new or reconditioned components on a part exchange basis - this can save a considerable amount of money.

Vehicle identification numbers

Although many individual parts, and in some cases sub-assemblies, fit a number of different models it is dangerous to assume that just because they look the same, they are the same. Differences are not always easy to detect except by serial numbers. Make sure therefore, that the appropriate identity number for the model or sub-assembly is known and quoted when a spare part is ordered.

The illustration below shows the *Vehicle Identification Plate* which will be found in the engine compartment, on top of the inner fender panel.

When buying a replacement part from a Ford (Mercury) dealer, decide which category that part fits into (eg; engine, trim, paint etc). Then record the relevant number from the vehicle identification plate. Quote this number and the vehicle number to the storeman; he will then be able to provide you with the correct part for your individual vehicle.

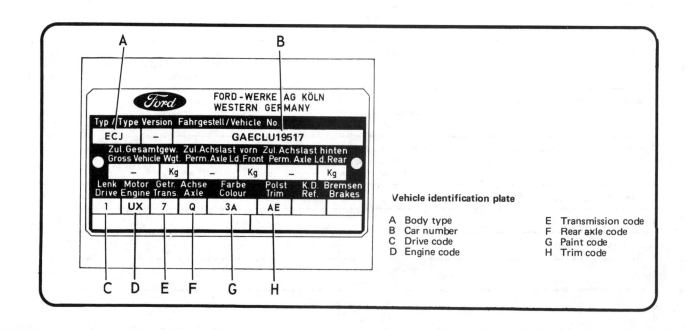

Vehicle identification plate

A Body type
B Car number
C Drive code
D Engine code
E Transmission code
F Rear axle code
G Paint code
H Trim code

As this book has been written in England, it uses the appropriate English component names, phrases, and spelling. Some of these differ from those used in America. Normally, these cause no difficulty, but to make sure, a glossary is printed below. In ordering spare parts remember the parts list will probably use these words:

Glossary

English	American	English	American
Accelerator	Gas pedal	Layshaft (of gearbox)	Counter shaft
Alternator	Generator (AC)	Leading shoe (of brake)	Primary shoe
Anti-roll bar	Stabiliser or sway bar	Locks	Latches
Choke/venturi	Barrel	Motorway	Freeway, turnpike etc.
Battery	Energizer	Number plate	Licence plate
Bonnet (engine cover)	Hood	Paraffin	Kerosene
Boot lid	Trunk lid	Petrol	Gasoline
Boot (luggage compartment)	Trunk	Petrol tank	Gas tank
Bottom gear	1st gear	'Pinking'	'Pinging'
Bulkhead	Firewall	Quarter light	Quarter window
Camfollower or tappet	Valve lifter or tappet	Retread	Recap
Carburettor	Carburetor	Reverse	Back-up
Catch	Latch	Rocker cover	Valve cover
Circlip	Snap ring	Roof rack	Car-top carrier
Clearance	Lash	Saloon	Sedan
Crownwheel	Ring gear (of differential)	Seized	Frozen
Disc (brake)	Rotor/disk	Side indicator lights	Side marker lights
Driveshaft	Propellor shaft	Side light	Parking light
Drop arm	Pitman arm	Silencer	Muffler
Drop head coupe	Convertible	Spanner	Wrench
Dynamo	Generator (DC)	Sill panel (beneath doors)	Rocker panel
Earth (electrical)	Ground	Split cotter (for valve spring cap)	Lock (for valve spring retainer)
Engineer's blue	Prussion blue	Split pin	Cotter pin
Estate car	Station wagon	Steering arm	Spindle arm
Exhaust manifold	Header	Sump	Oil pan
Fast back (Coupe)	Hard top	Tab washer	Tang; lock
Fault finding/diagnosis	Trouble shooting	Tailgate	Liftgate
Float chamber	Float bowl	Tappet	Valve lifter
Free-play	Lash	Thrust bearing	Throw-out bearing
Freewheel	Coast	Top gear	High
Gudgeon pin	Piston pin or wrist pin	Trackrod (of steering)	Tie-rod (or connecting rod)
Gearchange	Shift	Trailing shoe (of brake)	Secondary shoe
Gearbox	Transmission	Transmission	Whole drive line
Halfshaft	Axle-shaft	Tyre	Tire
Handbrake	Parking brake	Van	Panel wagon/van
Hood	Soft top	Vice	Vise
Hot spot	Heat riser	Wheel nut	Lug nut
Indicator	Turn signal	Windscreen	Windshield
Interior light	Dome lamp	Wing/mudguard	Fender

Miscellaneous points

An "Oil seal" is fitted to components lubricated by grease!

A "Damper" is a "Shock absorber" it damps out bouncing, and absorbs shocks of bump impact. Both names are correct, and both are used haphazardly.

Note that British drum brakes are different from the Bendix type that is common in America, so different descriptive names result. The shoe end furthest from the hydraulic wheel cylinder is on a pivot; interconnection between the shoes as on Bendix brakes is most uncommon. Therefore the phrase "Primary" or "Secondary" shoe does not apply. A shoe is said to be Leading or Trailing. A "Leading" shoe is one on which a point on the drum, as it rotates forward, reaches the shoe at the end worked by the hydraulic cylinder before the anchor end. The opposite is a trailing shoe, and this one has no self servo from the wrapping effect of the rotating drum.

Routine maintenance

The Routine Maintenance instructions listed are basically those recommended by the manufacturer. They are supplemented by additional maintenance tasks proven to be necessary.

It must be emphasised that if any part of the engine or its ancillary equipment involved with emission control is disturbed, cleaned or adjusted, the car must be taken to the local Capri dealer for checking.

Weekly, before a long journey, or every 250 miles (400 Km)

1 Remove the dipstick and check the engine oil level which should be up to the 'MAX' mark. Top up the oil with Castrol GTX. On no account allow the oil to fall below the 'MIN' mark on the dipstick.
2 Check the tyre pressures with an accurate gauge and adjust as necessary. As a safety precaution make sure that the tyre walls and treads are free from damage.
3 Check the battery electrolyte level and top up as necessary with distilled water. Make sure that the top of the battery is always kept clean and free from moisture.
4 Refill the windscreen washer bottle with soft water. Add a special anti-freeze satchet or methylated spirits in cold weather to prevent freezing (do not use ordinary anti-freeze). Check that the jets operate correctly.
5 Check all wheel nuts for tightness but take care not to overtighten.

Every 3000 miles (5000 Km) or 3 months

The following maintenance items must be carried out at this mileage/time interval if the car is being operated in severe conditions. These are considered to be:—
a) Outside temperature remains below 10°F (−12.2°C) for 60 days or more and most trips are less than 10 miles.
b) If a trailer having a total weight of more than 2000 lb. is towed over long distances.
c) Extended periods of idling or low speed operation.
For normal car operation these service items may be carried out at 6,000 mile (10,000 Km) or 6 month intervals.
Complete the service items in the weekly service check plus:
1 Check the level of coolant in the engine cooling system when cold. Remove the radiator pressure cap and check the level of coolant which should be 0.5 inch below the filler orifice. Over-filling will merely result in wastage. In very cold weather an anti-freeze solution must be used.
2 Run the engine until it is hot and then place a container under the engine sump drain plug. Unscrew and remove the drain plug and allow the oil to drain out for 10 minutes. Whilst this is being done change the oil filter as described in the next service operation. Clean the oil filler cap in petrol and shake dry. Refill

the engine with Castrol GTX and clean off any oil which may have been accidentally spilt over the engine or its components. Run the engine and check the oil level.
3 To renew the oil filter, unscrew the oil filter canister and discard it. Wipe the area around the filter location in the side of the cylinder block. Smear a little engine oil in the rubber 'O' ring located on the face of the new oil filter canister and screw on until it is hand-tight. Do not overtighten.
4 Remove the spark plugs, inspect and clean them as described in Chapter 4.

Every 6,000 miles (10,000 Km) or 6 months

Complete the service items in the 3000 mile service check plus:
1 Refer to Chapter 3 and renew the air cleaner element.
2 Refer to Chapter 5 and check the clutch pedal free play.
3 Manual gearbox: Wipe the area around combined filler and level plug. Undo and remove the plug and check the oil level which, when correct should be up to the bottom of the threaded hole, top up if necessary with Castrol Hypoy Light.
4 Automatic transmission only: Refer to Chapter 6 and check the transmission fluid level.
5 Wipe the area around the rear axle combined filler and level plug. Undo and remove the plug and check the oil level which, when correct, should be up to the bottom of the threaded hole. Top up if necessary with Castrol Hypoy.
6 Wipe the top of the brake master cylinder reservoir, unscrew the cap and top up with Castrol Girling Brake Fluid as necessary. Take care not to spill any hydraulic fluid on the paintwork as it acts as a solvent.
7 First 6,000 miles only: Check the tightness of the exhaust manifold securing bolts.
8 The fan belt adjustment must be tight enough to drive the alternator without overloading the bearings, including the water pump bearings. The method of adjusting the fan belt is described in Chapter 2. It is considered to be correct when it can be pressed in 0.5 inch (13 mm) at the mid point of its longest run.
9 Refer to Chapter 10 and check the battery electrolyte specific gravity.
10 Wipe the top of the battery free from dust and moisture. Clean off any corrosion round the battery terminals and clamps and lightly smear such areas with a trace of petroleum jelly such as vaseline. Check earth connection is firm.
11 Generally inspect radiator and heater hoses for signs of perishing and, if evident, fit new hoses. Check tightness of the hose clips.
12 Lubricate the accelerator pedal pivot and linkage with a little Castrol GTX.
13 Generally check the engine for signs of oil and water leaks and rectify as necessary.

14 Refer to Chapter 9 and check the thickness of the front disc brake pads and rear drum brake shoe linings. Make sure that the adjusting mechanism is functioning correctly. Remove traces of dust from each brake unit.

15 Generally check all brake lines and flexible hoses for signs of leaks. Also inspect the calipers and wheel cylinders for signs of leaks. Rectify as necessary.

16 Inspect the exhaust system for signs of blowing or excessive rusting. Replace defective components as necessary.

17 Check the operation of all controls, lights and instruments and rectify any fault found.

18 Lubricate all door locks, lock cylinders, bonnet safety catch pivot, door strikers, door check straps, hinges and all other oil can points.

19 Refer to Chapter 9 and check the handbrake adjustment. Lubricate the handbrake linkage.

20 Check the seat belts for signs of wear and the fixing points for security.

21 Check tightness of the rear spring 'U' bolts.

22 Refer to Chapter 6 and check the adjustment of the automatic transmission linkages and cables.

THE FOLLOWING SERVICE ITEMS SHOULD BE CHECKED BY THE LOCAL CAPRI DEALER.

23 Check correct function of the Decel valve.
24 Check correct operation of the carburettor and emission control system.

Every 12,000 miles (20,000 Km) or 12 months

Complete the service items in the 6,000 mile service check plus:

1 Refer to Chapter 3 and fit a new fuel line filter. Check all fuel lines for leakage and unions for tightness.

2 Check the seat belts for security of anchorages and the webbing for wear or damage.

3 Lubricate the clutch control cable and pedal pivots.

4 Inspect the steering and suspension linkages for signs of wear. Rectify as necessary.

5 Generally inspect all brake lines for rusting and hoses for deterioration. Rectify as necessary.

6 Spring back the two clips and remove the distributor cap. Lift off the rotor arm. Apply a smear of grease to the cam surface. Remove any excess oil or grease with a clean rag. Apply a few drops of oil through the hole in the contact breaker base plate to lubricate the automatic timing control.

7 Wipe the distributor cap, top of the coil and HT leads with a

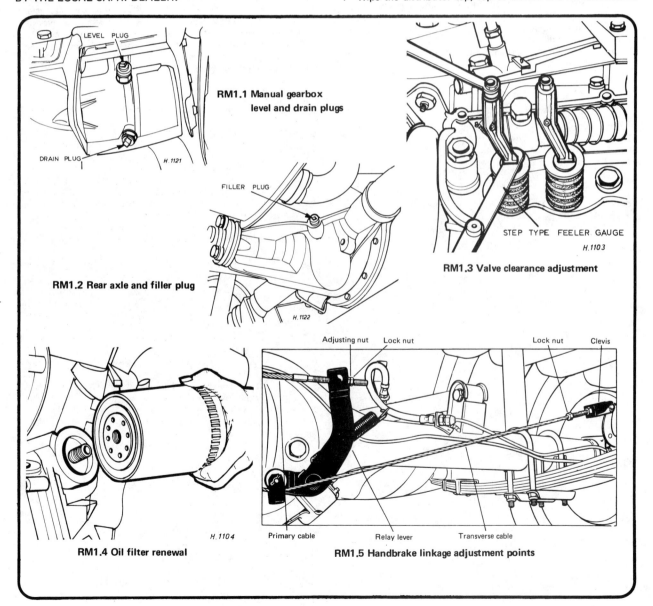

RM1.1 Manual gearbox level and drain plugs

LEVEL PLUG
DRAIN PLUG
H.1121

RM1.2 Rear axle and filler plug

FILLER PLUG
H.1122

RM1.3 Valve clearance adjustment

STEP TYPE FEELER GAUGE
H.1103

RM1.4 Oil filter renewal

H.1104

RM1.5 Handbrake linkage adjustment points

Adjusting nut   Lock nut   Lock nut   Clevis
Primary cable   Relay lever   Transverse cable

clean rag to remove traces of dust or oil. Check for signs of damage, tracking or deterioration of the HT leads.

8　Check the valve clearances and adjust if necessary as described in Chapter 1.

9　Fit new spark plugs as described in Chapter 4.

10　Fit new contact breaker points as described in Chapter 4.

11　Wash the bodywork and chromium fittings and clean out the interior of the car. Wax polish the bodywork including all chromium and bright metal trim. Force wax polish into any joints in the bodywork to prevent rust formation.

12　If it is wished change over the tyres to equalise wear. Balance the front wheels to eliminate any vibration, especially from the steering.

13　Lubricate the washer around the wiper spindles with several drops of glycerine. Fit new windscreen wiper blades.

14　Steam clean the underside of the body and clean the engine compartment and gearbox exterior as well as the whole of the front compartment.

THE FOLLOWING SERVICE ITEMS SHOULD BE CHECKED BY THE LOCAL CAPRI DEALER.

15　Check secondary ignition wire resistances.

16　Check correct operation of ignition control system advance/retard and vacuum cut in. Also check operation of thermal switch in air cleaner.

17　Check and adjust ignition timing.

18　Test ignition coil output.

19　Carry out an exhaust gas analysis. Also a full test on the fuel emission system.

Every 24,000 miles (40,000 Km) or 2 years

Complete the service items in the 12,000 mile service check plus:

1　Fit a new emission control canister and purge hose. For full information see Chapter 3.

2　Fit a new distributor cap, rotor arm and condenser.

3　Drain and completely flush out the cooling system as described in Chapter 2.

4　Examine the hub bearings for wear and replace as necessary. Full information will be found in Chapter 11.

5　Remove the starter motor, examine the brushes and replace as necessary. Clean the commutator and starter drive as described in Chapter 10.

6　Test the cylinder compressions, and if necessary remove the cylinder heads, decarbonise, grind in the valves and fit new valve springs. Full information will be found in Chapter 1.

Every 36,000 miles (65,000 Km) or 3 years

Completely drain the brake hydraulic fluid from the system. All seals and flexible hoses throughout the braking system should be examined and preferably renewed. The working surfaces of the master cylinder, wheel and caliper cylinders should be inspected for signs of wear or scoring and new parts fitted as considered necessary. Refill the hydraulic system with Castrol Girling Brake Fluid.

Recommended lubricants and fluids

COMPONENT	TYPE OF LUBRICANT OR FLUID	CASTROL PRODUCT
ENGINE	Multigrade engine oil	Castrol GTX
GEARBOX	SAE 80 E.P.	Castrol Hypoy Light
REAR AXLE	SAE 90 E.P.	Castrol Hypoy
STEERING GEAR	SAE 90 E.P.	Castrol Hypoy
FRONT WHEEL BEARINGS	Medium grade multi-purpose grease ...	Castrol LM Grease
DISTRIBUTOR, STARTER & GENERATOR BUSHES	Engine or light oil	Castrol GTX
DISTRIBUTOR CONTACT BREAKER CAM & BATTERY	Petroleum jelly	
HYDRAULIC PISTONS	Rubber grease	Castrol Rubber Grease
BRAKE MASTER CYLINDER FLUID RESERVOIR	Hydraulic fluid	Castrol Girling Universal Brake and Clutch Fluid
AUTOMATIC GEARBOX	Automatic-transmission fluid	Castrol TQF

Additional Castrol 'Everyman' oil can be used to lubricate door, boot and bonnet hinges, locks and pivots etc.

LUBRICATION CHART

CASTROL GTX
An ultra high performance motor oil approved for use in the engine in summer and winter.

CASTROL HYPOY LIGHT GEAR OIL
A powerful, extreme pressure lubricant recommended for the transmission and steering gear.

CASTROL HYPOY GEAR OIL
A powerful, extreme-pressure gear oil essential for the lubrication of the hypoid rear axle.

CASTROL LM GREASE
Recommended for the wheel bearings. May also be used for chassis lubrication.

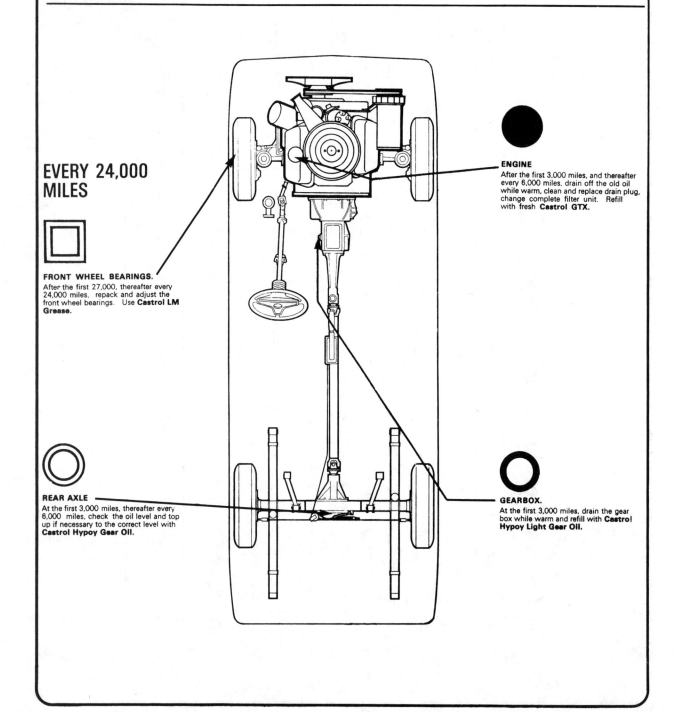

EVERY 24,000 MILES

FRONT WHEEL BEARINGS.
After the first 27,000, thereafter every 24,000 miles, repack and adjust the front wheel bearings. Use **Castrol LM Grease.**

ENGINE
After the first 3,000 miles, and thereafter every 6,000 miles, drain off the old oil while warm, clean and replace drain plug, change complete filter unit. Refill with fresh **Castrol GTX.**

REAR AXLE
At the first 3,000 miles, thereafter every 6,000 miles, check the oil level and top up if necessary to the correct level with **Castrol Hypoy Gear Oil.**

GEARBOX.
At the first 3,000 miles, drain the gear box while warm and refill with **Castrol Hypoy Light Gear Oil.**

Chapter 1 Engine

Contents

Specifications

Type	6 cylinder 60° V pushrod operated OHV	
Compression ratio	8.2 : 1	
Bore	3.545 in	(90.043 mm)
Stroke	2.630 in	(66.802 mm)
Capacity	155 cu in 2550 cc	
Oil pressure (hot)	40 - 55 lb/in^2	(2.82 - 3.87 kg/cm^2)
Firing order	1 4 2 5 3 6	

Cylinder block

Cylinder bore diameter (standard) Class 1	3.543 in	(89.9922 mm)
2	3.544 in	(90.0176 mm)
3	3.545 in	(90.043 mm)
4	3.546 in	(90.0684 mm)
Cylinder bore diameter (oversize) 0.020 service	3.564 in	(90.5256 mm)
0.040 service	3.584 in	(91.0336 mm)
Main bearing bore diameter Red	2.386 in	(60.6044 mm)
Blue	2.387 in	(60.6298 mm)
Thrust bearing width	0.890 - 0.892 in	(22.606 - 22.6568 mm)
Vertical inside diameter of fitted main bearing inserts standard:		
Red	2.2454 to 2.2548 in	(56.990 to 57.000 mm)
Blue	2.2450 to 2.2454 in	(56.980 to 56.990 mm)

Undersize:

0.010	...	...	...	...	...	...	...	2.235 in	(56.769 mm)
0.020	...	...	...	...	...	...	...	2.225 in	(56.515 mm)
0.030	...	...	...	...	...	...	...	2.215 in	(56.261 mm)
0.040	...	...	...	...	...	...	...	2.205 in	(56.007 mm)

Bores in cylinder block for camshaft bearings:

Front	...	...	...	...	...	...	...	1.773 in	(45.720 mm)
No. 2	...	...	...	...	...	...	...	1.758 in	(44.6532 mm)
No. 3	...	...	...	...	...	...	...	1.743 in	(44.2722 mm)
Rear	...	...	...	...	...	...	...	1.728 in	(43.8912 mm)

Crankshaft

Main bearing journal diameter: Standard

Red	...	...	...	...	...	...	...	2.244 in	(56.9976 mm)
Blue	...	...	...	...	...	...	...	2.243 in	(56.9722 mm)

Oversize:

0.010	...	...	...	...	...	...	...	2.234 in	(56.7436 mm)
0.020	...	...	...	...	...	...	...	2.224 in	(56.4896 mm)
0.030	...	...	...	...	...	...	...	2.214 in	(56.2356 mm)
0.040	...	...	...	...	...	...	...	2.204 in	(55.9816 mm)

Main journal to bearing insert clearance:

Standard	...	...	...	...	...	...	...	0.0005 - 0.002 in	(0.0127 - 0.508 mm)
Undersize	...	...	...	...	...	..	...	0.0005 - 0.002 in	(0.0127 - 0.508 mm)

Thrust bearing width:

Bearing journal		...	...	...	...	...	...	1.039 in	(26.3906 mm)
Bearing insert		...	...	...	...	...	...	1.034 in	(26.2636 mm)
Crankshaft end play	...	...	...	...	...	...		0.004 - 0.008 in	(0.1016 - 0.2032 mm)

Connecting rod bearing journal diameter standard:

Red	...	...	...	...	...	...	...	2.126 in	(54.0004 mm)
Blue	...	...	...	...	...	...	...	2.125 in	(53.975 mm)

Undersize:

0.010	...	...	...	...	...	...	...	2.116 in	(53.7464 mm)
0.020	...	...	...	...	...	...	...	2.106 in	(53.4924 mm)
0.030	...	...	...	...	...	...	...	2.096 in	(53.2384 mm)
0.040	...	...	...	...	...	...	...	2.086 in	(52.9844 mm)

Connecting rods

Connecting rod bearing insert vertical diameter standard:

Red	...	...	...	...	...	...	...	2.127 in	(54.0258 mm)
Blue	...	...	...	...	...	...	...	2.126 in	(53.7718 mm)

Undersize:

0.010	...	...	...	...	...	...	...	2.117 in	(53.7718 mm)
0.020	...	...	...	...	...	...	...	2.107 in	(53.5178 mm)
0.030	...	...	...	...	...	...	...	2.097 in	(53.2638 mm)
0.040	...	...	...	...	...	...	...	2.087 in	(53.0098 mm)

Journal bearing insert clearance:

Standard	...	...	...	...	...	...	...	0.0005 - 0.002 in	(0.0127 - 0.0508 m)
Undersize	..	...	...	...	...	...	...	0.0005 - 0.0025 in	(0.0127 - 0.0635 m)

Pistons

Diameter:

Standard	...	...	...	...	...	...	...	3.542 in	(89.9668 mm)

Oversize:

0.020	...	...	...	...	...	...	...	3.562 in	(90.4748 mm)
0.040	...	...	...	...	...	...	...	3.582 in	(90.9828 mm)
Clearance	...	...	...	...	...	...	...	0.001 - 0.003 in	(0.0254 - 0.0762 m)

Piston rings

Ring gap (fitted):

Upper compression	...	...	...	...	...	...		0.015 - 0.023 in	(0.381 - 0.5842 mm)
Lower compression	...	...	...	...	...	...		0.015 - 0.023 in	(0.381 - 0.5842 mm)
Oil control	...	...	...	...	...	...	...	0.015 - 0.055 in	(0.381 - 1.397 mm)

Camshaft

Number of bearings	...	...	...	...	...	...		4	

Bearing diameter:

Front	...	...	...	...	...	...	...	1.650 in	(42.291 mm)
No. 2	...	...	...	...	...	...	...	1.635 in	(41.783 mm)
No. 3	...	...	...	...	...	..	...	1.620 in	(41.275 mm)
Rear	...	...	..	...	...	...	...	1.605 in	(40.767 mm)

Bush inside diameter:

Front	...	...	...	...	...	...	...	1.652 in	(41.9608 mm)
No. 2	...	...	...	...	...	...	...	1.637 in	(41.5798 mm)

No. 3	1.622 in	(41.1988 mm)
Rear	1.607 in	(40.8178 mm)
End play	0.001 - 0.004 in	(0.254 - 0.1016 mm)
Thrust plate thickness standard:		
Red	0.156 in	(3.9624 mm)
Blue	0.157 in	(3.9874 mm)
Oversize:		
Red	0.161 in	(4.0894 mm)
Blue	0.162 in	(4.1148 mm)
Cam lift	0.255 in	(6.477 mm)
Cam heel to toe dimension	1.338 - 1.346 in	(33.9852 - 34.1884 mm)
Camshaft bearings:		
Distance from front face of cylinder block to rear side of assembled bearing		
Tolerance	± 0.010 in	(0.254 mm)
Front	0.831 in	(21.1074 mm)
No. 2	6.559 in	(166.5986 mm)
No. 3	11.319 in	(287.5026 mm)
Rear	17.091 in	(434.1114 mm)

Cylinder head

Valve seat angle	45°	
Valve stem diameter (inlet)		
Standard	0.316 in	(8.0264 mm)
Oversize:		
0.008	0.325 in	(8.2296 mm)
0.016	0.332 in	(8.4328 mm)
0.024	0.340 in	(8.636 mm)
0.032	0.348 in	(8.8392 mm)
Valve stem diameter (exhaust)		
Standard	0.315 in	(8.001 mm)
Oversize:		
0.008	0.323 in	(8.2042 mm)
0.016	0.331 in	(8.4074 mm)
0.024	0.339 in	(8.6106 mm)
0.032 ... ... -	0.347 in	(8.8138 mm)
Valve stem bore diameter:		
Standard	**0.318 in**	**(8.0772 mm)**
Oversize:		
0.008	0.326 in	(8.2804 mm)
0.016	0.334 in	(8.4836 mm)
Valve lift	0.373 in	(8.4742 mm)
Valve clearance (cold)		
Inlet	0.014 in	(0.355 mm)
Exhaust	0.016 in	(0.406 mm)

Inlet valve timing:		
Opens	20° BTDC	
Closes	56° ABDC	
Exhaust valve timing		
Opens	62° BBDC	
Closes	74° ATDC	
Valve tappet diameter	0.874 in	(22.1996 mm)

Torque wrench settings:	lb f ft	kg fm
Support bracket to engine	40 - 45	5.55 - 6.20
Support bracket to insulator	17 - 27	2.34 - 3.70
Insulator to frame	17 - 27	2.34 - 3.70
Crossmember to frame bracket	10 - 13	1.38 - 1.79
Insulator to crossmember	12 - 15	1.65 - 2.06
Insulator to transmission bracket	13 - 16	1.79 - 2.21
Transmission bracket securing bolt:		
Manual	20 - 30	2.77 - 4.15
Automatic	37 - 42	5.11 - 5.80
Main bearing caps	65 - 75	8.95 - 10.2
Connecting rod bearing caps	22 - 26	3.04 - 3.5
Crankshaft gear	32 - 36	4.4 - 4.8
Camshaft gear	32 - 36	4.4 - 4.8
Crankshaft pulley	32 - 36	4.4 - 4.8
Flywheel	45 - 50	6.22 - 6.9
Front cover	12 - 15	1.65 - 2.06
Water pump	6 - 9	0.82 - 1.24

Oil pump	10 - 12	1.38 - 1.6
Rocker shaft supports	43 - 49	5.94 - 6.80
Oil sump (final)	5 - 8	0.7 - 1.11
Rocker arm covers (final)	2 - 5	0.27 - 0.69
Inlet manifold (final)	15 - 18	2.07 - 2.49
Cylinder head (final)	65 - 80	8.95 - 11.06
Temperature sender unit	8 - 12	1.11 - 1.6
Spark plugs	15 - 22	2.06 - 3.03
Vibration damper bolt	92 - 104	12.57 - 14.37

1 General description

The Capri model covered by this manual has the 2600 German built V6 engine with the cylinders arranged in a 60 degree formation. It is a four stroke petrol engine.

The cylinder bores are machined directly into the cast iron cylinder block. The cylinder block is cast integral with the crankcase and incorporates full length water jackets. There are four large diameter main bearings each having removable caps.

A cast iron crankshaft runs in the main bearings which are fitted with detachable steel backed copper lead bearing shells. The end float of the crankshaft is controlled by thrust washers fitted on either side of the front intermediate bearing.

Pressed in oil seals are incorporated in the front cover and rear oil seal carrier so as to prevent oil leaks from either the front or the rear of the crankshaft pulley hub. The rear oil seal in the carrier runs directly onto the crankshaft flange.

A gear on the end of the camshaft is in direct mesh with a second gear on the end of the crankshaft and is driven by the crankshaft at half engine speed. The camshaft runs in steel backed white metal bushes. Incorporated on the camshaft behind the front bearing journal is a skew gear and this drives the oil pump and distributor. Forward of the camshaft gear and retained by the gear bolt is an eccentric which operates the mechanical lift fuel pump mounted onto the side of the front cover.

The valves are mounted overhead and are operated by a system of rockers, pushrods and tappets from the camshaft that is placed in the valley between the two banks of cylinders. The inlet valves are of a larger diameter than those of the exhaust valves to improve engine breathing. The rocker arms are mounted on a rocker shaft located on the top of each cylinder head. The valve springs are of an unusual form with close coils at one end with the close coil fitted adjacent to the cylinder head.

The connecting rods are H section forgings and the big ends are located by hollow dowels and secured with two bolts. Similar to the crankshaft main bearing the big end bearings are steel backed and copper lead lined.

The little end, sometimes called the small end, is not bearing lined but is shrunk onto the piston pin to secure the latter in position.

Mounted onto the rear end of the crankshaft is a cast iron flywheel machined to accept the 9.5 in (241.3 mm) clutch.

A steel starter ring gear is shrunk onto the outer periphery of the flywheel and engages with the starter motor driver during engine starting conditions. If an automatic transmission is fitted, the ring gear is shrunk onto an inertia ring which is attached to the torque converter. The torque converter is driven via a drive plate to the rear crankshaft flange instead of the normal flywheel.

The engine oil sump is a steel pressing having a rear well. The drain plug is on the left hand side of the pressing.

The hexagonal drive shaft from the distributor drives the oil pump which may be either of the sliding vane or eccentric bi-rotor design. Incorporated into the design of either pump is an oil pressure relief valve. Oil under pressure is directed via a full flow oil filter to the main, big end, camshaft bearings and to the tappets. As the tappets are hollow they control the amount of oil through the hollow pushrods to the rocker arms and valves.

There is a drilling in the cylinder block front face which supplies oil to the timing gears.

The oil from the rocker arms drains from the cylinder head and into the tappet chamber so lubricating the cams and distributor drive gear as it returns to the oil sump at the base of the engine.

The cylinder bores are lubricated by one squirt of oil every crankshaft revolution emitting from a small drilling in each connecting rod web. The piston pins are continuously lubricated by oil mist created by internal engine activity and also on the downward strokes by oil scraped by the oil control rings from the cylinder bores.

Located on the right hand rocker cover top is the oil filler cap and this incorporates the positive crankcase ventilation system. Any crankcase fumes are discharged into the inlet manifold under the control of an emission valve located in the right hand rocker cover.

2 Major operations with engine in place

The following major operations may be carried out without taking the engine from the car:-
1 Removal and replacement of the cylinder heads.
2 Removal and replacement of the timing gear.
3 Removal and replacement of the front engine mountings.
4 Removal and replacement of the engine - gearbox rear mounting.

3 Major operations with engine removed

Although it would be possible to carry out some of the following operations with the engine in the car if the gearbox and clutch were removed, it is deemed inadvisable.
1 Removal and replacement of the flywheel.
2 Removal and replacement of the rear main bearing oil seal.
3 Removal and replacement of the sump.
4 Removal and replacement of the big end bearings.
5 Removal and replacement of the pistons and connecting rods.
6 Removal and replacement of the oil pump.

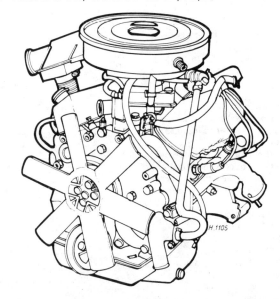

Fig. 1.1. Left hand view of engine

7 Removal and replacement of the crankshaft and crankshaft main bearings.

8 Removal and replacement of the camshaft and camshaft bushes.

4 Methods of engine removal

The engine may be lifted out together with the gearbox or separated from the gearbox and lifted out by itself. If the gearbox is left attached the disadvantage is that the engine has to be tilted to a very steep angle to get it out. Unless both the engine and gearbox are being repaired or overhauled together there is no other reason for removing them as a unit.

5 Engine removal without gearbox

1 This task takes about three hours. It is essential to have a good hoist. If an inspection pit is not available, two axle stands will also be required. In the later stages, when the engine is being separated from the gearbox and lifted, the assistance of another person is most useful.

2 Open the bonnet.

3 Place a container of suitable size under the radiator and one under the engine and drain the cooling system as described in Chapter 2. Do not drain the water in the garage or the place where the engine is to be removed if receptacles are not at hand to catch the water.

4 Place a container of 12 US pints/6 litres under the oil sump and remove the drain plug. Let the oil drain for 10 minutes and then refit the plug.

5 Place old blankets over the wings and across the cowl to prevent damage to the paintwork.

6 It is easier if two assistants are available so that the bonnet can be supported whilst the hinges are being released.

7 Using a pencil mark the outline of the hinges on the bonnet.

8 Undo and remove the four nuts and washers and bolt plates that secure the hinges to the bonnet.

9 Release the bonnet stay and carefully lift the bonnet up and over the front of the engine compartment.

10 Disconnect the battery, release the battery clamp and lift away from its tray.

11 Refer to Chapter 3 and remove the air cleaner and intake duct assembly.

12 Slacken the clips that secure the upper and lower radiator hoses and carefully remove the hoses.

13 Refer to Chapter 2 and remove the radiator and its shroud.

14 Detach the terminal connector at the rear of the alternator. Slacken the mounting bolts and push the alternator towards the engine. Lift away the fan belt. Remove the alternator mounting bolts and lift away the alternator.

15 Remove the alternator bracket securing bolts and spring washers and lift away the bracket and earth cable from the side of the cylinder block.

16 Slacken the heater hose clips at the cylinder block and water pump unions and detach the hoses.

17 Remove the engine earth cable securing bolt from the engine and move the earth cable to one side.

18 Disconnect the main fuel line from the inlet side of the fuel pump and plug the end of the line to prevent syphoning of petrol.

19 Detach the accelerator cable or linkage at the carburettor installation and inlet manifold. Further information will be found in Chapter 3.

20 When an automatic transmission is fitted, disconnect the downshift linkage.

21 Make a note of the cable connections to the ignition coil, water temperature sender unit and detach from the terminals. Also release the oil pressure gauge pressure pipe.

22 Detach the vacuum hose to the brake servo unit from the inlet manifold.

23 Undo and remove the nuts that secure each exhaust down pipe to the exhaust manifolds, release the clamp plates and move the downpipes to the sides of the engine compartment.

24 Chock the rear wheels, jack up the front of the car and support on firmly based axle stands. To give better access, remove the front wheels.

25 Make a note of the cable connections to the starter motor. Detach the cables from the starter motor terminals.

26 Undo and remove the bolts and spring washers that secure the starter motor to the engine. Lift away the starter motor.

27 Undo and remove the engine front mounting through bolts at the cylinder block.

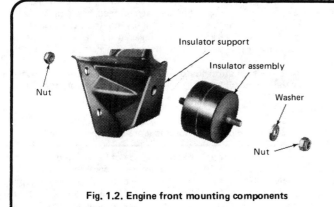

Fig. 1.2. Engine front mounting components

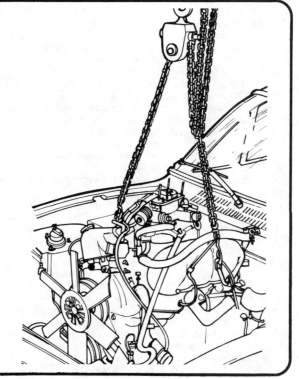

Fig. 1.3. Engine removal (less gearbox)

Automatic Transmission

28 Undo and remove the bolts and spring washers that secure the converter inspection cover to the housing. Lift away the inspection cover.

29 Undo and remove the bolts that secure the torque converter to the flywheel/adaptor plate. It will be necessary to rotate the crankshaft using a large spanner on the crankshaft pulley securing bolt.

30 Undo and remove the converter housing to engine block securing bolts and spring washers.

31 Detach the downshift rod from its bracket.

Manual Transmission

32 Pull back the clutch release arm rubber boot . Slacken the locknut and adjustment nut. Detach the inner cable from the release arm and withdraw the cable assembly.

33 Undo and remove the bolts and spring washers securing the bell housing to the engines.

All Models

34 Refit the wheel and lower the front of the car.

35 Wrap rope slings around the exhaust manifolds or if chains are to be used, mount brackets on the exhaust manifold and then attach the chain hooks to the brackets. Take up the slack.

36 Place a jack under the transmission unit to support its weight.

37 Check that all cables and controls have been detached and safely tucked out of the way.

38 Raise the engine slightly and then draw it forwards. When automatic transmission is fitted make sure that the torque converter remains attached to the transmission unit.

39 Continue lifting the engine taking care that the backplate does not foul the bodywork.

40 With the engine away from the engine compartment lower to the ground or bench and suitably support so that it does not roll over.

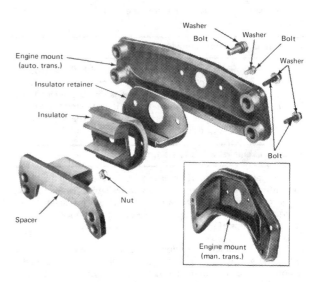

Fig. 1.4. Engine rear mounting components

---

6   Engine removal with manual gearbox attached

1   Proceed exactly as described in Section 5 up to and including paragraph 19, then 21 to 27 inclusive and finally paragraphs 32 and 33.

2   Unscrew the gearbox drain plug and allow the oil to drain away for five minutes. Replace the drain plug.

3   Working under the car detach the three remote control selector rods from the side of the gearbox. See Chapter 6.

4   Support the weight of the gearbox using a small jack located adjacent to the drain plug.

5   Undo and remove the centre bolt which locates the gearbox extension housing into the support member. Then making sure the gearbox support jack is firmly in position, undo and remove the four bolts and washers that secure the crossmember to the underside of the body. Lift away the crossmember.

6   With the crossmember removed it is now an easy task to disconnect the speedometer cable from the gearbox by removing the circlip and withdrawing the cable.

7   Detach the reverse light cable connector at its snap connector.

8   Wrap rope slings around the exhaust manifolds or if chains are to be used, mount brackets on the exhaust manifold and then attach the chain hooks to the brackets. Take up the slack.

9   Check that all cable and controls have been detached and safely tucked out of the way.

10 With the jack under the gearbox still in position start lifting and at the same time, once the front mountings have been cleared, move the engine forward until the propeller shaft drops on the ground but support it until clear, and then lower it and rest it on a suitable block so as not to strain the centre bearing.

11 Due to the fact that the gearbox is attached, the engine will have to be lifted out at a much steeper angle than for removing the engine on its own. As the weight is more towards the rear, it will be fairly easy to achieve the necessary angle.

12 Continue to raise the engine and move it forwards at the

necessary angle. At this stage the forward edge of the bellhousing is likely to catch against the front crossmember and the tail of the gearbox will need raising until the whole unit is forward and clear of it.

13 Finally the whole unit will rise clear and if the maximum height of the lifting tackle has been reached, it will be necessary to swing the unit so that the tail can be lifted clear whilst the hoist is moved away or the car lowered from its axle stands and pushed from under the unit. (It will be necessary to tie up the propeller shaft front end).

14 The whole unit should be lowered to the ground (or bench) as soon as possible and the gearbox may then be separated from the engine.

---

7   Engine removal with automatic transmission attached

It is recommended that the engine not be removed whilst still attached to the automatic transmission, because of the weight involved. If it is necessary to remove both units refer to Chapter 6, Section 11 (C4) or Section 19 (BW 35) and remove the transmission unit first. Then remove the engine as described in Section 5 but disregarding information on detachment from the transmission unit.

---

8   Engine dismantling - general

1   Ideally, the engine is mounted on a proper stand for overhaul but it is anticipated that most owners will have a strong bench on which to place it. If a sufficiently large strong bench is not available then the work can be done at ground level. It is essential, however, that some form of substantial wooden surface is available. Timber should be at least ¾ inch thick, otherwise the weight of the engine will cause projections to punch holes straight through it.

2 It will save a great deal of time later if the engine is thoroughly cleaned down on the exterior before any dismantling begins. This can be done by using paraffin and a stiff brush or more easily, by the use of a proprietary solvent which can be brushed on and then the dirt swilled off with a water jet. This will dispose of all the heavy muck and grit once and for all so that later cleaning of individual components will be a relatively clean process and the paraffin bath will not become contaminated with abrasive material.

3 As the engine is stripped down, clean each part as it comes off. Try to avoid immersing parts with oilways in paraffin as pockets of liquid could remain and cause oil dilution in the critical first few revolutions after reassembly. Clean oilways with pipe cleaners, or, preferably, an air jet.

4 Where possible avoid damaging gaskets on removal, especially if new ones have not been obtained. They can be used as patterns if new ones have to be specially cut.

5 It is helpful to obtain a few blocks of wood to support the engine whilst it is in the process of dismantling. Start dismantling at the top of the engine and then turn the block over and deal with the sump and crankshaft etc., afterwards.

6 Nuts and bolts should be replaced in their locations where possible to avoid confusion later. As an alternative keep each group of nuts and bolts (all the timing gear cover bolts for example) together in a jar or tin.

7 Many items dismantled must be replaced in the same position, if they are not being renewed. These include valves, rocker arms, tapets, pistons, pushrods, bearings and connecting rods.

Some of these are marked on assembly to avoid any possibility of mixing them up during overhaul. Others are not, and it is a great help if adequate preparation is made in advance to classify these parts. Suitably labelled tins or jars and, for small items, egg trays, tobacco tins and so on, can be used. The time spent in this preparation will be amply repaid later.

9 Engine ancillaries - removal

1 Before beginning a complete overhaul or if the engine is being exchanged for a works reconditioned unit the following items should be removed:-

Fuel system components:
Carburettor
Inlet and Exhaust manifolds
Fuel pump
Fuel lines

Ignition system components:
Spark plugs
Distributor
Coil

Electrical system components(if not removed already):
Alternator and mounting brackets
Starter motor

Cooling system components:
Fan and fan pulley
Water pump, Thermostat housing and thermostat
Water temperature sender unit

Engine:
Crankcase ventilation tube
Oil filter element
Oil pressure sender unit (if fitted)
Oil level dipstick
Oil filler cap
Engine mounting brackets

Clutch:
Clutch pressure plate and total assembly
Clutch friction plate and total assembly

Some of these items have to be removed for individual servicing or renewal periodically and details can be found under the appropriate Chapter.

10 Cylinder heads - removal with engine in car

1 For safety reasons disconnect the battery earth cable.
2 Remove the air cleaner from the carburettor installation as described in Chapter 3.
3 Disconnect the accelerator linkage from the carburettor.
4 Refer to Chapter 2 and drain the cooling system.
5 Detach the HT leads from the spark plugs, release the distributor cap securing clips and remove the distributor cap.
6 Slacken the clips and disconnect the hose from the water pump to the water outlet.
7 Detach the vacuum pipe from the distributor body and carburettor installation.
8 Refer to Chapter 3 and remove the carburettor and inlet manifold assembly. This will necessitate removal of the distributor.

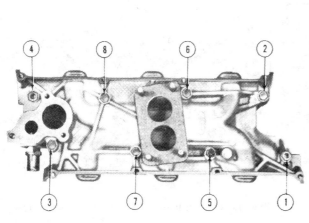

Fig. 1.5. Inlet manifold securing bolts slackening or tightening sequence

Notch downward for both banks

Fig. 1.6. Removal of rocker arm assembly

9 Remove the two rocker covers by undoing and removing the securing screws and lifting away together with their respective gaskets.

10 Undo and remove the three bolts and washers that secure each rocker shaft assembly to the top of each cylinder head. This must be done in a progressive manner. When the bolts are free lift away the rocker shaft assembly and oil baffles. Note to which each rocker shaft assembly was fitted.

11 With the rocker shaft assemblies away remove the pushrods and note the location from whence they came and also which way up. Keep them in order and the right way up by pushing them through a piece of stiff paper or cardboard with the valve numbers marked.

12 Detach the exhaust downpipes from the exhaust manifold and move the downpipes to the sides of the engine compartment. Leave the manifolds in place as they will act as a lever to assist removal of the heads.

13 Taking each cylinder head in turn, slacken the eight holding down bolts in the order shown. When all are free of tension remove all the bolts.

14 On occasions the heads may have stuck to the head gasket and cylinder block in which case if pulling up on the exhaust manifolds does not free them they should be struck smartly with a soft faced hammer in order to break the joints. Do NOT try to prise them off with a blade of any description or damage will be caused to the faces of the head or block or both.

15 Lift the heads off carefully. Note which side each head comes from as they are identical and it is essential to replace them on the same bank of cylinders. Place them where they cannot be damaged. Undo the bolts holding the exhaust manifold to each head if not previously removed.

16 Remove the cylinder head gaskets. New ones will be required for reassembly.

11 Cylinder heads - removal with engine out

Follow the sequence given in Section 10, paragraphs 5 to 16 inclusive, disregarding information on parts mentioned that have been previously removed.

12 Cylinder heads - dismantling of valves and springs

1 Lay the cylinder head on its side and using a proper valve spring compression place the 'U' shaped end over the spring retainer and screw on the valve head so as to compress the spring.

2 Sometimes the retainer will stick in which case the end of the compressor over the spring should be tapped with a hammer to release the retainer from the locks (collets).

3 As the spring is compressed two tapered locks will be exposed and should be taken from the recess in the retainer.

4 When the compressor is released the spring may be removed from the valve. Lift off the retainer, spring and oil seal. Withdraw the valve from the cylinder head. Note that the springs are fitted with the close coils towards the cylinder head.

5 It is essential that the valves, springs, retainers, locks and seals are all kept in order so that they may be refitted in their original positions.

13 Valve rocker shaft assembly - dismantling

1 With the rocker shaft assembly on the bench tap out the pin at each end of the rocker shaft using a suitable diameter parallel pin punch.

2 Withdraw the spring washer, rocker arm, support, rocker arm spring and subsequent parts in order. Keep all parts in that order so that they may be refitted in their original positions.

14 Tappet - removal

1 The tappets may now be removed from the cylinder block by pushing them up from the camshaft (which can be revolved if necessary to raise the tappets) and lifting them out.

2 If necessary the pushrod bearing caps in each tappet can be taken out by first extracting the retaining circlip.

3 Make sure that all the tappets are kept in order so that they may be replaced in the location they came from.

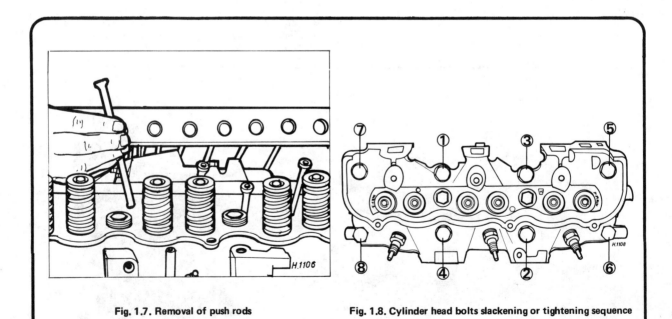

Fig. 1.7. Removal of push rods   Fig. 1.8. Cylinder head bolts slackening or tightening sequence

15 Crankshaft pulley wheel - removal

1 Remove the bolt and washer locating the pulley to the front of the crankshaft. The pulley is keyed to the crankshaft and must be drawn off with a proper sprocket puller. Attempts to lever it off with long bladed articles such as screwdrivers or tyre levers are not suitable in this case because the timing cover behind the pulley is a light and relatively fragile casting. Any pressure against it could certainly crack it and possibly break a hole in it.

2 The pulley may be removed with the engine in the car but it may be necessary to remove the radiator, depending on the type of pulley extractor used and the clearance it allows.

3 Recover the Woodruff key from the crankshaft nose.

16 Flywheel - removal

1 Remove the clutch assembly as described in Chapter 5, Section 3.

2 The flywheel is held in position to the crankshaft by six bolts. One of these bolts is spaced unevenly so that the flywheel will only fit one position.

3 Remove the six bolts, taking care to support the weight of the flywheel as they are slackened off in case it slips off the flange. Secure it carefully, taking care not to damage the mating surfaces on the crankshaft and flywheel.

17 Sump - removal

1 With the engine out of the car, first invert the engine and then remove the bolts which hold the sump in place.

2 The sump may be stuck quite firmly to the engine if sealing compound has been used on the gasket. It is in order to lever it off in this case. The gasket should be removed and discarded in

any case.

3 It is possible to remove the sump with the engine in the car. First withdraw the oil level dipstick.

4 Remove the bolts that secure the fan shroud to the radiator. Place the shroud over the fan.

5 Detach the battery earth cable.

6 Slacken the alternator mounting bolts and remove the fan belt.

7 Chock the rear wheels, jack up the front of the car and support on firmly based stands.

8 Drain the sump after placing a container of 12.009 US pints/5.682 litres under the drain plug and removing the plug. Allow to drain for five minutes and refit the plug.

9 Note the electrical cable connections to the starter motor and detach from their terminals.

10 Undo and remove the starter motor securing bolts and spring washers. Lift away the starter motor.

11 Undo and remove the bolts and spring washers that secure the splash shield.

12 Support the engine using an overhead hoist or crane and then undo and remove the engine front support nuts.

13 Raise the engine and place some wood blocks between the engine front supports and chassis brackets.

14 Undo and remove the bolts and spring washers that secure the clutch or converter housing cover. Lift away the cover.

15 Undo and remove the oil sump retaining bolts and lift away the oil sump. If stuck, refer to paragraph 2. Remove the sump gasket.

18 Front cover - removal

1 With the engine out of the car, remove the sump and crankshaft pulley wheel.

2 Undo and remove the water pump retaining bolts and lift the water pump from the front cover. It may be necessary to tap it

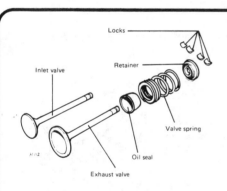

Fig. 1.9. Inlet and exhaust valve components

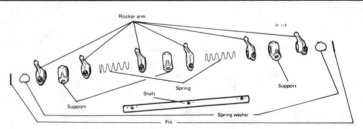

Fig. 1.10. Rocker arm and shaft assembly

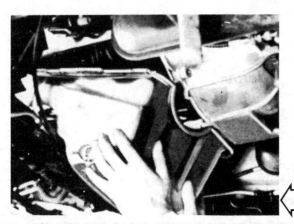

Fig. 1.11. Removal of sump (engine in car)

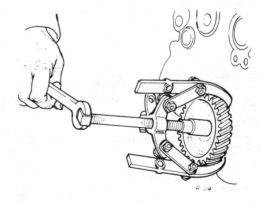

Fig. 1.12. Using universal puller to remove crankshaft timing gear

with a soft faced hammer if a jointing compound has been used.
3 Undo and remove the front cover securing bolts and lift away. If stuck, carry out the instructions in paragraph 2. Remove the front cover gasket.
4 If the engine is still in the car it will be necessary to remove the front sump bolts which run through the timing cover. It will also be necessary to remove the fan belt, crankshaft pulley wheel and fuel pump.

19 Timing gears - removal

1 Undo and remove the bolt and washer that secures the timing gear to the camshaft.
2 To remove the gear lightly tap it at the rear so releasing it from the camshaft. Lift away the gear and then the Woodruff key.
3 To remove the crankshaft gear use a universal puller and draw it from the end of the crankshaft. This is only necessary when the gear is to be renewed.
4 Recover the Woodruff key.

20 Camshaft - removal

1 The camshaft can be removed with the engine in the car. (Should camshaft renewal be necessary it will probably be necessary to overhaul other parts of the engine too. If this is the case engine removal should be considered).
2 Refer to Chapter 2 and remove the radiator.
3 Detach the spark plug leads from the spark plugs, release the cap securing clips and place the cap to one side.
4 Detach the distributor vacuum line and then remove the distributor as described in Chapter 4.
5 Remove the alternator as described in Chapter 10.
6 Undo and remove the screws that secure each rocker cover to

the cylinder heads. Lift away the rocker covers and gaskets.
7 Refer to Chapter 3 and remove the inlet manifold and carburettor installation.
8 Undo and remove the three bolts and washers that secure each rocker shaft assembly to the cylinder heads. This should be done in a progressive manner to avoid straining the shaft. Lift away each rocker shaft assembly noting from which head each was fitted.
9 Remove the pushrods and note the location from where they came and also which way up. Keep them in order and the right way up by pushing them through a piece of stiff paper with valve numbers marked.
10 Refer to Section 17 and remove the sump.
11 Refer to Section 18 and remove the front cover.
12 Refer to Section 19 and remove the camshaft timing gear.
13 Undo and remove the two screws which secure the camshaft thrust plate to the cylinder block face. Lift away the plate and spacer.
14 Using a magnet recover the tappets from the Vee in the cylinder block. Keep in order as they must be refitted in their original positions.
15 If any tappets cannot be removed, retain in their maximum height positions with clothes pegs.
16 The camshaft may now be drawn forwards through the cylinder block. Take care that the sharp edges of the cams do not damage the bearings.

21 Oil pump - removal

1 Refer to Section 17 and remove the sump.
2 Undo and remove the two bolts that secure the pump to the crankcase. Lift away the pump and recover the gasket.
3 The long hexagonal section drive shaft will come out with the pump. This is driven by the distributor shaft.

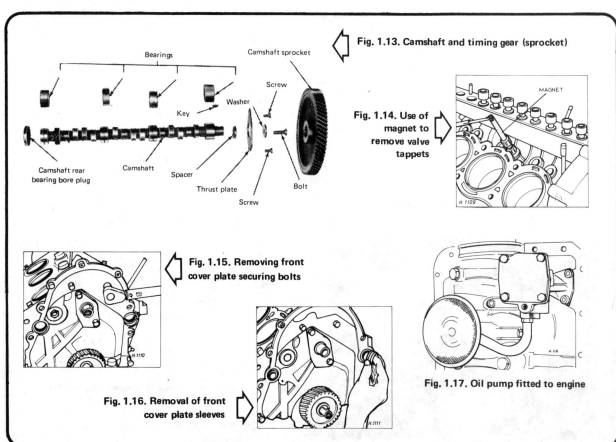

Fig. 1.13. Camshaft and timing gear (sprocket)

Fig. 1.14. Use of magnet to remove valve tappets

Fig. 1.15. Removing front cover plate securing bolts

Fig. 1.16. Removal of front cover plate sleeves

Fig. 1.17. Oil pump fitted to engine

22 Pistons, connecting rods and big end bearings - removal

1 Pistons and connecting rods may be removed with the engine in the car, provided the sump and cylinder heads are first removed. The bearing shells may be removed with the heads on.

2 Slacken the two nuts holding each bearing cap to the connecting rod. Use a good quality socket spanner for this work. A ring spanner may be used for removal only - not replacement which calls for a special torque spanner. Having slackened the nuts two or three turns tap the caps to dislodge them from the connecting rods. Completely remove the nuts and lift away the end caps.

3 Each bearing cap normally has the cylinder number etched on one end as does the connecting rod. However, this must be verified and if in doubt the cap should be marked with a dab of paint or punch mark to ensure that its relationship with the connecting rod is not altered.

4 The piston and connecting rod may then be pushed out of the top of each cylinder.

5 The big end bearing shells can be removed from the connecting rod and cap by sliding them round in the direction of the notch at the end of the shell and lifting them out. If they are not being renewed it is vital they are not interchanged - either between pistons or between cap and connecting rod.

23 Piston rings - removal

1 Remove the pistons from the engine.

2 The rings come off over the top of the piston. Starting with the top one, lift one end of the ring out of the groove and gradually ease it out all the way round. With the second and third rings an old feeler blade is useful for sliding them over the other grooves. However, as rings are only normally removed if they are going to be renewed it should not matter if breakages occur.

24 Gudgeon pin - removal

The gudgeon pins need removing if the pistons are being renewed. New pistons are supplied with new pins for fitting to the existing connecting rods. The gudgeon pin is semi-floating - that is it is a tight shrink fit with the connecting rod and a moving fit in the piston. To press it out requires considerable force and under usual circumstances a proper press and special tools are essential. Otherwise piston damage will occur. If damage to the pistons does not matter, then the pins may be pressed out using suitable diameter pieces of rod and tube between the jaws of a vice. However, this is not recommended as the connecting rod might be damaged also. It is recommended that gudgeon pins and pistons are removed from, and refitted to, connecting rods, by Capri dealers with the necessary facilities.

25 Crankshaft rear oil seal - removal

It is possible to remove the crankshaft rear oil seal with the engine in or out of the car. Where the engine is being completely removed, refer to Section 26 and remove the crankshaft. The seal can then be drawn from the end of the crankshaft. With the engine in the car proceed as follows:

1 Refer to Chapter 6 and remove the transmission.

2 Manual gearbox: Refer to Chapter 5 and remove the clutch assembly.

3 Refer to Section 16 and remove the flywheel.

4 Undo and remove the bolts and spring washers that secure the flywheel housing and rear plate where fitted.

5 Using an awl make two holes in the crankshaft rear oil seal. Punch holes on opposite sides of the crankshaft and just above the rear bearing cap to cylinder block split line.

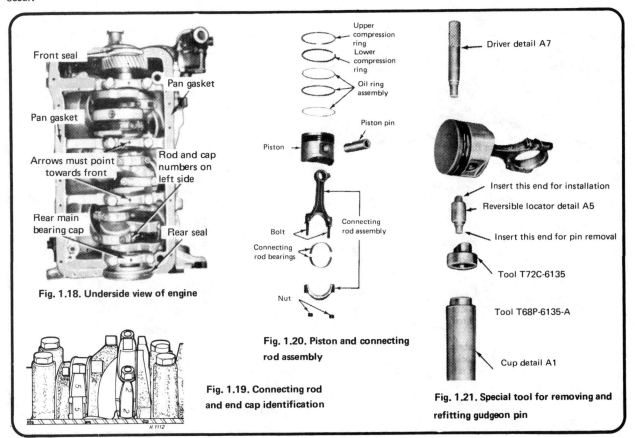

Fig. 1.18. Underside view of engine

Fig. 1.19. Connecting rod and end cap identification

Fig. 1.20. Piston and connecting rod assembly

Fig. 1.21. Special tool for removing and refitting gudgeon pin

6 Screw two long self tapping screws into the two holes and with pliers pull or lever out the oil seal. If tight it may be necessary to place small blocks of wood against the cylinder block to provide a fulcrum for the pliers when levering out.

7 Take extreme caution not to scratch the crankshaft oil seal surface.

26 Main bearings and crankshaft - removal

1 The engine should be taken from the car and the sump, cylinder heads, timing gears and pistons removed.

2 With a good quality socket spanner undo the eight bolts holding the four main bearing caps.

3 When all the bolts are removed lift out the caps. If they should be tight, tap the sides gently with a piece of wood or soft mallet to dislodge them.

4 Lift out the crankshaft.

5 Slide out the bearing shells from the caps and from the crankcase seats. Also take away the thrust washers on each side of the centre main bearing. The half which is on each side of the centre bearing cap is fitted with a tang to prevent rotation.

27 Lubrication and crankcase ventilation system - description

1 A general description of the oil circulation system is given in Section 1 of this Chapter.

2 The oil pump is of the eccentric bi-rotor type.

3 The oil is drawn through a gauze screen and tube which is below the oil level in the well of the sump. It is then pumped via the full flow oil filter to the system of oil galleries in the block as previously described. The oil filter cartridge is mounted externally on the left hand side of the block.

4 The crankcase is positively ventilated. Air enters through the oil filler cap in the left-hand rocker cover which is fitted with a washable gauze filter. Air enters directly under the rim of the cap or as in the closed system, the cap is connected to the carburettor air filter by a pipe so that filtration of the air is by existing air filter.

5 Air passes through the pushrod and oil drain channels in the tappet chamber and up the right-hand bank of the block to the right-hand rocker cover. The right-hand rocker cover is fitted with an outlet connected by a pipe to the engine intake manifold. A tapered valve in the rocker cover outlet controls the outlet of fumes so that when manifold depression is high the valve closes partially, thus reducing the flow proportionally.

28 Oil filter - removal and replacement

The oil filter is a complete throwaway cartridge screwed into the left-hand side of the engine block. Simply unscrew the old unit, clean the seating on the block, and screw the new one in, taking care not to cross the thread. Continue until the sealing ring just touches the block face. Then tighten one half turn. Always run the engine and check for signs of leaks after installation.

29 Engine components - examination for wear

When the engine has been stripped down and all parts properly cleaned decisions have to be made as to what needs renewal and the following sections tell the examiner what to look for. In any border line case it is always best to decide in favour of a new part. Even if a part may still be serviceable its life will have been reduced by wear and the degree of trouble needed to replace it in the future must be taken into consideration. However, these things are relative and it depends on whether a quick 'survival' job is being done or whether the car as a whole is being regarded as having many thousands of miles of useful and economical life remaining.

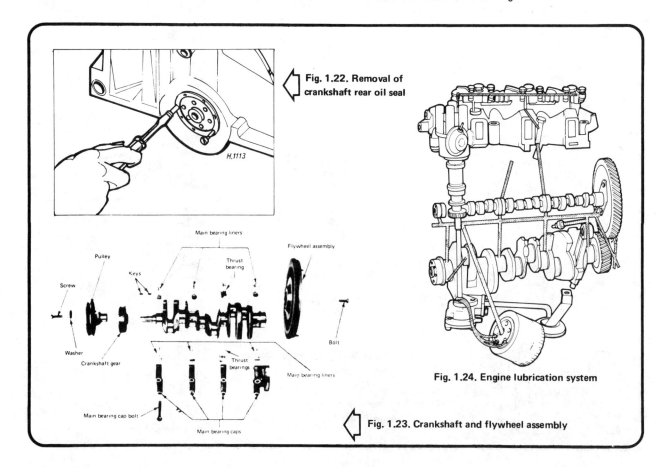

Fig. 1.22. Removal of crankshaft rear oil seal

H.1113

Fig. 1.24. Engine lubrication system

Main bearing liners

Pulley

Thrust bearing

Flywheel assembly

Keys

Screw

Washer

Crankshaft gear

Thrust bearings

Bolt

Main bearing liners

Main bearing cap bolt

Main bearing caps

Fig. 1.23. Crankshaft and flywheel assembly

30 Crankshaft - examination and renovation

1 Look at the three main bearing journals and the four crankpins and if there are any scratches or score marks then the shaft will need regrinding. Such conditions will nearly always be accompanied by similar deterioration in the matching bearing shells.

2 Each bearing journal should also be round and can be checked with a micrometer or calliper gauge around the periphery at several points. If there is more than 0.001 in (0.0254 mm) of ovality regrinding is necessary.

3 A main Capri agent or motor engineering specialist will be able to decide to what extent regrinding is necessary and also supply the special under-size shell bearings to match whatever may need grinding off the journals.

4 Before taking the crankshaft for regrinding check also the cylinder bores and pistons as it may be more convenient to have the engineering operations performed at the same time by the same engineer.

31 Crankshaft (main) bearings and big end (connecting rod) bearings - examination and renovation

1 With careful servicing and regular oil and filter changes bearings will last for a very long time but they can still fail for unforseen reasons. With big end bearings the indications are regular rhythmic loud knocking from the crankcase, the frequency depending on engine speed. It is particularly noticeable when the engine is under load. This symptom is accompanied by a fall in oil pressure although this is not normally noticeable unless an oil pressure gauge is fitted. Main bearing failure is usually indicated by serious vibration, particularly at higher engine revolutions, accompanied by a more significant drop in oil pressure and a 'rumbling' noise.

2 Bearing shells in good condition have bearing surfaces with a smooth, even, matt silver/grey colour all over. Worn bearings will show patches of a different colour where the bearing metal has worn away and exposed the underlay. Damaged bearings will be pitted or scored. It is nearly always well worthwhile fitting new shells as their cost is relatively low. If the crankshaft is in good condition it is merely a question of obtaining another set of standard size. A reground crankshaft will need new bearing shells as a matter of course.

32 Cylinder bores - examination and renovation

1 A new cylinder is perfectly round and the walls parallel throughout its length. The action of the piston tends to wear the walls at right angles to the gudgeon pin due to side thrust. This wear takes place principally on that section of the cylinder swept by the piston rings.

2 It is possible to get an indication of bore wear by removing the cylinder heads with the engine still in the car. With the piston down in the bore first signs of wear can be seen and felt just below the top of the bore where the top piston ring reaches and there will be a noticeable lip. If there is no lip it is fairly reasonable to expect that bore wear is low and any lack of compression or excessive oil consumption is due to worn or broken piston rings or pistons (see next section).

3 If it is possible to obtain a bore measuring micrometer measure the bore in the thrust plane below the lip and again at the bottom of the cylinder in the same plane. If the difference is more than 0.003 inch (0.0762 mm)/then a rebore is necessary. Similarly, a difference of 0.003 inch (0.0762 mm) or more across the bore diameter is a sign of ovality calling for a rebore.

4 Any bore which is significantly scratched or scored will need reboring. This symptom usually indicates that the piston or rings are damaged in that cylinder. In the event of only one cylinder being in need of reboring it will still be necessary for all four to be bored and fitted with new oversize pistons and rings.

Your Capri dealer or local engineering specialist will be able to rebore and obtain the necessary matched pistons. If the crankshaft is undergoing regrinding it is a good idea to let the same firm renovate and reassemble the crankshaft and pistons to the block. A reputable firm normally gives a guarantee for such work. In cases where engines have been rebored already to their maximum, new cylinder liners are available which may be fitted. In such cases the same reboring processes have to be followed and the services of a specialist engineering firm are required.

33 Pistons and piston rings - examination and renovation

1 Worn pistons and rings can usually be diagnosed when the symptoms of excessive oil consumption and low compression occur and are sometimes, though not always, associated with worn cylinder bores. Compression testers that fit into the spark plug holes are available and these can indicate where low compression is occuring. Wear usually accelerates the more it is left so when the symptoms occur early action can possibly save the expense of a rebore.

2 Another symptom of piston wear is piston slap - a knocking noise from the crankcase not to be confused with big end bearing failure. It can be heard clearly at low engine speed when there is no load (idling for example) and the engine is cold, and is much less audible when the engine speed increases. Piston wear usually occurs in the skirt or lower end of the piston and is indicated by vertical streaks in the worn area which is always on the thrust side. It can also be seen where the skirt thickness is different.

3 Piston ring wear can be checked by first removing the rings from the pistons as described in Section 23. Then place the rings in the cylinder bores from the top, pushing them down about 1.5 inches (38.1 mm) with the head of a piston (from which the rings have been removed) so that they rest square in the cylinder. Then measure the gap at the ends of the ring with a feeler gauge. If it exceeds 0.023 inch (0.584 mm) for the two top compression rings, or 0.055 inch (1.397 mm) for the oil control ring then they need renewal.

4 The grooves in which the rings locate in the piston can also become enlarged in use. The clearance between ring and piston, in the groove, should not exceed 0.004 inch (0.1016 mm) for the top two compression rings and 0.003 inch (0.0762 mm) for the lower oil control ring.

5 However, it is rare that a piston is only worn in the ring grooves and the need to replace them for this fault alone is hardly ever encountered. Wherever pistons are renewed the weight of the four piston/connecting rod assemblies should be kept within the limit variation of 8 gms. to maintain engine balance.

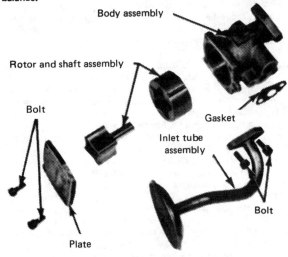

Fig. 1.25. Oil pump components

Body assembly

Rotor and shaft assembly

Bolt

Gasket

Inlet tube assembly

Bolt

Plate

34 Connecting rods and gudgeon pins - examination and renovation

1 Gudgeon pins are a shrink fit into the connecting rods. Neither of these would normally need replacement unless the pistons were being changed, in which case the new pistons would automatically be supplied with new gudgeon pins.
2 Connecting rods are not subject to wear but in extreme circumstances such as engine seizure they could be distorted. Such conditons may be visually apparent but where doubt exists they should be changed. The bearing caps should also be examined for indications of filing down which may have been attempted in the mistaken idea that bearing slackness could be remedied in this way. If there are such signs then the connecting rods should be renewed.

35 Camshaft and camshaft bearings - examination and renovation

1 The camshaft bearing bushes should be examined for signs of scoring and pitting. If they need renewal they will have to be dealt with professionally as although it may be relatively easy to remove the old bushes, the correct fitting of new ones requires special tools. If they are not fitted evenly and square from the very start they can be distorted thus causing localised wear in a very short time. See your Capri dealer or local engineering specialist for this work.
2 The camshaft itself may show signs of wear on the bearing journals, cam lobes or the skew gear. The main decision to take is what degree of wear justifies replacement, which is costly. Any signs of scoring or damage to the bearing journals must be rectified and as undersize bearing bushes are not supplied the journals cannot be reground. Renewal of the whole camshaft is the only solution. Similarly, excessive wear on the skew gear which can be seen where the distributor driveshaft teeth mesh will mean renewal of the whole camshaft.
3 The cam lobes themselves may show signs of ridging or pitting on the high points. If the ridging is light then it may be possible to smooth it out with fine emery. The cam lobes, however, are surface hardened and once this is penetrated wear will be very rapid thereafter. The cams are also offset and tapered to cause the tappets to rotate - thus ensuring that wear is even - so do not mistake this condition for wear.

36 Tappets - examination and renovation

1 The faces of the tappets which bear on the camshaft should show no signs of pitting, scoring or other forms of wear. They should also not be a loose fit in their housing. Wear is only normally encountered at very high mileages or in cases of neglected engine lubrication. Renew if necessary.

37 Valves and valve seats - examination and renovation

1 With the valves removed from the cylinder heads examine the heads for signs of cracking, burning away and pitting of the edge where it seats in the port. The seats of the valves in the cylinder head should also be examined for the same signs. Usually it is the valve that deteriorates first but if a bad valve is not rectified the seat will suffer and this is more difficult to repair.
2 The inlet valve heads are coated with diffused aluminium to increase their resistance to oxidisation and to give a hard wear resistant surface on the valve seat area. These valves should in no circumstances be ground as this will remove the aluminium coating. If the valves are worn or pitted they should be replaced with a new set. The inlet valve seats can however, be lapped with an old or dummy valve in the way as described below.
3 As far as the exhaust valves are concerned; provided there are no obvious signs of serious pitting the valve should be ground

with its seat. This may be done by placing a smear of carborundum paste on the edge of the valve and using a suction type valve holder grinding the valve in situ. This is done with a semi-rotary action, twisting the handle of the valve holder between the hands and lifting it occasionally to redistribute the paste. Use a coarse paste to start with and finish with a fine paste. As soon as a matt grey unbroken line appears on both the valve and the seat the valve is 'ground in'. All traces of carbon should also be cleaned from the head and the neck of the valve stem. A wire brush mounted in a power drill is a quick and effective way of doing this.
4 If an exhaust valve requires renewal it should be ground into the seat in the same way as an old valve.
5 Another form of valve wear can occur on the stem where it runs in the guide in the cylinder head. This can be detected by trying to rock the valve from side to side. If there is any movement at all it is an indication that the valve stem or guide is worn. Check the stem first with a micrometer at points all along and around its length and if they are not within the specified size new valves will probably solve the problem. If the guides are worn, however, they will need reboring for oversize valves or for fitting guide inserts. The valve seats will also need recutting to ensure they are concentric with the stems. This work should be given to your Capri dealer or local engineering works.
6 When valve seats are badly burnt or pitted, requiring replacement, inserts may be fitted - or replaced if already fitted once before - and once again this is a specialist task to be carried out by a suitable engineering firm.
7 When all valve grinding is completed it is essential that every trace of grinding paste is removed from the valves and ports in the cylinder head. This should be done with thorough washing in petrol or paraffin and blowing out with a jet of air. If particles of carborundum should work their way into the engine they would cause havoc with bearings or cylinder walls.

38 Timing gears - examination and renovation

Carefully inspect the gear teeth for signs of excessive wear which will cause noisy operation. When assembled to the engine the backlash must not exceed 0.004 in (0.1016 mm).

39 Flywheel ring gear - examination and renovation

1 If the ring gear is badly worn or has missing teeth it should be renewed. The old ring can be removed from the flywheel by cutting a notch between two teeth with a hacksaw and then splitting it with a cold chisel.
2 To fit a new ring gear requires heating the ring to 400°F (204°C). This can be done by polishing four equally spaced sections of the gear, laying it on a suitable heat resistant surface (such as fire bricks) and heating it evenly with a blow lamp or torch until the polished areas turn a light yellow tint. Do not overheat or the hard wearing properties will be lost. The gear has a chamfered inner edge which should go against the shoulder when put on the flywheel. When hot enough place the gear in position quickly, tapping it home if necessary and let it cool naturally without quenching in any way.

40 Oil pump - overhaul

1 The oil pump maintains a pressure of around 45 lbs in^2. An oil pressure gauge is fitted to give earlier warning of falling oil pressures due either to overheating, pump or bearing wear.
2 At a major engine overhaul it is as well to check the pump and exchange it for a reconditioned unit if necessary. The efficient operation of the oil pump depends on the finely machined tolerances between the moving parts of the rotor and the body and reconditioning of these is generally not within the competence of the non-specialist owner.
3 To dismantle the pump first remove it from the engine as

described in Section 21.

4 Remove the two bolts holding the end cover to the body and remove the cover and relief valve parts which will be released.

5 The necessary clearances may now be checked using a machined straight edge (a good steel rule) and a feeler gauge.

6 On bi-rotor type pumps the critical clearances are between the lobes of the centre rotor and convex faces of the outer rotor, between the outer rotor and the pump body, and between both rotors and the end cover plate.

7 The rotor lobe clearances may be checked as shown in Fig. 1.25. The clearances should not exceed 0.006 in (0.152 mm). The clearance between the outer rotor and pump body should not exceed 0.010 in (0.254 mm).

8 The endfloat clearance can be measured by placing a steel straight edge across the end of the pump and measuring the gap between the rotors and the straight edge. The gap on either rotor should not exceed 0.005 in (0.127 mm).

9 If the only excessive clearances are endfloat it is possible to reduce them by removing the rotors from the pump body and lapping away the face of the body on a flat bed until the necessary clearances are obtained. It must be emphasised, however, that the face of the body must remain perfectly flat and square to the axis of the rotor spindle otherwise the clearances will not be equal and the end cover will not be a pressure tight fit to the body. It is worth trying, of course, if the pump is in need of renewal any way but unless done properly it could seriously jeopardise the rest of an overhaul. Any variations in the other clearances should be overcome with an exchange unit.

10 When reassembling the pump and refitting the end cover make sure that the interior is scrupulously clean and that the pressure relief valve parts are assembled in the correct positions as indicated in the exploded drawings.

41 Cylinder heads and piston crowns - decarbonisation

1 When cylinder heads are removed either in the course of an overhaul or for inspection of bores or valve condition when the engine is in the car it is normal to remove all carbon deposits from the piston crowns and heads.

2 This is best done with a cup shaped wire brush and an electric drill and is fairly straightforward when the engine is dismantled and the pistons removed. Sometimes hard spots of carbon are not easily removed except by a scraper. When cleaning the pistons with a scraper take care not to damage the surface of the piston in any way.

3 When the engine is in the car certain precautions must be taken when decarbonising the piston crowns in order to prevent dislodged pieces of carbon falling into the interior of the engine which could cause damage to cylinder bores, pistons and rings - or if allowed into the water passages - damage to the water pump. Turn the engine, therefore, so that the piston being worked on is at the top of its stroke and then mask off the adjacent cylinder bore and all surrounding water jack orifices with paper and adhesive tape. Press grease into the gap all round the piston to keep carbon particles out and then scrape all carbon away by hand carefully. Do not use a power drill and wire brush when the engine is in the car as it will be virtually impossible to keep all the carbon dust clear of the engine. When completed carefully clear out the grease round the rim of the piston with a matchstick or something similar - bringing any carbon particles with it. Repeat the process on the other three piston crowns. It is not recommended that a ring of carbon is left round the edge of the piston on the theory that it will aid oil consumption. This was valid in the earlier days of long stroke low revving engines but modern engines, fuels and lubricants cause less carbon deposits any way and any left behind tends merely to cause hot-spots.

42 Rocker gear - examination and renovation

1 Check the shaft for straightness by rolling it on a flat surface.

It is most unlikely that it will deviate from normal, but if it does, then a judicious attempt may be made to straighten it. If this is not successful purchase a new shaft. The surface of the shaft should be free from any worn ridges caused by the rocker arms. If any wear is evident renew the rocker shaft. Wear is likely to have occurred only if the rocker shaft oil holes have become blocked.

2 Check the rocker arms for wear of the rocker bushes, for wear at the rocker arm face which bears on the valve stem, and for wear of the adjusting ball ended screws. Wear in the rocker arm bush can be checked by gripping the rocker arm tip and holding the rocker arm in place on the shaft, noting if there is any lateral rocker arm shake. If any shake is present, and the arm is loose on the shaft, remedial action must be taken. It is recommended that any worn rocker arm be taken to the local Capri dealer or automobile engineering works to have the old bush drawn out and a new bush fitted.

3 Check the tip of the rocker arm where it bears on the valve head, for cracking or serious wear on the case hardening. If none is present the rocker arm may be refitted. Check the pushrods for straightness by rolling them on a flat surface.

43 Engine reassembly - general

1 All components of the engine must be cleaned of oil sludge and old gaskets and the working area should also be clear and clean. In addition to the normal range of good quality socket spanners and general tools which are essential, the following must be available before reassembly begins:-
1) Complete set of new gaskets.
2) Supply of clean rags.
3) Clean oil can full of clean engine oil.
4) Torque spanner.
5) All new spare parts as necessary.

44 Engine reassembly - camshaft, crankshaft and oil pump

1 Insert the camshaft carefully into the block, taking care not to let any of the cam lobes damage the bearing bushes.

2 Refit the camshaft thrust plate and secure it with the two screws. These screws must be tightened firmly.

3 Select the halves of the four main bearing shells which have the oil hole and grooves and place them in position in the crankcase. The notches on the ends of the shells should locate in the cut-outs in the housings. It is essential that the two surfaces coming together are scrupulously clean.

4 Lubricate the bearings generously with clean engine oil.

5 Make sure that the crankshaft is scrupulously clean and lower it carefully into place on the bearings with the gearwheel towards the front of the engine.

6 Take the two halves of the thrust washers which do not have tags on and very carefully slide them into position round the side of the first intermediate main bearing. The grooves in the washers should face outwards from the bearing.

7 The end of the top half of the thrust washer can easily be pushed finally into position with a finger.

8 Fit the plain halves of the main bearing shells into the caps with the notches in the shells corresponding with the grooves in the caps.

9 The first intermediate bearing cap has machined recesses on each side to accept the lower halves of the thrust washers which have the tags on them to prevent rotation.

10 Hold the thrust washers in place while fitting the centre bearing cap and check that the grooves on the washer are facing away from the cap.

11 When the crankshaft and centre bearing cap is in position the endfloat may be checked by pushing the crankshaft as far as it will go in either direction and checking the gap between the thrust washer and the crankshaft web with a feeler gauge. The gap should be between 0.003 and 0.011 in (0.08 to 0.28 mm).

12 The front and rear main bearing caps do not automatically

line up for bolting down and it may be necessary to tap them with a hammer handle or other soft weight to enable the bolts to pick up the threads.

13 Make sure that the bolts are clean, and tighten them all down evenly to a torque of 65 to 75 lb ft. (8.95 - 10.2 kg.m) with a torque spanner.

14 Although not absolutely necessary it is best to renew the rear crankshaft oil seal - it is provided in the gasket set anyhow.

15 Place the new seal squarely in position with the open lip facing away from the shoulder in the bore. The seal can be tapped home squarely with a soft metal drift.

16 It is important to make sure that the seal is driven in square from the very start, otherwise it will buckle; so if one side tends to go in too far to start with pull it out and start afresh until it is squarely and firmly 'started' all round.

17 Lubricate the crankshaft flange well so that the seal will not run on a dry surface to start with and heat up.

18 Make sure the hexagonal drive shaft is located in the oil pump and replace the pump, tighten the two mounting bolts evenly to 10 -12 lb.ft. (1.38 - 1.6 kg.m) torque.

45 Engine reassembly - pistons, piston rings, connecting rods, big end bearings, end plates, timing gear and front cover

1 The subsequent paragraphs on assembly assume that all the checks described in Section 33 and 34 have been carried out. Also the engine has been partially assembled as described in Section 44.

2 The assembly of new pistons to connecting rods should have been carried out as recommended in Section 34. The new pistons should be supplied with rings already fitted.

3 If new rings are being fitted to existing pistons the following procedure should be followed. Having removed the old rings make sure that each ring groove in the piston is completely cleaned of carbon deposits. This is done most easily by breaking one of the old rings and using the sharp end as a scraper. Be careful not to remove any metal from the groove by mistake!

4 The new piston rings - three for each piston - must first be checked in the cylinder bores as described in Section 33. It is assumed that the gap at the ends could meet when normal operating temperatures are reached and the rings would then break.

5 The minimum gap for all three rings is 0.015 in (0.38 mm). If the gap is too small, one end of the ring must be filed to increase the gap. To do this the ring should be gripped in a vice between two thin pieces of soft metal in such a way that only the end to be filed is gripped and so that it only protrudes above the jaws of the vice a very small distance. This will eliminate the possibility of bending and breaking the ring while filing the end. Use a thin, fine file and proceed in easy stages - checking the gap by replacing the ring in the bore until the necessary minimum gap is obtained. This must be done with every ring - checking each one in the bore to which it will eventually be fitted. To avoid mistakes it is best to complete one set of rings at a time and replace the piston in the cylinder bore proceeding to the next.

6 To replace the rings on to the pistons calls for patience and care if breakages are to be avoided. The three rings for each piston must all be fitted over the crown so obviously the first one to go on is the slotted oil control ring. Hold the ring over the top of the piston and spread the ends just enough to get it around the circumference. Then, with the fingers, ease it down, keeping it parallel to the ring grooves by 'walking' the ring ends alternately down the piston. Being wider than the compression rings no difficulty should be encountered in getting it over the first two grooves in the piston.

7 The lower compression ring, which goes on next, must only be fitted one way up. It is marked 'TOP' to indicate its upper face.

8 Start fitting this ring by spreading the ends to get it located over the top of the piston.

9 The lower compression ring has to be guided over the top ring groove and this can be done by using a suitably cut piece of

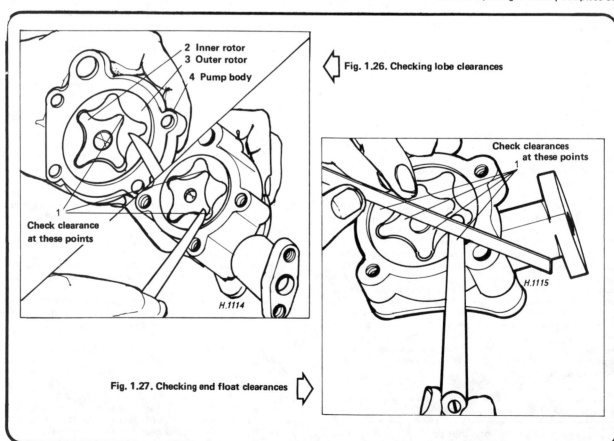

Fig. 1.26. Checking lobe clearances

Fig. 1.27. Checking end float clearances

2 Inner rotor
3 Outer rotor
4 Pump body

Check clearance at these points

H.1114

Check clearances at these points

H.1115

tin which can be placed so as to cover the top groove under the ends of the ring.

10 Alternatively, a feeler blade may be slid around under the ring to guide it into its groove.

11 The top ring may be fitted either way up as it is barrel faced.

12 With the rings fitted the piston/connecting rod assembly is ready for replacement in the cylinder.

13 Each connecting rod and bearing cap should have been marked on removal but in any case the cylinder number is etched lightly on the end of the cap and connecting rod alongside. The piston and connecting rod are also marked to show which side faces the front of the engine.

14 Start with No. 1 cylinder and remove the existing oil 'glaze' from the bore by rubbing it down with very fine emery. This will break down the hardened skin and permit the new piston rings to bed down more quickly.

15 Fit a new shell bearing half into the connecting rod of No. 1 piston so that the notch in the bearing shell locates in the groove in the connecting rod.

16 Push the piston into the cylinder bore (the correct way round) until the oil control ring abuts the face of the block. Then, using a piston ring compressor, contract the piston rings

and tap the piston into the cylinder. Take great care to be sure that a ring is not trapped on the top edge of the cylinder bore and when tapping the piston in do not use any force. If this is not done the rings could easily be broken.

17 When the piston has been fully located in the bore push it down so that the end of the connecting rod seats on the journal on the crankshaft. Make sure the journal is well lubricated with engine oil.

18 Maintaining absolute cleanliness all the time fit the other shell bearing half into the cap, once again with the notches in the bearing and cap lined up. Lubricate it with engine oil and fit it onto the connecting rod so that the holes in the cap fit to the dowels in the connecting rod.

19 Replace all pistons and connecting rods in a similar manner and do not make any mistakes locating the correct Number piston in the correct bore. Numbers 1, 2 and 3 cylinders are on the right hand bank and numbers 4, 5 and 6 on the left hand bank starting from the front of the engine. However, due to the Vee formation of the engine the big end journals on the crankshaft starting at the front run 1,4,2,5,3,6. Make sure you have it all clear in your mind to start with!

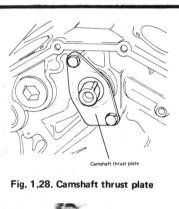

Fig. 1.28. Camshaft thrust plate

Fig. 1.29. Alignment of thrust bearing

Apply sealer to these surfaces

Fig. 1.30. Application of sealer to rear main bearing cap

Wedge seals

Fig. 1.31. Fitting rear main bearing cap wedge seals

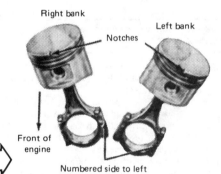

Fig. 1.32. Correct piston and connecting rod location

Fig. 1.34. Using a wood rod to refit piston

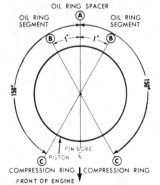

Fig. 1.33. Spacing of piston ring gaps

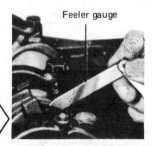

Feeler gauge

Fig. 1.35. Using a feeler gauge to check connecting rod side clearance

20 When all caps are correctly fitted tighten down the bolts to the correct torque of 22 -26 lb ft (3.04 - 3.5 kg m).

21 The timing gears are easily fitted but care must be taken to ensure that the marks line up properly. The camshaft and crankshaft gears are keyed to their respective shafts. The timing marks are in the form of a single dimple on one tooth of each gearwheel.

22 Before replacing the camshaft timing gear the front engine plate must be replaced. Select the new gasket and coat the clean face of the block with suitable sealing compound (Hermetite, Wellseal) and stick the gasket to it in position. Then offer up the cover plate.

23 Bolt the cover plate up tight to the block, not forgetting to fit the support plate behind the three centre bolts.

24 Fit the camshaft and crankshaft gears so that the timing marks line up. Replace the camshaft gear locking bolt and washer. Tighten the bolt to 32 - 36 lb ft (4.4 - 4.8 kg m)..

25 If the crankshaft pulley wheel oil seal is being replaced in the front cover it will be necessary to take care in driving out the old one as the cover is a light alloy casting which will not stand rough treatment. As the old seal must be driven out from the front it is essential to find two pieces of wood thicker than the depth of the cover so that the immediate area near the seal ring may be supported.

26 With the cover firmly supported inside, it can be laid on the bench and the old seal driven out with a punch.

27 Turn the cover over and carefully tap in the new seal evenly with the inner lip facing away from the shoulder in the bore.

28 Tap the seal home finally with a block of wood.

29 Select the front cover gasket and using a suitable sealing compound position it on the engine front plate and offer up the cover.

30 Place the front cover bolts in position and screw them up loosely. Then fit the crankshaft pulley wheel onto the keyway of the crankshaft. See that the boss of the pulley is lubricated where the oil seal runs.

31 The replacement of the crankshaft pulley, before tightening the cover bolts, centralises the seal to the pulley. The bolts holding the cover may then be tightened to the specified torque.

46 Engine reassembly - rear plate, crankshaft pulley wheel, sump and flywheel

1 If the engine rear plate has been removed it should now be replaced. Make sure that both metal faces are quite clean before refitting. No gasket is used.

2 Replace the bolt and washer which locate the crankshaft pulley wheel, block the crankshaft with a piece of wood against the side of the crankcase and tighten the bolt to the specified torque.

3 Trim the projecting pieces of the front cover and backplate gaskets at the sump face of the block and front cover.

4 Trim the projecting edge of the rear oil seal carrier on the sump face at the rear of the crankcase.

5 Clean all traces of old gasket which may remain from the sump joint faces and cover the faces of both the crankcase and sump with sealing compound. The sump gasket is in four sections which dovetail together and these should be carefully positioned and the joints interlocked.

6 The engine is then ready for the sump to be replaced.

7 Clean the interior of the sump thoroughly, apply sealer to the joint edge and place it in position.

8 Replace all the sump bolts and tighten them evenly to a final torque of 5 - 8 lb ft (0.7 - 1.11 kg m).

9 The flywheel may now be replaced. Make sure that the mating flanges are clean and free from burrs and line up the bolt holes correctly. They are so positioned that they will only line up in one position. Do not hammer the flywheel into position if it should be difficult to get it fully onto the flange. Support it squarely and replace the bolts, tightening them evenly so as to draw the flywheel squarely onto its seat. There are no washers

and the bolts should be tightened evenly and progressively to the final torque value given in the specifications.

47 Engine reassembly - valve gear, cylinder heads, and inlet manifold

1 When the cylinder heads have been decarbonised and the valves ground in as described in Sections 37 and 41, the cylinder heads may be reassembled. If the valves have been removed as described in Section 12 there will be no confusion as to which valve belongs in which position.

2 Make sure all traces of carbon and grinding paste have been removed, lubricate the valve stem with engine oil and place it in the appropriate guide.

3 It will then protrude through the top of the cylinder head.

4 Fit a new seal cup over the valve stem.

5 Place the valve spring over the valve stem with the close coils of the spring nearest the cylinder head.

6 Fit the circular retainer over the spring with the protruding centre boss retainer downwards.

7 Using a proper valve spring compressor tool, compress the spring down the valve stem sufficiently far to enable the two halves of the locks (collets) to be fitted into the groove in the valve stem. If necessary the locks should be smeared with grease to keep them in position. The spring compressor may then be released. Watch to ensure that the locks stay together in position as the retainer comes past them. If the retainer is a little off centre it may force one lock out of its groove in which case the spring must be recompressed and the lock repositioned. When the compressor is finally released tap the head of the valve stem with a soft mallet to make sure the valve assembly is securely held in position.

8 Stand the engine the right way up on the bench and replace the tappets if they have been removed from the block. If these have been kept in order on removal, as suggested, it will be a simple matter to replace them.

9 The two cylinder heads are identical so if they were marked left and right on removal they can be replaced on the same bank. If they have been muddled up no real harm will result but the pushrods will not be matched to their correct rocker arms. As they normally 'run in' together excessive wear could occur until such time as the two unfamiliar surfaces have bedded in again.

10 Select a new cylinder head gasket and place it in position on the block on one bank. These gaskets are identical and can fit either bank but they can only go on the bank one way - which is obvious from the way the bolt holes and cooling jack holes line up.

11 Locate the gasket over the protruding spigots in the block and then place the cylinder head in position.

12 Make sure the cylinder head bolts are clean and lightly oiled and replace them. Nip them all down lightly and then tighten them in the sequence shown in Fig. 1.8. The bolts should be tightened down to progressive torque loadings - all to 50 lb ft (6.9 kg m) then all to 60 lb ft (8.30 kg m) and finally to the specified requirement of 65 - 80 lb ft (8.95 - 11.06 kg m).

13 Now fit the pushrods into position, making sure that they are replaced the same way up as they came out and according to the original valve position. This will not be difficult if they have been kept in order. Reassemble the rocker shaft assembling the order being shown in Fig. 1.10.

14 Refit the rocker shaft assemblies to the cylinder heads and secure to the cylinder heads with the three bolts and washers.

15 The inlet manifolds may now be refitted to the cylinder heads. In view of the large area to be sealed for both air and water it is a safety measure - if not essential - to use a jointing compound such as 'Wellseal' in addition to the gasket on the mating surfaces.

16 Place the inlet manifold gasket in position in the Vee so that the single square hole is on the left hand cylinder head. The gasket is obviously incorrect if put on any other way but this is a positive guide.

17 Apply jointing compound to the mating faces of the inlet manifold. Note the square port which matches the gasket hole and port in the left hand cylinder head.

18 Place the manifold in position taking care not to disturb the gasket.

19 Replace the manifold securing bolts, ensuring that the gasket is lined up to permit them to pick up the threads in the cylinder heads, and screw them up lightly.

20 With a torque wrench tighten the bolts down evenly to 15 - 18 lb ft (2.07 - 2.49 kg m). This tightening should be done in stages - all being tightened to 5 lb ft (0.7 kg m) then to 10 lb ft (1.38 kg m) before finally reaching the specified figure. Any uneven or excessive tightening may crack the manifold casting so take care (Fig. 1.40).

48 Valve to rocker clearance - adjustment

1 The valve stem to rocker clearance, which is in effect the mechanical free play between the camshaft and the end of the valve stem, is important to the correct operation and performance of the engine. If the clearance is too great the valve opening is reduced with consequent reduction in gas flow - and is also very noisy. If the clearance is too little the valve could open too much with the danger of it hitting the crown of the piston. The clearance is checked when the tappet is on the heel of the cam (opposite the highest point) and the valve therefore closed. This position coincides with certain other valves being fully open with their tappets on the high point of the cam. This can be seen easily when the valve spring is fully compressed.

2 The table below shows the relationship between the fully open valves and the closed valves which are to be checked.

valves open	adjust valves
No. 5 Cylinder	No. 1 Cylinder
No. 3 Cylinder	No. 4 Cylinder
No. 6 Cylinder	No. 2 Cylinder
No. 1 Cylinder	No. 5 Cylinder
No. 4 Cylinder	No. 3 Cylinder
No. 2 Cylinder	No.6 Cylinder

3 The clearances should be set at 0.014 in (0.355 mm) for the inlet valves and 0.016 in (0.406 mm) for the exhaust valves. After the engine has been run for a short time and then allowed to cool, the clearances should be checked again.

4 The actual adjustment procedure is straightforward. With the appropriate valve ready for checking place a feeler gauge of the required thickness (for exhaust or inlet valve) between the top of the valve stem and the rocker arm. If it will not go in or it is too loose slacken the locknut and reset the adjustment by screwing the adjusting screw in or out until the required setting is

obtained. Retighten the locknut.

49 Engine reassembly - fitting ancillary components

1 The exhaust manifolds are best replaced before putting the engine back into the car as they provide very useful holds if the engine has to be manhandled at all. Select the new gaskets and fit them the correct way, as they are not symmetrical.

2 Replace each manifold and tighten the bolts evenly.

3 The ancillary engine components must be replaced and the method of doing this is detailed in the appropriate Chapters. Section 9 of this Chapter gives a full list of the items involved. When this has been done the engine is ready to be put back in the car.

50 Engine replacement - without gearbox

1 The engine must be positioned suitably so that the sling used to remove it can be easily refitted and the lifting tackle hooked on. Position the engine the right way round in front of the car and then raise it so that it may be brought into position over the car or the car rolled into position underneath it.

2 The gearbox should be jacked up to its approximately normal position.

3 Lower the engine steadily into the engine compartment, keeping all ancillary wires, pipes and cables well clear of the sides. It is best to have a second person guiding the engine while it is being lowered.

4 The tricky part is finally mating the engine to the gearbox, which involves locating the gearbox input shaft into the clutch housing and flywheel. Provided that the clutch friction plate has been centred correctly as described in Chapter 5, there should be little difficulty. Grease the splines of the gearbox input shaft first. It may be necessary to rock the engine from side to side in order to get the engine fully home. Under no circumstances let any strain be imparted onto the gearbox input shaft. This could occur if the shaft was not fully located and the engine was raised or lowered more than the amount required for very slight adjustment of position.

5 As soon as the engine is fully up to the gearbox bellhousing replace the bolts holding the two together.

6 Now finally lower the engine onto its mounting brackets at the front and replce and tighten down the nuts and washers.

7 Replace all electrical connections; the fuel lines and carburettor linkages, cooling system hoses and radiator in the reverse order to that described in Section 5.

8 Reconnect the clutch cable as described in Chapter 5, replace the exhaust pipes and reconnect them to the manifold extensions, replace the plate covering the lower half of the bellhousing and remove the supporting jack.

9 Fill the engine with fresh oil and replace the coolant.

51 Engine replacement - with manual gearbox

1 The gearbox should be refitted to the engine, taking the same precautions as regards the input shaft as mentioned in Section 50.

2 The general principles of lifting the engine/gearbox assembly are the same as for the engine above but the gearbox will tilt everything to a much steeper angle as shown in the photos for Section 7. Replacement will certainly require the assistance of a second person.

3 Lift the gearbox end of the unit into the engine compartment (unless you are fortunate enough to have a hoist with a very high lift) and then lower and guide the unit down. One of the first things to be done is to reconnect the propeller shaft into the gearbox rear extension casing so someone should be ready to lift and guide the propeller shaft into position as soon as the gearbox is near enough. This cannot be done after the unit has been lowered beyond a certain position.

4 If a trolley jack is available this is the time to place it under the gearbox so that as the engine is lowered further the rear end can be supported and raised as necessary - at the same time being able to roll back as required. Without such a jack, support the rear in such a way that it can slide if possible. In any case the gearbox will have to be jacked and held up in position when the unit nears its final position.

5 Locate the front mounting brackets on the locating bolts as described in Section 50.

6 Refit the speedometer drive cable with the gearbox drive socket and refit the circlip and bolt. This MUST be done before the gearbox supporting crossmember is in place.

7 Jack up the rear of the gearbox and position the cross-member to the bodyframe. Then replace and tighten down the four retaining bolts and the centre bolt to the gearbox extension.

8 Replace the gearbox remote control change lever and housing as described in Chapter 6.

9 Reconnect the clutch cable and adjust as described in Chapter 5 and reconnect the reversing light wire. The final connections should then be made as described in Section 50 and in addition to the engine lubricant and coolant the gearbox should also be refilled with fresh oil.

52 Engine - initial start up after overhaul or major repair

1 Make sure that the battery is fully charged and that all lubri-cants, coolants and fuel are replenished.

2 If the fuel system has been dismantled it will require several revolutions of the engine on the starter motor to get the petrol up to the carburettor. An initial 'prime' of about 1/3 of a cupful of petrol poured down the choke of the carburettor will help the engine to fire quickly, thus relieving the load on the battery. Do not overdo this however, as flooding may result.

3 As soon as the engine fires and runs keep it going at a fast tickover only (no faster) and bring it up to normal working temperature.

4 As the engine warms up there will be odd smells and some smoke from parts getting hot and burning off oil deposits. The signs to look for are leaks of oil or water which will be obvious if serious. Check also the clamp connections of the exhaust pipes to the manifolds as these do not always 'find' their exact gas tight position until the warmth and vibration have acted on them and it is almost certain that they will need tightening further. This should be done of course with the engine stopped.

5 When running temperature has been reached adjust the idling speed as described in Chapter 3.

6 Stop the engine and wait a few minutes to see if any lubri-cants or coolant is dripping out when the engine is stationary.

7 Road test the car to check that the timing is correct and giving the necessary smoothness and power. Do not race the engine - if new bearings and/or pistons and rings have been fitted it should be treated as a new engine and run in at reduced revolutions for 500 miles (800 km).

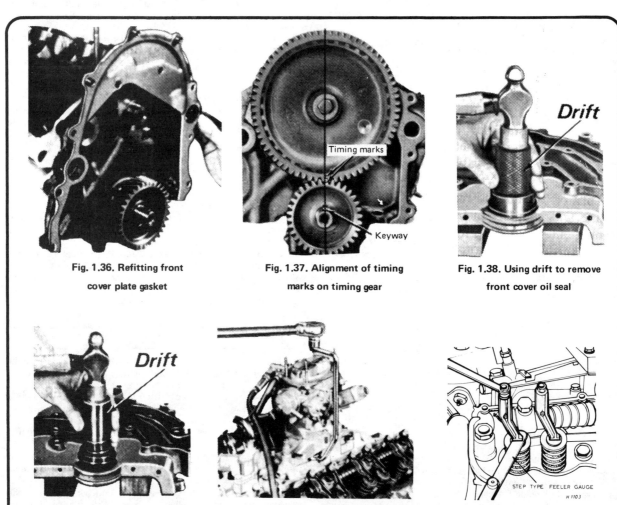

Fig. 1.36. Refitting front cover plate gasket

Fig. 1.37. Alignment of timing marks on timing gear

Fig. 1.38. Using drift to remove front cover oil seal

Fig. 1.39. Using drift to refit front cover oil seal

Fig. 1.40. If possible use a shaped spanner to tighten inlet manifold bolt

Fig. 1.41. Adjustment of valve clearances

Fault Finding Chart - Engine

Symptom	Reason/s	Remedy
Engine will not turn over when starter switch is operated	Flat battery Bad battery connections Bad connections at solenoid switch and/or starter motor	Check that battery is fully charged and that all connections are clean and tight.
	Starter motor jammed	Turn the square headed end of the starter motor shaft with a spanner to free it.
	Defective solenoid	Bridge the main terminals of the solenoid switch with a piece of heavy duty cable in order to operate the starter.
	Starter motor defective	Remove and overhaul starter motor.
Engine turns over normally but fails to fire and run	No spark at plugs	Check ignition system according to procedures given in Chapter 4.
	No fuel reaching engine	Check fuel system according to procedures given in Chapter 3.
	Too much fuel reaching the engine (flooding)	Check the fuel system as above.
Engine starts but runs unevenly and	Ignition and/or fuel system faults	Check the ignition and fuel systems as though the engine had failed to start.
	Incorrect valve clearances	Check and reset clearances.
	Burnt out valves Blown cylinder head gasket	Remove cylinder heads and examine and overhaul as necessary.
	Worn out piston rings Worn cylinder bores	Remove cylinder heads and examine pistons and cylinder bores. Overhaul as necessary.
Lack of power	Ignition and/or fuel system faults	Check the ignition and fuel systems for correct ignition timing and carburettor settings.
	Incorrect valve clearances	Check and reset the clearances.
	Burnt out valves Blown cylinder head gasket	Remove cylinder heads and examine and overhaul as necessary.
	Worn out piston rings Worn cylinder bores	Remove cylinder heads and examine pistons and cylinder bores. Overhaul as necessary.
	Oil leaks from crankshaft rear oil seal, timing cover gasket and oil seal, rocker cover gasket, oil filter gasket, sump gasket, sump plug washer.	Identify source of leak and renew seal as appropriate.
	Worn piston rings or cylinder bores resulting in oil being burnt by engine Smoky exhaust is an indication	Fit new rings or rebore cylinders and fit new pistons, depending on degree of wear.
	Worn valve guides and/or defective valve stem seals Smoke blowing out from the rocker cover vents is an indication	Remove cylinder heads and recondition valve stem bores and valves and seals as necessary.
Excessive mechanical noise from engine	Wrong valve to rocker clearances	Adjust valve clearances.
	Worn crankshaft bearings. Worn cylinders (piston slap) Worn timing gears	Inspect and overhaul where necessary.

NOTE: When investigating starting and uneven running faults do not be tempted into snap diagnosis. Start from the beginning of the check procedure and follow it through. It will take less time in the long run. Poor performance from an engine in terms of power and economy is not normally diagnosed quickly. In any event the ignition and fuel systems must be checked first before assuming any further investigation needs to be made.

Chapter 2 Cooling system

Contents

Specifications

Type ... ...   Pressurised, assisted by pump and fan

Thermostat

Type	Wax
Location	Lower left hand corner of cylinder block front cover
Starts to open	185º to 192º F (85º to 72.1º C)
Fully open	178º to 199º F (63.4º to 75.0º C)

Radiator

Type	Corrugated fin.
Pressure cap opens	13 lb/sq in (0.91 kg/cm^2)

Water pump

Type	Centrifugal

Fan

Number of blades	6
Tension	50 lb (22.68 kg)
Free play of belt	0.5 inch (12.7 mm)
Cooling system capacity	8.25 US quarts

Torque wrench settings:

	lb f ft	kg f m
Fan securing bolts	7 - 9	1.0 - 1.2
Water pump	6 - 12	0.83 - 1.6
Alternator attachment	15 - 18	2.07 - 2.49

1 General description

The engine cooling system may be considered as a three stage, positive circulation pressurised system incorporating a centrifugal water pump and thermostat, the latter being mounted at the lower left hand corner of the cylinder block front cover.

Circulation of coolant through the system is as follows and is shown diagrammatically in Figs. 2.1 and 2.2. The coolant from the engine is passed through the top hose to the top ot the radiator and being cooled by the air flow through the radiator matrix, becomes more dense and flows to the bottom of the radiator. This action is assisted by the induced circulation by the water pump.

The thermostat is located in the lower hose as opposed to the more usual position in the upper hose; it controls the coolant flow from the radiator rather than to the radiator.

With the thermostat front end open the coolant is able to flow to the water pump where it is passed onto the coolant passages in the front cover and thereafter around the cylinder block and heads back to the radiator top hose.

Coolant for circulation through the heater unit is drawn from the coolant outlet housing on the inlet manifold, providing the heater control therefore the regulation valve is set to the hot or open position. It passes through the heater and is returned by the heater return hose which is connected to the coolant inlet or thermostat housing.

Because operation of the carburettor automatic choke is reliant on the temperature of the coolant, a small bore separate hose is also connected to the coolant outlet housing on the inlet manifold. This is a continuous circuit because the hose is connected to the heater return hose for recirculation through the cooling system.

A by-pass circuit which is in operation whilst the engine is warming up from cold comprises a hose from the coolant outlet housing on the inlet manifold and is connected to the coolant inlet housing on the front cover. During this time three distinct stages may be considered to have occurred:

1 The radiator to water pump is closed whilst all other circuits are open. The front end of the thermostat is closed and the back side is open.

2 When the engine reaches normal operating temperature all circuits are open with the thermostat open at both ends so providing a controlled coolant temperature. This commences to occur at 185°F (85°C).

3 If the engine is running hot the front end of the thermostat remains open but the rear side is closed so shutting off the by-pass circuit. This gives additional cooling action by directing all coolant to the radiator.

2 Cooling system - draining

With the car on level ground drain the system as follows:

1 If the engine is cold remove the filler cap by turning the cap in an anti-clockwise direction. Should the engine be hot, having just been run, then turn the filler cap, suitably padded with a large amount of cloth over the top until the pressure in the system has had time to disperse. If, with the engine very hot, the cap is released suddenly, the drop in pressure can result in the coolant boiling. With the pressure released the cap can be removed.

2 If anti-freeze is in the cooling system drain it into a clean container for re-use.

3 There are three drain plugs, one at the base of the radiator and one on each side of the cylinder block. These should next be opened. (Fig. 2.3).

4 When the water has finished running out, probe the drain plug orifices with a short piece of wire to dislodge any particles of rust or sediment which may be blocking the holes so preventing all the coolant draining out.

3 Cooling system - flushing

1 With time the cooling system will gradually lose its efficiency as the radiator matrix becomes choked with rust scale, deposits from the water and other sediment.

2 To clean the system out, remove the pressure cap from the radiator and open the drain plugs fully. Leave a hose in the cap neck for ten to fifteen minutes with water running through.

3 In very bad cases the radiator should be reverse flushed. This can be done in the car but is better if the radiator can be removed as described in Section 5 of this Chapter.

4 Invert the radiator and place a hose pipe in the radiator lower hose pipe connection, the gap between hose and connection suitably padded with cloth. Water under slight pressure is then forced through the radiator matrix in the reverse direction to normal flow so loosening any particles and passing them out through the radiator top hose connection.

5 The hose is then removed from the lower hose connection and, with the radiator in its normal, instead of inverted position fit the hose and padding to the top hose connection and flush in the normal coolant flow direction.

6 If the radiator still appears to be partially blocked a proprietary radiator cleaner may be used.

7 Once the radiator is clean it may be refitted.

4 Cooling system - filling

1 Close all three drain plugs.

2 Move the heater temperature control to the 'HOT' position.

3 Disconnect the heater hose at the coolant outlet housing and hold the hose end at a position the same height as the elbow, to ensure that there are no air locks.

4 Fill the cooling system slowly. The best type of water to use in the cooling system is rain water; if just water is being used instead of an anti-freeze solution, continue filling until the coolant starts to flow from the elbow and hose end. Quickly reconnect the hose and tighten the clip.

5 Resume refilling the cooling system until the level is 0.25 inch (6.35 mm) from the top of the filler neck.

6 Replace the filler cap and turn it firmly in a clockwise direction to lock it in position.

7 Start the engine and allow to idle for two minutes and carefully remove the filler cap. Check the level and top up using warm water or anti-freeze or alternatively allow to cool. If cold coolant is added to hot water in the cooling system it can cause internal strains in the metal surrounding the water jackets due to sudden temperature changes.

8 Finally inspect for water leaks especially if any part of the cooling system has been disturbed for new part fitment or overhaul.

5 Radiator - removal, inspection, cleaning and replacement

1 To remove the radiator first drain the cooling system as described in Section 2 of this Chapter.

2 Detach the radiator upper splash shield.

3 Slacken the clips securing the hoses to the top and bottom of the radiator and carefully detach the hoses.

4 If an automatic transmission oil cooler is incorporated in the radiator wipe the areas around the unions to the oil cooler and detach the oil cooler pipes. Quickly plug the ends to stop loss of transmission fluid and dirt ingress.

5 The radiator is retained in position with four bolts with spring washers and flat washers, two each side of the radiator. These should be removed next.

6 The radiator may now be lifted up and away from the car, taking extreme care not to touch the matrix with the fan blades.

7 With the radiator away from the car any leaks can be soldered up or repaired with suitable patching substance: Clean

Fig. 2.1. The flow of coolant in the cooling system

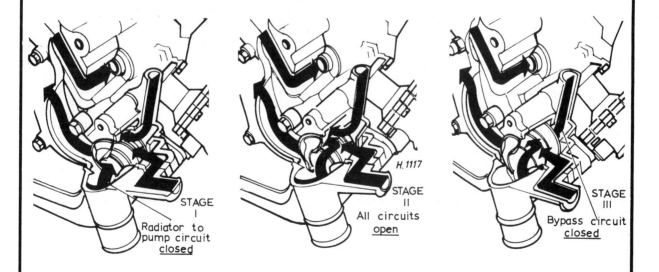

STAGE
I
Radiator to
pump circuit
closed

H.1117

STAGE
II
All circuits
open

STAGE
III
Bypass circuit
closed

Fig. 2.2. Three stages of thermostat operation

out the inside of the radiator by flushing as described in Section 3.

8   Clean the exterior of the radiator by hosing down the matrix with a strong jet of water to clear away any road dirt, dead flies etc.

9   Inspect the radiator hoses for cracks, internal or external perishing, damage caused by overtightening securing clips and examine hose securing clips for rust and/or distortion. Renew components as necessary. Renew drain plug if leaking.
The drain plug should be renewed if leaking.

10 Refitting the radiator is the reverse sequence to removal but the following additional points should be noted:
a) Refill the cooling system as described in Section 4.
b) If an automatic transmission oil cooler is fitted check the oil level as described in Chapter 6.

6   Thermostat - removal, testing and replacement

1   To remove the thermostat first drain the cooling system as described in Section 2.

2   Slacken the clips that secure the radiator bottom hose and heater return hose to the thermostat housing. Carefully detach the hoses from the thermostat housing.

3   Undo and remove the three bolts and spring washers that secure the thermostat housing cover to the front cover.

4   Draw the housing from the front cover. Tap the side very gently if it has stuck to the gasket and front cover. Recover the gasket.

5   Using a screwdriver ease out the thermostat retainer washer (if fitted) and lift away the thermostat noting which way round it is fitted.

6   Test the thermostat for correct functioning by suspending it in a saucepan of cold water together with a thermometer.

7   Heat the water and note when the thermostat begins to open which should be between 185° to 192°F (85° to 72.1°C) at fully open at 178° to 199°F (63.4° to 75.0°C).

8   Discard the thermostat if it opens too early. Allow the thermostat to cool down naturally and if it does not close it should be discarded and a new one obtained.

9   If the thermostat is stuck open when cold this will be apparent when removing it from the housing.

10 Replacing the thermostat is the reverse sequence to removal. It is recommended that a new gasket is fitted between the housing and the front cover.

11 Clean the faces of the housing and the front cover to ensure a water tight joint. If the housing has corroded badly a new one should be fitted.

12 Refill the cooling system as described in Section 4 and finally check for water leaks.

7   Fan - removal and refitting

1   Unscrew and remove the four bolts and washers and lift away the fan blade assembly.

2   Refitting the fan blade assembly is the reverse sequence to removal. Tighten the bolts to a torque wrench setting of 7 to 9 lbf ft (1.0 - 1.2 kg fm).

8   Fan belt - adjustment

1   It is important to keep the fan belt correctly adjusted. Check the adjustment at the first 600 miles (1,000 km), then at 3,000 miles (5,000 km) and thereafter every 6,000 miles (10,000 km) intervals.

2   If the belt is too loose it will slip, wear rapidly and cause the alternator and water pump to malfunction. If the belt is too tight the alternator and water pump bearings will wear rapidly causing premature failure of these components.

3   The fan belt tension is considered correct when there is 0.5 inch (12.7 mm) free movement at the mid-way point between the alternator and water pump pulleys, this being the longest run of the belt (Fig. 2.4.) .

4   To adjust the fan belt slacken the three alternator securing bolts and move the unit either in or out until the correct tension is obtained. It is easier if the bolts are only slackened a little so that it requires some force to move it. In this way the tension of the belt can be arrived at more quickly than by making frequent adjustments.

5   If difficulty is experienced in moving the alternator away from the engine a piece of wood serves as a lever and can be held in this position whilst the bolts are tightened.

9   Fan belt - renewal and refitting

1   If the fan belt is worn or has stretched unduly it should be replaced. The most usual reason for replacement is that the belt has broken in service. It is therefore recommended that a spare belt is always carried. Replacement is a reversal of the removal sequence, but as replacement due to breakage is the most usual operation it is described below:

2   Slacken the three alternator mounting bolts and push the unit towards the engine.

3   Slip the belt over the crankshaft, water pump and alternator pulleys.

4   Adjust the belt tension as described in Section 8 and tighten the three bolts securely.

5   After 600 miles (1,000 km) recheck the fan belt tension.

10 Anti-freeze mixture

1   In circumstances where it is likely that the temperature will drop to below freezing, it is essential that some of the water is drained and an adequate amount of ethylene glycol anti-freeze is added to the cooling system.

2   Never use an anti-freeze with an alcohol base as evaporation is too high.

3   Either of the above mentioned anti-freezes can be left in the cooling system for up to two years, but after six months it is advisable to have the specific gravity of the coolant checked at your local garage and topped up with the same type of anti-freeze already in use. Thereafter check once every three months. three months.

4   Below are the amounts of anti-freeze by percentage volume which should be added to ensure adequate protection down to the temperature given:-

Amount of anti-freeze	Protection to
50%	- 37°C (-34°F)
40%	- 25°C (-13°F)
30%	- 16°C (+3°F)
25%	- 13°C (+9°F)
20%	- 9°C (+15°F)
15%	- 7°C (+20°F)
10%	- 4°C (+25°F)

11 Water pump - removal and refitting

1   Refer to Section 2 and completely drain the cooling system.

2   Slacken the clips that secure the lower radiator hose and the heater return hose to the thermostat housing. Carefully detach the hoses from the thermostat housing.

3   Refer to Section 10 and remove the fan belt.

4   Refer to Section 7 and remove the fan. Lift away the pulley from the front of the water pump spindle.

5   Unscrew and remove the bolts and washers that secure the water pump assembly. Note the location of the bolts as they are of different lengths.

6   Lift away the water pump assembly. Recover the gasket if not stuck to the casting. If necessary also remove the thermostat housing from the water pump.

7   Before refitting the water pump assembly remove all traces of the old gasket and sealing compound from the front cover and water pump assembly.

8   Carefully apply a sealer to both sides of a new gasket and accurately position on the water pump.

9   Hold the water pump in position and screw in two bolts and washers so retaining it to the front cover.

10 Remove all gasket material from the thermostat housing mating faces. Apply a sealer to both sides of the new gasket and position on the water pump. Secure in position with the two bolts and washers.

11 Refit all remaining securing bolts and washers ensuring they are located in their original positions. Tighten in a diagonal and progressive manner to the correct torque wrench settings - see specifications.

12 Refit the fan and pulley as described in Section 7.
13 Refit and adjust the fan belt tension as described in Sections 8 and 9.
14 Refill the cooling system as described in Section 4.

12 Water pump - overhaul

It is recommended that if the water pump requires overhaul as indicated by leaks, excessive movement of the spindle or noisy operation it be removed and a replacement unit fitted. Besides requiring the use of special tools not normally found in a home mechanics kit difficulty could be experienced in obtaining individual parts without a long wait as these would not normally be kept by the smaller dealers.

13 Temperature gauge sender unit - removal and refitting

1   Partially drain the cooling system as described in Section 2.
2   Detach the terminal connector from the sender unit which is located on the inlet manifold.
3   Unscrew the old sender unit using a suitable size socket or box spanner.
4   Apply a little conductive water resistant sealer (part number C2AZ - 19554 - B) to the threads of the new sender unit and screw into position. Take care not to overtighten.
5   Refit the terminal connector and top up the cooling system as described in Section 4.

Belt free play   Adjusting arm bolt   Mounting bolt

Fig. 2.3. Coolant drain plugs

Fig. 2.4. Fan belt adjustment

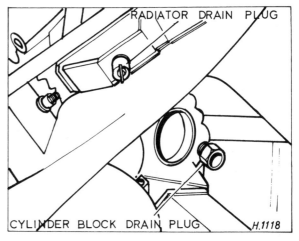

Chapter 3 Fuel system and carburation

Contents

Specifications

Fuel pump

Type	Mechanical driven from eccentric on camshaft via pushrod.
Delivery pressure	3.75 - 5.0 lb/in^2 (0.26 - 0.35 Kg/cm^2)
Inlet vacuum	8.5 in (21.60 cm) Hg

Fuel tank

Location	Rear of car in luggage compartment
Capacity	12 US gallons/41.34 litres

Carburettor

Type	Motocraft 5200. dual barrel

Air cleaner element

Type	Replacement paper element
Duct and valve actuation temperature	90 - 100°F (32.2 - 37.8°C)

Fuel evaporative emission system

Type	4 unit system

Decel valve timing ... ... | 1.5 - 3.5 seconds

TORQUE WRENCH SETTINGS	lb ft	Kg fm
Exhaust silencer clamps	25 35	3.4 - 4.8
Inlet pipe flange nuts	17 - 25	2.35 - 3.4
'O' ring insulator brackets to floor panel	9	1.2

1 General description

The fuel system comprises a 12 US gallons/41.34 litres fuel tank, a mechanically operated fuel pump and a motorcraft twin venturi downdraught carburettor, together with the necessary fuel lines, in line filter air cleaner assembly, fuel contents gauge and transmitter unit.

To confirm to the regulations imposed in the USA for controlling engine emission, the fuel system has been modified and further information will be found in the relevant sections of this Chapter. Before starting any work on the fuel system refer to Section 2.

2 US Federal regulations - emission control

The fuel system has been modified so that the car will comply with the USA Federal Regulations covering emission of hydrocarbons and carbon monoxide. To achieve this the ignition system must be accurately set using special equipment (See Chapter 4) before any attempt is made to adjust the carburettor or its controls. Thereafter the fuel system may be reset but once again special equipment must be used. The information contained in this chapter is given to assist the reader to clean and/or overhaul the various components but when completed the car must be taken to the local Capri dealer for final adjustments to be made. Failure to do this will probably mean that the car does not comply with the regulations.

3 Air cleaner - removal, element renewal and replacement

1 With the bonnet open, first detach the pipe from the side of the air cleaner body. This is the pipe that goes to the carbon canister used in the Fuel Evaporative Emission system.
2 Undo and remove the four wing nuts and plain washers that secure the air cleaner body to the carburettor.
3 The air cleaner may now be drawn from the four carburettor mounted studs.
4 Lift off the lid and withdraw the element. If the car has covered 6,000 miles (10,000 Km) or 6 months has passed since element renewal, the element should be discarded and a new one obtained.
5 Wipe out the air cleaner body and fit a new element. Refit the lid.
6 Located in the air cleaner inlet is a special duct and valve assembly. Inspect this and ensure that the spring is secured at both ends. Lubricate the flat valve pivot with a few drops of Castrol GTX. If operation of the thermostatic bulb is suspect refer to Section 4 for further information.
7 Refit the air cleaner to the carburettor studs and secure with the four wing nuts and plain washers.

4 Air cleaner duct and valve assembly - testing and adjustment

The air cleaner assembly incorporates a temperature operated valve and duct mechanism which must function correctly otherwise performance will be affected, as well as failure of the car to meet Federal Regulations. The unit is designed to provide the carburettor with air at a temperature of between 90 and 100°F (32.2 and 37.8°C).

When assembled and the temperature of the engine compartment is less than 100°F (37.8°C) the valve plate must be in the 'HEAT ON' position. Should this not be the case check for possible interference of the plate and duct. Lubricate the pivot. If it should still stick the plate may be realigned by bending slightly.

To test the operation of the thermostat capsule remove the unit from the carburettor and withdraw the element. Immerse the duct assembly in water until the capsule is totally covered with water. Heat the water until it reaches 100°F (37.8°C) and hold at this temperature for 5 minutes. The valve must be in the 'HEAT ON' position.

Now raise the temperature to 135°F (39.5°C) and hold at this new temperature for 5 minutes. The valve should now be in the 'HEAT OFF' position. If the valve does not meet these requirements and yet the valve plate is free to pivot the duct and valve assembly should be removed and reset or dismantled and new parts fitted.

To reset the thermostat, leave the locknut slack and carrying out the previously described tests whilst making small adjustments until the correct action is obtained.

5 In line fuel filter - renewal

If the filter has become blocked or the renewal period reached the filter should be removed and discarded. To do this, proceed as follows:
1 Refer to Section 3 and remove the air cleaner assembly.
2 Slacken the clamp that secures the fuel inlet hose to the fuel filter.
3 Unscrew the fuel filter from the carburettor. Detach the fuel filter from the hose and discard the retaining clamp.
4 To fit a new filter place a new clamp on the inlet hose and connect the hose to the filter.
5 Screw the filter into the carburettor inlet port and tighten.
6 Place a second clip on the fuel line hose and clip the clamp securely. If the original type of clamps are not available use small hose clips.
7 Refit the air cleaner, start the engine and check for leaks.

6 Fuel pump - description

1 The mechanical fuel pump is mounted on the left hand side of the cylinder block at a position behind the water pump and is connected to the fuel tank and carburettor by a system of metal and flexible pipes.
2 The fuel pump is actuated by a rod driven by an eccentric on the camshaft.
3 The unit is of a semi sealed type and it is only possible to clean out sediment.
4 The pump operates in the following manner: As the engine camshaft rotates, the eccentric on the camshaft moves the rod which in turn operates the diaphragm. By a system of internal valves fuel is passed to the carburettor float chamber.
5 When the carburettor float chamber is full the needle valve will close to prevent further fuel flowing from the pump. It will continue in this condition until the needle valve in the carburettor opens to admit more fuel.

7 Fuel pump - sediment removal

1 Remove the centre screw and fibre washer securing the metal dome to the top of the pump body. Lift away the metal dome and sealing washer.
2 Wash out the sediment chamber with several changes of clean petrol.
3 Make sure the sealing washer is in good order and refit the metal dome. Secure with the screw and fibre washer. This must not be overtightened otherwise the dome will distort or the screw threads strip.

8 Fuel pump - testing

Presuming that the fuel lines and unions are in good condition and that there are no leaks anywhere, check the performance of the fuel pump in the following manner: Disconnect the fuel pipe at the carburettor inlet and the high tension lead from the coil. With a suitable container or a large rag in position to catch the ejected fuel, turn the engine over on the starter motor. A good spurt of petrol should emerge from the end of the pipe every second revolution.
If this condition exists after engine overhaul check that the operating rod has not been inadvertently left out.
Any internal fault in a pump necessitates the fitting of a new pump as described in Section 9.

9 Fuel pump - removal and replacement

1 Slacken the clip and detach the inlet and outlet pipes from the pump.
2 Undo and remove the two securing bolts and washers. Lift away the pump and its gasket. The latter should be discarded and a new one obtained ready for refitting.
3 To refit the fuel pump first make sure that all traces of the old gasket have been removed from the mounting pad and pump.
4 Smear some oil resistant cement onto both sides of a new gasket and place on the flange. Check that the rod is correctly located and replace the pump. Secure with the two bolts and washers.
5 Reconnect the two pipes and check for fuel leaks.

10 Carburettor - general description

The carburettor fitted is the Motorcraft 5200 series which is a two stage, two venturi type. The primary stage or venturi is smaller than the secondary venturi.
The primary stage includes a curb idle system, an accelerator pump system, an idle transfer system, a metering system and power enrichment system.
The secondary stage includes a transfer system, a main metering system and a power system. The secondary system is actuated by a mechanical linkage.
The primary and secondary systems draw fuel from a common fuel bowl and float chamber.
Located in the carburettor spacer is a hot idle compensator which increases the idle speed during periods of prolonged running when the operating temperature rises.

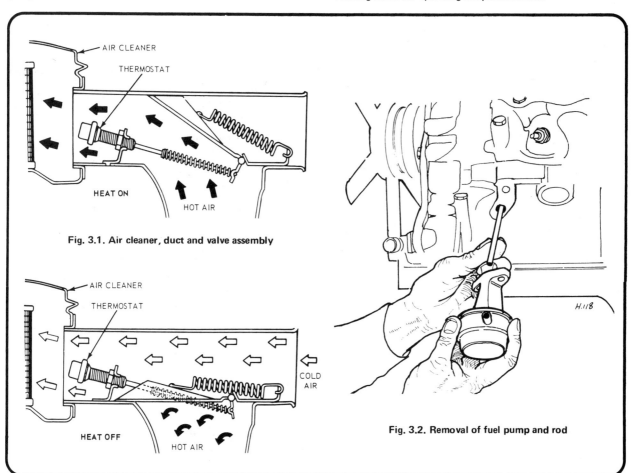

Fig. 3.1. Air cleaner, duct and valve assembly

Fig. 3.2. Removal of fuel pump and rod

11 Carburettor - dismantling and reassembly - general

1 With time the component parts of the carburettor will wear and petrol consumption will increase. The diameter of drillings and jets may alter, and air and fuel leaks may develop round spindles and other moving parts. Because of the high degree of precision involved it is best to purchase an exchange carburettor. This is one of the few instances where it is better to take the latter course rather than to rebuild the component oneself.

2 It may be necessary to partially dismantle the carburettor to clear a blocked jet or to renew a choke diaphragm. The accelerator pump itself may need attention and gaskets may need renewal. Providing care is taken there is no reason why the carburettor may not be completely reconditioned at home, but ensure a full repair kit can be obtained before you strip the carburettor down. NEVER poke out jets with wire or similar to clean them but blow them out with compressed air or air from a car tyre pump.

3 When a carburettor has been refitted or the controls adjusted it is imperative that the car be taken to the local Capri dealer to have any adjustments made so that it complies with the Federal Regulations.

12 Carburettor - removal and refitting

1 Open the bonnet and remove the air cleaner assembly as described in Section 3.

2 Refer to Chapter 2 and partially drain the cooling system.

3 Slacken the clips securing the hoses to the automatic choke housing and carefully separate the hoses from the housing.

4 Disconnect the throttle linkage from the carburettor installation.

5 Release the distributor automatic advance pipe from the side of the carburettor.

6 Slacken the fuel pipe retaining clip at the float chamber and detach the pipe.

7 Detach the ventilation tube from the top of the float chamber (if fitted).

8 Undo the four nuts that secure the carburettor flange and remove the nuts and spring washers.

9 Carefully lift away the carburettor and its gasket.

10 Replacement is a straightforward reversal of the removal sequence but note the following additional points:-

a) Remove all traces of the old carburettor gasket. Clean the mating flanges and fit a new gasket in place.

b) Refill the cooling system as described in Chapter 2.

c) Refer to Section 11, paragraph 3 and also Section 2 in connection with the USA Federal Regulations.

13 Carburettor - dismantling, overhaul and reassembly

1 Before dismantling wash the exterior of the carburettor and wipe dry using a non fluffy rag. Select a clean area of the workbench and lay several layers of newspaper on the top. Obtain several small containers for putting in some of the small parts that could easily be lost. Whenever a part is to be removed look at it first so that it may be refitted in its original position. As each part is removed place it in order along one edge of the newspaper so that by using this method reassembly is made easier.

2 All parts of the carburettor are shown in Fig. 3.4.

3 Undo and remove the fuel inlet filter plug and filter screen assembly.

4 Undo and remove the bowl cover securing screws and spring washers.

5 Carefully remove the choke rod retaining clips and lift away the bowl cover.

6 Withdraw the choke rod sealing plug and seal.

7 Remove the float pivot shaft, float assembly and needle valve.

8 Undo and remove the three screws and spring washers that secure the vacuum diaphragm cover. Lift away the cover, spring and diaphragm from the choke housing.

9 Undo and remove the screw and fibre washer that secures the choke water housing to the choke housing. Lift away the water cover and its gasket.

10 Undo and remove the three screws and spring washers that secure the choke thermostatic spring housing retaining ring to the choke housing. Lift away the retaining ring, choke thermostatic spring housing and gasket.

11 Undo and remove the three long screws that secure the choke housing to the carburettor body. Withdraw the housing from the carburettor body. Detach the fast idle rod. Be careful to make a note of the location of the longest screw.

12 Lift away the 'O' ring from the vacuum passage.

13 Undo and remove the choke shaft nut and lock washer. Note the position of the fast idle cam spring.

14 Detach the spring loop from the choke lever and then remove the choke lever and spring. Also remove the spring retainer.

15 Remove the choke shaft washer and then the choke shaft, lever and the Teflon bearing.

16 Undo and remove the fast idle lever and shaft securing screw. Lift away the bushing and spring washer. Remove the fast idle lever and flat spacer. Also remove the adjustment screw and spring.

17 Undo and remove the three vacuum diaphragm screws and lift away the washers and diaphragm.

18 If necessary remove the choke housing diaphragm cover plug screw, and adjustment screw.

19 Undo and remove the four accelerator pump cover screws and pump cover assembly. Remove the pump diaphragm assembly and pump return spring.

20 Remove the pump discharge valve assembly, the pump discharge nozzle and the two gaskets. Unscrew and remove the pump channel plug screw.

21 Now turning to the main body remove the primary main well on bleed plug and main well tube.

22 Remove the secondary main well air bleed plug and main well tube. It is very important to note the size of the air bleed plugs and main well tubes so that they are refitted in their correct locations.

23 Remove the primary and secondary main metering jets. Again note the different sizes of jets so that they are refitted in their correct locations.

24 Unscrew and remove the power valve and its gasket.

25 Remove the primary and secondary idle jet retainer plugs and idle jets which are located on the sides of the carburettor body.

26 Rotate in the idle limiter cap to the stop. Now remove the idle limiter cap. Count the number of turns required to lightly seat the idle adjustment needle. This must be counted to the nearest 1/16 turn.

27 Remove the secondary operating lever return spring.

28 Undo and remove the primary throttle lever nut and lock washer. Remove the primary lever and flat washer.

29 Lift away the secondary operating lever assembly and the lever bushing.

30 Remove the idle adjusting lever spring and shaft washer. Make a note of how the primary throttle return spring is hooked over the idle adjustment lever and carburettor body.

31 Unscrew the idle speed screw and spring from the idle adjustment lever.

32 Undo and remove the secondary throttle lever securing nut, lock washer, plain washer and secondary throttle lever. Finally remove the secondary idle adjusting screw.

33 Dismantling is now complete and all parts should be thoroughly washed and cleaned in petrol. Remove any sediment in the float chamber and drillings but take care not to scratch the fine drillings whilst doing so. Remove all traces of old gaskets using a sharp knife.

34 Reassembly of the carburettor is the direct reversal of the dismantling process. During reassembly it will be necessary to adjust the following parts and information will be found in the relevant Sections.

a) Choke thermostatic spring housing - Section 14.
b) Secondary throttle stop screw - Section 15.
c) Float setting - Section 16.
d) De-choke clearance - Section 17.

e) Fast idle speed - Section 18.
f) Fast idle cam clearance - Section 19.
g) Chokeplate vacuum pull-down - Section 20.
h) Idle speed and fuel mixture - Section 21.

14 Choke thermostatic spring housing - adjustment

1 Refer to Section 3 and remove the air cleaner assembly.
2 Slacken the three choke cover retaining screws. It is permissible for the cover to be rotated slightly without partially draining the cooling system.
3 Move the choke cover to 0.125 inch (3.175 mm) weak (anti-clockwise) from the index mark. It will be observed that a small punch mark indicates the correct location.
4 Retighten the three cover retaining screws and finally refit the air cleaner.

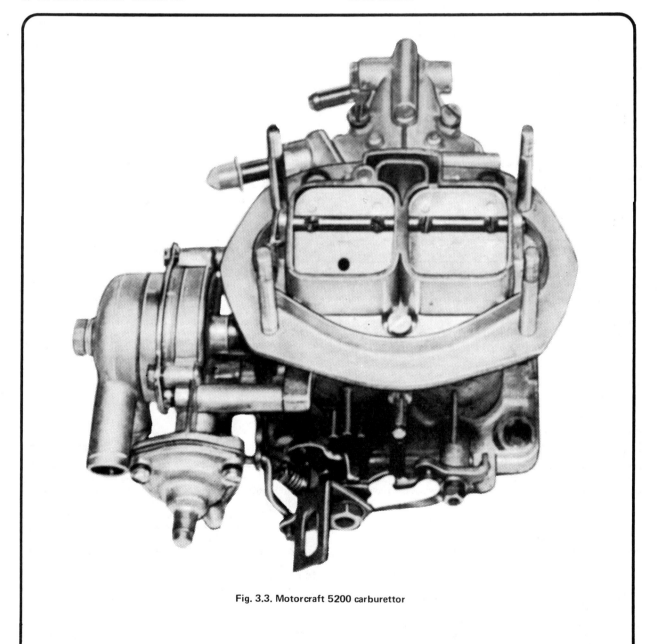

Fig. 3.3. Motorcraft 5200 carburettor

15 Secondary throttle stop screw - adjustment

1 With the air cleaner removed, unscrew the secondary throttle stop screw until the secondary throttle plate seats in its bore.
2 Slowly turn in the screw until it just touches the tab on the secondary throttle lever. Now screw in an additional ¼ turn.

16 Float level - adjustment

1 This job may be done once the bowl cover has been removed.
2 Hold the bowl cover vertically and with the float tang resting lightly on the spring loaded fuel inlet needle, carefully measure the clearance between the edge of the float and the bowl cover. The distance between the top of the float and the cover flange should be 5.5 to 6.0 mm. For this job a ruler or drill is necessary. If this reading is not correct carefully adjust it by bending the arm between the pivot and the float at the float end.
3 Pull the float outwards and check that it moves another 8 to 8.5 mm to give a total reading of 14 mm maximum. If this is not correct adjust the position of the tab which abuts the needle valve housing until the correct travel is obtained.

17 De-choke clearance - adjustment

1 Gently hold the throttle lever in the fully open position and then apply pressure to the top edge of the choke plate so eliminating any slack in the choke linkage.
2 Measure the distance between the lower edge of the choke plate and the air intake wall. This should be between 3.5 and 4.0 mm. If adjustment is necessary bend the tab on the fast idle lever where it touches the fast idle cam.

18 Fast idle speed - adjustment

1 To adjust the engine fast idle speed first run the engine until it reaches its normal operating temperature.
2 Adjust the position of the fast idle screw positioned on the second step of the fast idle cam until it is against the shoulder on the first step.
3 The fast idle speed should now be set as necessary by adjusting the screw in or out.

19 Fast idle cam clearance - adjustment

1 With the air cleaner removed insert a 0.156 inch (3.969 mm) drill between the lower edge of the choke plate and the air intake wall.
2 Hold the fast idle screw on the second step of the fast idle cam and measure the clearance between the tang of the choke lever and the arm on the fast idle cam. Should the clearance not be correct bend the choke lever tang up or down as necessary.

20 Choke plate vacuum pull-down - adjustment

1 Undo and remove the three hexagonal screws and then the ring that retains the choke thermostatic spring cover. Do not disturb the water cover securing screw.
2 Pull the water cover and thermostatic spring cover assembly away from the housing.
3 Adjust the fast idle cam until it is on the top step.
4 With a screwdriver carefully push the diaphragm stem back against its stop.
5 Measure the distance between the lower edge of the choke

plate and the air intake wall. This should be 0.8 to 0.9 mm. It may be necessary to remove any slack from the choke linkage by applying a little finger pressure to the top edge of the choke plate.
6 If adjustment is necessary remove the screwed plug from the diaphragm and turn the adjusting screw in or out as necessary.
7 Refit the choke water cover and its gasket securing with the retaining ring and three screws.

21 Idle speed and fuel mixture - adjustment

1 To carry out these adjustments it is necessary to use specialist tuning equipment so that the results will be within the Federal Requirements. Full information is given in this section to enable the engine to be started and the car driven to the local Capri dealer.
2 The carburettor fitted is equipped with idle fuel mixture adjustment limiters which control the maximum idle richness thereby preventing over rich idle adjustment. The plastic idle limiter cap is filled on the head of the idle fuel mixture adjustment screw. Any adjustment to be made   must therefore be within the range of the limiter and no attempt may be made to render the limiter inoperative. If it is not possible to obtain a satisfactory idle speed then the ignition and engine settings must be checked as well as other parts of the fuel system.
3 Start the engine and with the bonnet in the half raised position run the engine at a speed of 1500 rpm for a period of at least 20 minutes. This may be achieved by positioning the fast idle screw or cam follower on the kickdown step of the fast idle cam.
4 The ignition timing and distributor advance/retard system must now be checked for correct operation. This work requires specialist equipment.
5 Disconnect the carburettor-to-decel valve hose at the decel valve. Plug the decel valve fitting, (see Section 22).
6 Manual gearbox. The gear change lever must be in the neutral position.
7 Automatic transmission. The selector lever must be in the Drive position except when an exhaust gas analyser is in use. Take CARE not to open the throttle wide and CHOCK all wheels.
8 Adjust the engine curb idle speed until the engine runs evenly at a reasonable idle speed.
9 Now turn the mixture idle adjustment screw inwards to obtain the smoothest running condition within the range of the idle limiter.
10 Check the exhaust gas CO content using an exhaust gas analyser.

22 Decel valve - description and servicing

The decel valve is mounted on the inlet manifold adjacent to the carburettor. The purpose of this valve is to meter the engine an additional amount of fuel and air during engine deceleration conditions. This additional amount of fuel and air, together with other modifications permits a more complete combustion with resultant lower levels of exhaust emissions. During periods of engine deceleration, manifold vacuum faces the diaphragm assembly against the spring which in turn raises (or opens) the decel valve. With the valve now open existing manifold vacuum pulls a metered amount of fuel and air from the carburettor and passes through the valve body assembly into the inlet manifold. The decel valve remains open and continues to supply additional air and fuel for a specified time of 1.5 - 3.5 seconds.

Special test equipment is required to check the operation of this valve so if its performance is suspect take the car to the local Capri dealer.

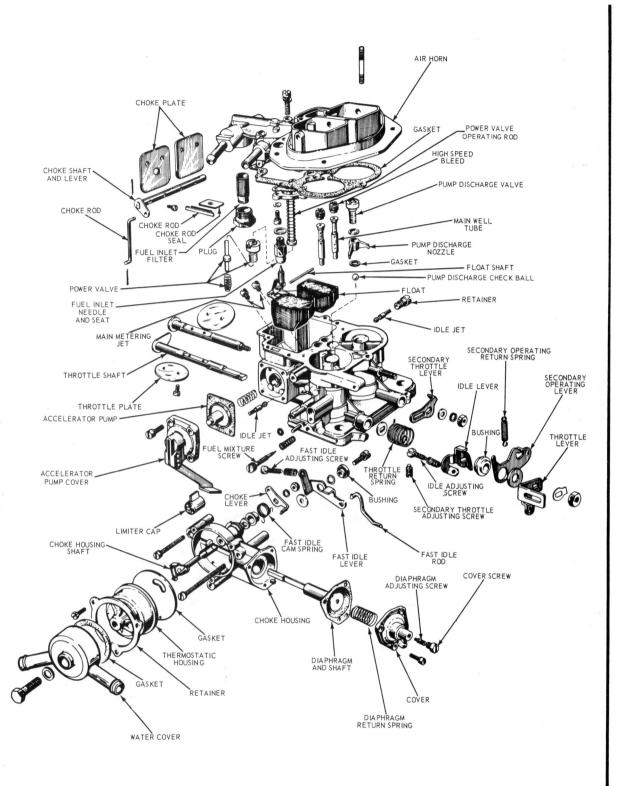

Fig. 3.4. Carburettor component parts

23 Fuel tank - removal and replacement

1 The fuel tank is located in the rear luggage compartment with the filler pipe connected to the flush filling pressure and vacuum sensitive filler cap located in the right hand quarter panel. The filler pipe is connected to the vertically mounted tank by a convoluted hose.

2 Remove the filler cap and using a length of rubber hose approximately ½ inch bore, syphon out as much petrol as possible.

3 Disconnect the battery earth terminal for safety reasons.

4 Slacken the clip that secures the flexible hose to the fuel tank neck.

5 Disconnect the fuel and vapour lines from the tank.

6 Undo and remove the four bolts and spring washers that secure the fuel tank and partially lower the tank.

7 Disconnect the fuel tank sender unit cable and lift away the fuel tank.

8 If necessary detach the sender unit by rotating the lock ring. Carefully withdraw the sender unit ensuring the float arm is not bent. Recover the sealing ring. It may be necessary to the unit to assist removal. Note the float arm hangs down when in the fitted position.

9 Refitting the sender unit and the fuel tank is the reverse sequence to removal. Test the operation of the sender unit by switching on the ignition. Wait 30 seconds and observe the gauge reading.

24 Fuel tank - cleaning

1 With time it is likely that sediment will collect in the bottom of the fuel tank. Condensation, resulting in rust and other impurities will usually be found in the fuel tank of any car more than three or four years old.

2 When the tank is removed it should be vigorously flushed out and turned upside down and, if facilities are available, steam cleaned.

3 Never weld or bring a naked light close to an empty fuel tank unless it has been steamed out for at least two hours or washed internally with boiling water and detergent several times. If using the latter method finally fill the tank with boiling water and detergent and allow to stand for at least three hours.

4 Any small holes may be repaired using a special preparation which gives satisfactory results provided the instructions are rigidly adhered to.

25 Fuel evaporative emission system - general description

A fuel evaporative emission system is fitted to Capri models to limit the emission of fuel vapour into the atmosphere and to prevent neat fuel from escaping from the fuel tank.

It comprises four major units:

a) Fuel tank.
b) Pressure and vacuum sensitive fuel tank.
c) A 0.040 inch (1.016 mm) restrictor.
d) A vapour absorbing charcoal canister.

The rear mounted fuel tank is mounted vertically behind the bulkhead. The filler neck is double sealed and in addition to direction fuel to the tank it also provides a means of venting air through a secondary concentric chamber and sensing the fuel fill level. This is obtained by using a twin tube neck. The outer neck comprises two seamless tubes joined together by an edge cut seal.

The lower of the tubes is welded to the top of the tank at its point of entry and then protrudes into the tank where it receives the fill control tube.

The fuel filler cap incorporates two valves, one to release excess pressure in the tank should the vapour line become blocked, and a vacuum relief valve to admit air to the tank as fuel is used.

When the level of fuel in the tank rises vapours are discharged to the atmosphere through the fill control tube and the annular space between the inner filler tube and the outer neck. When the fuel level covers the fill control tube, vapour can no longer escape and the filler tube will begin to fill up. Under these conditions a vapour lock will be formed by the restrictor and neither vapour nor fuel can flow through the vapour line to the charcoal canister. The fuel level is therefore controlled by the level of the fill control tube which is positioned to keep an expansion volume of approximately 10% of the tank capacity at the top of the tank.

On very hot days when petrol expands in the tank a vapour flow will commence and will be forced through the restrictor. This will allow the vapour passing through the system to be absorbed by charcoal contained in a canister which is mounted in the engine compartment.

The canister is open to the atmosphere on one side and connected to the air filter by a length of rubber hose on the other. Fuel vapour absorbed by the charcoal when the vehicle is stationary is extracted by the flow of air through the canister into the air filter when the engine is restricted.

If a restrictor develops in the vapour line between the tank and charcoal canister causing the vapour pressure in the system to reach 0.7 to 1.5 lb/sq in the pressure relief valve in the fuel tank filler cap will open and allow the vapour to discharge to the atmosphere.

When the fuel level in the tank drops or the ambient temperature drops the resultant vacuum opens the vacuum valve in the fuel tank filler cap. This will allow air to enter the fuel tank cap body until the balance of pressure is restored whereupon the valve closes.

26 Accelerator pedal - removal and replacement

1 Release the throttle cable clip and detach the throttle cable from the lever on the accelerator pedal shaft.

2 Carefully disconnect the accelerator petal return spring.

3 Withdraw the retaining pins from each side of the right hand bush.

4 The accelerator pedal and shaft may now be withdrawn from the pedal mounting bracket.

5 Refitting the accelerator pedal is the reverse sequence. Lubricate the bushes and cable attachment with a little Castrol LM Grease.

6 It is now necessary to adjust the accelerator pedal position.

7 Manual transmission: Place a 0.015 in (0.381 mm) feeler gauge between the return stop and the pedal arm. Adjust the return stop located under the instrument panel until the front face of the accelerator pedal pad is 4.5 inch (114.3 mm) from the floor panel. Now adjust the accelerator cable to remove slackness.

8 Automatic transmission: Detach the accelerator cable at the bell crank ball joint. Now adjust the accelerator pedal pad height to 4.5 inches (114.3 mm) from the top face of the pedal to the floor by turning the pedal stop adjustment bolt which is located under the instrument panel. If necessary reset the engine idle speed. Adjust the accelerator cable until it just slides onto the bell crank ball joint and reconnect. Finally remove the air cleaner (Section 3) and ensure that the carburettor throttle plates open fully and return to the idle position when the pedal is released.

27 Accelerator cable - removal and replacement

1 Open the bonnet and detach the accelerator cable from the accelerator lever ball stud.

2 Slacken the two cable adjustment nuts at the bracket and slip the cable from the bracket.

3 Detach the cable from the accelerator pedal shaft lever.

4 Remove the cable retainer at the dash panel and remove the cable.

5 Refitting the cable is the reverse sequence to removal.

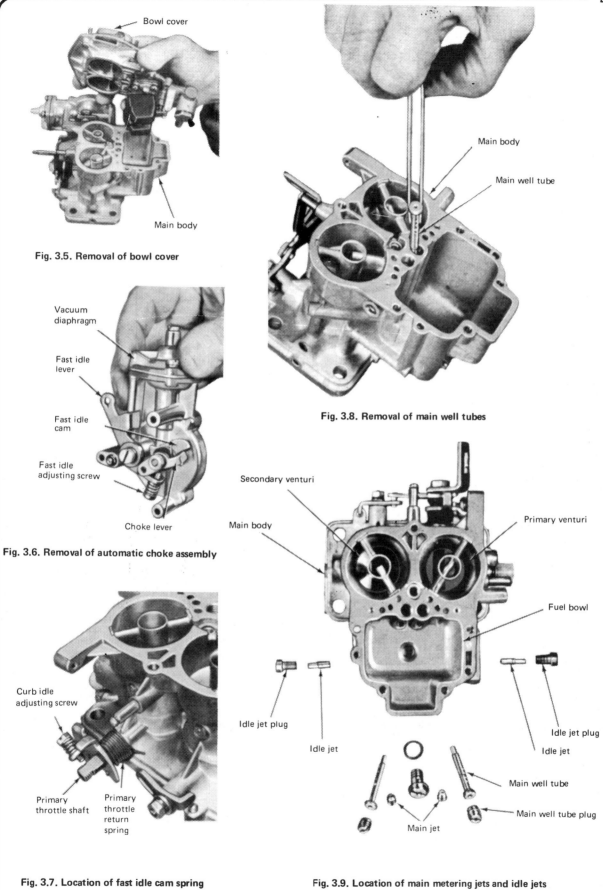

Bowl cover

Main body

Fig. 3.5. Removal of bowl cover

Vacuum diaphragm

Fast idle lever

Fast idle cam

Fast idle adjusting screw

Choke lever

Fig. 3.6. Removal of automatic choke assembly

Curb idle adjusting screw

Primary throttle shaft

Primary throttle return spring

Fig. 3.7. Location of fast idle cam spring

Main body

Main well tube

Fig. 3.8. Removal of main well tubes

Secondary venturi

Main body

Primary venturi

Fuel bowl

Idle jet plug

Idle jet

Idle jet plug

Idle jet

Main well tube

Main well tube plug

Main jet

Fig. 3.9. Location of main metering jets and idle jets

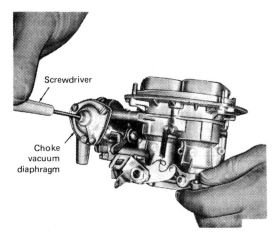

Screwdriver

Choke
vacuum
diaphragm

**Fig. 3.10. ADJUSTMENT OF AUTOMATIC CHOKE
DURING REASSEMBLY**

The threads must be flush with inside of cover.

28 Kickdown cable (C4 automatic transmission) - removal, replacement and adjustment

1 Detach the kickdown cable from the throttle lever bell crank.
2 Slacken the two cable adjustment nuts at the bracket. The cable may now be withdrawn sideways from the bracket.
3 Chock the front wheels, jack up the rear of the car and support on firmly based stands.
4 Working under the car disconnect the kickdown cable from the transmission unit.
5 The cable may now be removed from the car.
6 Refitting the cable is the reverse sequence to removal. It will however, be necessary to adjust the linkage.
7 Move the throttle to the wide open position and locate the kickdown cable so that the tang just contacts the throttle shaft. This condition is obtained by repositioning the nuts and then tightening.

29 Downshift valve control cable (BW35 Automatic transmission) - removal, replacement and adjustment.

1 Detach the downshift valve control cable from the bell crank assembly.
2 Slacken the cable to bracket retaining nut and withdraw the cable sideways from the bracket.
3 Chock the front wheels, jack up the rear of the car and support on firmly based stands.
4 Wipe the area around the transmission unit drain plug and unscrew. Allow the fluid to drain into a clean container. If the car has just been run take extreme care as the fluid will be extremely hot and can cause severe burns.
5 Undo and remove the bolts and washers that secure the oil pan to the transmission unit body. Lift away the oil pan and its gasket.
6 Rotate the cam sufficiently for the downshift control cable to be detached.
7 Unscrew the outer cable from the transmission body and lift away the cable from the car.
8 To refit the cable first screw the cable into the transmission body and fully tighten.
9 Rotate the cam and connect the downshift control cable to the cam.
10 Fit a new oil pan gasket and replace the oil pan. Secure with the bolts and washers.

11 Lower the car and position the cable in the bracket. Secure with the retaining nut.
12 Reconnect the cable to the bell crank assembly. If a new cable is being fitted, crimp the sliding collar so as to provide a clearance of 0.030 inch (0.762 mm) between the collar and housing.
13 Refill the transmission unit as described in Chapter 6 and then road test.

30 Fuel system - fault finding

There are three main types of fault that the fuel system is prone to, and they may be summarised as follows:-
a) Lack of fuel at engine.
b) Weak mixture.
c) Rich mixture.
It can be difficult to diagnose the cause of a fuel system or engine malfunction because of the modifications made to comply with the US Federal Regulations. Because of this the condition of the engine, the efficiency of the ignition system, ignition timing, and the operation of the fuel system are very much interdependent. To save a considerable amount of time if a fault is suspected, other than complete failure, the car should be taken to the local Capri dealer who will have special diagnostic equipment which will enable him to find quickly the cause of any trouble.
The recommendations given in the following three sections are to be used as a guide to serious faults of the major units. Emission modification faults are purposely not covered.

31 Lack of fuel at engine

1 If it is not possible to start the engine, first positively check that there is fuel in the fuel tank, and then check the ignition system as detailed in Chapter 4. If the fault is not in the ignition system then disconnect the fuel inlet pipe from the carburettor and turn the engine over by the starter switch.
2 If petrol squirts from the end of the inlet pipe, reconnect the pipe and check that the fuel is getting to the float chamber. This is done by unscrewing the bolts from the top of the float chamber, and lifting the cover just enough to see inside.
3 If fuel is there then it is likely that there is a blockage in the starting jet, which should be removed and cleaned.
4 No fuel in the float chamber, is caused either by a blockage in the pipe between the pump and float chamber or a sticking float chamber valve. Alternatively the filter may be blocked.
5 If it is decided that it is the float chamber valve that is sticking, the carburettor should be partially dismantled and the valve inspected for signs of dirt or gum causing it to stick in the closed position.
6 If no petrol squirts from the end of the pipe leading to the carburettor then disconnect the pipe leading to the inlet side of the fuel pump. If fuel runs out of the pipe then there is a fault in the fuel pump, and the pump should be checked.
7 No fuel flowing from the tank when it is known that there is fuel in the tank indicates a blocked pipe line. The line to the tank should be blown out. It is unlikely that the fuel tank vent would become blocked, but this could be a reason for the reluctance of the fuel to flow. To test for this, blow into the tank down the fill orifice. There should be no build up of pressure in the fuel tank, as the excess pressure should be carried away down the vent pipe.

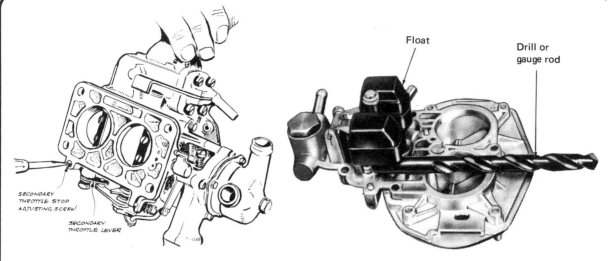

Fig. 3.11. Adjustment of secondary throttle stop

SECONDARY THROTTLE STOP ADJUSTING SCREW

SECONDARY THROTTLE LEVER

Float

Drill or gauge rod

Fig. 3.12. Float setting

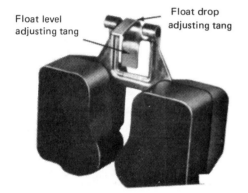

Float level adjusting tang

Float drop adjusting tang

Fig. 3.13. Adjustment of float assembly

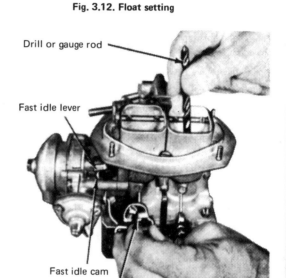

Drill or gauge rod

Fast idle lever

Fast idle cam

Throttle lever

Fig. 3.14. Adjustment of de-choke

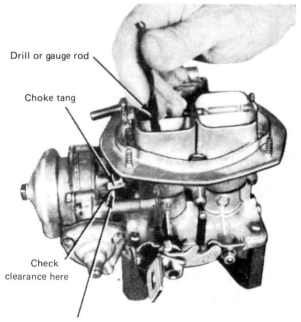

Drill or gauge rod

Choke tang

Check clearance here

Fast idle cam

Fig. 3.15. Adjustment of fast idle speed

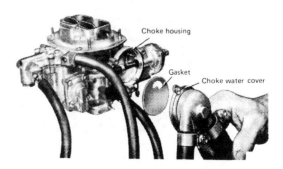

Choke housing

Gasket

Choke water cover

Fig. 3.16. Removal of choke water cover

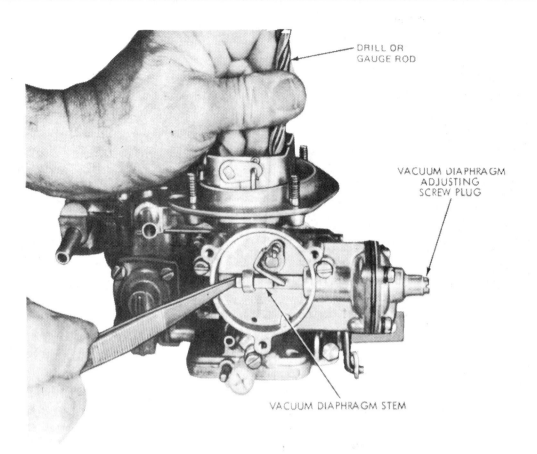

DRILL OR
GAUGE ROD

VACUUM DIAPHRAGM
ADJUSTING
SCREW PLUG

VACUUM DIAPHRAGM STEM

Fig. 3.17. Pushing in vacuum diaphragm stem to enable measurement of choke plate pull down

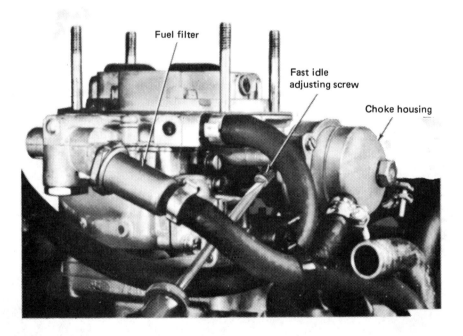

Fuel filter

Fast idle
adjusting screw

Choke housing

Fig. 3.18. Adjustment of fast idle speed

Fig. 3.19. Engine idle mixture adjustment

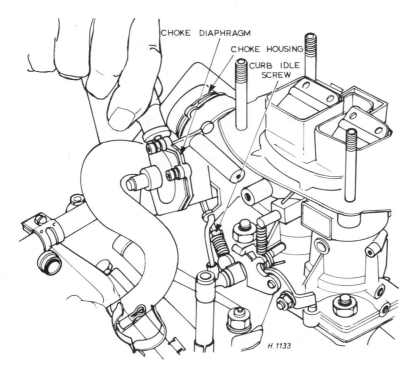

Fig. 3.20. Adjustment of curb idle

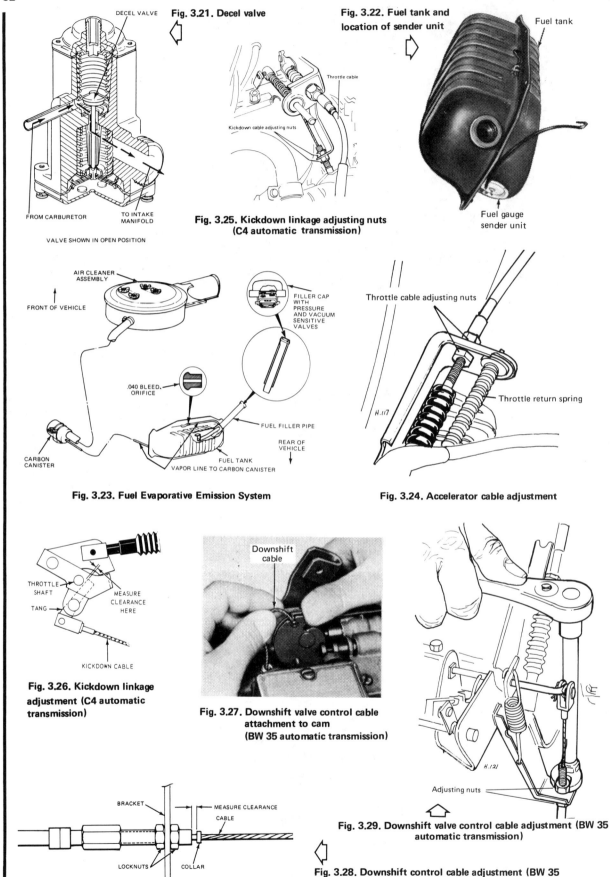

Fig. 3.21. Decel valve

DECEL VALVE

FROM CARBURETOR

TO INTAKE MANIFOLD

VALVE SHOWN IN OPEN POSITION

Fig. 3.22. Fuel tank and location of sender unit

Fuel tank

Fuel gauge sender unit

Throttle cable

Kickdown cable adjusting nuts

Fig. 3.25. Kickdown linkage adjusting nuts (C4 automatic transmission)

AIR CLEANER ASSEMBLY

FRONT OF VEHICLE

FILLER CAP WITH PRESSURE AND VACUUM SENSITIVE VALVES

.040 BLEED ORIFICE

FUEL FILLER PIPE

REAR OF VEHICLE

CARBON CANISTER

FUEL TANK

VAPOR LINE TO CARBON CANISTER

Fig. 3.23. Fuel Evaporative Emission System

Throttle cable adjusting nuts

Throttle return spring

H.117

Fig. 3.24. Accelerator cable adjustment

THROTTLE SHAFT

TANG

MEASURE CLEARANCE HERE

KICKDOWN CABLE

Fig. 3.26. Kickdown linkage adjustment (C4 automatic transmission)

Downshift cable

Fig. 3.27. Downshift valve control cable attachment to cam (BW 35 automatic transmission)

Adjusting nuts

H.121

Fig. 3.29. Downshift valve control cable adjustment (BW 35 automatic transmission)

BRACKET

MEASURE CLEARANCE

CABLE

LOCKNUTS

COLLAR

Fig. 3.28. Downshift control cable adjustment (BW 35 automatic transmission)

32 Weak mixture

1 If the fuel/air mixture is weak there are six main clues to this condition:-
a) The engine will be difficult to start.
b) The engine will overheat easily.
c) If the spark plugs are examined (as detailed in the section on engine tuning), they will have a light grey/white deposit on the insulator nose.
d) The fuel consumption may be light.
e) There will be a noticeable lack of power.
f) During acceleration and on the over-run there will be a certain amount of spitting back through the carburettor.

2 As the carburettor is of the fixed jet type, these faults are invariably due to circumstances outside the carburettor. The only usual fault likely in the carburettor is that one or more of the jets may be partially blocked. If the car will not start easily but runs well at speed, then it is likely that the starting jet is blocked, whereas if the engine starts easily but will not rev, then it is likely that the main jets are blocked.

3 If the level of petrol in the float chamber is low this is usually due to a sticking valve or incorrectly set floats.

4 Air leaks either in the fuel lines, or in the induction system should also be checked for. Also check the distributor vacuum pipe connection as a leak in this is directly felt in the inlet manifold.

5 The fuel pump may be at fault and should be checked.

33 Rich mixture

1 If the fuel/air mixture is rich there are also six main clues to this condition:-
a) If the spark plugs are examined they will be found to have a black sooty deposit on the insulator nose.
b) The fuel consumption will be heavy.
c) The exhaust will give off a heavy black smoke, especially when accelerating.
d) The interior deposits on the exhaust pipe will be dry, black and sooty (if they are wet, black and sooty this indicates worn bores, and much oil being burnt).
e) There will be a noticeable lack of power.
f) There will be a certain amount of back-firing through the exhaust system.

2 The faults in this case are usually in the carburettor and the most usual is that the level of petrol in the float chamber is too high. This is due either to dirt behind the needle valve, or a leaking float (metallic type only) which will not close the valve properly, or a sticking needle.

3 With a very high mileage (or because someone has tried to clean the jets out with wire), it may be that the jets have become enlarged.

4 If the air correction jets are restricted in any way the mixture will tend to become very rich.

5 Occasionally it is found that the automatic choke control is sticking or has been maladjusted.

6 Again, occasionally the fuel pump pressure may be excessive so forcing the needle valve open slightly until a higher level of petrol is reached in the float chamber.

34 Fuel gauge and sender unit - fault finding

1 If the fuel gauge fails to give a reading with the ignition on or reads 'FULL' all the time, then a check must be made to see if the fault is in the gauge, sender unit, or wire in between.

2 Turn the ignition on and disconnect the wire from the fuel tank sender unit. Check that the fuel gauge needle is on the empty mark. To check if the fuel gauge is in order now earth the fuel tank sender unit wire. This should send the needle to the full mark.

3 If the fuel gauge is in order, check the wiring for shorts or loose connections. If none can be found, then the sender unit will be at fault and must be renewed.

4 Should both the fuel gauge, and the temperature gauge fail to work, or if they both give unusually high readings, then a check must be made of the instrument voltage regulator.

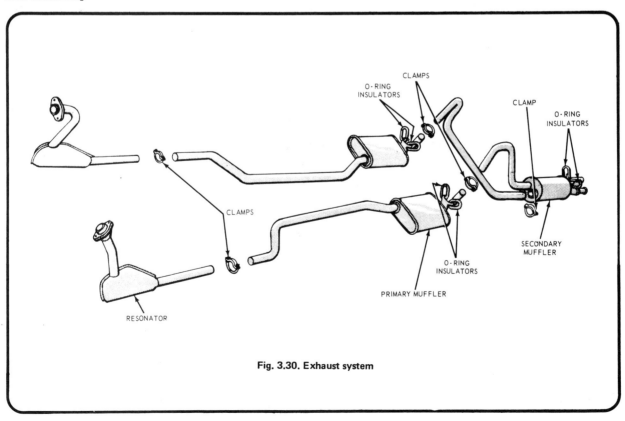

Fig. 3.30. Exhaust system

Chapter 4 Ignition system

Contents

Specifications

Spark plugs

Make	Autolite, AG 32
Plug gap	See 'tune up' sticker on inner wing under bonnet

Coil

Type	oil filled
Resistance at 20°C (68°F)	
Primary	3.1 to 3.5 ohms
Secondary	4.750 to 5.750 ohms
Output	30 kv

Distributor

Type	Bosch series 12127
Contact points gap setting	0.025 inch (0.64 mm)
Rotation	Clockwise
Ignition advance	Centrifugal and vacuum controlled
Dwell angle	30° to 40°
Static advance (initial)	12° BTDC
Firing order	1 4 2 5 3 6
Resistance	
Identification	Grey
Resistance	1.4 - 1.6 ohms

Electronic distributor control

Type	Imco transmission spark control or electronic spark control system

Torque wrench settings:

	lb f ft	kg fm
Spark plugs	24 to 28	3.32 to 3.87

Spark plug and cylinder numbering sequence:

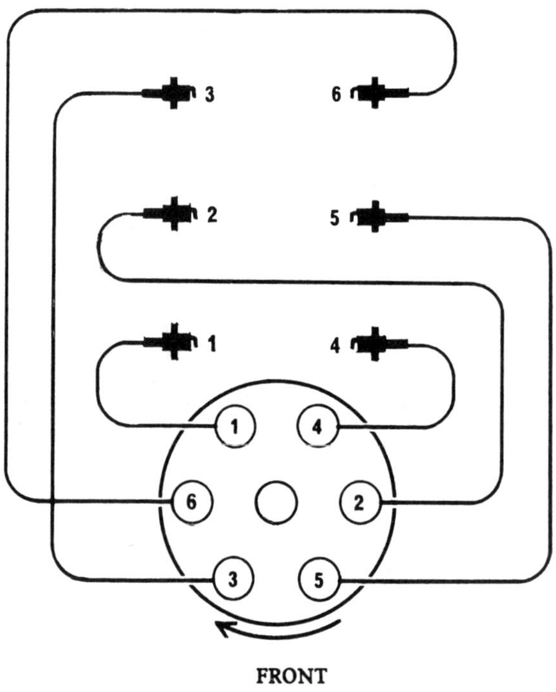

FRONT

Fig. 4.S1 Plug/Distributor connections

1 General description

In order that the engine can run correctly it is necessary for an electrical spark to ignite the fuel/air mixture in the combustion chamber at exactly the right moment in relation to engine speed and load. The ignition system is based on feeding low tension voltage from the battery to the coil where it is converted to high tension voltage. The high tension voltage is powerful enough to jump the spark plug gap in the cylinders many times a second under high compression, providing that the system is in good condition and that all adjustments are correct.

The ignition system is divided into two circuits, low tension and high tension.

The low tension circuit (sometimes known as the primary) consists of the battery, lead to the control box, lead to the ignition switch, lead from the ignition switch to the low tension or primary coil windings (terminal BAT), and the lead from the low tension coil windings (coil terminal DIST) to the contact breaker points and condenser in the distributor.

The high tension circuit consists of the high tension or secondary coil windings, the heavy ignition lead from the centre of the coil windings, the heavy ignition lead from the centre of the coil to the centre of the distributor cap, the rotor arm, and the spark plug leads and spark plugs.

The system functions in the following manner. Low tension voltage is changed in the coil into high tension voltage by the opening and closing of the contact breaker points in the low tension circuit. High tension voltage is then fed via the carbon brush in the centre of the distributor cap to the rotor arm of the distributor cap, and each time it comes in line with one of the four metal segments in the cap, which are connected to the spark plug leads, the opening and closing of the contact breaker points causes the high tension voltage to build up, jump the gap from the rotor arm to the appropriate metal segment and so via the spark plug lead to the spark plug, where it finally jumps the spark plug gap before going to earth.

The ignition is advanced and retarded automatically, to ensure the spark occurs at just the right instant for the particular load at the prevailing engine speed.

The ignition advance is controlled both mechanically and by a vacuum operated system. The mechanical governor comprises two weights, which move out from the distributor shaft as the engine speed rises due to centrifugal force. As they move outwards they rotate the cam relative to the distributor shaft, and so advance the spark. The weights are held in position by two light springs and it is the tension of the springs which is largely responsible for correct spark advancement.

The vacuum control consists of a diaphragm, one side of which is connected via a small bore tube to the carburettor, and the other side to the contact breaker plate. Depression in the inlet manifold and carburettor, which varies with engine speed and throttle opening, causes the diaphragm to move, so moving the contact breaker plate, and advancing or retarding the spark. A fine degree of control is achieved by a spring in the vacuum assembly.

The wiring harness includes a high resistance wire in the ignition coil feed circuit and it is very important that only a 'ballast resistor' type ignition coil is used. This lead is identified by its grey colour tracer colour coding and has a resistance of 1.4 - 1.6 ohms. The starter solenoid has an extra terminal so that a wire from the solenoid to the coil supplies current direct to the coil when the starter motor is operated. The ballast resistor wire is therefore by-passed and battery voltage is fed to the ignition system so giving easier starting.

2 Ignition system servicing and Federal Regulations

In order to conform with the Federal Regulations which govern the emission of hydrocarbons and carbon monoxide from car exhaust systems, the engine, carburation and ignition system have been suitably modified.

It is critically important that the ignition system is kept in good operational order and to achieve this accurate analytical equipment is needed to check and reset the distributor function. This will be found at your local dealer.

Information contained in this Chapter is supplied to enable the home mechanic to set the ignition system roughly so enabling starting the engine. Thereafter the car must be taken to the local Capri dealer for final tuning. Failure to do this can result in heavy penalties.

3 Contact breaker points - adjustment

1 To adjust the contact breaker points to the correct gap first release the two clips securing the distributor cap to the distributor body, and lift away the cap. Clean the cap inside and out with a dry cloth. It is unlikely that the six segments will be badly burned or scored, but if they are the cap will have to be renewed.
2 Inspect the contact located in the top of the cap and make sure it is serviceable.
3 Gently prise the contact breaker points open to examine the condition of their faces. If they are rough, pitted or dirty it will be necessary to remove them for refacing or for a replacement points assembly to be fitted.
4 Presuming that the points are satisfactory, or that they have been cleaned and refitted, measure the gap between the points by turning the engine over until the heel of the breaker arm is on the highest point of the cam.
5 A 0.025 inch (0.64 mm) feeler gauge should now just fit between the points.
6 If the gap varies from this amount, slacken the lockscrew and adjust the contact gap by inserting a screwdriver in the notched hole in the breaker plate. Turn clockwise to increase and anti clockwise to decrease the gap. When the gap is correct, tighten the securing screw and check the gap again.
7 Make sure the rotor is in position, replace the distributor cap and clip the spring blade retainers into position.

4 Contact breaker points - removal and replacement

1 If the contact breaker points are burned, pitted or badly worn they must be removed and renewed.
2 Lift off the rotor arm by pulling it straight up from the spindle.
3 Detach the contact breaker point wire from the condenser and coil terminal.
4 Undo and remove the single contact breaker point assembly lock screw and lift out the breaker point assembly.
5 Refitting the contact breaker points is the reverse sequence to removal. The gap must be reset as described in Section 3.
6 Finally replace the rotor arm and then the distributor cap.
NOTE: Should the contact points be badly worn a new assembly must be fitted. As an emergency measure clean the faces with fine emery paper folded over a thin steel rule. It is necessary to remove completely the built up deposits, but not necessary to rub the fitted point right down to the stage where all the pitting has disappeared. When the surfaces are flat a feeler gauge can be used and the gap reset.

5 Condenser - removal, testing and replacement

1 The purpose of the condenser, (sometimes known as a capacitor) is to ensure that when the contact breaker points open there is no sparking across them which would waste voltage and cause wear.
2 The condenser is fitted in parallel with the contact breaker points. If it develops a short circuit, it will cause ignition failure as the points will be prevented from interrupting the low tension circuit.

3 If the engine becomes very difficult to start or begins to miss after several miles running and the breaker points show signs of excessive burning, then the condition of the condenser must be suspect. A further test can be made by separating the points by hand with the ignition switched on. If this is accompanied by a flash it is indicative that the condenser has failed.

4 Without special test equipment the only sure way to diagnose condenser trouble is to replace a suspected unit with a new one and note if there is any improvement.

5 To remove the condenser from the distributor take off the distributor cap and rotor arm.

6 Detach the condenser lead from the contact breaker point and coil lead terminal.

7 Undo and remove the one screw that secures the condenser to the distributor body.

8 Carefully work the wire grommet from the distributor body and lift away condenser.

9 Refitting the condenser is the reverse sequence to removal.

6 Distributor - lubrication

1 It is important that the distributor cam is lubricated with petroleum jelly at the specified mileages, and that the breaker arm, governor weights, and cam spindle, are lubricated with engine oil once every 6,000 miles.

2 Great care should be taken not to use too much lubricant, as any excess that finds its way onto the contact breaker points could cause burning and misfiring.

3 To gain access to the cam spindle, lift away the rotor arm. Drop no more than two drops of enigne oil onto the felt pad. This will run down the spindle when the engine is hot and lubricate the bearings.

4 To lubricate the automatic timing control allow a few drops of oil to pass through the hole in the contact breaker base plate through which the four sided cam emerges. Apply not more than one drop of oil to the pivot post and remove any excess.

7 Distributor - removal

1 To remove the distributor first release the two clips that secure the distributor cap to the distributor body. Lift away the distributor cap.

2 Detach the vacuum lines from the vacuum advance diaphragm.

3 To make refitting simpler rotate the crankshaft until the timing notch in the crankshaft pulley is at the 12° BTDC mark on the plate. Ascertain that the No 1 cylinder is on the compression stroke by removing the spark plug and feeling the compression with a thumb as the piston rises in the cylinder. The distributor rotor should now point to No 1 cylinder.

4 Undo and remove the distributor hold down bolt and withdraw the distributor.

8 Distributor - dismantling, overhaul and reassembly

1 With the distributor on the bench, release the two spring clips retaining the cap and lift away the cap.

2 Pull the rotor arm off the distributor cam spindle.

3 Remove the contact breaker points as described in Section 4.

4 Unscrew and remove the condenser securing screw and lift away the condenser and connector.

5 Next carefully remove the 'U' shaped clip from the pull rod of the vacuum unit.

6 Undo and remove the two screws that secure the vacuum unit to the side of the distributor body. Lift away the vacuum unit.

7 Undo and remove the screws that secure the distributor cap spring clip retainer to the side of the distributor body. Lift away the two clips and retainers. This will also release the breaker plate assembly.

8 Lift away the contact breaker plate assembly from the inside of the distributor body.

9 Separate the breaker plate by removing the spring clip that holds the lower and upper plates together.

10 It is important that the primary and secondary springs of the automatic advance system are refitted in their original position during reassembly to the springs, weights and upper plate must be marked accordingly.

11 Unhook the springs from the posts on the centrifugal weights.

12 Using a screwdriver, release the cam from the cam spindle and recover the felt pad, lock ring, and thrust washers from the cam. Release the two springs from the cam plate and lift away the centrifugal weights and washers.

13 Should it be necessary to remove the drive gear, using a suitable diameter parallel pin punch tap out the gear lock pin.

14 The gear may now be drawn off the shaft with a universal puller. If there are no means of holding the legs these must be bound together with wire to stop them springing apart during removal.

15 Finally withdraw the shaft from the distributor body.

16 Check the contact breaker points for wear. Check the distributor cap for signs of tracking indicated by a thin black line between the segments. Renew the cap if any signs of tracking are found.

17 If the metal portion of the rotor arm is badly burned or loose, renew the arm. If only slightly burned clean the end with a fine file. Check that the contact spring has adequate pressure and the bearing surface is clean and in good condition.

18 Check that the carbon brush in the distributor cap is unbroken and stands proud of its holder.

19 Examine the centrifugal weights and pivots for wear and the advance springs for slackness. They can best be checked by comparing with new parts. If they are slack they must be renewed.

20 Check the points assembly for fit on the breaker plate, and the cam follower for wear.

21 Examine the fit of the spindle in the distributor body. If there is excessive side movement it will be necessary to either fit a new bush or obtain a new body.

22 To reassemble first refit the two centrifugal weight washers onto the cam spindle. Smear a little Castrol LM Grease onto the centrifugal weight contact faces and pivots and replace the weights in their original positions.

23 Lubricate the upper end of the spindle with Castrol GTX and slide on the cam. Hook the two springs onto the weight retainers so that they are refitted in their original positions.

24 Position the thrust washer and lock ring in the cam. Carefully manipulate the lock ring into position using a thin electrician's screwdriver.

25 Refit the felt pad and thoroughly soak with Castrol GTX.

26 Lubricate the distributor spindle with Castrol GTX and insert it into the housing. The gear may now be tapped into position taking care to line up the lock pin holes in the gear and spindle. Support the spindle whilst performing this operation.

27 Fit a new lock pin to the gear and spindle and make sure that it is symmetrically positioned.

28 Locate the lower breaker plate in the distributor body. Place the distributor cap retaining spring clip and retainers on the outside of the distributor body and secure the retainers and lower breaker plate with the two screws.

29 Position the contact breaker point assembly in the breaker plate in such a manner that the entire lower surface of the assembly contacts the plate. Refit the contact breaker point assembly securing screw but do not fully tighten yet.

30 Hook the diaphragm assembly pull rod into contact with the pivot pin.

31 Secure the diaphragm to the distributor body with the two screws. Also refit the condenser to the terminal side of the diaphragm bracket securing screw. The condenser must firmly contact its lower stop on the housing.

32 Apply a little Castrol LM Grease or vaseline to the cam and also to the heel of the breaker lever.

33 Reset the contact breaker points as described in Section 3 and then replace the rotor arm and distributor cap.

9 Distributor - replacement

1 Replacement is a reversal of the removal procedure given in Section 7.

2 Provided the engine timing has not been altered no difficulty should be encountered.

3 Insert the distributor, making sure that the rotor lines up with the No 1 cylinder mark on the distributor body when the distributor is in the proper position on the engine and the drive gears in mesh.

4 Secure the distributor hold down bolt.

5 Refit the distributor cap and secure with the two clips.

6 Refer to Section 10 and reset the ignition timing.

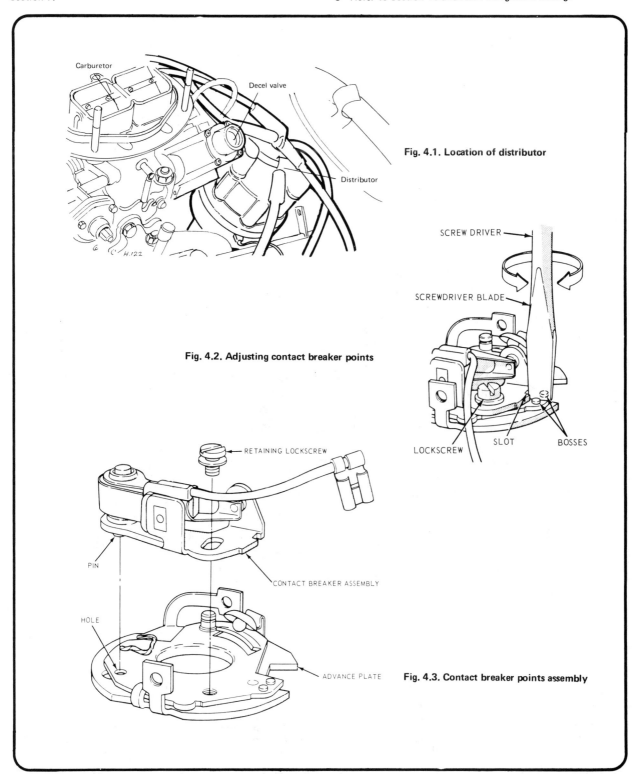

Fig. 4.1. Location of distributor

Fig. 4.2. Adjusting contact breaker points

Fig. 4.3. Contact breaker points assembly

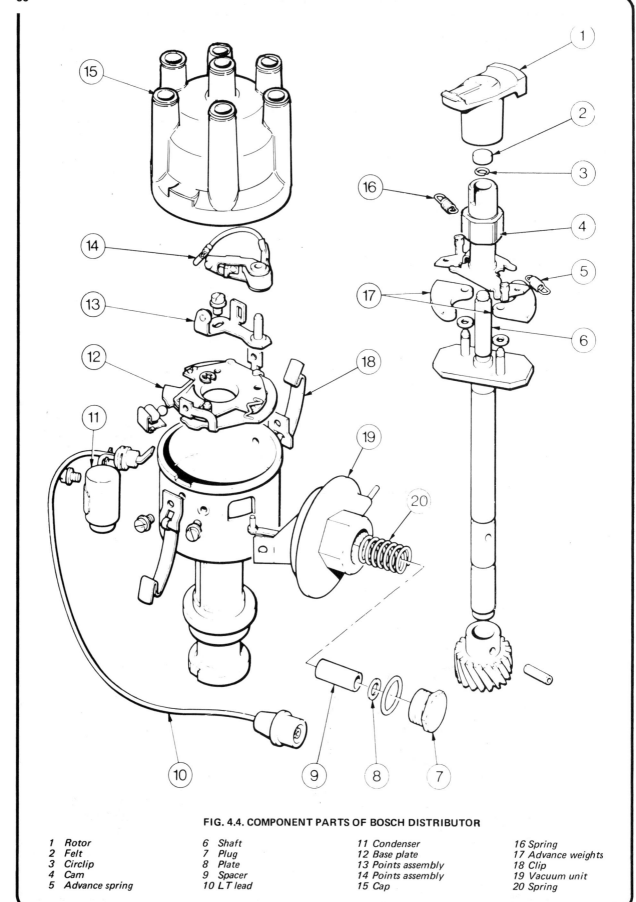

FIG. 4.4. COMPONENT PARTS OF BOSCH DISTRIBUTOR

1	Rotor	6	Shaft	11	Condenser	16	Spring
2	Felt	7	Plug	12	Base plate	17	Advance weights
3	Circlip	8	Plate	13	Points assembly	18	Clip
4	Cam	9	Spacer	14	Points assembly	19	Vacuum unit
5	Advance spring	10	LT lead	15	Cap	20	Spring

Fig. 4.5. Springs located on centrifugal weights

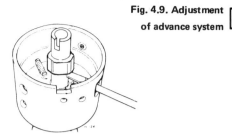

Fig. 4.6. Removal of cam from spindle

Fig. 4.9. Adjustment of advance system ⇨

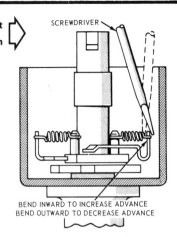

SCREWDRIVER

BEND INWARD TO INCREASE ADVANCE
BEND OUTWARD TO DECREASE ADVANCE

TDC

12° BTC

Fig. 4.10. Location of resistance wire (arrowed) ⇨

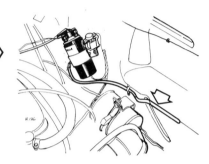

⇦ Fig. 4.7. Timing marks

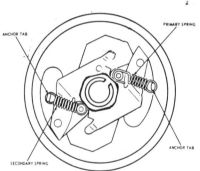

ANCHOR TAB

PRIMARY SPRING

SECONDARY SPRING

ANCHOR TAB

Fig. 4.8. Mechanical advance assembly

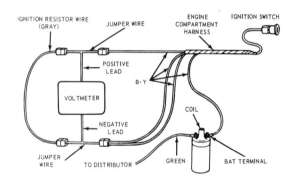

IGNITION RESISTOR WIRE (GRAY)   JUMPER WIRE   ENGINE COMPARTMENT HARNESS   IGNITION SWITCH

POSITIVE LEAD

B-Y

VOLTMETER

NEGATIVE LEAD

COIL

JUMPER WIRE   TO DISTRIBUTOR   GREEN   BAT TERMINAL

Fig. 4.11. Circuit for testing ignition resistance wire

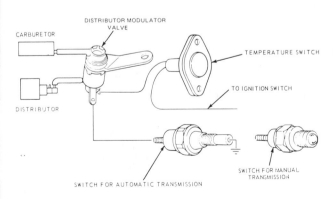

CARBURETOR

DISTRIBUTOR MODULATOR VALVE

TEMPERATURE SWITCH

TO IGNITION SWITCH

DISTRIBUTOR

SWITCH FOR AUTOMATIC TRANSMISSION

SWITCH FOR MANUAL TRANSMISSION

Fig. 4.12. Layout of transmission regulated spark control system (TRS)

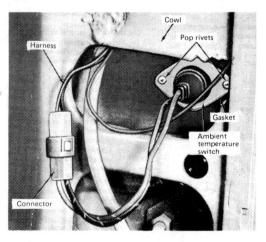

Cowl
Pop rivets
Harness
Gasket
Ambient temperature switch
Connector

Fig. 4.13. Location of Temperature Switch (TRS and ESC systems)

62

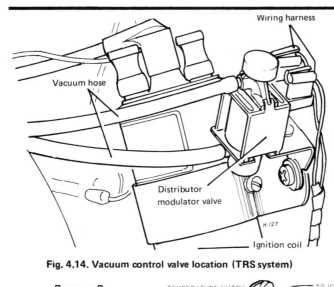

Vacuum hose

Wiring harness

Distributor
modulator valve

Ignition coil

Fig. 4.14. Vacuum control valve location (TRS system)

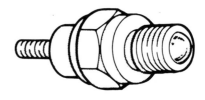

Fig. 4.15. Transmission switch (TRS system)

TEMPERATURE SWITCH

TO IGNITION SWITCH

CARBURETOR

AMPLIFIER

DISTRIBUTOR
MODULATOR
VALVE

DISTRIBUTOR

SPEED SENSOR

Fig. 4.16. Layout of Electronic Spark Control System (ESC system)

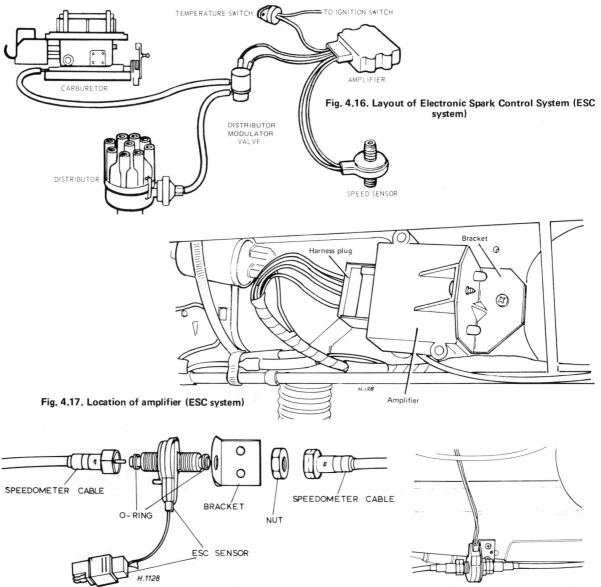

Harness plug

Bracket

Amplifier

Fig. 4.17. Location of amplifier (ESC system)

SPEEDOMETER CABLE

O-RING

BRACKET

NUT

SPEEDOMETER CABLE

ESC SENSOR

Fig. 4.18. Speed sensor and related parts (ESC system)

Fig. 4.19. Speed sensor location (ESC system)

10 Ignition timing

1 Refer to Section 3 and check the contact breaker points gap.
2 Rotate the crankshaft until the timing notch in the crankshaft pulley is at the 12° BTDC mark on the plate. Remove the distributor cap and check that the rotor is pointing to No 1 spark plug lead. If the distributor is away from the engine remove No 1 spark plug and feel the compression with a thumb as the piston rises in the cylinder.
3 Slacken the distributor clamp bolt and rotate the distributor body as necessary until the contact breaker points are just opening.
4 If this position cannot be reached check that the drive gear has meshed on the correct tooth by lifting out the distributor and resetting its position.
5 Tighten the distributor body clamp bolt, but do not over-tighten.
6 Set in this way the timing should be approximately correct but is not sufficient to comply with Federal Requirements - see Section 2.

11 Vacuum and mechanical advance - adjustments

1 The distributor is designed so that the vacuum and mechanical advance characteristics may be altered.
2 Normally no adjustment is necessary and should not be attempted. However, if a new shaft is fitted for example, the spring anchor tabs on the action plate may be in a relatively different position and thus could alter the tension on the springs. These tabs can be altered by bending them. This, however, is quite futile without specialist test and setting equipment so should not be attempted.

12 Ignition resistance wire - testing

To promote longer ignition system life the actual running voltage used in the system is reduced by means of a resistance wire positioned between the ignition switch and the ignition coil.

This circuit is alive when the ignition switch is on in the normal running position but is bypassed while the ignition switch is in the start position thereby applying full battery voltage for easier engine starting.

If the condition exists where the engine will start but will not run with the switch in the running position the resistance wire should be suspect and checked. To carry out this check proceed as follows:
1 Connect up a voltmeter as shown in Fig. 4.12.
2 Fit a jump wire from the distributor terminal of the coil to a good earth.
3 Make sure that all the accessories and lights are switched off.
4 Turn on the ignition.
5 The voltmeter should read between 6.6 and 4.5 volts. If the reading is above or below these limits the resistance wire should be renewed.

13 Electronic distributor controls

It is possible that one of two devices will be fitted into the ignition system to regulate the distributor by changing the vacuum forces applied to the distributor diaphragm. These devices are used because of exhaust emission control requirements.

The operation, testing and renewal of any of the parts are definitely beyond the scope of this manual. Any suspected malfunction of the system fitted must be referred to the local dealer for further investigation.

14 Spark plugs and leads

1 The correct functioning of the spark plugs are vital for the corect running and efficiency of the engine.
2 At intervals of 6,000 miles the plugs should be removed, examined, cleaned, and if worn excessively, renewed. The condition of the spark plugs will also tell much about the overall condition of the engine.
3 If the insulator nose of the spark plug is clean and white, with no deposits, this is indicative of a weak mixture, or too hot a plug. (A hot plug transfers heat away from the electrode slowly - a cold plug transfers it away quickly).
4 The plugs fitted as standard are as listed in specifications at the head of this Chapter. If the tip and insulator nose is covered with hard black looking deposits, then this is indicative that the mixture is too rich. Should the plug be black and oily, then it is likely that the engine is fairly worn, as well as the mixture being too rich.
5 If the insulator nose is covered with light tan to greyish brown deposits, then the mixture is correct and it is likely that the engine is in good condition.
6 If there are any traces of long brown tapering stains on the outside of the white portion of the plug, then the plug will have to be renewed, as this shows that there is a faulty joint between the plug body and the insulator, and compression is being allowed to leak away.
7 Plugs should be cleaned by a sand blasting machine, which will free them from carbon more thoroughly than cleaning by hand. The machine will also test the condition of the plugs under compression. Any plug that fails to spark at the recommended pressure should be renewed.
8 The spark plug gap is of considerable importance, as, if it is too large or too small, the size of the spark and its efficiency will be seriously impaired. The spark plug gap should be set to the figure given in specifications at the beginning of this Chapter.
9 To set it, measure the gap with a feeler gauge, and then bend open, or close, the outer plug electrode until the correct gap is achieved. The centre electrode should never be bent as this may crack the insulation and cause plug failure if nothing worse.
10 When replacing the plugs, remember to use new plug washers, and replace the leads from the distributor in the correct firing order.
11 The plug leads require no routine attention other than being kept clean and wiped over regularly.

At intervals of 6,000 miles, however, pull the leads off the plugs and distributor one at a time and make sure no water has found its way onto the connections. Remove any corrosion from the brass ends, wipe the collars on top of the distributor, and refit the leads.

15 Ignition system - fault symptoms

There are two main symptoms indicating faults. Either the engine will not start or fire, or the engine is difficult to start and misfires. If it is a regular misfire, i.e. the engine is only running on two or three cylinders the fault is almost sure to be in the secondary, or high tension circuit. If the misfiring is intermittent, the fault could be in either the high or low tension circuits. If the car stops suddenly or will not start at all, it is likely that the fault is in the low tension circuit. Loss of power and overheating, apart from faulty carburation settings, are normally due to faults in the distributor or incorrect ignition timing.

It must however, be pointed out that due to the engine being modified to comply with Federal Regulations the performance of the engine is dependent on the correct functioning of all systems. If a fault arises in one system it is possible that it will show up in another system. Therefore other than a major fault which will be obvious any intermittent or minor fault will probably require the use of electronic diagnostic equipment to quickly and accurately find the cause.

The suggestions given in the following two sections are for guidance purposes and should not be considered to cover every aspect of the ignition system. The obvious ommission is the electronic distributor control.

16 Fault diagnosis - engine fails to start

1   If the engine fails to start and the car was running normally when it was last used, first check there is fuel in the petrol tank. If the engine turns over normally on the starter motor and the battery is evidently well charged then the fault may be in either the high or low tension circuits. First check the HT circuit. NOTE: If the battery is known to be fully charged; the ignition light comes on, and the starter motor fails to turn the engine CHECK THE TIGHTNESS OF THE LEADS ON THE BATTERY TERMINALS also the secureness of the earth lead to its CONNECTION TO THE BODY. It is quite common for the leads to have worked loose, even if they look and feel secure. If one of the battery terminal posts gets very hot when trying to work the starter motor this is a sure indication of a faulty connection to that terminal.

2   One of the commonest reasons for bad starting is wet or damp spark plug leads and distributor. Remove the distributor cap. If condensation is visible internally dry the cap with a rag and also wipe over the leads. Replace the cap.

3   If the engine still fails to start, check that current is reaching the plugs, by disconnecting each plug lead in turn at the spark plug end, and hold the end of the cable about 0.187 in (4.76 mm) away from the cylinder block. Spin the engine on the starter motor.

4   Sparking between the end of the cable and the block should be fairly strong with a regular blue spark. (Hold the lead with rubber gloves to avoid electric shocks). If current is reaching the plugs, then remove them and clean and regap them to 0.025 in (0.64 mm). The engine should now start.

5   If there is no spark at the plug leads take off the HT lead from the centre of the distributor cap and hold it to the block as before. Spin the engine on the starter once more. A rapid succession of blue sparks between the end of the lead and the block indicate that the coil is in order and that the distributor cap is cracked the rotor arm faulty or the carbon brush in the top of the distributor cap is not making good contact with the spring on the rotor arm. Possibly the points are in bad condition. Clean and reset them as described in Section 3 of this Chapter.

6   If there are no sparks from the end of the lead from the coil check the connections at the coil end of the lead. If it is in order start checking the low tension circuit.

7   Use a 12v voltmeter or a 12v bulb and two lengths of wire. With the ignition switch on and the points open, test between the low tension wire to the coil (it is marked BAT) and earth. No reading indicates a break in the supply from the ignition switch. Check the connections at the switch to see if any are loose. Refit them and the engine should run. A reading shows a faulty coil or condenser or broken lead between the coil and the distributor.

8   Take the condenser wire off the points assembly and with the points open test between the moving point and earth. If there is now a reading, then the fault is in the condenser. Fit a new one and the fault is cleared.

9   With no reading from the moving point to earth, take a reading between earth and the DIST terminal of the coil. A reading here shows a broken wire which will need to be replaced between the coil and distributor. No reading confirms that the coil has failed and must be renewed, after which the engine will run once more. Remember to refit the condenser wire to the points assembly. For these tests it is sufficient to separate the points with a piece of dry paper while testing with the points open.

17 Fault diagnosis - engine misfires

1   If the engine misfires regularly, run it at a fast idling speed. Pull off each of the plug caps in turn and listen to the note of the engine. Hold the plug cap in a dry cloth or with a rubber glove as additional protection against a shock from the HT supply.

2   No difference in engine running will be noticed when the lead from the defective circuit is removed. Removing the lead from one of the good cylinders will accentuate the misfire.

3   Remove the plug lead from the end of the defective plug and hold it about 0.187 in (4.76 mm) away from the block. Restart the engine. If the sparking is fairly strong and regular the fault must lie in the spark plug.

4   The plug may be loose, the insulation may be cracked, or the points may have burnt away giving too wide a gap for the spark to jump. Worse still, one of the points may have broken off. Either renew the plug, or clean it, reset the gap, and then test it.

5   If there is no spark at the end of the plug lead, or if it is weak and intermittent, check the ignition lead from the distributor to the plug. If the insulation is cracked or perished, renew the lead. Check the connections at the distributor cap.

6   If there is still no spark, examine the distributor cap carefully for tracking. This can be recognised by a very thin black line running between two or more electrodes, or between an electrode and some other part of the distributor. These lines are paths which now conduct electricity across the cap thus letting it run to earth. The only answer is a new distributor cap.

7   Apart from the ignition timing being incorrect, other causes of misfiring have already been dealt with under section dealing with the failure of the engine to start. To recap - these are that:-
a) The coil may be faulty giving an intermittent misfire.
b) There may be a damaged wire or loose connection in the low tension circuit.
c) The condenser may be short circuiting.
d) There may be a mechanical fault in the distributor (broken driving spindle or contact breaker spring).

8   If the ignition timing is too far retarded, it should be noted that the engine will tend to overheat, and there will be a quite noticeable drop in power. If the engine is overheating and the power is down, and the ignition timing is correct, then the carburettor should be checked, as it is likely that this is where the fault lies.

White deposits and damaged porcelain insulation indicating overheating

Broken porcelain insulation due to bent central electrode

Electrodes burnt away due to wrong heat value or chronic pre-ignition (pinking)

Excessive black deposits caused by over-rich mixture or wrong heat value

Mild white deposits and electrode burnt indicating too weak a fuel mixture

Plug in sound condition with light greyish brown deposits

Fig. 4.20. The condition of spark plugs is a guide to the condition of the engine

Chapter 5 Clutch

Contents

Specifications

Type (clutch)	Single dry plate diaphragm spring
Actuation	Cable
Number of damper springs	6
Lining - outside diameter	9.5 inch (24.1 cm)
Lining - inside diameter	6.13 inch (15.56 cm)
Pressure plate diameter	9.5 inch (24.1 cm)
Total friction area	83 sq in (536 sq cm)
Free travel (at release bearing)	0.138 - 0.144 inch (3.505 - 3.658 mm)

Torque wrench settings:

	lbf ft	kg fm
Clutch to flywheel	11 to 14	1.53 to 1.94
Clutch housing to transmission case	40 to 47	5.5 to 6.47

1 General description

The clutch unit is of the single dry plate diaphragm spring type which comprises a steel cover dowelled and bolted to the rear face of the flywheel. It contains the pressure plate, diaphragm spring and fulcrum rings.

The clutch disc is free to slide along the splined first motion shaft and is held in position between the flywheel and the pressure plate by the pressure of the pressure plate spring. Friction lining material is riveted to the clutch disc and it has a spring cushioned hub to absorb transmission shocks and to help ensure a smooth take-off.

The circular diaphragm spring is mounted on shoulder pins and held in place in the cover by two fulcrum rings. The spring is also held to the pressure plate by three spring steel clips which are riveted in position.

The clutch is actuated by a cable controlled by the clutch pedal. The clutch release mechanism consists of a release fork and bearing which are in permanent contact with the release fingers on the diaphragm spring. There should therefore, never be any free play at the release fork. Wear of the friction material in the clutch is adjusted out by means of a cable adjuster at the lower end of the cable where it passes through the bellhousing.

Depressing the clutch pedal actuates the clutch release arm by means of the cable.

The release arm pushes the release bearing forwards to bear against the release fingers, so moving the centre of the diaphragm spring inwards. The spring is sandwiched between two annular rings which act as fulcrum points. As the centre of the spring is pushed in the outside of the spring is pushed out, so moving the pressure plate backwards and disengaging the pressure plate from the clutch disc.

When the clutch pedal is released the diaphragm spring forces the pressure plate into contact with the high friction linings on the clutch disc and at the same time pushes the clutch disc a fraction of an inch forwards on its splines so engaging the clutch disc with the flywheel. The clutch disc is now firmly sandwiched between the pressure plate and the flywheel so the drive is taken up.

2 Clutch adjustment

1 Every 6,000 miles (10,000 km), adjust the clutch cable to compensate for wear in the linings.

2 The clutch should be adjusted until there is a clearance of 0.138 to 0.144 inch (3.5 to 3.7 mm) between the adjusting nut and its abutment on the bellhousing as indicated in Fig. 5.3. When correctly adjusted there should be 0.50 to 0.75 inch (12.7 to 19.1 mm) free play at the clutch pedal.

3 To obtain the correct adjustment, slacken off the locknut (A in Fig. 5.3) and get an assistant to pull the clutch pedal onto its stop, then move the adjusting nut 'B' until the correct clearance has been obtained as mentioned in paragraph 2 above.

4 Hold the adjusting nut 'B' steady to prevent it moving and retighten the locknut 'A' then recheck the clearance and the pedal free movement.

5 When fitting a new friction plate it will be found that the cable will need fairly extensive adjustment particularly if the old friction plate was well worn.

3 Clutch - removal

1 Remove the gearbox as described in Chapter 6.

2 Scribe a mating line from the clutch cover to the flywheel to ensure identical positioning on replacement and then remove the clutch assembly by unscrewing the six bolts holding the cover to the rear face of the flywheel. Unscrew the bolts diagonally half a turn at a time to prevent distortion to the cover flange.

3 With all the bolts and spring washers removed lift the clutch assembly off the locating dowels. The driven plate or clutch disc may fall out at this stage as it is not attached to either the clutch cover assembly or the flywheel.

4 Clutch - overhaul

1 It is not practical to dismantle the pressure plate assembly and the term 'clutch dismantling and replacement' is a term usually used for simply fitting a new clutch friction plate.

2 If a new clutch disc is being fitted it is a false economy not to renew the release bearing at the same time. This will preclude having to replace it at a later date when wear on the clutch linings is still very small.

3 If the pressure plate assembly requires renewal (see Section 5) an exchange unit must be purchased. This will have been accurately set up and balanced to very fine limits.

5 Clutch - inspection

1 Examine the clutch disc friction linings for wear and loose rivets and the disc for rim distortion, cracks, broken hub springs, and worn splines. The surface of the friction linings may be highly glazed, but as long as the clutch material pattern can be clearly seen this is satisfactory. Compare the amount of lining wear with a new clutch disc at the stores in your local garage, and if the linings are more than three quarters worn renew the disc.

2 It is always best to renew the clutch driven plate as an assembly to preclude further trouble, but, if it is wished to merely renew the linings, the rivets should be drilled out and not knocked out with a punch. The manufacturers do not advise that only the linings are renewed and personal experience dictates that it is far more satisfactory to renew the driven plate complete than to try and economise by only fitting new friction linings.

3 Check the machined faces of the flywheel and the pressure plate. If either are grooved they should either be machined until smooth, or renewed.

4 If the pressure plate is cracked or split it is essential that an exchange unit is fitted, also if the pressure of the diaphragm spring is suspect.

5 Check the release bearing for smoothness of operation. There should be no harshness and no slackness in it. It should spin reasonably freely bearing in mind it has been pre-packed with grease.

6 Clutch - replacement

1 It is important that no oil or grease gets on the clutch disc friction linings, or the pressure plate and flywheel faces. It is advisable to replace the clutch with clean hands and to wipe down the pressure plate and flywheel faces with a clean dry rag before assembly begins.

2 Place the clutch disc against the flywheel, ensuring that it is the correct way round. The flywheel side of the clutch disc is clearly marked near the centre. If the disc is fitted the wrong way round, it will be quite impossible to operate the clutch.

3 Replace the clutch cover assembly loosely on the dowels. Replace the six bolts and spring washers and tighten them finger tight so that the clutch disc is gripped but can still be moved.

4 The clutch disc must now be centralised so that when the engine and gearbox are mated, the gearbox input shaft splines will pass through the splines in the centre of the driven plate hub.

5 Centralisation can be carried out quite easily by inserting a round bar or long screwdriver through the hole in the centre of the clutch, so that the end of the bar rests in the small hole in the end of the crankshaft containing the input shaft bearing bush. Ideally an old Ford input shaft should be used.

6 Using the input shaft bearing bush as a fulcrum, moving the bar sideways or up and down will move the clutch disc in whichever direction is necessary to achieve centralisation.

7 Centralisation is easily judged by removing the bar and viewing the driven plate hub in relation to the hole in the centre of the clutch cover plate diaphragm spring. When the hub appears exactly in the centre of the hole all is correct. Alternatively the input shaft will fit the bush and centre of the clutch hub exactly obviating the need for visual alignment.

8 Tighten the clutch bolts firmly in a diagonal sequence to ensure that the cover plate is pulled down evenly and without distortion of the flange. Finally tighten the bolts down to a torque of 11 to 14 lb ft (1.53 to 1.94 kg m).

7 Clutch release bearing - removal and replacement

1 With the gearbox and engine separated to provide access to the clutch, attention can be given to the release bearing located in the bellhousing, over the input shaft.

2 The release bearing is a relatively inexpensive but important component and unless it is nearly new it is a mistake not to renew it during an overhaul of the clutch.

3 To remove the release bearing first pull off the release arm rubber gaiter.

4 The release arm and bearing assembly can then be withdrawn from the clutch housing.

5 To free the bearing from the release arm simply unhook it, and then with the aid of two blocks of wood and a vice press off the release bearing from its hub.

6 Replacement is a straightforward reversal of these instructions.

8 Clutch cable - removal and replacement

1 Place chocks behind the rear wheels, jack up the front of the car, and place stands under the front crossmember.

2 Loosen the locknut on the cable adjuster on the bellhousing and slacken off the adjuster.

3 Spring off the clip (A in Fig. 5.4) from the top of the clutch pedal, push out the pivot pin (B) and pull the cable into the engine compartment.

4 Under the car, pull the rubber gaiter clear of the release arm and push the cable towards the gearbox and then out sideways through the slot in the outer end of the arm (See Fig. 5.5).

5 Replacement is a straightforward reversal of the removal sequence. Ensure the pivot pin is lubricated.

9 Clutch pedal - removal and replacement

1 The clutch pedal is removed and replaced in exactly the same way and the brake pedal.

2 A full description of how to remove and replace the brake pedal can be found in Chapter 9.

10 Clutch faults

There are four main faults to which the clutch and release mechanism are prone. They may occur by themselves or in conjunction with any of the other faults. They are clutch squeal, slip, spin and judder.

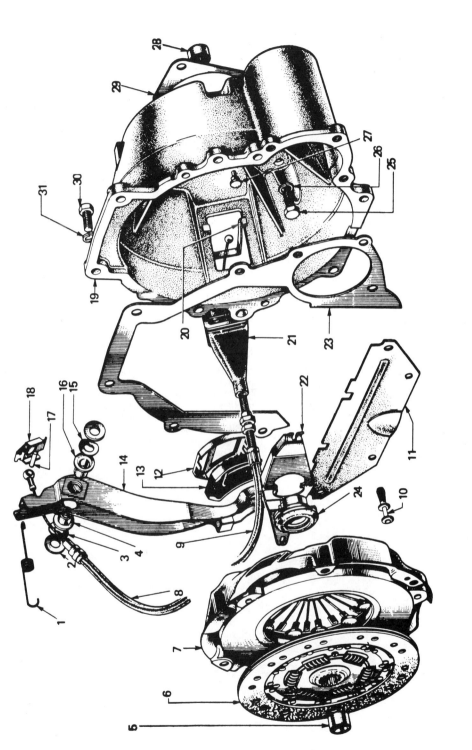

FIG. 5.1. THE CLUTCH ASSEMBLY

1 Spring
2 Washer
3 Washer
4 Bush
5 Bearing

6 Friction plate
7 Pressure plate and dia-
 phragm spring assembly
8 Clutch operating cable
9 Clutch operating cable

10 Inspection plate retainer
11 Inspection plate
12 Cover for pedal rubber
13 Pedal rubber
14 Pedal assembly

15 Washer
16 Bush
17 Pin
18 Clip
19 Bellhousing
20 Retaining spring clip

21 Rubber gaiter
22 Clutch release lever
23 Flywheel housing cover
24 Clutch release bearing
 assembly
25 Bolt

26 Spring washer
27 Dowel
28 Bearing
29 Gasket
30 Bolt
31 Spring washer

11 Clutch squeal - diagnosis and cure

1   If on taking up the drive or when changing gear, the clutch squeals, this is a sure indication of a badly worn clutch release bearing.

2   As well as regular wear due to normal use, wear of the clutch release bearing is much accentuated if the clutch is ridden, or held down for long periods in gear, with the engine running. To minimise wear of this component the car should always be taken out of gear at traffic lights and for similar hold-ups.

3   The clutch release bearing is not an expensive item, but difficult to get at.

12 Clutch slip - diagnosis and cure

1   Clutch slip is a self evident condition which occurs when the clutch friction plate is badly worn, oil or grease have got onto the flywheel or pressure plate faces, or the pressure plate itself is faulty.

2   The reason for clutch slip is that, due to one of the faults listed above, there is either insufficient pressure from the pressure plate, or insufficient friction from the friction plate to ensure solid drive.

3   If small amounts of oil get onto the clutch, they will be burnt off under the heat of clutch engagement, and in the process, gradually darkening the linings. Excessive oil on the clutch will burn off leaving a carbon deposit which can cause quite bad slip, or fierceness, spin and judder.

4   If clutch slip is suspected, and confirmation of this condition is required, there are several tests which can be made.

5   With the engine in second or third gear and pulling lightly up a moderate incline, sudden depression of the accelerator pedal may cause the engine to increase its speed without any increase in road speed. Easing off on the accelerator will then give a definite drop in engine speed without the car slowing.

6   In extreme cases of clutch slip the engine will race under normal acceleration conditions.

7   If slip is due to oil or grease on the linings a temporary cure can sometimes be effected by squirting carbon tetrachloride into the clutch. The permanent cure is, of course, to renew the clutch driven plate and trace and rectify the oil leak.

13 Clutch spin - diagnosis and cure

1   Clutch spin is a condition which occurs when the release arm travel is excessive, there is an obstruction in the clutch either on the primary gear splines, or in the operating lever itself, or the oil may have partially burnt off the clutch linings and have left a resinous deposit which is causing the clutch disc to stick to the pressure plate or flywheel.

2   The reason for clutch spin is that due to any, or a combination of, the faults just listed, the clutch pressure plate is not completely freeing from the centre plate even with the clutch pedal fully depressed.

3   If the clutch spin is suspected, the condition can be confirmed by extreme difficulty in engaging first gear from rest, difficulty in changing gear, and very sudden take-up of the clutch drive at the fully depressed end of the clutch pedal travel as the clutch is released.

4   Check that the clutch cable is correctly adjusted and if in order then the fault lies internally in the clutch. It will then be necessary to remove the clutch for examination, and to check the gearbox input shaft.

14 Clutch judder - diagnosis and cure

1   Clutch judder is a self evident condition which occurs when the gearbox or engine mountings are loose or too flexible, when there is oil on the faces of the clutch friction plate, or when the clutch pressure plate has been incorrectly adjusted during assembly.

2   The reason for clutch judder is that due to one of the faults just listed, the clutch pressure plate is not freeing smoothly from the friction disc, and is snatching.

3   Clutch judder normally occurs when the clutch pedal is released in first or reverse gears, and the whole car shudders as it moves backwards or forwards.

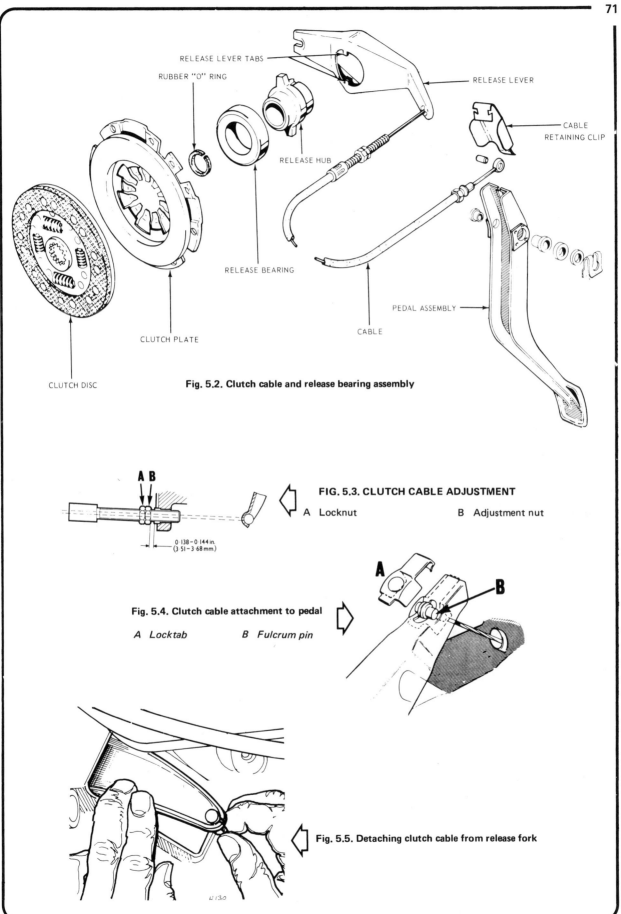

RELEASE LEVER TABS

RUBBER "O" RING

RELEASE LEVER

CABLE RETAINING CLIP

RELEASE HUB

RELEASE BEARING

PEDAL ASSEMBLY

CABLE

CLUTCH PLATE

CLUTCH DISC

Fig. 5.2. Clutch cable and release bearing assembly

A B

0·138 – 0·144 in.
(3·51 – 3·68 mm.)

FIG. 5.3. CLUTCH CABLE ADJUSTMENT

A Locknut   B Adjustment nut

Fig. 5.4. Clutch cable attachment to pedal

A Locktab   B Fulcrum pin

A

B

Fig. 5.5. Detaching clutch cable from release fork

Chapter 6 Gearbox and automatic transmission

Contents

Specifications

Manual gearbox

Number of gears	4 forward, 1 reverse
Type of gears	Helical, constant mesh
Synchromesh	All forward gears
Oil capacity	2.8 US pints/1.278 litres
Ratios:	
First	3.65 : 1
Second	1.97 : 1
Third	1.37 : 1
Fourth (top)	1.00 : 1
Reverse	3.66 : 1
Countershaft gear train end float	0.006 - 0.018 in (0.15 - 0.45 mm)

Automatic transmission

Type:	
Up to November 1967	C4
After November 1967	BW35
Torque converter ratio range	Infinitely variable between 1 : 1 and 2 : 1
Refill capacity*	
C4	15.6 US pints/7.387 litres
BW35	13.21 US pints/6.23 litres

C4

Gear ratios:	
First	2.46 : 1
Second	1.46 : 1
Third	1 : 1
Reverse	2.20 : 1
Model type	PED
Torque converter type	Hydro-Kinetic three element
Turbine and stator end float	0.060 in (1.524 mm) maximum
Normal operating temperature	66°C (150°F)
Band adjustment:	
Intermediate (front)	10 lb f ft (1.382 kg fm) back off 1.75 turns
Low/reverse (rear)	10 lb f ft (1.382 kg fm) back off 3 turns

BW35

Gear ratios:	
First	2 393 : 1
Second	1.450 : 1
Third	1.000 : 1
Reverse	2.094 : 1
Normal operating temperature	100 to 115°C (212 - 236°F)

Refill procedure C4 only ...   .

Add 0.6 US pint/0.28 litre if oil cooler fitted.
Add 1.5 US pints/0.65 litre if unit dry

Refill with 7.2 US pints/3.4 litres.
Add remainder after running engine. Select all ranges to charge valve bodies screws and clutches.
Disconnect the return pipe to bleed oil cooler if fitted.

Torque wrench settings:

	lb f ft	kg fm
Manual gearbox		
Drain and filler plugs	25 - 30	3.4 - 4.146
Cover to gearbox case	12 - 14	1.658 - 1.94
Clutch housing to gearbox case	40 - 47	5.528 - 6.47
Clutch housing to engine	22 27	3.04 - 3.7
Extension housing to gearbox case	30 - 35	4.146 - 4.8
Automatic transmission		
C4		
Converter to flywheel	23 - 28	3.18 - 3.870
Converter housing to transmission case	28 - 40	3.9 - 5.5
Oil sump to transmission case	12 - 16	1.658 - 2.211
Converter cover to converter housing	12 - 16	1.658 - 2.211
Engine to transmission	23 - 33	3.18 - 4.6
Converter drain plug (if fitted)	20 - 30	2.764 - 4.146
Downshift lever to shaft	12 - 16	1.658 - 2.211
Filler tube to engine	20 - 25	2.77 - 3.4
Filler tube to sump	32 - 42	4.4 - 5.81
Neutral switch to case	55 - 75	7.6 - 10.2
Oil cooler line connections	80 - 120	11.06 - 16.60
BW35		
Transmission case to converter housing	30 - 33	4.15 - 4.6
Torque converter to drive plate	40 - 45	5.5 - 6.22
Neutral switch locknut	4 - 6	0.55 - 0.83
Oil sump drain plug	9 - 12	1.2 - 1.658

1 General description

The manual gearbox fitted to all models contains four forward constant mesh helically cut gears and one reverse straight out gear. Synchromesh is fitted between 1st/2nd, 2nd/3rd, and 3rd/4th. The individual cast bellhousing and gearbox casings are bolted together as is the extension housing.

Gear selector levers are located on the left hand side of the gearbox and connect with a remote control gear change lever mounted on the floor of the car.

The gearbox is of a simple design using a minimum number of components. Where close tolerances and limits are required, manufacturing tolerances are compensated for and excessive end float or backlash is eliminated by fitting selective circlips (snap rings). When overhauling the gearbox always use new circlips, never replace ones that have already been used.

Gear selection is by means of the remote gear change lever and operates through three selector rods and six selector levers.

Automatic transmission is fitted as a factory option on models covered by this manual. Further information on the unit will be found in Sections 8 to 21 inclusive.

2 Gearbox - removal and replacement

1 The gearbox can be removed in unit with the engine through the engine compartment as described in Chapter 1. Alternatively the gearbox can be separated from the rear of the engine at the bellhousing and the gearbox lowered from under the car. The latter method is easier and quicker than the former.

2 If a hoist or an inspection pit are not available then run the back of the car up a pair of ramps or jack it up and fit axle stands. Next jack up the front of the car and support on axle stands.

3 For safety reasons disconnect the battery earth terminal.

4 Mark the propeller shaft and rear axle flanges so that they may be reconnected in their original positions. Undo and remove the four securing bolts and lower the rear half of the propeller shaft.

5 Undo and remove the two bolts that secure the centre bearing carrier to its bracket.

6 Carefully lower the front half of the propeller shaft whilst at the same time sliding the front yoke from the rear of the gearbox extension housing.

7 Wrap some polythene around the end of the gearbox and secure with string or wire to stop any oil running out.

8 Using a pair of circlip pliers or a small screwdriver remove the speedometer cable securing clip from the side of the gearbox extension housing. Withdraw the speedometer cable and tie back.

9 Detach the exhaust pipe securing bracket from the side of the gearbox and swing it clear.

10 Ease back the clutch release lever boot from the side of the gearbox bellhousing. Slacken the locknut to detach the inner cable from the release lever. Withdraw the clutch cable and tie back.

11 Carefully release the spring retainers and detach the selector rods from the selector levers on the left hand side of the gearbox.

12 Make a note of the electrical connections to the starter motor and then detach the connectors from the terminals.

13 Undo and remove the three bolts and spring washers that secure the starter motor. Withdraw the starter motor from its aperture and lift away.

14 Undo and remove the six bolts and spring washers that secure the clutch bellhousing to the rear of the engine.

15 Undo and remove the bolts and spring washers that secure the engine back plate to the front lower half of the flywheel housing.

16 Support the weight of the gearbox using a small jack. Use a second jack to support the rear of the engine.

17 Undo and remove the four bolts and spring washers that secure the gearbox crossmember to the underside of the body.

18 The gearbox may now be drawn rearwards from the engine. Because of its weight the help of a second person should now be enlisted. Be very careful not to allow the weight of the gearbox to hang on the gearbox input shaft. To give clearance between the gearbox and body, the jacks will have to be lowered.

19 The crossmember may now be detached from the gearbox by undoing and removing the two securing bolts and spring washers.

20 If major work is to be undertaken on the gearbox it is recommended that the exterior be washed with paraffin and dried with a non fluffy rag.

21 Refitting the gearbox is the reverse sequence to removal but the following aditional points should be noted:

a) Adjust the clutch control cable in such a manner that after two pedal applications there is a clearance of 0.138 - 0.144 inch (3.505 - 3.658 mm) between the adjustment nut and clutch housing.

b) Before reconnecting the selector rods to the selector levers grease the ends of the rods. Also lubricate the ball end of the clutch operating cable.

c) Check the correct operation of the gear selector linkage. If necessary readjust as described in Section 7.

3 Gearbox - dismantling

1 Place the complete unit on a firm bench or table and ensure that you have the following tools available, in addition to the normal range of spanners etc.,

a) Good quality circlip pliers, 2 pairs - 1 expanding and 1 contracting.

b) Copper headed hammer, at least 2 lb.

c) Selection of steel and brass drifts.

d) Small containers.

e) Engineer's vice mounted on firm bench.

f) Selection of steel tubing.

2 Any attempt to dismantle the gearbox without the foregoing is not impossible, but will certainly be very difficult and inconvenient.

3 Read the whole of this section before starting work.

4 Unscrew and remove the drain plug and allow the oil to drain out into a container of 3.603 US pints/1.705 litres. Refit the drain plug.

5 To dismantle first slide off the clutch release bearing and release fork.

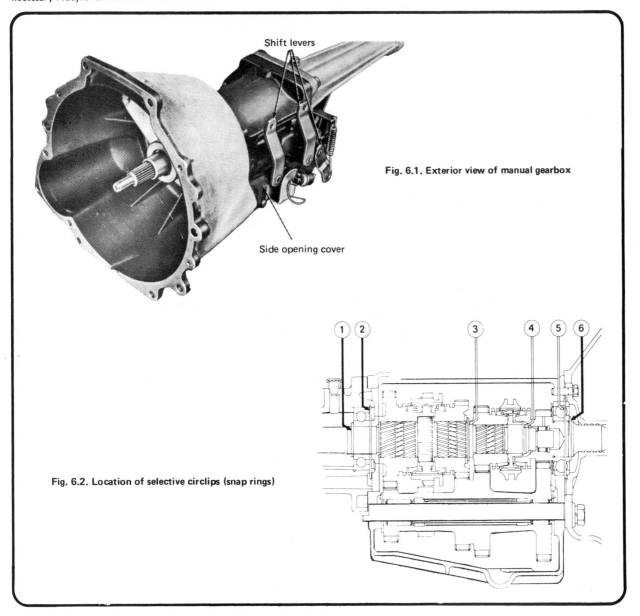

Fig. 6.1. Exterior view of manual gearbox

Shift levers

Side opening cover

Fig. 6.2. Location of selective circlips (snap rings)

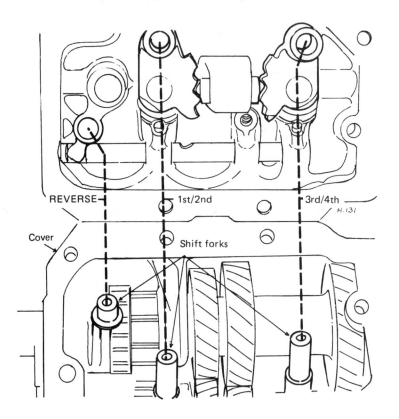

REVERSE   1st/2nd   3rd/4th   H.131

Cover

Shift forks

Fig. 6.3. Selector forks and cover

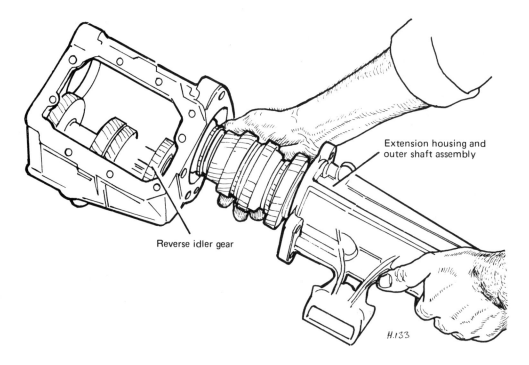

Extension housing and
outer shaft assembly

Reverse idler gear

H.133

Fig. 6.4. Removal of extension housing and output shaft assembly

6 Undo and remove the four bolts and spring washers that secure the clutch housing to the gearbox casing. Lightly tap the clutch housing and separate from the gearbox casing. Also remove the three bolts and spring washers securing the input shaft bearing retainer. Lift away the retainer and its gasket.

7 Undo and remove the seven bolts and spring washers that secure the gear change cover. Lift away the cover. Make a note of the location of the selector forks (shift forks). Lift away the selector forks.

9 Undo and remove the four bolts and spring washers that secure the gearbox extension housing to the gearbox casing.

10 Rotate the extension housing until the end of the countershaft becomes fully visible.

11 Using a suitable diameter drift drive out the countershaft from the front towards the extension housing. Once the countershaft is removed the cluster gear may now drop into the bottom of the gearbox casing.

12 Using a soft faced hammer, gently tap the input shaft from the front of the gearbox casing.

13 The extension housing complete with output shaft may now be drawn rearwards from the gearbox casing.

14 Lift out the cluster gear and recover the needle rollers and roller spacers from inside the cluster gear bore.

15 Also lift out the cluster gear thrust washers noting which way round they are fitted.

16 It will now be necessary to make up an offset drift as shown in Fig. 6.5. Using this drift drive out the reverse idler gear shaft towards the rear of the gearbox casing. Do not attempt to remove the shaft by drifting inwards.

17 The gearbox is now completely stripped out from the main casing.

18 Clean out the interior thoroughly and check for dropped needle rollers.

19 The output shaft may now be dismantled.

20 Remove the snap ring located in front of the 3rd/4th gear synchronizer. Withdraw the synchronizer assembly and 3rd gear from the output shaft.

21 Using circlip pliers remove the snap ring and thrust washer located in front of the 2nd gear. Pull off the 2nd gear and blocking ring.

22 Slide off the 1st/2nd gear synchronizer sleeve and synchronizer inserts. It will be observed that the synchronizer hub is splined to the output shaft and cannot be pressed off.

23 Unscrew the speedometer drive retainer and withdraw the speedometer driven gear and its retainer.

24 A snap ring located behind the 1st gear and extension housing must next be released. This can be a little difficult due to limited working space.

25 The output shaft can now be tapped out of the extension housing using a soft faced hammer.

26 The speedometer drive gear should next be removed. This may be done using a long leg puller or a soft metal drift and hammer.

27 Remove the snap ring located in front of the output shaft bearing. Using a press or bench vice and suitable packing pieces remove the bearing. Note which way round it is fitted.

28 Slide off the spacer and 1st gear including the blocking ring. Remove the insert spring.

29 The input shaft assembly may be dismantled by first removing the circlip using a pair of circlip pliers.

30 Place the input shaft gear on the top of the vice with the outer track of the race resting on soft faces.

31 Using a soft faced hammer drive the input shaft through the race inner track. The strain placed on the bearing does not matter, as the bearing would not be removed unless it was being renewed. Alternatively use a three legged universal puller.

32 Lift away the race from the input shaft noting the circlip groove on the outer track is offset towards the front.

33 To assemble the input shaft, place the race against soft metal faces (old shell bearing suitably straightened) on the top of the jaws of the vice and, using a drift located in the output spigot bearing hole in the rear of the input shaft, drift the shaft into the bearing. Make quite sure the bearing is the correct way round.

Alternatively use a piece of long tube of suitable diameter.

34 Refit the circlip that secures the bearing and also the one located in the bearing outer track.

4 Gearbox - inspection

1 It is assumed that the gearbox has been dismantled for reasons of excessive noise, lack of synchromesh action on certain gears, or for failure to stay "in gear". If anything more drastic than this exists (ie. total failure, seizure, or gear case cracked) it would be better to leave well alone and look for a replacement, either a second hand, or an exchange unit.

2 Examine all gears for excessively worn, chipped or damaged teeth. Any such gears should be renewed. It will usually be found that if a tooth is damaged in the countershaft gear train the mating gears teeth on the output shaft will also be damaged.

3 Check all synchronizer sleeves for wear on the bearing surface which normally have clearly defined oil reservoir grooves in them. If these are smooth or obviously uneven, renewal is essential. Also, when fitted to their mating cones - as they would be in operation there should be no rock. This would signify ovality, or lack of concentricity. One of the most satisfactory ways of checking is by comparing the fit of a new sleeve on the hub with the old one. If the grooves of the sleeve are obviously worn or damaged (causing engagement difficulties) the sleeve should be renewed.

4 All ball bearings should be checked for chatter. It is advisable to replace these anyway, even though they may not appear to be too badly worn.

5 Circlips which in this particular gearbox are all important in locating bearings, gears and hubs, should also be checked to ensure that they are not distorted or damaged. In any case a selection of new circlips of varying thickness should be obtained to compensate for variations in new components fitted, or wear in old ones.

6 The thrust washers at the ends of the countershaft gear train should also be replaced as they will almost certainly have worn if the gearbox is well used.

7 The caged needle roller bearing between the input shaft and output shaft will usually be found in good order, but if any doubt renew the bearing.

8 The sliding hubs themselves are also subject to wear and where the fault has been failure of any gear to remain engaged, or actual difficulty in engagement, then the hub is one of the likely suspects.

9 The ends of the splines are machined in such a way as to form a 'Keystone' effect on engagement with the corresponding mainshaft gear. Do not confuse this with wear. Check also that the blocker bars (sliding keys) are not sloppy and move freely. If there is any rock or backlash between the inner and outer sections of the hub, the whole assembly must be renewed, particularly if there has been a complaint of jumping out of gear.

5 Gearbox - reassembly

1 Make sure that all parts are clean and when assembled are well lubricated with Castrol Hypoy Light (EP 80). Where the threads of a securing bolt extend into the gearbox casing or extension housing apply a little oil resistant sealer to the threads.

2 Slide the insert spring, blocking ring, first gear and spacer onto the rear of the output shaft. The broad side of the spacer must point towards the output shaft bearing.

3 Slide a new extension housing circlip onto the output shaft.

4 Carefully press or drift the bearing onto the output shaft and secure it to the output shaft with a new snap ring.

5 If a new bearing or output shaft is being fitted a retaining circlip which fits exactly in the groove must be used.

6 Using a tubular drift drive the speedometer drive gear onto the output shaft. The gear must be accurately positioned as shown in Fig. 6.11. This is very important because there is no locking device for the gear on the shaft.

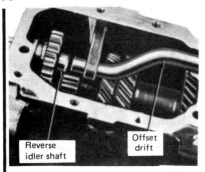

Fig. 6.5. Removal of reverse idler shaft

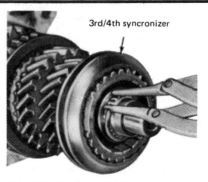

Fig. 6.6. Removal of 3rd gear snap ring

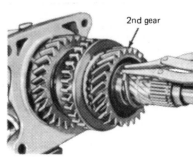

Fig. 6.7. Removal of 2nd gear snap ring

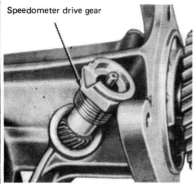

Fig. 6.8. Removal of speedometer drive gear

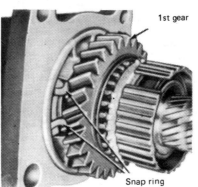

Fig. 6.9. Location of output shaft bearing snap ring

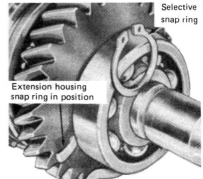

Fig. 6.10. Selecting output shaft bearing snap ring

Fig. 6.11. Fitted position of speedometer gear

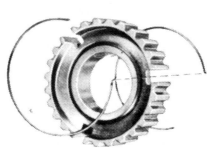

Fig. 6.12. Correct fitting position of insert springs

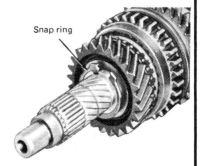

Fig. 6.13. Fitting second gear snap ring

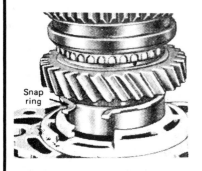

Fig. 6.14. Fitting output shaft into extension housing

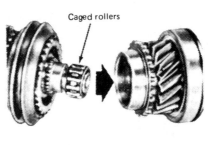

Fig. 6.15. Fitting caged roller bearing to input shaft

Fig. 6.16. Input shaft bearing retainer. Note location of drain slot

7 Position the 1st and 2nd gear synchronizer springs offset in the synchronizer hub so that their individual tensions oppose each other. This is achieved by placing one end of each spring into the same insert groove.

8 Locate the inserts in their grooves and slide the 1st and 2nd gear synchronizer sleeve onto the synchronizer hub with the selector fork collar facing towards the forward end of the output shaft.

9 Now slide the blocking ring, second gear and thrust washer on the output shaft. Fit the retaining circlip (snap ring).

10 Obtain a metal bucket or old oil drum of a sufficient size to accommodate the extension housing. Put the extension housing in, place on a stove, fill with water and heat up to near boiling point.

11 Using thick rags remove the extension housing and slide the output shaft and bearing into the extension housing bore. Do NOT press or drift the output shaft into the extension housing as it will cause the machined bore to become oversize and the bearing outer track will be a loose fit.

12 Fit the snap ring, previously positioned on the output shaft, into the extension housing. This will require a little patience.

13 Position the 3rd and 4th gear synchronizer springs offset in the synchronizer as previously described in paragraph 7.

14 Locate the inserts in their groove and slide the 3rd and 4th gear synchronizer sleeve onto the synchronizer hub with the narrow shoulder facing rearwards.

15 Slide the third gear and third/fourth gear synchronizer assembly on the output shaft. Refit the retaining snap ring.

16 Fit the input shaft and gear assembly to the gearbox casing and using a soft metal drift on the bearing outer track make sure it is fully home.

17 Inspect the seal in the input shaft bearing retainer and if it shows signs of deterioration prise out with a screwdriver and fit a new one. The lip must face towards the gearbox casing when fitted.

18 Fit the front bearing retainer and a new gasket to the front of the gearbox casing. The oil groove in the retainer must be in line with the transmission case and the gasket must not cover this passage. Apply a little sealer to the three cover retaining screws and tighten in a progressive manner.

19 Locate the reverse idler gear in the main casing so that the collar for the selector fork faces rearwards. Slide the shaft into position until it is in position and flush with the wall of the main casing.

20 Assemble the cluster gear bearings by first inserting the spacer tube and inner rings into the bore. Apply some thick grease to the needle roller locations and replace the needle rollers. Finally replace the pair of outer rings.

21 Make up a piece of tube the exact length of the cluster gear and the same diameter as the shaft. Slide this into the countershaft bore.

22 Position new cluster gear thrust washers in the main casing retaining with thick grease.

23 Smear a little jointing compound to both faces of the extension housing gasket and fit to the main casing.

24 Slide the extension housing and output shaft assembly into position taking care not to damage the caged roller bearing on the end of the output shaft.

25 With the extension housing in position and located so that the countershaft can be refitted invert the assembly so that the cluster gear is uppermost. Rotate the input and output shafts until the countershaft can be inserted. The offset lug on the shaft must be correctly positioned at the rear when finally fitted in the main casing. As the shaft is inserted it will eject the dummy shaft.

26 Turn the extension housing until it is the correct way up and secure with the four bolts and spring washers. Apply a little oil resistant sealer to these bolts. Tighten the bolts to a torque wrench setting of 30 - 35 lb ft (4.15 - 4.8 kg m).

27 Refit the speedometer driven gear to the side of the extension housing.

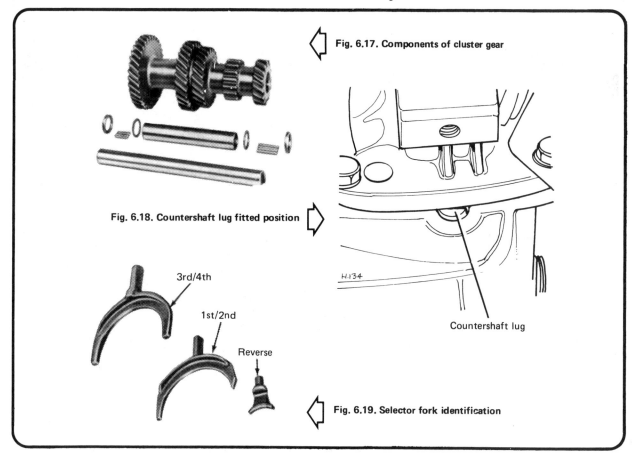

Fig. 6.17. Components of cluster gear

Fig. 6.18. Countershaft lug fitted position

H.134

Countershaft lug

3rd/4th

1st/2nd

Reverse

Fig. 6.19. Selector fork identification

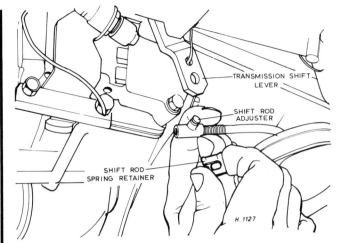

Fig. 6.20. Disconnecting selector rods

Fig. 6.21. Gear change lever assembly securing screws

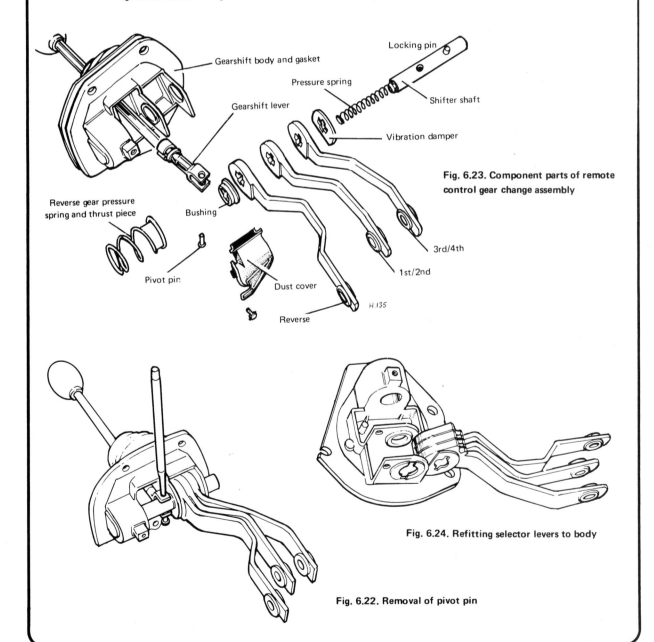

Fig. 6.23. Component parts of remote control gear change assembly

Fig. 6.24. Refitting selector levers to body

Fig. 6.22. Removal of pivot pin

28 Refer to Fig. 6.19 to identify the selector forks and fit the first/second and third/fourth selector forks with the number stamped on them facing towards the FRONT of the gearbox. The reverse selector fork must be fitted with the number facing rearwards. It should be observed that the short leg of the first/second selector fork must be fitted towards the bottom of the gearbox.

29 Apply a little sealer to the gear change housing gasket and fit to the side of the main casing. Replace the gear change housing and secure with the bolts and spring washers. These should be tightened to a torque wrench setting of 12 - 14 lb ft (1.6 - 1.94 Kg m).

30 Before proceeding further check that all forward and the reverse gears can be obtained by operating the two side levers. If one or more gears are unobtainable, remove the housing and investigate the cause.

31 Refit the gearbox bell housing and secure with the four bolts and spring washers. These should be tightened to a torque wrench setting of 40 - 47 lb ft (5.5 - 6.22 kg m).

32 Replace the clutch release lever, hub and bearing.

33 The gearbox is now ready for refitting. Do not forget to refill with 2.8 US pints/1.278 litres of Castrol Hypoy Light (EP 80).

6 Gear change lever - removal and replacement

1 Chock the front wheels, jack up the rear of the car and support on firmly based axle stands.

2 Using a pair of pliers or a screwdriver remove the clips retaining the gear change rods to the levers. Detach the rods.

3 Working inside the car carefully detach the wood grain panel located at the rear of the console. For this use a strong knife.

4 Undo and remove the two screws that secure the plastic cross panel. Slide the plastic cross panel forwards and lift away.

5 Ease up the rear corners of the handbrake lever rubber boot which will give access to two screws. Undo and remove these two screws.

6 Carefully ease up the rear edge of the front wood grain panel and remove the centre retaining screw.

7 Undo and remove the two screws, one each side of the forward lower edge of the console, unscrew the gear change lever knob and move the console to one side.

8 Undo and remove the three screws that secure the gear change lever assembly to the floor panel. The gear change lever assembly may now be lifted up and away from the floor.

9 Should it be necessary to dismantle the assembly first drive out the pivot pin using a parallel pin punch.

10 Pull the gear change lever up from the assembly.

11 Move all three selector levers towards the rear into the horizontal until it is possible for the grooved pin to be moved through the respective cut outs in the selector levers and shaft retainers.

12 Pull the selector lever shaft out and then drift out the locking pin with a suitable diameter parallel pin punch.

13 Lift away the pressure springs, thrust piece and bushings.

14 To reassemble first smear all sliding surfaces with Castrol LM Grease.

15 Position the reverse gear pressure spring on the thrust piece and slide both parts into the main body.

16 Place the bush with the larger diameter towards the change levers.

17 Refit the change levers and vibration dampers.

18 The shaft complete with locking pin and pressure spring may now be inserted into the shaft retainers and change levers. Allow the change levers to swing into the vertical position.

19 Refit the gear change lever and rubber boot and retain it in position with the pivot pin.

20 Refitting the gear change lever assembly is the reverse sequence to removal. It will however, be necessary to check the adjustment as described in Section 7.

7 Gear change linkage - adjustment

1 Refer to Fig. 6.26 and make up an alignment pin to the dimensions given.

2 Chock the front wheels, jack up the rear of the car and support on firmly based stands.

3 Using a pair of pliers or a screwdriver remove the clips retaining the gear change rods to the levers.

4 Insert the previously made alignment pin into the change levers as shown in Fig. 6.27. This ensures that they are accurately positioned.

5 Move the gearbox selector levers to the neutral position.

6 Adjust the length of the selector rods until they fit into the holes in the gearbox selector levers.

7 Refit the selector rods to the gearbox selector levers and retain with the spring retainers. Lubricate the moving parts with a little Castrol LM Grease.

8 Remove the alignment pin and lower the car to the ground. Road test to ensure that all gears are easily obtainable.

8 Automatic transmission - general description

Special towing or recovery information:

Towing. If a caravan, boat or trailer is being towed, always select the 'L' position before ascending or descending steep hills to stop overheating of the special transmission fluid, and to receive benefit from engine braking.

Recovery towing. Should it be necessary to have the car towed to a garage it must not be longer than 20 miles (32.19 Km) away and the speed should not exceed 30 mph (48.28 kph). Towing is permitted provided the transmission is not damaged and that the oil level is correct. Put the selector lever in the 'N' position. If there are noises emitting from the transmission, or the towing distance is greater than 20 miles (32.19 Km), the propeller shaft should be disconnected and completely removed and the end of the transmission sealed to prevent oil loss and dirt ingress. As an alternative, the car can be suspended and towed with the rear wheels off the ground.

Tow starting. Due to the design characteristics of the automatic transmission it is not possible to tow start the car.

An automatic transmission unit may be fitted as a factory option to all models covered by this manual. Early cars were fitted with the C4 dual range three speed automatic transmission unit and later cars were fitted with the well proved Borg Warner type 35.

The system comprises two main components:-

1 A three element hydrokinetic torque converter coupling, capable of torque multiplication at an infinitely variable ratio between 2:1 and 1:1.

2 A torque/speed responsive and hydraulic epicyclic gearbox comprising a planetary gearset providing three forward ratios and one reverse ratio.

Due to the complexity of the automatic transmission unit, if performance is not up to standard, or overhaul is necessary, it is imperative that this be left to the local Capri dealer who will have the special equipment and knowledge for fault diagnosis and rectification.

The content of the following Sections is therefore confined to supplying general information and any service information and instruction that can be used by the owner.

9 Automatic transmission - fluid level

It is important that the transmission fluid manufactured to the correct specification such as Castrol TQF is used. The refill capacity of the unit is:

C4   15.6 US pints/7.387 litres
BW35   13.21 US pints/6.25 litres

The total capacity will be more as some fluid is retained in the torque converter. Complete   draining and refilling should not be necessary except for repairs.

10 Maintenance

1 Every 6,000 miles (10,000 Km) or more frquently, check the automatic transmission fluid level. With the engine at its normal operating temperature, move the selector to the 'P' position and allow to idle for 2 minutes. Remove the dipstick, wipe it clean and, with the engine idling, insert the dipstick and quickly withdraw it again. If necessary, add enough oil of clean correct grade to bring the level to the 'high' mark. The difference between the two dipstick graduations is approximately 1.2 US pints/0.568 litres.
2 If the unit has been drained, it is recommended that only new fluid is used. Fill up to the correct 'HIGH' level, gradually refilling the unit; the exact amount will depend on how much was left in the converter after draining.
3 On the C4 automatic transmission unit, at 36,000 miles, and thereafter every 36,000 miles (60,000 Km), it will be necessary to check the adjustment of the intermediate band. At the same time, check the adjustment of the low and reverse band, but because of the amount and type of motoring encountered, it is difficult to give an exact period this check will be required.
4 Ensure that the exterior of the converter housing and gearbox is always kept free from dust or mud, otherwise over-heating will occur.

11 Automatic transmission - removal and replacement (C4)

Any suspected faults must be referred to the local Capri dealer before unit removal, as with this type of transmission the fault must be confirmed, using specialist equipment.

1 Open the engine compartment lid and place old blankets over the wings to prevent accidental damage to the paintwork.
2 For safety reasons disconnect the battery earth cable.
3 Raise the car on a hoist or drive over a pit. If neither are available raise the car as high as possible and support on axle stands. Make sure they are very firmly located.
4 Place a container of 16 US pints, (7.5 litres) under the trans-mission fluid sump. Slacken the sump securing bolts commen-cing at the rear and working to the front. Allow the fluid to drain out.
CAUTION: If the car has just been driven the fluid will be extremely hot and can cause severe burns. Allow to cool down before draining.
5 Make a note of the electrical cable connections to the starter motor. Remove the connectors from their terminals.
6 Undo and remove the three bolts and spring washers to the engine. Lift away the starter motor from the converter housing.
7 Undo and remove the bolts and spring washers that secure the access cover to the lower end of the converter housing. Lift away the access cover.

12 Mechanical linkage - adjustment (C4)

1 Move the selector lever to the 'D' position.
2 Chock the front wheels, jack up the rear of the car and support on firmly based stands.
3 Remove the clevis pin and disconnect the cable and bushing from the transmission lever.
4 With selector lever in the 'D' position, move the transmission lever to the 'D' position, this being the third detent position from the rear of the unit.
5 Adjust the cable length until the clevis pin holes in the manual lever and the end of the cable are in alignment.
6 Reconnect the cable and secure with the clevis pin and clip.
7 Lower the car to the ground and road test to ensure correct operation in all selector lever positions.
8 Undo and remove the converter to flywheel securing nuts. To do this fit a spanner to the crankshaft pulley securing bolt and turn the crankshaft (therefore the converter) to gain access to these nuts.
9 Again turn the converter until the drain plug is accessible. Remove the plug and allow fluid to drain from the converter. Refit the plug once all fluid has drained out.
10 Mark the propeller shaft and rear axle flanges so that they may be reconnected in their original positions. Undo and remove the four securing bolts and lower the rear half of the propeller shaft.
11 Undo and remove the two bolts that secure the centre bearing carrier to its bracket.
12 Carefully lower the front half of the propeller shaft whilst at the same time sliding the front yoke from the rear of the transmission unit.
13 Wrap some rag around the end of the unit to prevent dirt ingress or accidental damage to the splines.
14 Release the speedometer cable from the extension housing.
15 Detach the shift cable from the manual lever at the transmission unit end.
16 Undo and remove the two bolts and spring washers that secure the shift cable bracket to the converter housing. Move the cable and bracket to one side.
17 Detach the downshift cable from the transmission downshift lever bracket.
18 Make a note of the electrical cable connections at the switch end and detach the connectors. Disconnect the cables from the support clamps and move out of the way.
19 Detach the vacuum line from the transmission vacuum unit.
20 Using a suitable jack support the weight of the unit and then remove the insulator to extension housing bracket bolt.
21 Undo and remove the crossmember-to-frame securing bolts. Lift away the crossmember.
22 Wipe the ends of the oil cooler pipes at the transmission and detach the pipes. Wrap the ends in rags to stop dirt ingress.
23 Undo and remove the bolt that secures the transmission filler tube to the cylinder block. Lift the tube from the case.
24 Undo and remove the converter housing to engine securing bolts.
25 Check that no cables or securing bolts have been left in position.
26 The assistance of at least one other person is now required because of the weight of the complete unit.
27 Carefully pull the unit rearwards and downwards. Draw away from under the car.
28 Refitting the unit is the reverse sequence to removal. It will be necessary to adjust the controls and also the inhibitor switch as described later in this chapter. Do not forget to refill the unit. Refer to Sections 9 and 10 for further information. Do not race the engine for a period of 5 minutes to allow complete circulation of the hydraulic fluid.

13 Throttle and downshift linkage adjustment (C4 and BW 35)

For full information refer to Chapter 3.

14 Neutral start switch - removal, refitting and adjustment (C4)

1 Detach the downshift cable from the transmission unit downshift lever.
2 Apply some penetrating oil to the downshift lever shaft and nut.
3 Undo and remove the transmission downshift outer lever retaining nut and lever.
4 Undo and remove the two neutral start switch securing bolts.
5 Detach the multi pin connector from the neutral switch and remove the switch from the transmission unit.
6 To refit the switch, place in position on the transmission unit and replace the two retaining bolts. Do not fully tighten yet.
7 Move the transmission manual lever to the neutral position, rotate the switch and insert a No 43 drill into the gauge pin hole. It must be inserted to a full 0.2031 inch (5.159 mm) into the three holes in the switch.
8 Tighten the switch securing bolts to a torque wrench setting of 55 - 57 lb ft (7.4 - 7.85 Kg m) and remove the drill.
9 Refit the outer downshift lever and securing nut, which should be tightened to a torque wrench setting of 8 - 9 lb ft (1.11 - 1.2 Kg m).
10 Reconnect the downshift cable to the downshift lever.
11 Reconnect the switch wires. Check the operation of the switch in each detent position. The engine should only start when the selector lever is in the N or P position.

15 Intermediate band - adjustment (C4)

The intermediate or front band is used to hold the sungear stationary so as to give the second gear ratio. If it is not correctly adjusted there will be noticeable slip during first to second gearchange or from third to second gearchange. The first symptoms of these conditions will be a very sluggish gearchange instead of the usual crisp action.

To adjust the intermediate band, undo and remove the adjustment screw locknut located on the left hand side of the transmission case. Tighten the adjusting screw using a torque wrench set to 10 lb ft (1.38 Kg m). Then slacken the adjusting screw exactly 1.75 turns. A new locknut must be fitted and tightened to a torque wrench setting of between 35 and 45 lb ft (4.8 and 6.22 Kg m).

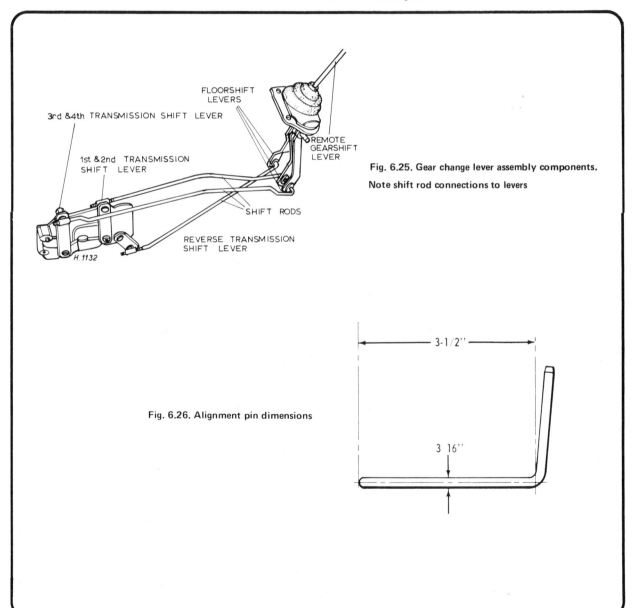

FLOORSHIFT LEVERS

3rd &4th TRANSMISSION SHIFT LEVER

1st &2nd TRANSMISSION SHIFT LEVER

REMOTE GEARSHIFT LEVER

SHIFT RODS

REVERSE TRANSMISSION SHIFT LEVER

H.1132

Fig. 6.25. Gear change lever assembly components.

Note shift rod connections to levers

3-1/2''

3 16''

Fig. 6.26. Alignment pin dimensions

16 Low and reverse band adjustment (C4)

The low and reverse band or rear band is in action when 'L' or 'R' position of the selector lever has been obtained to hold the low and reverse pinion carrier stationary. If it is not correctly adjusted, there will be a noticeable malfunction of the automatic transmission unit, whereby there will be no drive with the selector lever in the 'R' position, also associated with no engine braking on first gear when the selector lever is in the 'L' position.

To adjust the rear band undo and remove the adjusting screw locknut located on the left hand side of the automatic transmission casing and tighten the adjusting screw to a torque wrench setting of 10 lb ft (1.38 Kg m). Then slacken the adjusting screw exactly three turns and fit a new locknut. Tighten to a torque wrench setting of between 35 and 45 lb ft (4.8 and 6.22 Kg m).

17 Selector lever - removal and replacement

1   Chock the front wheels, jack up the rear of the car and support on firmly based stands.
2   Withdraw the clevis pin and disconnect the selector lever cable and bushing from the selector lever operating arm.
3   Working inside the car carefully detach the woodgrain panel at the rear of the console. A strong knife is the best tool to use.
4   Undo and remove the two screws that retain the plastic cross panel. Slide the panel forwards and lift away.
5   Lift up the rear corners of the handbrake rubber boot thereby revealing two screws. Undo and remove these screws.
6   Carefully prise up the rear edge of the front wood grain panel and remove the centre retaining screw.
7   Undo and remove the two screws located one each side of the forward lower edge of the console, and move the console to the side.

8   Lift the selector lever indicator bezel upwards.
9   Undo and remove the three selector lever housing to floor panel securing bolts. Detach the indicator light and remove the selector lever and housing assembly.
10 Slacken the set screw that retains the handle to the selector lever. Fully depress the push button and remove the handle.
11 Remove the plug from the side of the selector housing and remove the retaining nut located at the base of the selector lever.
12 The selector lever and bushings are next removed by lightly tapping the operating arm shaft with a copper drift and hammer.
13 Using a suitable diameter parallel pin punch drift out the cable retaining pin located at the top of the selector lever.
14 Remove the cable adjustment nut from the cable at the lower end of the selector lever and remove the detent plunger, spring and bushing.
15 The cable may now be withdrawn from the selector lever.
16 Reassembly and refitting is the reverse sequence to removal. During reassembly of the selector lever it is necessary to turn the cable adjustment nut until a clearance of 0.005 - 0.010 inch (0.127 - 0.254 mm) is obtained between the bottom of the pawl and detent.

18 Manual linkage control cable - removal and replacement

1   Chock the front wheels, jack up the rear of the car and support on firmly based stands.
2   Withdraw the clevis pin and disconnect the selector lever cable and bushing from the selector lever operating arm located.
3   Slacken the cable retaining nut at the body bracket and release the cable from the bracket.
4   Withdraw the clevis pin and disconnect the cable and bushing from the transmission unit.
5   Slacken the cable adjustment and locknut at the transmission bracket and lift the cable from the car.
6   Refitting the cable is the reverse sequence to removal. It will be necessary to adjust the cable as described in Section 12.

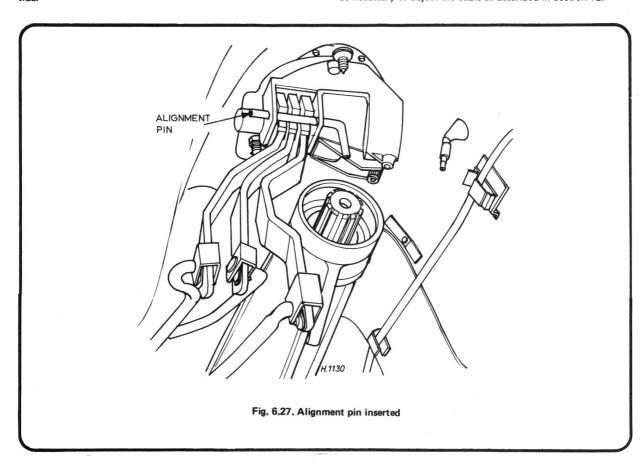

ALIGNMENT PIN

H.1130

Fig. 6.27. Alignment pin inserted

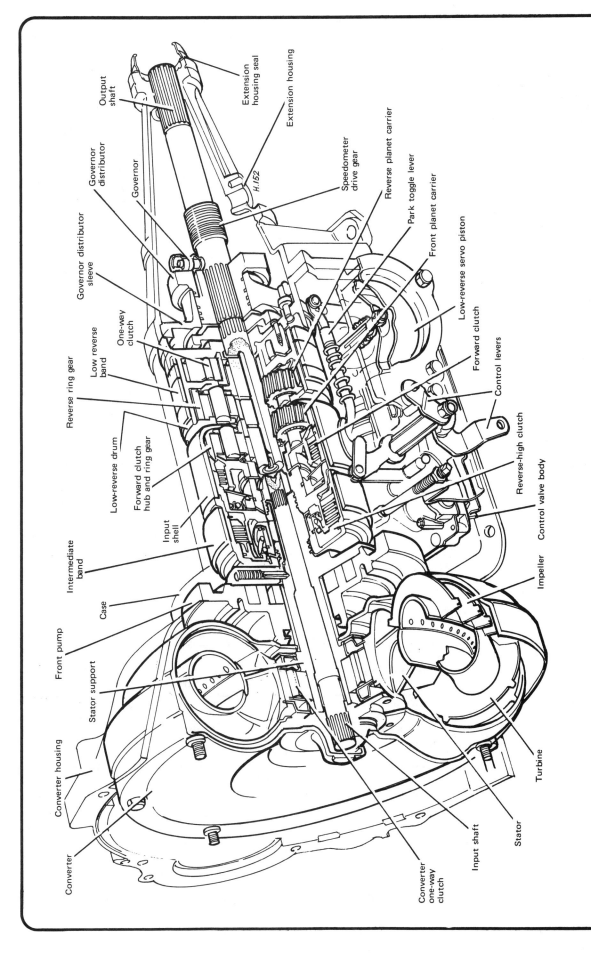

Fig. 6.28. Cross sectional view of C4 Automatic Transmission

Output shaft

Extension housing seal

Extension housing

Governor distributor

Governor

Speedometer drive gear

Reverse planet carrier

Park toggle lever

Front planet carrier

Governor distributor sleeve

One-way clutch

Low-reverse servo piston

Forward clutch

Reverse ring gear

Low reverse band

Control levers

Low-reverse drum

Forward clutch hub and ring gear

Reverse-high clutch

Input shell

Control valve body

Intermediate band

Impeller

Control valve body

Case

Front pump

Turbine

Stator support

Stator

Converter housing

Input shaft

Converter

Converter one-way clutch

H.152

19 Automatic transmisstion - removal and replacement (BW 35)

1 Refer to Section 11, paragraphs 1 to 3 inclusive.

2 Withdraw the transmission unit dipstick and put to one side.

3 Detach the throttle linkage downshift valve control cable.

4 Place a container having a capacity of 13.5 US pints/6.25 litres under the drain plug. Remove the drain plug and allow the fluid to drain out. Refit the plug.

CAUTION: If the car has just been driven the fluid will be extremely hot and can cause severe burns. Allow to cool down before draining.

5 Detach the propeller shaft as described in Section 11, paragraphs 10 to 13 inclusive.

6 Disconnect the exhaust pipe bracket from the transmission bracket. Slacken the bracket at the exhaust pipe and rotate it to the side.

7 Using a pair of circlip pliers release the speedometer cable at the transmission extension and withdraw the speedometer cable.

8 Make a note of the cable connections at the starter motor and detach from the terminals. Undo and remove the bolts and spring washers that secure the starter motor to the engine and withdraw from the converter housing.

9 Undo and remove the bolts and spring washers that secure the front lower cover to the converter housing.

10 Undo and remove the four bolts that secure the flex plate to the converter.

11 Refer to Fig. 6.32 and detach the manual linkage control from the transmission unit.

12 Make a note of the cable connections to the starter neutral switch terminals. Detach the cable connectors.

13 Support the weight of the transmission unit with a suitable jack.

14 Undo and remove the four bolts that secure the engine support to the underside of the body.

15 Undo and remove the six bolts and spring washers that secure the converter housing to the engine.

16 Carefully withdraw the transmission fluid filter tube. Check that all securing bolts and cables have been detached from the unit.

17 The assistance of at least one other person is now required because of the weight of the complete unit.

18 Using a large tyre lever exert pressure between the flex plate and converter so as to prevent the converter becoming disengaged from the transmission unit as it is drawn rearwards. It will also be full of hydraulic fluid.

19 Carefully pull the unit rearwards and lift it away from under the car. Place on wooden blocks so that the selector lever is not damaged or bent.

20 To separate the converter housing from the transmission unit first lift off the converter from the transmission unit, taking suitable precautions to catch the fluid upon separation. Undo and remove the six bolts and spring washers that secure the converter housing to the transmission case. Lift away the converter housing.

21 Refitting the automatic transmission unit is the reverse sequence to removal but there are several additional points which will assist:

a) If the torque converter has been removed before refitting it will be necessary to align the front pump drive tangs with the slots in the inner gear and then carefully replace the torque converter. Take extreme precautions not to damage the oil seal.

b) Adjust the manual selector linkage, the throttle downshift cable and the inhibitor switch. Full details will be found in this and also Chapter 3.

c) Do not forget to refill the unit. Refer to Sections 9 and 10 for full information. Do not race the engine for a period of 5 minutes to allow complete circulation of the hydraulic fluid.

20 Neutral start switch - adjustment (BW 35)

1 Select the 'D' position. Make a note of the starter inhibitor and reverse lamp switch cable connections and disconnect the cables from the switch.

2 Connect a test lamp and battery across the small starter inhibitor terminals and a further test lamp and battery across the two larger reverse light terminals.

3 Undo the locknut and screw out the switch about two turns. Slowly screw in the switch again until the test light connected to the reverse light terminal goes out. Mark the relative position of the switch.

4 Continue screwing in the switch until the test lamp connected to the starter inhibitor terminals lights. Mark the relative position of the switch again.

5 Unscrew the switch until it is half way between the two positions and tighten the locknut.

6 Reconnect the cables and check that the starter motor only operates when the selector lever is in the 'P' or 'N' position. Also check that the reverse light only operates with the selector in the 'R' position. If the switch does not operate it should be renewed.

Fault finding - manual gearbox

Symptom	Reason/s	Remedy
Ineffective synchromesh	Worn baulk rings or synchro hubs	Dismantle and renew.
Jumps out of one or more gears (on drive or over-run)	Weak springs or worn selector forks or worn gears	Dismantle and renew.
Noisy, rough, whining and vibration	Worn bearings and/or thrust washers (initially) resulting in extended wear generally due to play and backlash. Broken gear teeth	Dismantle and renew countershaft.
Noisy and difficult engagement of gears	Clutch fault	Examine clutch operation.

NOTE: It is sometimes difficult to decide whether it is worthwhile removing and dismantling the gearbox for a fault which may be nothing more than a minor irritant. Gearboxes which howl, or where the synchromesh can be 'beaten' by a quick gear change, may continue to perform for a long time in this stage. A worn gearbox usually needs a complete rebuild to eliminate noise because the various gears, if re-aligned on new bearings will continue to howl when different wearing surfaces are presented to each other.

The decision to overhaul therefore, must be considered with regard to time and money available, relative to the degree of noise or malfunction that the driver has to suffer.

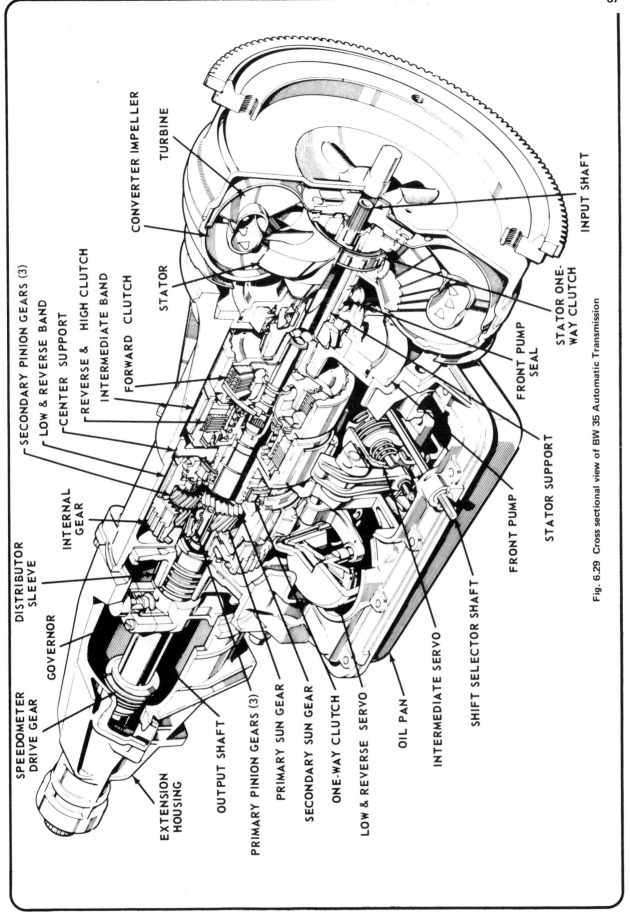

SPEEDOMETER
DRIVE GEAR

DISTRIBUTOR
SLEEVE

GOVERNOR

INTERNAL
GEAR

SECONDARY PINION GEARS (3)

LOW & REVERSE BAND

CENTER SUPPORT

REVERSE & HIGH CLUTCH

INTERMEDIATE BAND

FORWARD CLUTCH

STATOR

CONVERTER IMPELLER

TURBINE

INPUT SHAFT

STATOR ONE-
WAY CLUTCH

FRONT PUMP
SEAL

STATOR SUPPORT

FRONT PUMP

SHIFT SELECTOR SHAFT

INTERMEDIATE SERVO

OIL PAN

LOW & REVERSE SERVO

ONE-WAY CLUTCH

SECONDARY SUN GEAR

PRIMARY SUN GEAR

PRIMARY PINION GEARS (3)

OUTPUT SHAFT

EXTENSION
HOUSING

Fig. 6.29 Cross sectional view of BW 35 Automatic Transmission

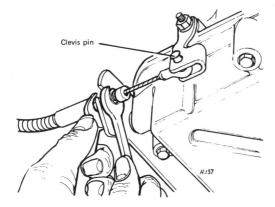

Fig. 6.30. Manual linkage control cable adjustment

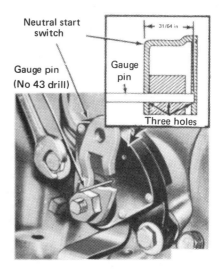

Fig. 6.31. Adjustment of neutral start switch (C4)

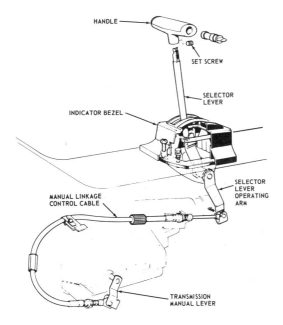

Fig. 6.32. Layout of selector lever assembly and control cable

Fig. 6.33. Removal of selector lever bezel

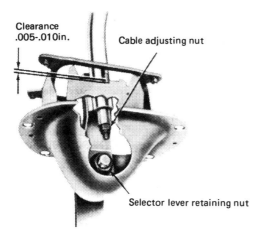

Fig. 6.34. Manual selector lever - adjustment

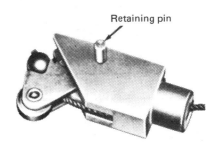

Fig. 6.35. Cable retaining pin

Fault finding - automatic transmission

As has been mentioned elsewhere in this Chapter no service repair to the automatic transmission unit should be considered by anyone without the specialist knowledge and equipment required to undertake such work. Information is however given on the various adjustments which the author considers may be completed without any difficulty.

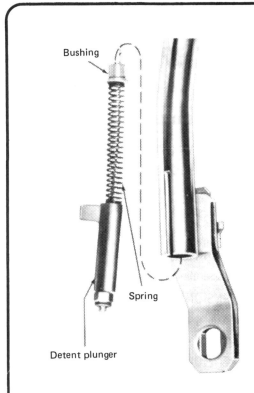

Fig. 6.36. Detent plunger removal

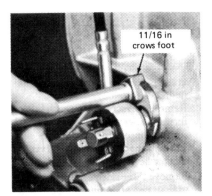

Fig. 6.37. Removal of neutral start switch (BW 35). Note crows foot wrench being used

Chapter 7 Propeller shaft and universal joints

Contents

Specifications

Torque wrench setting:

	lbf ft	kg fm
Centre bolt	28	3.9

1 General description

Drive is transmitted from the gearbox to the rear axle by means of a finely balanced tubular propeller shaft split into two halves and supported at the centre by a rubber mounted bearing.

Fitted to the front centre and rear of the propeller shaft assembly are universal joints which allow for vertical movement of the rear axle and slight movement of the complete power unit on its rubber mountings. Each universal joint comprises a four legged centre spider, four needle roller bearings and two yokes.

Fore and aft movement of the rear axle is absorbed by a sliding spline located at the gearbox end. The yoke flange of the rear universal joint is fitted to the rear axle and is secured to the pinion flange by four bolts and lock washers.

The universal joints at the front, centre and rear of the propeller shaft are obtainable as a kit. They are of the sealed type and require no maintenance once assembled.

2 Propeller shaft - removal and replacement

1 Jack up the rear of the car, or position the rear of the car over a pit or on a ramp.
2 If the rear of the car is jacked up, supplement the jack with support blocks so that danger is minimised, should the jack collapse.
3 If the rear wheels are off the ground place the car in gear or put the handbrake on to ensure that the propeller shaft does not turn when an attempt is made to loosen the four bolts securing the propeller shaft to the rear axle companion flange.
4 Unscrew and remove the four lock bolts and securing washers which hold the flange on the propeller shaft to the flange on the rear axle.
5 The propeller shaft is carefully balanced to fine limits and it is important that it is replaced in exactly the same position it was in prior to its removal. Scratch a mark on the propeller shaft

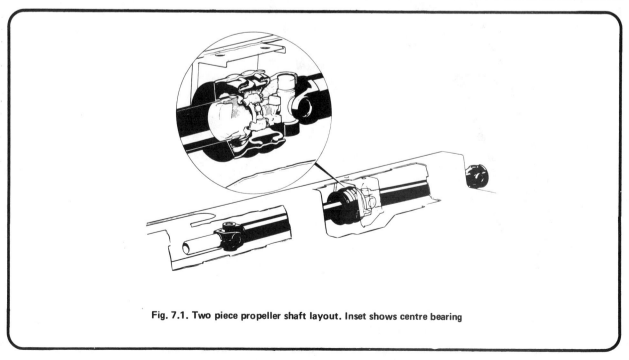

Fig. 7.1. Two piece propeller shaft layout. Inset shows centre bearing

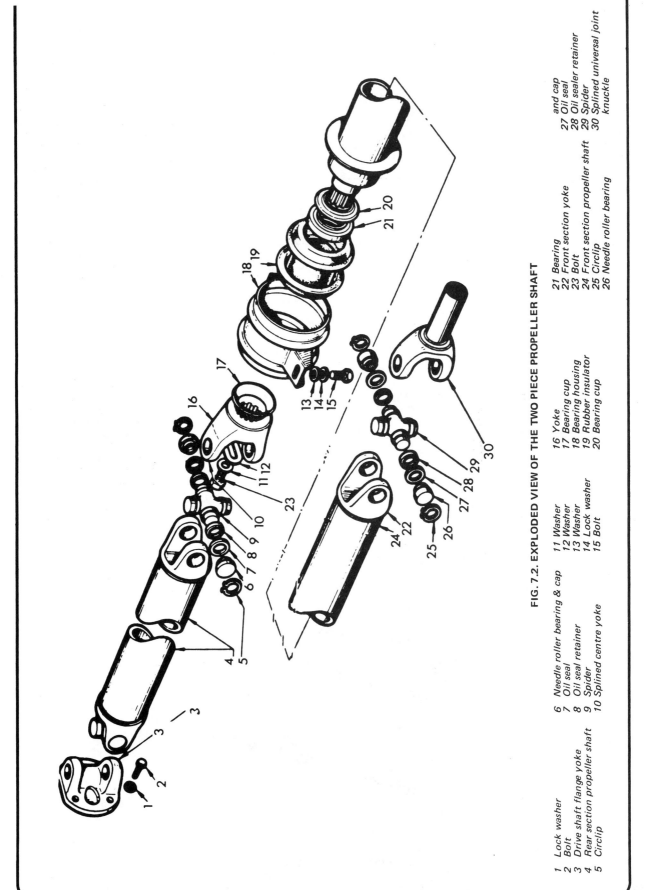

FIG. 7.2. EXPLODED VIEW OF THE TWO PIECE PROPELLER SHAFT

1 Lock washer
2 Bolt
3 Drive shaft flange yoke
4 Rear section propeller shaft
5 Circlip

6 Needle roller bearing & cap
7 Oil seal
8 Oil seal retainer
9 Spider
10 Splined centre yoke

11 Washer
12 Washer
13 Washer
14 Lock washer
15 Bolt

16 Yoke
17 Bearing cup
18 Bearing housing
19 Rubber insulator
20 Bearing cup

21 Bearing
22 Front section yoke
23 Bolt
24 Front section propeller shaft
25 Circlip
26 Needle roller bearing

27 Oil seal
28 Oil sealer retainer
29 Spider
30 Splined universal joint
   knuckle

and cap

and rear axle flanges to ensure accurate mating when the time comes for reassembly.

6 Undo and remove the two bolts holding the centre bearing housing to the underframe.

7 Slightly push the shaft forward to separate the two flanges at the rear, then lower the end of shaft and pull it rearwards to disengage it from the gearbox mainshaft splines.

8 Place a large can or tray under the rear of the gearbox extension to catch any oil which is likely to leak through the spline lubricating holes when the propeller shaft is removed.

9 Replacement of the two piece propeller shaft is a reversal of the above procedure. Ensure that the mating marks scratched on the propeller shaft and rear axle flanges line up.

3 Propeller shaft, centre bearing - removal and replacement

1 Prior to removing the centre bearing from the front section of the two piece propeller shaft, carefully scratch marks on the rear yoke and on the shaft just forward of the bearing housing to ensure correct alignment on reassembly.

2 Knock back the tab washer on the centre bolt located in the jaws of the rear yoke. Slacken off the nut and remove the 'U' washer from under it.

3 With the 'U' washer removed the rear yoke can now be drawn off the splines of the front section. The centre bolt and its washer remain attached to the splined front section.

4 Slide the bearing housing with its rubber insulator from the shaft. Bend back the six metal tabs on the housing and remove the rubber insulator.

5 The bearing and its protective caps should now be withdrawn from the splined section of the propeller shaft by careful levering with two large screwdrivers or tyre levers. If a suitable puller tool is available this should always be used in preference to any other method as it is less likely to cause damage to the bearing.

6 To replace the bearing, select a piece of piping or tubing that is just a fraction smaller in diameter than the bearing, place the splined part of the drive shaft upright in a vice, position the bearing on the shaft and using a soft hammer on the end of the piece of tubing drive the bearing firmly and squarely onto the shaft.

7 Replace the rubber insulator in the bearing housing ensuring that the boss on the insulator is at the top of the housing and will be adjacent to the underframe when the propeller shafts are replaced.

8 When the insulator is correctly positioned bend back the six metal tabs and slide the housing and insulator assembly over the bearing.

9 Slide the splined end of the shaft into the rear yoke ensuring that the previously scribed mating marks are correctly aligned.

10 Replace the 'U' washer under the centre bolt with its smooth surface facing the front section of the propeller shaft. Tighten down the centre bolt to a torque of 28 lb ft (3.9 kg m) and bend up its tab washer to secure it.

4 Universal joints - inspection and repair

1 Wear in the needle roller bearings is characterised by vibration in the transmission, 'clonks' on taking up the drive, and in extreme cases of lack of lubrication, metallic squeaking, and ultimately grating and shrieking sounds as the bearings break up.

2 It is easy to check if the needle roller bearings are worn with the propeller shaft in position, by trying to turn the shaft with one hand, the other hand holding the rear axle flange when the rear universal is being checked, and the front half coupling when the front universal is being checked. Any movement between the propeller shaft and the front and the rear half couplings is indicative of considerable wear. If worn, the old bearings and spiders will have to be discarded and a repair kit, comprising new universal joint spiders, bearings, oil seals, and retainers purchased. Check also by trying to lift the shaft and noticing any movement in the joints.

3 Examine the propeller shaft splines for wear. If worn it will be necessary to purchase a new front half coupling, or if the yokes are badly worn, an exchange propeller shaft. It is not possible to fit oversize bearings and journals to the trunnion bearing holes.

5 Universal joints - dismantling

1 Clean away all traces of dirt and grease from the circlips located on the ends of the bearing cups, and remove the clips by pressing them out with a screwdriver. NOTE: If they are difficult to remove tap the bearing cup face resting on top of the spider with a mallet which will ease the pressure on the circlip.

2 Take off the bearing cups on the propeller shaft yoke. To do this select two sockets from a socket spanner set, one large enough to fit completely over the bearing cup and the other smaller than the bearing cup (photo).

3 Open the jaws of the vice and with the sockets opposite each other and the universal joint in between tighten the vice and so force the narrower socket to move the opposite cup partially out of the yoke (photo) into the larger socket.

4 Remove the cup with a pair of pliers (photo). Remove the opposite cup, and then free the yoke from the propeller shaft.

5 To remove the remaining two cups now repeat the instructions in paragraph 3, or use a socket and hammer as illustrated.

6 Universal joints - reassembly

1 Thoroughly clean out the yokes and journals.

2 Fit new oil seals and retainers on the spider journals, place the spider on the propeller shaft yoke, and assemble the needle rollers in the bearing races with the assistance of some thin grease. Fill each bearing about a third full with Castrol LM Grease and fill the grease holes in the spider journal making sure all air bubbles are eliminated.

3 Refit the bearing cups on the spider and tap the bearings home so they lie squarely in position. Replace the circlips.

7.3 Removal of circlip

7.4 Two different size sockets are required

7.5 Movement of cup from yoke

7.6 Using pliers to remove cup

7.7 Using socket to remove remaining two cups

Chapter 8 Rear axle

Contents

Specifications

Type	... ...	Semi floating hypoid	
Ratio	... ...	3.22 : 1	
Number of teeth:			
Crownwheel	... ...	29	
Pinion	... ...	9	
Crownwheel/pinion backlash	... ...	0.0047 to 0.0087 in	(0.12 to 0.22 mm)
Drive pinion bearing pre-load	... ...	6.8 to 30 lb f in	(8 to 30 kg f cm)
Differential side gear play	... ...	0.0004 to 0.006 in	(0.01 to 0.15 mm)
Differential bearing pre load	... ...	0.0012 to 0.0031 in	(0.03 to 0.08 mm)
Oil capacity	... ...	2.3 US pints (1.1 litres)	

Torque wrench settings:

	lb f ft	kg fm
Bearing cap bolts	43 - 49	6 - 6.8
Drive pinion self locking nut	71 - 86	10 - 12
Crownwheel securing bolts	57 - 62	8 - 8.7
Rear axle housing cover	22 - 29	3 - 4
Halfshaft to side flange retainer plate	29 - 36	4 - 5
Propeller shaft to drive pinion flange	43 - 47	6 - 6.5
Propeller shaft centre bearing to securing bolt	13 - 17	1.8 - 2.3

1 General description

The rear axle is of the semi floating type and is held in place by semi-elliptic springs. These springs provide the necessary lateral and longitudinal location of the axle. The rear axle incorporates a hypoid crownwheel and pinion, and a two pinion differential. All repairs to the rear axle can be made without removing the axle casing from the car but from experience, other than removing the half shafts, it is better to remove the axle casing.

As the rear axle differential unit is a particularly sensitive component needing a variety of special tools to set it up correctly, it is not recommended for the owner to attempt any ambitious repairs. It is simpler and probably cheaper to fit a guaranteed second hand axle from a wrecker's yard than attempt only complicated repair work. This is of course, provided that a similar rear axle can be found. Factory exchange axles may be available.

All nuts and bolts on this axle assembly have metric threads so it will be necessary to obtain a set of metric sockets and spanners before starting work.

2 Half shaft - removal and replacement

1 Place the car on level ground, chock the front wheels, loosen the rear wheel nuts on the side bearing worked on, or both sides if both half shafts are to be removed, then jack up the rear of the car and remove the wheels.
2 Release the handbrake then remove the brake drum securing screw and take off the brake drum.
3 Undo and remove the four bolts retaining the half shaft bearing housing to the axle casing. These bolts are accessible with a socket on an extension through the holes in the half shaft flange (Fig. 8.2).
4 It should be possible at this stage to remove the half shaft by simply pulling on the flange, but if this fails replace the road wheel on the studs and tighten down two opposite nuts just enough to prevent movement of the wheel on the studs.
5 Sitting on the ground, with one leg either side of the wheel and braced on the spring, get a firm hold on the outer edge of the tyre and pull straight outwards as hard as possible.
6 Care must be taken not to damage the splines on the end of the half shaft when withdrawing by this method as its release

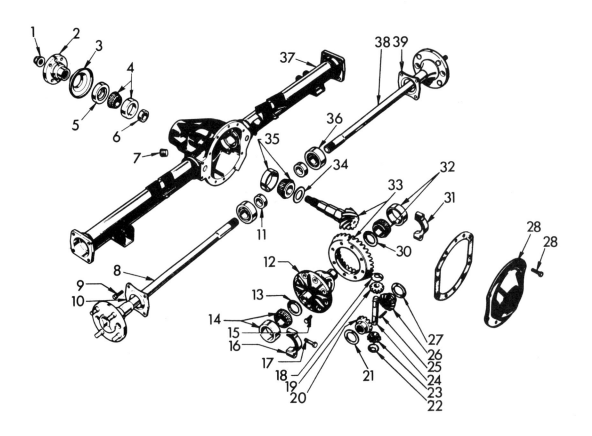

FIG. 8.1. THE REAR AXLE ASSEMBLY

1 Pinion nut	11 Retainer ring	21 Selective spacer	31 Bearing cap
2 Flange	12 Differential housing	22 Pinion thrust washer	32 Bearing assembly
3 Deflector	13 Selective spacer	23 Differential pinion	33 Crown wheel and
4 Bearing assembly	14 Bearing assembly	24 Spider shaft	pinion assembly
5 Seal	15 Bolt	25 Pinion shaft lock pin	34 Selective spacer
6 Selective spacer	16 Bearing cap	26 Differential gear	35 Bearing assembly
7 Filler/level plug	17 Bolt	27 Selective spacer	36 Half shaft bearing
8 Half shaft	18 Pinion thrust washer	28 Bolt	37 Axle housing
9 Bolt	19 Differential pinion	29 Rear axle housing cover	38 Half shaft
10 Bearing retainer	20 Differential gear	30 Selective spacer	39 Bearing retainer

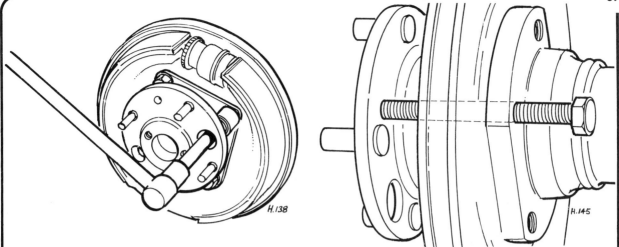

Fig. 8.2. Removal of bearing retainer plate securing bolts

Fig. 8.3. Using long bolts to assist withdrawal of half shaft —
alternative method

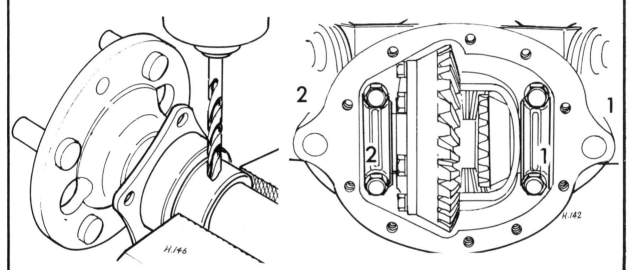

Fig. 8.4. Drilling hole in bearing inner ring prior to cutting
with chisel

Fig. 8.5. Differential casing and end cap identification marks

Fig. 8.6. Differential housing internal components

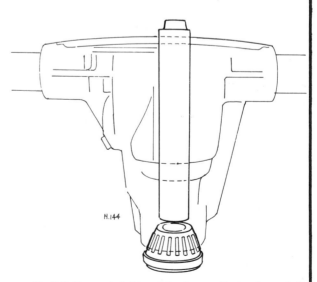

Fig. 8.7. Removal of drive pinion taper roller bearing and oil
seal

from the axle casing may be a bit sudden.

7 Replacement is a reversal of the removal procedure, but once again care should be taken not to damage the splines on the end of the half shaft. The half shaft bearing housing bolts should be replaced at a torque of 20 to 23 lb ft (2.7 to 3.2 kg m).

3 Half shaft bearing - removal and replacement

1 Refer to Section 2 and remove the half shaft assembly.
2 Using a 0.315 in (8 mm) diameter drill, bore a hole in the bearing inner ring. Using a sharp chisel cut the ring across the hole and slide off the ring. A new ring will be required during reassembly.
3 Place the half shaft upside down in a vice so that the bearing retainer is on the top of the jaws and the half shaft flange is under them and using a soft faced hammer drive the half shaft through the bearing. This may also be done using a universal puller in reverse using the feet to push the bearing retainer. It will be necessary to bind the legs together to stop them springing out. Lift away the bearing and retainer noting which way round they are fitted.
4 To fit the new bearing first slide the bearing along the half shaft followed by the bearing (the oil seal inside the bearing must be furthermost away from the half shaft flange).
5 Slide on a new inner ring.
6 Place the half shaft vertically between the jaws of a bench vice - flange uppermost, so that the inner ring is resting on the top of the vice jaws. Using a soft faced hammer drive the half shaft through the bearing and inner ring until it is seating fully on the bearing. Alternatively, a universal two leg puller can be used and if it has a hexagon head on the end of the centre screw it should be tightened to a torque wrench setting of 43 to 58 lb ft (6 to 8 kg m).
7 Refit the half shaft assembly as described in Section 2.

4 Rear cover - removal and replacement

1 Wipe down the rear of the final drive housing to prevent the possibility of dirt entering the rear axle.
2 Release the handbrake cross cable from the rear of each brake backplate by pulling out the small spring clips and withdrawing the clevis pins.
3 To give more room to work in, release the handbrake return spring from its bracket on the axle casing and then detach the operating lever from the casing.
4 Place a container of 3 US pints (2 litres) capacity under the rear axle casing to catch the oil as the rear cover is released.
5 Undo and remove the ten bolts and spring washers that secure the rear cover to the final drive housing. Lift away the rear cover and its gasket.
6 Before refitting the rear cover make sure that the mating faces are free of the old gasket or jointing compound.
7 Fit a new gasket and then the rear cover and secure with the ten bolts and spring washers. As the cover bolts protrude into the final drive housing it is important that a suitable oil resistant sealing compound is smeared onto the threads of each bolt before it is fitted.
8 Tighten the cover securing bolts to a torque wrench setting of 22 to 29 lb ft (3 to 4 kg m).
9 Reconnect the handbrake operating lever, cross cable and return spring.
10 Refill the rear axle with 2.3 US pints (1.065 litres) of Castrol Hypoy (EP 90).

5 Drive pinion oil seal - removal and replacement

1 This operation may be performed with the rear axle in position or on the bench.
2 Undo and remove the two bolts, spring and plain washers that secure the centre bearing support to the underside of the body.
3 With a scriber or file mark a line across the propeller shaft and pinion driving flanges so that they may be refitted together in their original positions.
4 Undo and remove the four bolts and spring washers securing the propeller shaft and pinion driving flanges and carefully lower the propeller shaft to the floor.
5 Carefully clean the front of the final drive housing as there will probably be a considerable amount of oil and dirt if the seal has been leaking for a while.
6 Using a mole wrench or large wrench grip the drive pinion flange and with a socket undo and remove the pinion flange retaining self locking nut. This nut must be discarded and a new one obtained ready for reassembly.
7 Place a container under the front of the final drive housing to catch any oil that may issue once the oil seal has been removed.
8 Using a universal puller and suitable thrust pad pull off the drive pinion flange from the drive pinion.
9 Using a screwdriver or small chisel carefully remove the old oil seal. It will probably be necessary to partially dismantle it. Note the correct way round it is fitted with the lip facing inwards.
10 Before fitting a new seal apply some grease to the inner face between the two lips of the seal.
11 Apply a little jointing compound to the outer face of the seal.
12 Using a tubular drift of suitable diameter carefully drive the oil seal into the final drive housing. Make quite sure that it is fitted squarely into the housing.
13 Replace the drive pinion flange and once again hold squarely with a mole wrench or large wrench. Fit a new self locking nut and tighten to a torque wrench setting of 71 to 86 lb ft (10 to 12 kg m).
14 Reconnect the propeller shaft aligning up the previously made marks on the flanges, and refit the bolts with new spring washers. Tighten to a torque wrench setting of 43 to 47 lb ft (6 to 6.5 kg m).
15 Refit the centre bearing support securing bolts, spring and plain washers and tighten to a torque wrench setting of 13 to 17 lb ft (1.8 to 2.3 kg m).
16 Finally check the oil level in the rear axle and top up if necessary with Castrol Hypoy (EP 90).

6 Rear axle - removal and replacement

1 With the car on level ground, chock the front wheels and slacken the rear wheel nuts.
2 Raise and support the rear of the body and the differential casing with chocks or jacks so that the rear wheels are clear of the ground. This is most easily done by placing a jack under the centre of the differential, jacking up the axle and then fitting chocks under the mounting points at the front of the rear springs to support the body.
3 Remove both rear wheels.
4 Undo and remove the two bolts and spring and plain washers that secure the centre bearing support to the underside of the body.
5 With a scriber or file mark a line across the propeller shaft and pinion driving flanges so that they may be refitted together in their original positions.
6 Undo and remove the four bolts and spring washers that the propeller shaft and pinion driving flanges and carefully lower the propeller shaft to the floor.

99

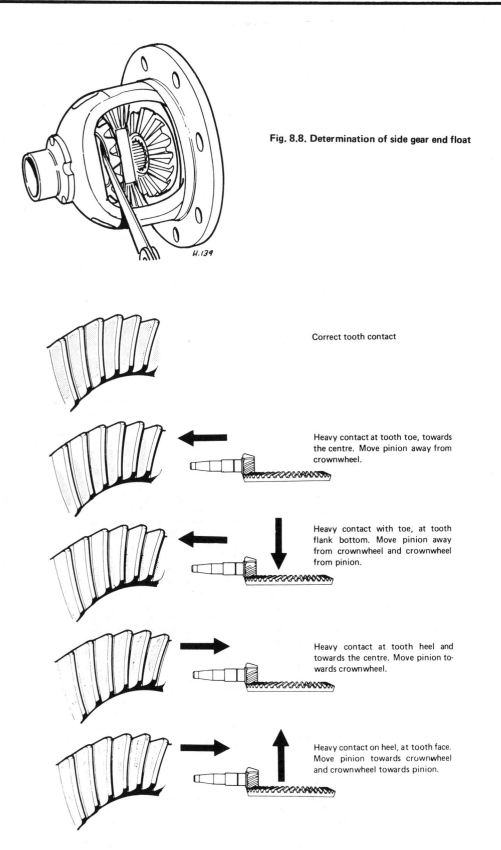

Fig. 8.8. Determination of side gear end float

Correct tooth contact

Heavy contact at tooth toe, towards the centre. Move pinion away from crownwheel.

Heavy contact with toe, at tooth flank bottom. Move pinion away from crownwheel and crownwheel from pinion.

Heavy contact at tooth heel and towards the centre. Move pinion towards crownwheel.

Heavy contact on heel, at tooth face. Move pinion towards crownwheel and crownwheel towards pinion.

Fig. 8.9. Correct meshing of crownwheel and pinion and re-positioning guide for incorrect tooth meshing

7 Release the handbrake and by undoing the adjusting nut, disconnect the cable at the pivot point at the rear of the axle casing.

8 Wipe the area around the union of the brake pipe at the junction on the rear axle and detach the brake pipe. Plug the end with a piece of tapered wood.

9 Undo and remove the nuts, bolts and spring washers that hold the shock absorbers to the spring seats. It may be found necessary to adjust the jack under the axle casing to free the bolts.

10 Unscrew and remove the nuts and through bolts that retain the radius arms to the rear axle casing brackets. Ease each radius arm upwards from the rear axle casing.

11 Unscrew and remove the four nuts from under each spring 'U' bolt plate. These nuts screw onto the ends of the inverted 'U' bolts which retain the axle to the spring.

12 Tap away the 'U' bolt plates and 'U' bolts. Lift each end of the axle and recover the upper insulator and upper 'U' bolt plate.

13 The axle will now be resting free on the jack and can be removed by lifting it through one of the wheel arches.

14 Refitting is the reverse sequence to removal but the following additional points should be noted:
a) Tighten the nuts on the 'U' bolts to a torque wrench setting of 18 to 26 lb ft (2.49 to 3.60 kg m).
b) With the car resting on the ground the radius arm nuts and shock absorber lower mounting bolts should be tightened to the following torque wrench settings:

Radius arm   22 to 27 lb ft (3.04 to 3.73 kg m)
Shock absorber   40 to 45 lb ft (5.54 to 6.22 kg m)

c) Bleed the brakes after reconnection as described in Chapter 9. Also check the handbrake adjustment.
d) After axle overhaul do not forget to refill with Castrol Hypoy. The capacity is 2.3 US pints (1.065 litres).

7 Differential - removal, overhaul and replacement

1 It is recommended that for complete overhaul the rear axle be removed from the car as described in Section 6. Before commencing work refer to the second paragraph of Section 1.

2 Refer to Section 4 and remove the rear cover and then to Section 2 and withdraw the half shafts by about 6 inches (1.52.4 mm).

3 Working inside the axle casing undo and remove the four bolts that hold the two 'U' shaped differential bearing caps in the casing.

4 With a scriber mark the relative positions of the two bearing caps so that they may be refitted in their original positions. Lift away the two end caps.

5 Obtain two pieces of 2 inch (50 mm) square wood at least 12 inches (304.8 mm) long and with a sharp knife, taper the ends along a length of 6 inches (152.4 mm).

6 Place the tapered ends of the wood levers in the two cut-aways of the differential casing and using the rear cover face of the final drive housing as a fulcrum carefully lever the differential assembly from the final drive housing.

7 If it is necessary to remove the two differential case bearings these may be removed next using a universal two leg puller and suitable thrust pad. Carefully ease each bearing from its location. Recover the shim packs from behind each bearing noting from which side they came.

8 Using a scriber mark the relative positions of the crownwheel and differential housing so that the crownwheel may be refitted in its original position, unless, of course, it is to be renewed.

9 Undo and remove the eight bolts that secure the crownwheel to the differential housing. Using a soft faced hammer tap the crownwheel from its location on the differential housing.

10 Using a suitable diameter parallel pin punch, tap out the pin that locks the differential pinion gear shaft to the differential housing. NOTE: The hole into which the peg fits is slightly tapered, and the opposite end may be lightly peened over and should be cleaned with a suitable diameter drill.

11 Using a soft metal drift tap out the differential pinion gear shaft. Lift away the differential pinion gears, side gears and thrust washers taking care to ensure that the thrust washers are kept with their relative gears.

12 Professional fitters at the dealer's use a special tool for holding the pinion drive flange stationary whilst the nut in the centre of the flange is unscrewed. As it is tightened to a torque wrench setting of 71 to 86 lb ft (10 to 12 kg m) it will require some force to undo it. The average owner will not normally have the use of this special tool so, as an alternative method clamp the pinion flange in a vice and then undo the nut. Any damage caused to the edge of the flange by the vice should be carefully filed smooth. This nut must not be used again so a new one will be required during reassembly.

13 Using a universal two leg puller and suitable thrust pad draw the pinion drive flange from the end of the pinion shaft.

14 The pinion shaft may now be removed from the final drive housing. Carefully inspect the large taper roller bearing behind the pinion gear and if it shows signs of wear or fitting on the rollers or cage the bearing must be renewed.

15 Using a universal two leg puller and suitable thrust pad draw the bearing from the pinion shaft.

16 The smaller taper roller bearing and oil seal may next be removed from the final drive housing, pinion drive flange end. To do this use a soft metal drift with a tapered end or suitable diameter tube and working inside the housing tap the bearing circumference outwards so releasing first the oil seal and then the bearing.

17 Again using the soft metal drift and working inside the housing drift out the bearing cups. These must not be used with new bearings.

18 The final drive assembly is now dismantled and should be washed and dried with a clean non-fluffy rag ready for inspection.

19 Carefully inspect all the gear teeth for signs of pitting or wear and if evident new parts must be obtained. The crownwheel and pinion are a matched pair so if one of the two requires renewal a new matched pair must be obtained. If wear is evident on one or two of the differential pinion gears or side gears it is far better to obtain all four gears rather than just replace the worn one.

20 Inspect the thrust washers for signs of score marks or wear and if evident obtain new ones. Before the bearings were removed they should have been inspected for wear and usually if one bearing is worn it is far better to fit a complete new set.

21 When new parts have been obtained as required, reassembly can begin. First fit the thrust washers to the side gears and place them in position in the differential housing.

22 Place the thrust washers behind the differential pinion gears and mesh these two gears with the side gears through the two apertures in the differential housing. Make sure they are diametrically opposite to each other. Rotate the differential pinion gears through 90° so bringing them into line with the pinion gear shaft bore in the housing.

23 Insert the pinion gear shaft with the locking pin hole in line with the pin hole.

24 Using feeler gauges measure the end float of each side gear. The correct clearance is 0.006 inch (0.15 mm) and if this figure is exceeded new thrust washers must be obtained. Dismantle the assembly again and fit the new thrust washers.

25 Lock the pinion gear shaft using the pin which should be tapped fully home using a suitable diameter parallel pin punch. Peen over the end of the pin hole to stop the pin working its way out.

26 The crownwheel may next be refitted. Wipe the mating faces of the crownwheel and differential housing and if original parts are being used place the crownwheel into position with the previously made marks aligned. Refit the eight bolts that secure the crownwheel and tighten these in a progressive and diagonal manner to a final torque wrench setting of 57 to 62 lb ft (8 to 8.7 kg m).

27 Place the shim packs back in their original fitted position on the differential housing bearing location. Using a piece of suitable diameter tube very carefully fit the differential housing bearings with the smaller diameter of the taper outwards. The

bearing cage must not in any way be damaged.

28 Place the shim behind the head of the pinion gear and using a suitable diameter tube very carefully fit the larger taper roller bearing onto the pinion shaft. The larger diameter of the bearing must be next to the pinion head.

29 Using suitable diameter tubes fit the two taper roller bearing cones into the final drive housing making sure that they are fitted the correct way round.

30 Slide the shim and spacer onto the pinion shaft and insert into the final drive housing.

31 Refit the second and smaller diameter taper roller bearing onto the end of the pinion shaft and follow this with a new oil seal. Before the seal is actually fitted apply some grease to the inner face between the two lips of the seal.

32 Apply a little jointing compound to the outer face of the seal.

33 Using a tubular drift of suitable diameter carefully drive the oil seal into the final housing. Make quite sure that it is fitted squarely into the housing.

34 Replace the drive pinion flange and hold securely in a bench vice. Fit a new self locking nut and tighten to a torque wrench setting of 71 to 86 lb ft (10 to 12 kg m).

35 Fit the bearing cones to the differential housing bearings and carefully ease the housing into position in the final drive housing.

36 Replace the bearing caps in their original positions. Smear a little jointing compound on the threads of each cap securing bolt and fit into position. When all four bolts have been replaced tighten these up in a diagonal and progressive manner to a final torque wrench setting of 43 to 49 lb ft (6 to 6.8 kg m).

37 If possible mount a dial indicator gauge so that the probe is resting on one of the teeth of the crownwheel and determine the backlash between the crownwheel and pinion. The backlash may be varied by decreasing the thickness of the shims behind one bearing and increasing the thickness of shims behind the other thus moving the crownwheel into or out of mesh as required. The total thickness of the shims must not be changed.

38 The best check the do-it-yourself owner can make to ascertain the correct meshing of the crownwheel and pinion is to smear a little engineer's blue onto the crownwheel and pinion and then rotate the pinion. The contact mark should appear right in the middle of the crownwheel teeth. Refer to Fig. 8.9 where the correct tooth pattern is shown. Also given are incorrect tooth patterns and the method of obtaining the correct pattern. Obviously this will take time and further dismantling but will be worth it.

39 Before refitting the rear cover make sure that the mating faces are free from traces of the old gasket or jointing compound.

40 Fit a new gasket and then the rear cover and secure with the ten bolts and spring washers. As the cover bolts protrude into the final drive housing it is important that a suitable oil resistant sealing compound is smeared onto the threads of each bolt before it is fitted.

41 Tighten the cover securing bolts to a torque wrench setting of 22 to 29 lb ft (3 to 4 kg m).

42 Refit the half shafts as described in Section 2 and then the complete rear axle assembly as described in Section 6.

43 Do not forget to refill with Castrol Hypoy. The capacity is 2.3 US pints (1.065 litres).

8 Wheel stud - removal and replacement

1 The usual reasons for renewal of a wheel stud are either the threads have been damaged or the stud has broken, this usually being caused by overtightening of the wheel nuts. To renew a wheel stud, remove the half shaft assembly as described in Section 2.

2 Using a parallel pin punch of suitable diameter drive the old stud through the flange towards the bearing.

3 To fit a new stud place it in its hole from the rear of the flange and using a bench vice with a socket placed in front of the stud press it fully home in the flange.

Chapter 9 Braking system

Contents

Specifications

Type of system	Disc at front, drum at rear
Footbrake	Hydraulic on all four wheels
Handbrake	Mechanical to rear wheels only
Front brake layout	Trailing calipers
Hydraulic system	Dual line, tandem master cylinder and servo assisted

Brake dimensions

Front:

Disc diameter	9.625 in (24.45 cm)
Disc thickness	0.50 in (12.70 mm)
Disc runout	0.0035 in (0.089 cm)
Pad swept area	189.5 sq in (1.230 sq in)
Pad colour code	Blue/white/white/white/blue
Cylinder diameter	2.125 in (5.39 cm)

Rear:

Drum diameter	9 in (22.9 cm)
Lining width	1.75 in (44.5 mm)
Lining thickness	0.188 in (4.78 mm)
Total swept area	99 sq in (639.0 sq cm)
Cylinder diameter	0.75 in (19.05 cm)

Vacuum servo unit

Boost ratio	2.2 : 1
Diaphragm area	38 sq in (245.161 sq cm)

Torque wrench settings:

	lbf ft	kg f m
Caliper to suspension leg	45 - 50	6.22 - 6.91
Disc to hub	30 - 34	4.15 - 4.70
Rear backplate to axle housing	15 - 18	2.07 - 2.49
Hydraulic pipe unions	5 - 7	0.7 - 1.0
Bleed screws	5 - 7	0.7 - 1.0

1 General description

Disc brakes are fitted to the front wheels and drum brakes to the rear. All are operated under servo assistance from the brake pedal, this being connected to the master cylinder and servo assembly mounted on the bulkhead.

The hydraulic system is of the dual line principle whereby the front disc brake calipers have a separate hydraulic system to that of the rear drum brake wheel cylinders so that if failure of the hydraulic pipes to the front or rear brakes occurs half the braking system still operates. Servo assistance in this condition is still available.

The front brake disc is secured to the hub flange and the caliper mounted on the suspension strut and wheel stub assembly, so that the disc is able to rotate in between the two halves of the caliper. Inside each half of the caliper is a hydraulic cylinder, this being interconnected by a drilling which allows hydraulic fluid pressure to be transmitted to both halves. A piston operates in each cylinder, and is in contact with the outer face of the brake pad. By depressing the brake pedal, hydraulic fluid pressure is increased by the servo unit and transmitted to the caliper by a system of metal and flexible hoses whereupon the pistons are moved outwards so pushing the pads onto the face of the disc so slowing down the rotational speed of the disc.

The rear drum brakes have one cylinder operating two shoes. When the brake pedal is depressed, hydraulic fluid pressure, increased by the servo unit, is transmitted to the rear brake wheel cylinders by a system of metal and flexible pipes. The pressure moves the pistons outwards so pushing the shoe linings into contact with the inside circumference of the brake drum and slowing down the rotational speed of the drum.

The handbrake provides an independent means of rear brake application.

Also attached to each of the brake units is an automatic adjuster which operates in conjunction with the handbrake mechanism.

2 Bleeding the hydraulic system

1 Removal of all the air from the hydraulic system is essential to the correct working of the braking system, and before undertaking this, examine the fluid reservoir cap to ensure that the vent hole is clear. Check the level of fluid in the reservoir and top up if required.

2 Check all brake line unions and connections for possible seepage, and at the same time check the condition of the rubber hoses which may be perished.

3 If the condition of a caliper or wheel cylinder is in doubt, check for possible signs of fluid leakage.

4 If there is any possibility that incorrect fluid has been used in the system, drain all the fluid out and flush through with methylated spirits. Renew all piston seals and cups as they will be affected and could possibly fail under pressure.

5 Gather together a clean jar, a 12 inch length of tubing which fits tightly over the bleed screws and a tin of the correct brake fluid.

6 To bleed the system, clean the area around the bleed valves and start on the front right hand bleed screw by first removing the rubber cup over the end of the bleed screw.

7 Place the end of the tube in the clean jar which should contain sufficient fluid to keep the end of the tube emersed during the operation.

8 Open the bleed screw ¼ turn with a spanner and depress the brake pedal. After slowly releasing the pedal, pause for a moment to allow the fluid to recoup in the master cylinder and

depress it again. This will force air from the system. Continue until no more air bubbles can be seen coming from the tube. At intervals make sure that the reservoir is kept topped up, otherwise air will enter at this point again.

9 Finally depress the pedal down fully and hold it there whilst the bleed screw is tightened. To ensure correct seating it should be tightened to a torque wrench setting of 5 to 7 lb ft (0.70 to 1.0 kg m).

10 Repeat this operation on the second front brake, and then the rear brakes, starting with the right hand brake unit first.

11 When completed check the level of fluid in the reservoir and then check the feel of the brake pedal, which should be firm and free from any 'spongy' action, which is normally associated with air in the system.

12 It will be noticed that during the bleeding operation the effort required to depress the pedal the full stroke will increase because of loss of vacuum assistance as it is destroyed by repeated operation of the servo unit. Although the servo unit will be inoperative as far as assistance is concerned it does not affect the brake bleed operation.

3 Flexible hose - inspection, removal and replacement

1 Inspect the condition of the flexible hydraulic hoses leading to each of the front disc brake calipers and the one at the front of the rear axle. If they are swollen, damaged or chafed, they must be renewed.

2 Wipe the top of the brake master cylinder reservoir and unscrew the cap. Place a piece of polythene sheet over the top of the reservoir and refit the cap. This is to stop hydraulic fluid syphoning out during subsequent operations.

3 To remove a flexible hose wipe the union and any supports free from dust and undo the union nuts from the metal pipe ends.

4 Undo and remove the locknuts and washers securing each flexible hose end to the support and lift away the flexible hose.

5 Refitting is the reverse sequence to removal. It will be necessary to bleed the brake hydraulic system as described in Section 2. If one hose has been removed it is only necessary to bleed either the front or rear brake hydraulic system.

4 Front brake pads - inspection, removal and replacement

1 Apply the handbrake, remove the front wheel trim, slacken the wheel nuts, jack up the front of the car and place on firmly based axle stands. Remove the front wheel.

2 Inspect the amount of friction material left on the pads. The pads must be renewed when the thickness has been reduced to a minimum of 0.12 inches (3.00 mm).

3 If the fluid level in the master cylinder reservoir is high, when the pistons are moved into their respective bores to accomodate new pads the level could rise sufficiently for the fluid to overflow. Place absorbent cloth around the reservoir or syphon a little fluid out so preventing paintwork damage caused by the hydraulic fluid.

4 Using a pair of long nozed pliers, extract the two small clips that hold the main retaining pins in place.

5 Remove the main retaining pins which run through the caliper and the metal backing of the pads and the shims.

6 The friction pads can now be removed from the caliper. If they prove difficult to remove by hand a pair of long nosed pliers can be used. Lift away the shims and tension springs.

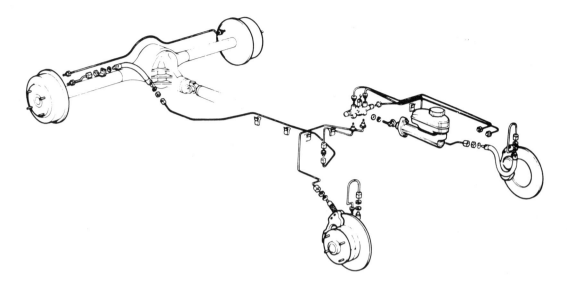

Fig. 9.1. Brake hydraulic system

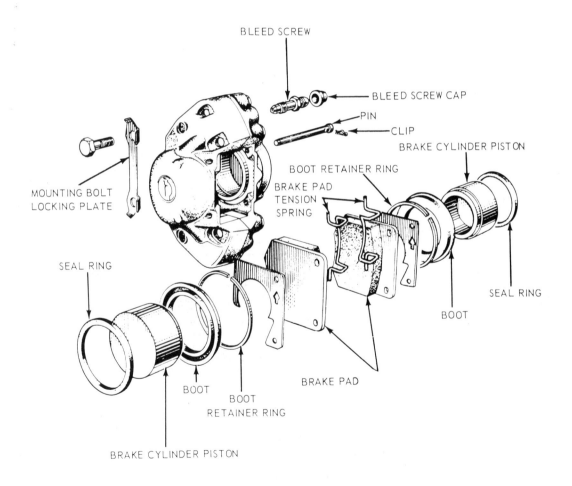

Fig. 9.2. Component parts of caliper

7 Carefully clean the recesses in the caliper in which the friction pads and shims lie, and the exposed faces of each piston from all traces of dirt or rust.

8 Using a piece of wood carefully retract the pistons

9 Place the brake pad tension springs on the brake pads and shims (these can be fitted either way up) and locate in the caliper. Insert the main pad retaining pins making sure that the tongs of the tension springs are under the retaining pins. Secure the pins with the small wire clips.

10 Refit the road wheel and lower the car. Tighten the wheel nuts securely and replace the wheel trim.

11 To correctly seat the pistons pump the brake pedal several times and finally top up the hydraulic fluid level in the master cylinder reservoir as necessary.

5 Front brake caliper - removal and refitting

1 Apply the handbrake, remove the front wheel trim, slacken the wheel nuts, jack up the front of the car and place on firmly based axle stands. Remove the front wheel.

2 Wipe the top of the master cylinder reservoir and unscrew the cap. Place a piece of polythene sheet over the top of the reservoir and refit the cap.

3 Remove the friction pads as described in Section 4.

4 If it is intended to fit new caliper pistons and/or the seals, depress the brake pedal to bring the pistons into contact with the disc and so assist subsequent removal of the pistons.

5 Wipe the area clean around the flexible hose bracket and detach the pipe as described in Section 3. Tape up the end of the pipe to stop the possibility of dirt ingress.

6 Using a screwdriver or chisel bend back the tabs on the locking plate and undo the two caliper body mounting bolts. Lift away the caliper from its mounting flange on the suspension leg.

7 To refit the caliper, position it over the disc and move it until the mounting bolt holes are in line with the two front holes in the suspension leg mounting flange.

8 Fit the caliper retaining bolts through the two holes in a new locking plate and insert the bolts through the caliper body. Tighten the bolts to a torque wrench setting of 45 to 50 lb ft (6.22 - 6.91 kg m).

9 Using a screwdriver, pliers or chisel bend up the locking plate tabs so as to lock the bolts.

10 Remove the tape from the end of the flexible hydraulic pipe and reconnect it to the union on the hose bracket. Be careful not to cross the thread of the union nut during the initial turns. The union nut should be tightened securely, if possible using a torque wrench and special slotted end ring spanner attachment set to 5 to 7 lb ft (0.70 to 1.00 kg m).

11 Push the pistons into their respective bores so as to accommodate the pads. Watch the level of hydraulic fluid in the master cylinder reservoir as it can overflow if too high whilst the pistons are being retracted. Place absorbent cloth around the reservoir or syphon a little fluid out so preventing paintwork damage.

12 Fit the pads, shims and tension springs as described in Section 4.

13 Bleed the hydraulic system as described in Section 2. Replace the road wheel and lower the car.

6 Front brake caliper - dismantling and reassembly

1 The pistons should be removed first. To do this half withdraw one piston from its bore in the caliper body.

2 Carefully remove the securing circlip and extract the sealing

bellows from its location in the lower part of the piston skirt. Completely remove the piston.

3 If difficulty is experienced in withdrawing the pistons use a jet of compressed air or a foot pump to move it out of its bore.

4 Remove the sealing bellows from its location in the annular ring which is machined in the cylinder bore.

5 Remove the piston sealing ring from the cylinder bore using a small screwdriver but do take care not to scratch the fine finish of the bore.

6 To remove the second piston repeat paragraphs 1 to 5 inclusive.

7 It is important that the two halves of the caliper are not separated under any circumstances. If hydraulic fluid leaks are evident from the joint, the caliper must be renewed.

8 Thoroughly wash all parts in methylated spirits or correct hydraulic fluid. During reassembly new rubber seals must be fitted; these should be well lubricated with clean hydraulic fluid.

9 Inspect the pistons and bores for signs of wear, score marks or damage, and, if evident new parts should be obtained ready for fitting or a new caliper obtained.

10 To reassemble, fit one of the piston seals into the annulus groove in the cylinder bore.

11 Fit the rubber bellows to the cylinder bore groove so that the lip is turned outwards.

12 Lubricate the seal and rubber bellows with correct hydraulic fluid. Push the piston, crown first, through the rubber sealing bellows and then into the cylinder bore. Take care as it is easy for the piston to damage the rubber bellows.

13 With the piston half inserted into the cylinder bore fit the inner edge of the bellows into the annular groove in the piston skirt.

14 Push the piston down the bore as far as it will go. Secure the rubber bellows to the caliper with the circlip.

15 Repeat paragraphs 10 to 14 inclusive for the second piston.

16 The caliper is now ready for refitting. It is recommended that the hydraulic pipe end is temporarily plugged to stop any dirt ingress whilst it is being refitted, before the pipe connection is made.

7 Front brake disc and hub - removal and replacement

1 After jacking up the car and removing the front wheel, remove the caliper as described in Section 5.

2 By judicious tapping and levering remove the dust cap from the centre of the hub.

3 Remove the split pin from the nut retainer and lift away the adjusting nut retainer.

4 Unscrew the adjusting nut and lift away the thrust washer and outer taper bearing.

5 Pull off the complete hub and disc assembly from the stub axle.

6 From the back of the hub assembly carefully prise out the grease seal and lift away the inner tapered bearing.

7 Carefully clean out the hub and wash the bearings with petrol making sure that no grease or oil is allowed to get onto the brake disc.

8 Should it be necessary to separate the disc from the hub for renewal or regrinding, first bend back the locking tabs and undo the four securing bolts. With a scriber mark the relative positions of the hub and disc to ensure refitting in their original positions and separate the disc from the hub.

9 Thoroughly clean the disc and inspect for signs of deep scoring, cracks or excessive corrosion. If these are evident, the disc may be reground but no more than a maximum total of 0.060 inch (1.524 mm) may be removed. It is however, desirable to fit a new disc if at all possible.

Fig. 9.3. Brake pad retaining pins and clips

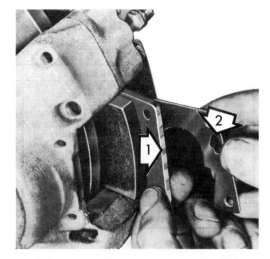

FIG. 9.4. WITHDRAWING PAD AND SHIM

Note   1   Pad colour coding on edge
*   2   Arrow in shim*

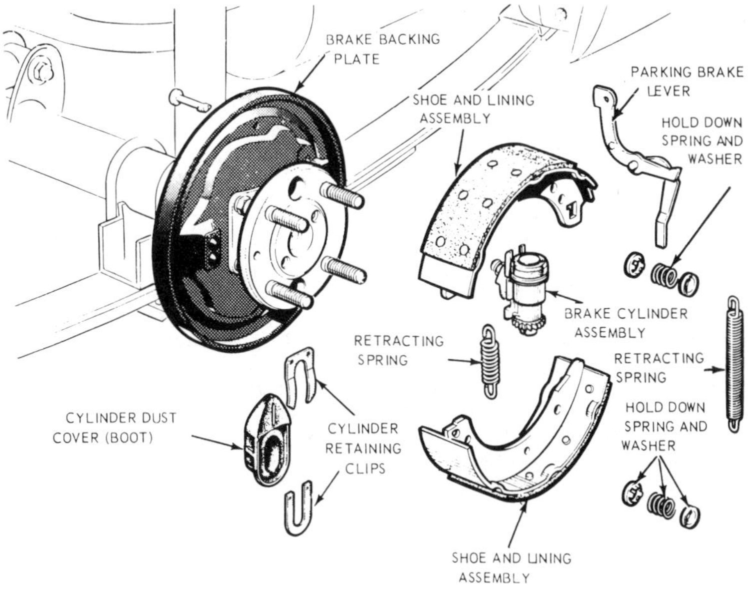

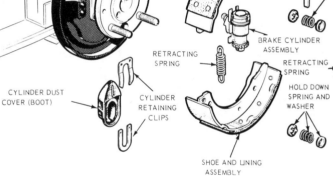

BRAKE BACKING
PLATE

SHOE AND LINING
ASSEMBLY

PARKING BRAKE
LEVER

HOLD DOWN
SPRING AND
WASHER

Fig. 9.5. Rear drum brake components

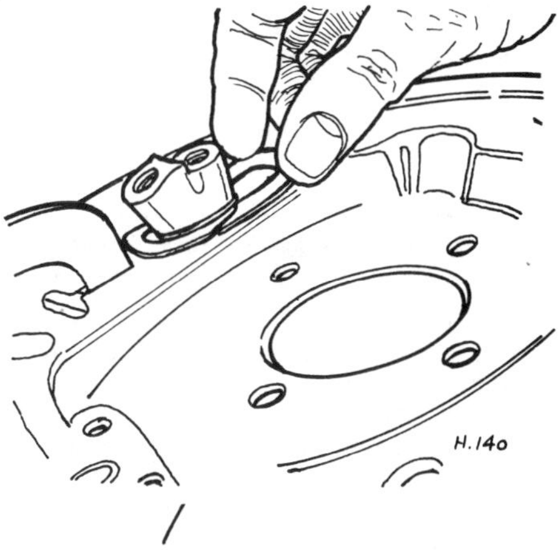

BRAKE CYLINDER
ASSEMBLY

RETRACTING
SPRING

RETRACTING
SPRING

CYLINDER DUST
COVER (BOOT)

CYLINDER
RETAINING
CLIPS

HOLD DOWN
SPRING AND
WASHER

SHOE AND LINING
ASSEMBLY

Fig. 9.6. Withdrawing rear wheel cylinder retaining plate

CYLINDER RETAINING PLATE

BLEED SCREW

CYLINDER RETAINING PLATE

PISTON RETURN SPRING

PISTON

BOOT

SEAL

CYLINDER ASSEMBLY

ADJUSTER

Fig. 9.7. Component parts of rear wheel cylinder

BOOT RETAINER

PARKING BRAKE LEVER

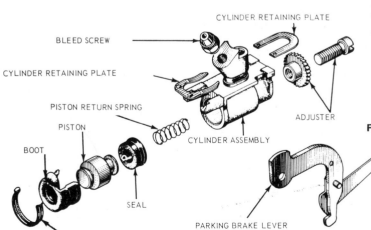

H.140

10 To reassemble make quite sure that the mating faces of the disc and hub are very clean and place the disc on the hub, lining up any previously made marks.

11 Fit the four securing bolts and two new tab washers and tighten the bolts in a progressive and diagonal manner to a final torque wrench setting of 30 to 34 lb ft (4.15 to 4.70 kg m). Bend up the locking tabs.

12 Work some Castrol LM Grease well into the bearing, fully pack the bearing cages and rollers. NOTE: leave the hub and grease seal empty to allow for subsequent expansion of the grease.

13 To reassemble the hub, first fit the inner bearing and then gently tap the grease seal back into the hub. A new seal must always be fitted as, during removal it was probably damaged. The lip must face inwards to the hub.

14 Replace the hub and disc assembly onto the stub axle and slide in the outer bearing and thrust washer.

15 Refit the adjusting nut and tighten it to a torque wrench setting of 27 lb ft (3.7 kg m) whilst rotating the hub and disc to ensure free movement and centralisation of the bearings. Slacken the nut back by 90° which will give the required end float of 0.001 - 0.005 in (0.03 - 0.13 mm). Fit the nut retainer and a new split pin, but at this stage do not lock the split pin.

16 If a dial indicator gauge is available, it is advisable to check the disc for run-out. The measurement should be taken as near to the edge of the worn yet smooth part of the disc as possible, and must not exceed 0.002 in (0.05 mm). If the figure obtained is found to be excessive, check the mating surfaces of the disc and hub for dirt or damage and check the bearings and cups for excessive wear or damage.

17 If a dial indicator gauge is not available the run-out can be checked by means of a feeler gauge placed between the casting of the caliper and the disc. Establish a reasonably tight fit with the feeler gauge between the top of the casting and the disc and rotate the disc and hub. Any high or low spots will immediately become obvious by extra tightness or looseness of the fit of the feeler gauge. The amount of runout can be checked by adding or subtracting feeler gauges as necessary.

18 Once the disc runout has been checked and found to be correct bend the ends of the split pin back and replace the dust cap.

19 Reconnect the brake hydraulic pipe and bleed the brakes as described in Section 2 of this Chapter.

6 Note which way round and into which holes in the shoes the two retracting springs fit and detach the retracting springs.

7 Lift away the two brake shoes and retracting springs.

8 If the shoes are to be left off for a while, place a warning on the steering wheel. Also place an elastic band around the wheel cylinder to stop the piston falling out.

9 Withdraw the ratchet wheel assembly from the wheel cylinder and rotate the ratchet wheel until it abuts the slot head bolt shoulder. If this is not done difficulty will arise in refitting the brake drum.

10 Thoroughly clean all traces of dust from the shoes, backplates and brake drums using a stiff brush. It is recommended that compressed air is not used as it blows up dust which should not be inhaled. Brake dust can cause judder, or squeal and, therefore, it is important to clean out as described.

11 Check that the piston is free in the cylinder, that the rubber dust covers are undamaged and in position, and that there are no hydraulic fluid leaks.

12 Prior to reassembly smear a trace of Castrol PH Brake Grease on the shoe support pads, brake shoe pivots and on the ratchet wheel face and threads.

13 To reassemble first fit the retracting springs to the shoe webs in the same position as was noted during removal.

14 Fit the shoe assembly to the backplate by first positioning the rear shoe in its location on the fixed pivot and over the parking brake link. Follow this with the front shoe.

15 Secure each shoe to the backplate with the spring and dished washer, dish facing inwards and turning through 90° to lock in position. Make sure that each shoe is firmly seated on the backplate.

16 Refit the brake drum and push it up the studs as far as it will go. Secure with the retaining screw.

17 The shoes must next be centralised by the brake pedal being depressed firmly several times.

18 Pull on and then release the handbrake several times until it is no longer possible to hear the clicking noise of the ratchet being turned by the adjusting arm. It is important to note that with the ratchet wheel in the fully off adjustment position, it is possible for the indexing lever on the parking brake link to over-ride the ratchet wheel and stay in this position. When operating the link lever it is necessary to ensure that it always returns to the fully off position each time.

19 Refit the road wheel and lower the car. Road test to ensure correct operation of the brakes.

8 Drum brake shoes - inspection, removal and refitting

After high mileages, it will be necessary to fit replacement shoes with new linings. Refitting new brake linings to shoes is not considered economic, or possible, without the use of special equipment. However, if the services of a local garage or workshop having brake relining equipment are available then there is no reason why the original shoes should not be relined successfully. Ensure that the correct specification linings are fitted to the shoes.

1 Chock the front wheels, jack up the rear of the car and place on firmly based axle stands. Remove the road wheel.

2 Release the handbrake retaining screw, and using a soft faced hammer on the outer circumference of the brake drum remove the brake drum.

3 The brake linings should be renewed if they are so worn that the rivet heads are flush with the surface of the lining. If bonded linings are fitted, they must be renewed when the lining material has worn down to 0.6 in (1.52 mm) at its thinnest part.

4 Depress each shoe holding down spring and rotate the spring retaining washer through 90° to disengage it from the pin secured to the back plate. Lift away the washer and spring.

5 Ease each shoe from its location slot in the fixed pivot and then detach the other end of each shoe from the wheel cylinder.

9 Drum brake wheel cylinder - removal, inspection and overhaul

If hydraulic fluid is leaking from the brake wheel cylinder, it will be necessary to dismantle it and renew the seal. Should brake fluid be found running down the side of the wheel, or if it is noticed that a pool of liquid forms alongside one wheel or the level of fluid in the master cylinder drops it is also indicative of failed seals.

1 Refer to Section 8 and remove the brake drum and shoes. Clean down the rear of the backplate using a stiff brush. Place a quantity of rag under the backplate to catch any hydraulic fluid that may issue from the open pipe or wheel cylinder.

2 Wipe the top of the brake master cylinder reservoir and unscrew the cap. Place a piece of polythene sheet over the top of the reservoir and replace the cap.

3 Using an open ended spanner carefully unscrew the hydraulic pipe connection union to the rear of the wheel cylinder. To prevent dirt ingress tape over the end of the pipe.

4 Withdraw the split pin and clevis pin from the handbrake lever at the rear of the backplate.

5 Using a screwdriver carefully ease the rubber dust cover from the rear of the backplate and lift away.

6 Pull off the two 'U' shaped retainers holding the wheel cylinder to the backplate noting that the spring retainer is fitted from the handbrake link end of the wheel cylinder and the flat retainer from the other end, the flat retainer being located between the spring retainer and the wheel cylinder.

7 The wheel cylinder and handbrake link can now be removed from the brake backplate.

8 To dismantle the wheel cylinder first remove the small metal clip holding the rubber dust cap in place then prise off the dust cap.

9 Take the piston complete with its seal out of the cylinder bore and then withdraw the spring. Should the piston and seal prove difficult to remove gentle pressure will push it out of the bore.

10 Inspect the cylinder bore for score marks caused by impurities in the hydraulic fluid. If any are found the cylinder and piston will require renewal together, as a replacement unit.

11 If the cylinder bore is sound thoroughly clean it out with fresh hydraulic fluid.

12 The old rubber seal will probably be visibly worn or swollen. Detach it from the piston, smear a new rubber seal with hydraulic fluid and assemble it to the piston with the flat face of the seal next to the piston rear shoulder.

13 Reassembly is a direct reversal of the dismantling procedure. If the rubber dust cap appears to be worn or damaged it should also be renewed.

14 Before commencing refitting smear the area where the cylinder slides on the backplate and the brake shoe support pads, brake shoe pivots, ratchet wheel face and threads with Castrol PH White Brake Grease or other approved brake grease.

15 Replacement is a straightforward reversal of the removal sequence but the following points should be checked with extra care.

16 After fitting the rubber boot, check that the wheel cylinder can slide freely in the backplate and that the handbrake link operates the self adjusting mechanism correctly.

17 It is important to note that the self adjusting ratchet mechanism on the right hand rear brake is right hand threaded and the mechanism on the left hand rear brake is left hand threaded.

18 When replacement is complete, bleed the braking system as described in Section 2.

10 Drum brake backplate - removal and refitting

1 To remove the backplate refer to Chapter 8 and remove the half shaft.

2 Detach the handbrake cable from the handbrake relay lever on the backplate.

3 Wipe the top of the brake master cylinder reservoir and unscrew the cap. Place a piece of polythene sheet over the top of the reservoir and replace the cap.

4 Using an open ended spanner, carefully unscrew the hydraulic pipe connection union to the rear of the wheel cylinder. To prevent dirt ingress tape over the pipe ends.

5 The brake backplate may now be lifted away.

6 Refitting is the reverse sequence to removal. It will be necessary to bleed the brake hydraulic system as described in Section 2.

11 Handbrake - adjustment

1 Chock the front wheels, jack up the rear of the car and support on firmly based axle stands located under the rear axle. Release the handbrake.

2 Slide under the car and check that the primary cable follows its correct run and is held correctly in its guides. The cable guides must be left well greased at all times.

3 First adjust the effective length of the primary cable by slackening the locknut on the end of the cable adjacent to the relay lever on the rear axle.

4 Adjust the nut until the primary cable has no slack in it and the relay lever is just clear of the slot on the banjo casing. Retighten the locknut.

5 Slacken the locknut on the end of the transverse cable adjacent to the right hand rear brake. Check that the parking brake operating levers are in the fully 'off' position, that is back on their stops, and adjust the cable so that there is no slack. Check that the operating levers are still on their stops and tighten the locknut.

6 It should be appreciated that once the handbrake system has been correctly set adjustment will only be necessary in the event of cable or component renewal, wear of the various linkage components or after high mileages due to cable stretch. Handbrake cable adjustment does not compensate for rear brake shoe lining wear.

7 Remove the axle stands and lower the car to the ground.

12 Handbrake lever - removal and replacement

1 Chock the front wheels, jack up the rear of the car and support on firmly based axle stands. Release the handbrake.

2 Working inside the car remove the carpeting from around the area of the handbrake lever.

3 Remove the split pin and withdraw the clevis pin that connects the primary cable to the lower end of the handbrake lever. This protrudes under the floor panels.

4 Undo and remove the six self tapping screws which secure the handbrake lever rubber boot to the floor. Draw the rubber boot up the lever.

5 Undo and remove the two bolts that secure the handbrake lever assembly to the floor. Lift away the lever assembly.

6 Refitting the lever assembly is the reverse sequence to removal. The following additional points should be noted:

a) Apply some Castrol LM Grease to the primary cable clevis pin.

b) Adjust the primary cable as described in Section 11.

13 Handbrake cables - removal and replacement

Two cables are used for the handbrake system these are known as the Primary cable and the Transverse cable and located as shown in Fig. 9.9.

Primary cable

1 Chock the front wheels, jack up the rear of the car and support on firmly based axle stands. Release the handbrake.

2 Working under the car unscrew and remove the nuts that secure the end of the primary cable to the relay lever located at the rear of the axle casing.

3 Detach the primary cable from the end of the handbrake lever by removing the split pin and withdrawing the clevis pin.

4 Detach the cable from its underbody guides and lift away.

5 Refitting the Primary cable is the reverse sequence to removal but the following additional points should be noted:

a) Apply some Castrol LM Grease to the cable guides and insert

the cable. Also lubricate the front clevis pin.
b) Refer to Section 11 and adjust the primary cable.

Transverse cable

1 Chock the front wheels, jack up the front of the car and support on firmly based axle stands. Release the handbrake.
2 Working under the car remove the split pin and withdraw the clevis pin that secures the transverse cable to the left hand backplate.
3 Detach the cable from the right hand rear backplate by removing the locknut and unscrewing the cable from the clevis.
4 Remove the pulley pins, split pin and withdraw the pulley pin. Lift away the little pulley wheel and transverse cable.
5 Refitting the transverse cable is the reverse sequence to removal but the following aditional points should be noted:
a) Apply some Castrol LM Grease to the pulley and pivot pin, the threaded end of the cable and the clevis pin.
b) Adjust the transverse cable as described in Section 11.

---

14 Brake master cylinder - removal and replacement

1 Apply the handbrake and chock the front wheels. Drain the fluid from the master cylinder reservoir and master cylinder by attaching a plastic bleed tube to one of the front brake bleed screws. Undo the screw one turn and then pump the fluid out into a clean glass container by means of the brake pedal. Hold the brake pedal against the floor at the end of each stroke and tighten the bleed screw. When the pedal has returned to its normal position loosen the bleed screw and repeat the process. The above sequence should now be carried out on one of the rear brake bleed screws.
2 Wipe the area around the two union nuts on the side of the master cylinder body and using an open ended spanner undo the two union nuts. Tape over the ends of the pipes to stop dirt ingress.
3 Undo and remove the two nuts and spring washers that secure the master cylinder to the rear of the servo unit. Lift away the master cylinder taking care not to damage the servo unit seal and ensure that no hydraulic fluid is allowed to drip onto the paintwork.
4 Refitting the master cylinder is the reverse sequence to removal. Always start the union nuts before finally tightening the master cylinder nuts. It will be necessary to bleed the complete hydraulic system: full details will be found in Section 2.

---

15 Brake master cylinder - dismantling, examination and reassembly

1 The component parts are shown in Fig. 9.10.
2 Prior to dismantling wipe the exterior of the master cylinder clean.
3 Using a clean metal rod of suitable diameter depress the primary piston until it reaches the stop so that the pressure of the intermediate piston is removed from the stop screw.
4 Unscrew the stop screw and remove the sealing washer. Release the pressure on the piston.
5 Lightly depress on the primary piston again to relieve the pressure on the circlip located in the bore at the flanged end of the cylinder. With a pair of pointed pliers remove the circlip taking care not to scratch the finely finished bore.
6 Lift away the stop washer, and withdraw the primary piston assembly.
7 Undo and remove the connecting screw and withdraw the

deep spring retainer, spring, flat spring retainer, seal retainer, primary seal, seal protector and secondary seal from the piston.
8 The intermediate piston assembly may now be removed by lightly tapping the master cylinder against a wooden base.
9 Withdraw the spring, spring retainer, seal retainer, primary seal, seal protector and the two separating seals from the piston.
10 Thoroughly wash all parts in either methylated spirits or clean approved hydraulic fluid and place in order ready for inspection.
11 Examine the bores of the master cylinder carefully for any signs of scoring, ridges or corrosion and, if it is found to be smooth all over, new seals can be fitted. If there is any doubt as to the condition of the bore, then a new cylinder must be fitted.
12 If examination of the seals shows them to be apparently oversize or very loose on their seats, suspect oil contamination in the system. Oil will swell these rubber seals, and if one is found to be swollen it is reasonable to assume that all seals in the braking system will require attention.
13 Before reassembly again wash all parts in methylated spirits or clean approved hydraulic fluid. Do not use any other type of oil or cleaning fluid or the seals will be damaged.
14 Commence reassembling by lubricating the bores with Red Rubber Grease.
15 Smear the new secondary seal with hydraulic fluid and fit this to the primary piston.
16 Locate the primary seal protector and then lubricate and fit a new primary seal. Refit the seal retainer, flat spring retainer, spring, deep spring retainer and connecting screw.
17 Lubricate and fit two new separating seals to the intermediate piston. These seals may be identified as having a silver band. Refit thesprimary seal protector and then lubricate and fit a new primary seal. Reassemble the seal retainer, spring retainer and the spring with its narrow end against the retainer.
18 Position the master cylinder between soft faces and clamp in a vice in such a manner that the main bore is inclined with the open end downwards.
19 Insert the intermediate piston assembly and primary piston assembly. To avoid any damage to the cup seals a flattened needle should be passed around the lip of each seal to assist entry into the cylinder bore.
20 Reposition the master cylinder so that it is now vertical with the open end upwards and place the stop washer in position. Depress the primary piston slightly and fit the circlip.
21 Next fully depress the primary piston and fit the stop screw with a new sealing washer. Tighten the stop screw to a torque wrench setting of 4.3 to 7.0 lb ft (0.6 to 1.0 kg m).
22 The master cylinder is now ready for refitting to the servo unit. Bleed the complete hydraulic system and road test the car.

---

16 Brake servo unit - removal and replacement

1 Slacken the clip securing the vacuum hose to the servo unit and carefully draw the hose from its union.
2 Refer to Section 13 and remove the master cylinder.
3 Using a pair of pliers remove the split pin on the end of the brake pedal to pushrod clevis. Lift away the clevis.
4 Undo and remove the bolts and spring washers that secure the servo unit to the dash panel. Lift away the servo unit and bracket.
5 Undo and remove the four nuts and spring washers that secure the bracket to the servo unit.
6 Refitting the servo unit is the reverse sequence to removal. It will be necessary to bleed the brake hydraulic system as described in Section 2.

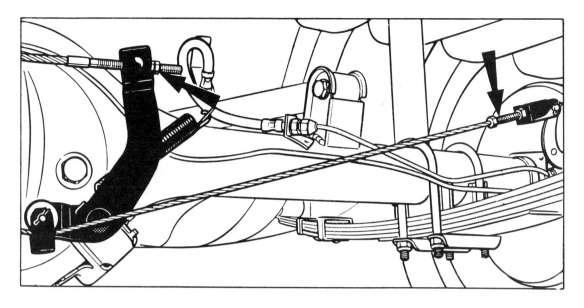

Fig. 9.8. Handbrake linkage adjustment points

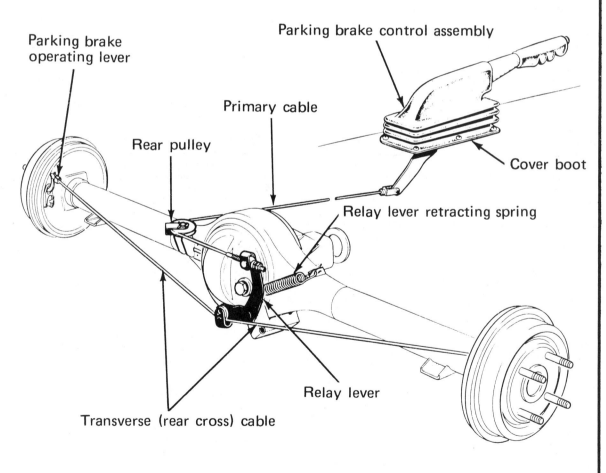

Parking brake operating lever

Parking brake control assembly

Primary cable

Rear pulley

Cover boot

Relay lever retracting spring

Relay lever

Transverse (rear cross) cable

Fig. 9.9. Handbrake assembly

17 Vacuum servo unit - description

1 A vacuum servo unit is fitted into the brake hydraulic circuit in series with the master cylinder, to provide assistance to the driver when the brake pedal is depressed. This reduces the effort required by the driver to operate the brakes under all braking conditions.

2 The unit operates by vacuum obtained from the induction manifold and comprises basically a booster diaphragm and check valve. The servo unit and hydraulic master cylinder are connected together so that the servo unit piston rod acts as the master cylinder pushrod. The drivers braking effort is transmitted through another pushrod to the servo unit piston and its built in control system. The servo unit piston does not fit tightly into the cylinder, but has a strong diaphragm to keep its edges in constant contact with the cylinder wall, so assuring an air tight seal between the two parts. The forward chamber is held under the vacuum conditions created in the inlet manifold of the engine and, during periods when the brake pedal is not in use, the controls open a passage to the rear chamber so placing it under vacuum conditions as well. When the brake pedal is depressed, the vacuum passage to the rear chamber is cut off and the chamber opened to atmospheric pressure. The consequent rush of air pushes the servo piston forward in the vacuum chamber and operates the main pushrod to the master cylinder.

3 The controls are designed so that assistance is given under all conditions and, when the brakes are not required, vacuum in the rear chamber is established when the brake pedal is released. All air from the atomosphere entering the rear chamber is passed through a small air filter.

4 Under normal operating conditions the vacuum servo unit is very reliable and does not require overhaul except at very high mileages. In this case it is far better to obtain a service exchange unit, rather than repair the original unit.

18 Vacuum servo unit - dismantling, inspection and reassembly

Thoroughly clean the outside of the unit using a stiff brush and wipe with a non fluffy rag. It cannot be too strongly emphasised that cleanliness is important when working on the servo. Before any attempt be made to dismantle, two items of equipment are required. Firstly, a base plate must be made to enable the unit to be safely held in a vice. Secondly, a lever must be made similar to the form shown. Without these items it is impossible to dismantle satisfactorily.

To dismantle the unit proceed as follows:

1 Using a file or scriber, make a line across the two halves of the unit to act as a datum for alignment.

2 Fit the previously made base plate into a firm vice and attach the unit to the plate using the master cylinder studs.

3 Fit the lever to the four studs on the rear shell as shown in Fig. 9.13.

4 Use a piece of long rubber hose and connect one end to the adaptor on the engine inlet manifold and the other end to the non return valve. Start the engine and this will creat a vacuum in the unit so drawing the two halves together.

5 Rotate the lever in an anti clockwise direction until the front shell indentations are in line with the recesses in the rim of the rear shell. Then press the lever assembly down firmly whilst an assistant stops the engine and quickly removes the vacuum pipe from the inlet manifold connector. Depress the operating rod so as to release the vacuum, whereupon the front and rear halves should part. If necessary, use a soft faced hammer and lightly tap the front half to break the bond.

6 Lift away the rear shell followed by the diaphragm return spring, the dust cap, end cap and the filter. Also withdraw the diaphragm. Press down the valve rod and shake out the valve retaining plate. Then separate the valve rod assembly from the diaphragm plate.

7 Gently ease the spring washer from the diaphragm plate and withdraw the pushrod and reaction disc.

8 The seal and plate assembly in the end of the front shell are a press fit. It is recommended that, unless the seal is to be renewed, they be left in situ.

9 Thoroughly clean all parts. Inspect all parts for signs of damage, stripped threads etc., and obtain new parts as necessary. All seals should be renewed and for this a 'Major Repair Kit' should be purchased. This kit will also contain two separate greases which must be used as directed and not interchanged.

10 To reassemble first smear the seal and bearing with suitable grease and refit the rear shell positioning it such that the flat face of the seal is towards the bearing. Press into position and refit the retainer.

11 Lightly smear the disc and hydraulic pushrod with the same grease. Refit the reaction disc and pushrod to the diaphragm plate and press in the large spring washer. The small spring washer supplied in the 'Major Repair Kit' is not required. It is important that the length of the pushrod is not altered in any way and any attempt to move the adjustment bolt will strip the threads. If a new hydraulic pushrod has been required, the length will have to be reset. Details of this operation are given at the end of this Section.

12 Lightly smear the outer diameter of the diaphragm plate neck and the bearing surfaces of the valve plunger with the same grease. Carefully fit the valve rod assembly into the neck of the diaphragm plate and fix with the retaining plate.

13 Fit the diaphragm into position and also the non return valve to the front shell. Next smear the seal and plate assembly with the same grease and press into the front shell with the plate facing inwards.

14 Fit the front shell to the base plate and the lever to the rear shell. Reconnect the vacuum hose to the non return valve and the adaptor on the engine inlet manifold. Position the diaphragm return spring in the front shell. Lightly smear the outer head of the diaphragm with the same grease and locate the diaphragm assembly in the rear shell. Position the rear shell assembly on the return spring and line up the previously made scribe marks.

15 The assistant should start the engine. Watching one's fingers very carefully, press the two halves of the unit together and, using the lever tool, turn clockwise to lock the two halves together. Stop the engine and disconnect the hose.

16 Press a new filter into the neck of the diaphragm plate, refit the end cap and position the dust cover onto the special lugs of the rear shell.

17 Hydraulic pushrod adjustment only applies if a new pushrod has been fitted. It will be seen that there is a bolt screwed into the end of the pushrod. The amount of protrusion has to be adjusted in the following manner: Remove the bolt and coat the threaded portion with Loctite Grade B. Reconnect the vacuum hose to the adaptor on the inlet valve and non return valve. Start the engine and screw the preparted bolt into the end of the pushrod. Adjust the position of the bolt head so that it is 0.011 to 0.016 in (0.28 to 0.40 mm) below the face of the front shell as shown by dimension A in Fig. 9.14. Leave the unit for a minimum of 24 hours to allow the Loctite to set hard.

18 Refit the servo unit to the car as described in the previous Section. To test the servo unit for correct operation after overhaul, first start the engine and run for a minimum period of two minutes and then switch off. Wait for ten minutes and apply the footbrake very carefully, listening to hear the rush of air into the servo unit. This will indicate that vacuum was retained and, therefore, operating correctly.

19 Pressure differential warning actuator - centralisation

1 If the shuttle in the pressure differential actuator has moved, either because air has got into one of the braking circuits or because one of the circuits has failed it will be necessary to centralise the shuttle.

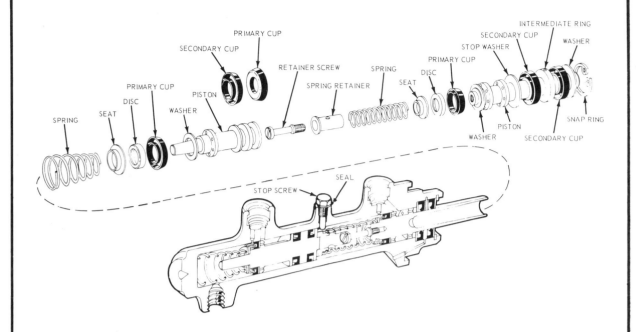

Fig. 9.10. Component parts of tendem master cylinder

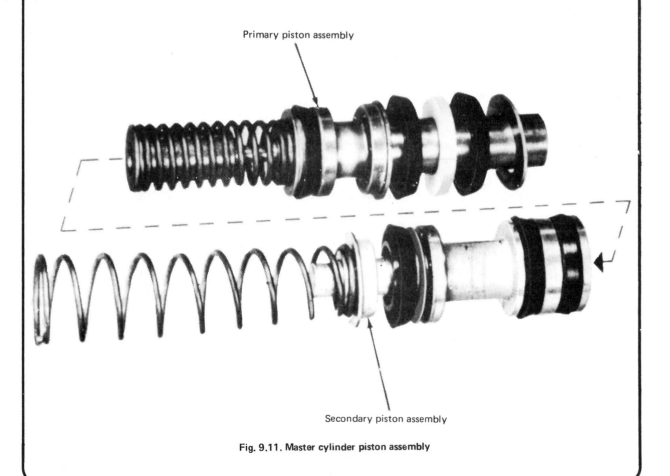

Primary piston assembly

Secondary piston assembly

Fig. 9.11. Master cylinder piston assembly

2 This can be done by obtaining an old screwdriver and cutting it down or grinding it into a tool of the dimensions shown in Fig. 9.15.

3 The rubber cover should be removed from the bottom of the pressure differnetial warning actuator and the tool inserted through the hole where it will engage in a slot in the larger piston thus drawing it into a central position.

4 During bleeding of the brakes the piston must be held in this position throughout the operation or it will prove very difficult to get the warning light to go out and stay out.

20 Pressure differential warning actuator - dismantling, examination and reassembly

1 Disconnect the five hydraulic pipes at their unions on the pressure differential warning actuator and to prevent too much loss of hydraulic fluid either place a piece of polythene under the cap of the master cylinder and screw it down tightly or plug the ends of the two pipes leading from the master cylinder.

2 Referring to Fig. 9.16 disconnect the wiring from the switch assembly (2).

3 Undo the single bolt holding the assembly to the rear of the engine compartment and remove it from the car.

4 To dismantle the assembly start by undoing the end plug (4) and discarding the copper gasket (5). Then undo the adaptor (8) and also discard its copper gasket as they must be renewed.

5 Unscrew the switch assembly (2) from the top of the unit then push the small and large pistons (7) out of their bores taking extreme care not to damage the bores during this operation.

6 Take the small seals (1 and 3) from their pistons making a careful note that the seals are slightly tapered and that the large diameter on each seal is fitted to the slotted end of the pistons. Discard the seals as they must be renewed.

7 Pull the dust cover (6) off the bottom of the unit and also discard this component for the same reasons as above.

8 Carefully examine the pistons (7) and the bore of the actuator for score marks scratches or damage; if any are found the complete unit must be exchanged.

9 To test if the switch assembly (2) is working correctly reconnect the wiring and press the plunger against any part of the bare metal of the engine or the bodywork when the warning light should come on. If it does not come on check the switch by substitution and also check the warning lamp bulb.

10 To reassemble the unit, start by fitting new seals (1 and 3) to the pistons (7) making sure that they are correctly fitted as detailed in paragraph 6 of this Section.

11 With the slotted end outwards, gently push the larger piston into the bore until the groove in the other end of the piston is opposite the hole in which the switch assembly (2) is fitted.

12 Screw the switch assembly (2) into position and tighten it down to a torque of 2 to 2.5 lb ft (0.28 to 0.34 kg m). Then gently push the shorter piston, with the slotted end outwards into the other end of the actuator.

13 Fit new copper washers (5) to the adaptor (8) and the end plug (4) and replace them in the assembly tightening them down to a torque of 16 to 20 lb ft (2.22 to 2.80 kg m). Fit a new dust cover (6) over the bottom aperture.

14 Replacement of the pressure differential warning actuator on the car is a direct reversal of the removal sequence. The brakes must be bled after replacement.

21 Brake pedal - removal and replacement

1 Disconnect the servo pushrod from the brake pedal by removing the small spring clip from the clevis pin then withdraw the clevis pin and bushes.

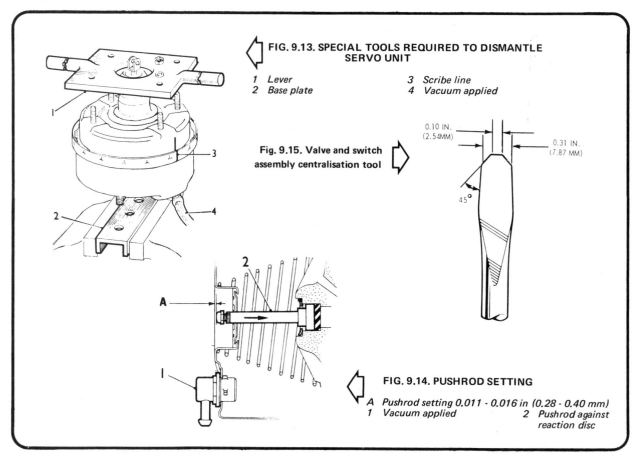

FIG. 9.13. SPECIAL TOOLS REQUIRED TO DISMANTLE SERVO UNIT

1 Lever
2 Base plate
3 Scribe line
4 Vacuum applied

Fig. 9.15. Valve and switch assembly centralisation tool

0.10 IN. (2.54MM)

0.31 IN. (7.87 MM)

45°

FIG. 9.14. PUSHROD SETTING

A Pushrod setting 0.011 - 0.016 in (0.28 - 0.40 mm)
1 Vacuum applied
2 Pushrod against reaction disc

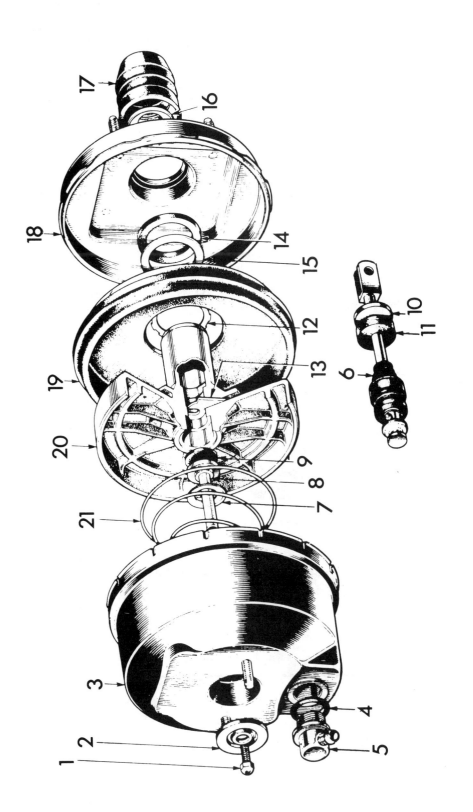

FIG. 9.12. THE SERVO UNIT — COMPONENT PARTS

1 Bolt
2 Seat assembly
3 Front shell
4 Seal

5 Valve assembly
6 Pushrod assembly
7 Dished washer
8 Brake servo pushrod

9 Reaction disc
10 Washer
11 Filter
12 Castellated washer

13 Stop key
14 Seal
15 Piston guide
16 Filter retainer

17 Dust cover
18 Rear shell
19 Diaphragm
20 Diaphragm plate

21 Spring

2   Take off the spring clip holding the clutch cable to the top of its pedal and withdraw the short pivot pin.

3   Remove the circlip from its groove on the pivot pin between the two pedals. The groove is situated between the brake pedal and the right hand side of the pedal mounting bracket.

4   Withdraw the pedal pivot pin from the clutch pedal end, then remove the two pedals carefully, noting the position of the bushes at either end and the single spacer washer.

5   Replacement is a direct reversal of the removal procedure detailed above, but when refitting the servo pushrod to the brake pedal ensure that the yellow paint mark on the pushrod yoke is facing towards the centre line of the car.

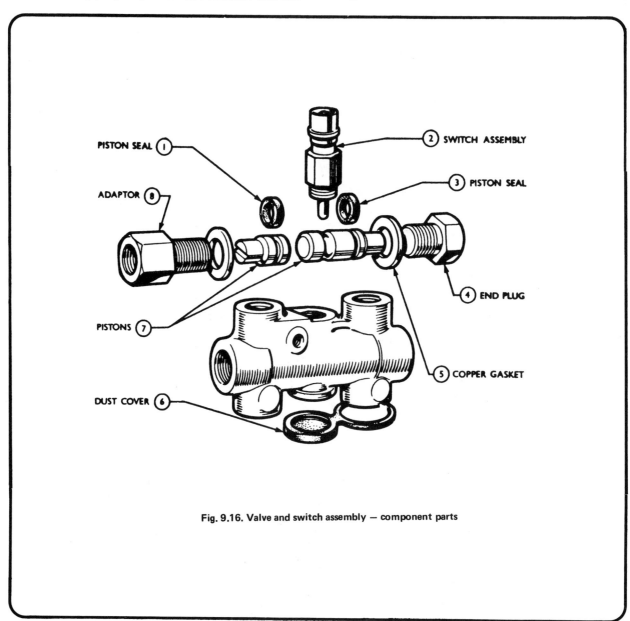

Fig. 9.16. Valve and switch assembly — component parts

Chapter 10 Electrical system

Contents

Specifications

Battery

Type	Lead acid 12 volt
Earthed terminal	Negative (−ve)
Capacity at 20 hr rate	66 amp/hr
Plates per cell	13
Specific gravity charged	1.275 to 1.290
Electrolyte capacity	7.7 pints (9.3 US pints, 4.3 litres)

Alternator

Type	Bosch K1
Speed (ratio to engine)	1.88 to 1
Maximum charge	35 amps
Brush spring pressure	10.6 - 14.1 oz

Regulator

Operating speed	5000 rpm
Alternator output	Not exceeding 10 amps
Voltage setting	14.1 to 14.4 volts

Starter motor

Lucas:

Type	Pre-engaged
Number of teeth on pinion	11
Number of teeth on ring gear	132
Gear ratio	12 : 1
Minimum brush length	0.375 inch (9.52 mm)
Brush spring pressure	28 oz (0.805 kg)
Minimum commutator thickness	0.8 in (2.05 mm)

Lock torque ...   .   7 lb f ft (097 kg fm) with 350 to 375 amps
Torque at 1000 rpm   ...   .   4.4 lb f ft (0.61 kg fm) with 260 to 375 amps
Light running current   ...   .   65 amp at 8,000 to 10,000 rpm
Maximum armature end float   ...   .   0.010 in (0.25 mm)

Solenoid:
Closing (series) winding resistance   ...   .   0.21 to 0.025 ohms
Hold-on (shunt) winding resistance   ...   .   0.9 to 1.1 ohms

Bosch:
Type ...   .   Pre-engaged
Teeth on pinion   10
Teeth on ring gear   135
Ratio ...   .   13.5 : 1
Number of brushes   4
Minimum brush length   ...   .   0.375 in (9.52 mm)
Brush spring pressure   ...   .   42.3 oz (1.190 kg)
Current draw (mounted on engine)   ...   .   100 - 130 amps at 68°F (20°C)
Engine cranking speed   ...   .   180 rpm (approx)

Fuse unit
Number of fuses   7
Fuse rating   ...   .   8 amps

Bulbs   C.P. or Wattage
Reverse light   ...   .   21 cp
Clock   ...   .   1.2 cp
Cluster illumination 2.2
Courtesy light   ...   .   6 cp
Front direction indicator   ...   .   32/4 cp
Headlights (high beam) ...   .   37.5 watts
Headlight (high and low beam)   ...   .   40 and 50 watts
Indicator lights ...   .   1.0 cp
Number plate lights   ...   .   5 cp
Rear direction indicator   ...   .   32 cp
Tail and stop light   ...   .   32/4 cp

Torque wrench settings:

	lb f ft	kg fm
Starter motor retaining bolts	20 to 25	2.76 to 3.46
Alternator mounting bolts	15 to 18	2.07 to 2.49
Alternator mounting bracket	20 to 25	2.76 to 3.46
Pulley nut	20 to 25	2.76 to 3.46

1 General description

The electrical system is of the 12 volt negative earth type. The major components comprise a 12 volt battery of which the negative terminal is earthed, an alternator which is driven from the crankshaft pulley, and a starter motor.

The battery supplies a steady amount of current for the ignition, lighting and other electrical circuits and provides a reserve of electricity when the current consumed by the electrical equipment exceeds that being produced by the alternator.

The alternator has its own integral regulator which ensures a high output if the battery is in a low state of charge or the demand from the electrical equipment is high, and a low output if the battery is fully charged and there is little demand for the electrical equipment.

When fitting electrical accessories to cars with a negative earth system it is important, if they contain silicone diodes or transistors, that they are connected correctly, otherwise serious damage may result to the components concerned. Items such as radios, tape recorders, electronic ignition systems, electronic tachometer, automatic dipping etc, should all be checked for correct polarity.

It is important that the battery positive lead is always disconnected if the battery is to be boost charged, also if the body repairs are to be carried out using electric welding equipment - the alternator must be disconnected otherwise serious damage can be caused to the more delicate instruments. Whenever the battery has to be disconnected it must always be reconnected with the negative terminal earthed.

2 Battery - removal and replacement

1 The battery is on a carrier fitted to the left hand wing valance of the engine compartment. It should be removed once every three months for cleaning and testing. Disconnect the positive and then the negative leads from the battery terminals by undoing and removing the plated nuts and bolts (photo). Note that two cables are attached to the positive terminal.

2 Unscrew and remove the bolt, and plain washer that secures the battery clamp plate to the carrier. Lift away the clamp plate. Carefully lift the battery from its carrier and hold it vertically to ensure that none of the electrolyte is spilled.

3 Replacement is a direct reversal of this procedure. NOTE: Replace the negative lead before the positive lead and smear the terminals with vaseline to prevent corrosion. NEVER use an ordinary grease.

3 Battery - maintenance and inspection

1 Normal weekly battery maintenance consists of checking the electrolyte level of each cell to ensure that the separators are covered by ¼ inch (6 mm) of electrolyte. If the level has fallen, top up the battery using distilled water only. Do not overfill. If a battery is overfilled or any electrolyte spilled, immediately wipe away the excess as electrolyte attacks and corrodes any metal it comes into contact with very rapidly.

2 If the battery has the Auto-fil device fitted, a special topping up sequence is required. The white balls in the Auto-fil battery are part of the automatic topping up device which ensures correct electrolyte level. The vent chamber should remain in position at all times except when topping up or taking specific gravity readings. If the electrolyte level in any of the cells is below the bottom of the filling tube top up as follows:

a) Lift off the vent chamber cover.

b) With the battery level, pour distilled water into the trough until all the filling tubes and trough are full.

c) Immediately replace the cover to allow the water in the trough and tubes to flow into the cells. Each cell will automatically receive the correct amount of water.

3 As well as keeping the terminals clean and covered with petroleum jelly, the top of the battery, and especially the top of the cells, should be kept clean and dry. This helps prevent corrosion and ensures that the battery does not become partially discharged by leakage through dampness and dirt.

4 Once every three months remove the battery and inspect the battery securing bolts, the battery clamp plate, tray and battery leads for corrosion (white fluffy deposits on the metal which are brittle to touch). If any corrosion is found clean off the deposit with ammonia and paint over the clean metal with an anti-rust anti-acid paint.

5 At the same time inspect the battery case for cracks. If a crack is found, clean and plug it with one of the proprietary compounds marketed by such firms as Holts for this purpose. If leakage through the crack has been excessive then it will be necessary to refill the appropriate cell with fresh electrolyte as detailed later. Cracks are frequently caused to the top of the battery cases by pouring in distilled water in the middle of winter AFTER instead of BEFORE a run. This gives the water no chance to mix with the electrolyte and so the former freezes and splits the battery case.

6 If topping up the battery becomes excessive and the case has been inspected for cracks that could cause leakage, but none are found, the battery is being overcharged and the voltage regulator will have to be checked and reset.

7 With the battery on the bench at the three monthly interval check, measure the specific gravity with a hydrometer to determine the state of charge and condition of the electrolyte. There should be very little variation between the different cells and, if a variation in excess of 0.025 is present it will be due to either:

a) Loss of electrolyte from the battery at some time caused by spillage or a leak, resulting in a drop in the specific gravity of the electrolyte when the deficiency was replaced with distilled water instead of fresh electrolyte.

b) An internal short circuit caused by buckling of the plates or similar malady pointing to the likelihood of total battery failure in the near future.

8 The specific gravity of the electrolyte for fully charged conditions, at the electrolyte temperature indicated, is listed in Table A. The specific gravity of a fully discharged battery at different temperatures of the electrolyte is given in Table B.

TABLE A — Specific gravity - battery fully charged

1.268 at 100°F or 38°C electrolyte temperature
1.272 at 90°F or 32°C electrolyte temperature
1.276 at 80°F or 27°C electrolyte temperature
1.280 at 70°F or 21°C electrolyte temperature
1.284 at 60°F or 16°C electrolyte temperature
1.288 at 50°F or 10°C electrolyte temperature
1.292 at 40°F or 4°C electrolyte temperature
1.296 at 30°F or -1.5°C electrolyte temperature

TABLE B — Specific gravity - battery fully discharged

1.098 at 100°F or 38°C electrolyte temperature
1.102 at 90°F or 32°C electrolyte temperature
1.106 at 80°F or 27°C electrolyte temperature
1.110 at 70°F or 21°C electrolyte temperature
1.114 at 60°F or 16°C electrolyte temperature
1.118 at 50°F or 10°C electrolyte temperature
1.122 at 40°F or 4°C electrolyte temperature
1.126 at 30°F or -1.5°C electrolyte temperature

4 Battery - electrolyte replenishment

1 If the battery is in a fully charged state and one of the cells maintains a specific gravity reading which is 0.025 or more lower than the others and a check of each cell has been made with a voltage meter to check for short circuits (a four to seven second test should give a steady reading of between 1.2 and 1.8 volts), then it is likely that electrolyte has been lost from the cell with the low reading at some time.

2 Top the cell up with a solution of 1 part sulphuric acid to 2.5 parts of water. If the cell is already fully topped up draw some electrolyte out of it with a pipette. The total capacity of each cell is ¾ pint (0.426 litre, 0.901 US pint).

3 When mixing the sulphuric acid and water NEVER ADD WATER TO SULPHURIC ACID — always pour the acid slowly onto the water in a glass container. IF WATER IS ADDED TO SULPHURIC ACID IT WILL EXPLODE.

4 Continue to top up the cell with the freshly made electrolyte and then recharge the battery and check the hydrometer readings.

5 Battery charging

1 In winter time when heavy demand is placed upon the battery, such as when starting from cold and much electrical equipment is continually in use, it is a good idea to occasionally have the battery fully charged from an external source at the rate of 3.5 to 4 amps.

2 Continue to charge the battery at this rate until no further rise in specific gravity is noted over a four hour period.

3 Alternatively, a trickle charger charging at the rate of 1.5 amps can be safely used over night.

4 Specially rapid 'boost' charges which are claimed to restore the power of the battery in 1 to 2 hours are most dangerous as they can cause serious damage to the battery plates through overheating.

5 While charging the battery note that the temperature of the electrolyte should never exceed 100°F (37.8°C).

6 Alternator - general description

The main advantage of an alternator over a dynamo lies in its ability to provide a high charge at low revolutions. Driving slowly in heavy traffic with a dynamo invariably means no charge is reaching the battery. In similar conditions even with the wiper, heater, lights and perhaps radio switched on the alternator will ensure a charge reaches the battery.

The alternator is of rotating field, ventilated design. It comprises, principally, a laminated stator on which is wound a star connected 3-phase output winding; a twelve pole rotor carrying the field windings - each end of the rotor shaft runs in ball race bearings which are lubricated for life; natural finish aluminium die cast end brackets, incorporating the mounting lugs; a rectifier pack for converting the AC output of the machine to DC for battery charging; and an output control regulator.

The rotor is belt driven from the engine through a pulley keyed to the rotor shaft. A pressed steel fan adjacent to the pulley draws cooling air through the machine. This fan forms an integral part of the alternator specification. It has been designed to provide adequate air flow with a minimum of noise, and to withstand the high stresses associated with the maximum speed. Rotation is clockwise viewed on the drive end. Maximum continuous rotor speed is 12,500 rpm.

Rectification of an alternator output is achieved by six silicone diodes housed in a rectifier pack and connected as a 3-phase full wave bridge. The rectifier pack is attached to the outer face of the slip ring end bracket and contains also three 'field' diodes; at normal operating speeds, rectified current from the stator output windings flows through these diodes to provide the self excitation of the rotor field, via brushes bearing on face type slip rings.

The slip rings are carried on a small diameter moulded drum attached to the rotor shaft outboard of the slip ring end bearing. The inner ring is centred on the rotor shaft axle, while the outer ring has a mean diameter of ¾ inch approximately. By keeping the mean diameter of the slip rings to a minimum, relative speeds between brushes and rings, and hence wear, are also minimal. The slip rings are connected to the rotor field winding by wires carried in grooves in the rotor shaft.

The brush gear is housed in a moulding screwed to the outside of the slip ring and bracket. This moulding thus encloses the slip ring and brush gear assembly, and together with the shielded bearing, protects the assembly against the entry of dust and moisture.

The regulator is set during manufacture and is located on the right hand inner wing panel. It requires no further attention but should its operation be suspect it must be renewed as a complete unit.

7 Alternator - routine maintenance

1 The equipment has been designed for the minimum amount of maintenance in service, the only items subject to wear being the brushes and bearings.

2 Brushes should be examined after about 75,000 miles (120,000 Km) and renewed if necessary. The bearings are pre-packed with grease for life, and should not require further attention.

3 Check the fan belt every 6,000 miles (10,000 Km) for correct adjustment which should be 0.5 in (13 mm) total movement at the centre of the run between the alternator and water pump pulleys.

8 Alternator - special procedures

Whenever the electrical system of the car is being attended to, or external means of starting the engine are used, there are certain precautions that must be taken otherwise serious and expensive damage can result.

1 Always make sure that the negative terminal of the battery is earthed. If the terminal connections are accidentally reversed or if the battery has been reverse charged the alternator diodes will burn out.

2 The output terminal on the alternator marked 'BAT' or B+ must never be earthed but should always be connected directly to the positive terminal of the battery.

3 Whenever the alternator is to be removed or when disconnecting the terminals of the alternator circuit always disconnect the battery earth terminal first.

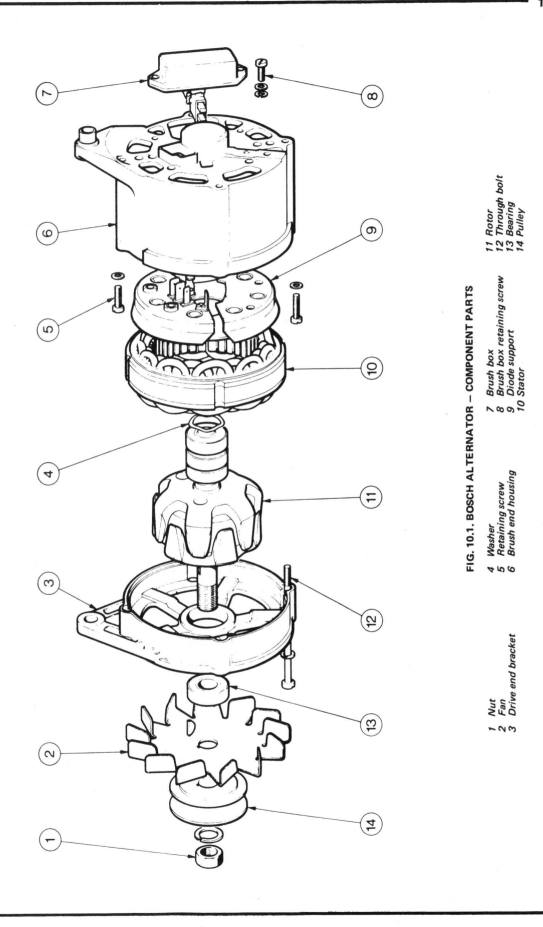

FIG. 10.1. BOSCH ALTERNATOR — COMPONENT PARTS

1 Nut
2 Fan
3 Drive end bracket

4 Washer
5 Retaining screw
6 Brush end housing

7 Brush box
8 Brush box retaining screw
9 Diode support
10 Stator

11 Rotor
12 Through bolt
13 Bearing
14 Pulley

4 The alternator must never be operated without the battery to alternator cable connected.

5 If the battery is to be charged by external means always disconnect both battery cables before the external charge is connected.

6 Should it be necessary to use a booster charger or booster battery to start the engine always double check that the negative cable is connected to negative terminal and the positive cable to positive terminal.

9 Alternator - removal and refitting

1 Disconnect the battery leads.

2 Note the terminal connections at the rear of the alternator and disconnect the plug or multi pin connector.

3 Remove the carburettor air cleaner and exhaust heat duct to gain better access to the alternator.

4 Undo and remove the alternator adjustment arm bolt, slacken the alternator mounting bolts and push the alternator inwards towards the engine. Lift away the fan belt from the pulley.

5 Remove the remaining two mounting bolts and carefully lift the alternator away from the car.

6 Take care not to knock or drop the alternator otherwise this can cause irreparable damage.

7 Refitting the alternator is the reverse sequence to removal. Adjust the fan belt so that it has 0.5 in (13 mm) total movement at the centre of the run between the alternator and water pump pulleys.

10 Alternator - fault finding and repair

Due to the specialist knowledge and equipment required to test or service an alternator it is recommended that if the performance is suspect, the car be taken to an automobile electrician who will have the facilities for such work. Because of this recommendation, information is limited to the inspection and renewal of the brushes. Should the alternator not charge or the system be suspect the following points may be checked before seeking further assistance.

1 Check the fan belt tension as described in Section 7.

2 Check the battery as described in Section 3.

3 Check all electrical cable connections for cleanliness and security.

11 Alternator brushes - inspection, removal and refitting

1 Undo and remove the two screws, spring and plain washers that secure the brush box to the rear of the brush end housing (see Fig.10.3). Lift away the brush box.

2 Check that the carbon brushes are able to slide smoothly in their guides without any sign of binding.

3 Measure the length of the brushes and if they have worn down to 0.02 in (0.5 mm) or less, they must be renewed.

4 Hold the brush wire with a pair of engineer's pliers and unsolder it from the brush box. Lift away the two brushes.

5 Insert the new brushes and check to make sure that they are free to move in their guides. If they bind lightly polish with a very fine file.

6 Solder the brush wire ends to the brush box taking care that solder is allowed to pass to the stranded wire.

7 Whenever new brushes are fitted new springs should be fitted.

8 Refitting the brush box is the reverse sequence to removal.

12 Starter motor - general description

The starter motor is of the pre-engaged type and is of either Lucas or Bosch Manufacture. The motor assembly comprises a solenoid, a lever, starter drive gear and motor. It can be seen that the solenoid is fitted to the front of the motor. The plunger inside the solenoid is connected to a centre pivoting lever, the other end of which is in contact with the drive sleeve and drive gear.

When the starter motor switch is operated, the solenoid is energised causing the plunger to move into the solenoid and the pinion to move into mesh with the starter ring gear on the flywheel (manual gearbox) or drive plate ring gear (automatic transmission). Upon the pinion being in full mesh with the ring gear, heavy duty contacts in the rear of the solenoid are closed and current is supplied to the motor.

Once the engine has started, the starter switch is released and, under spring action, the plunger is moved from the centre of the solenoid and, by means of the pivoting lever, the pinion is moved out of mesh with the ring gear.

13 Starter motor - testing on engine

1 If the starter motor fails to operate then check the condition of the battery by turning on the headlamps. If they glow brightly for several seconds and then gradually dim, the battery is in an uncharged condition.

2 If the headlamps continue to glow brightly and it is obvious that the battery is in good condition, check that tightness of the earth lead from the battery terminal to its connection on the body frame particularly, and other battery wiring. Check the tightness of the connections at the rear of the solenoid. Check the wiring with a voltmeter for breaks or short circuits.

3 If the battery is fully charged, the wiring in order and the motor electrical circuit checked for continuity, and it still fails to operate then it will have to be removed from the car for examination. Before this is done, however, ensure that the pinion gear has not jammed in mesh with the flywheel due either to a broken solenoid spring or dirty pinion gear splines. To release the pinion, engage a low gear and with the ignition switched off, rock the car backwards and forwards which should release the pinion from mesh with the ring gear. If the pinion still remains jammed, the starter motor must be removed for further examination.

14 Starter motor - removal and replacement

1 Chock the rear wheels, apply the handbrake, and jack up the front of the car. Support on firmly based axle stands.

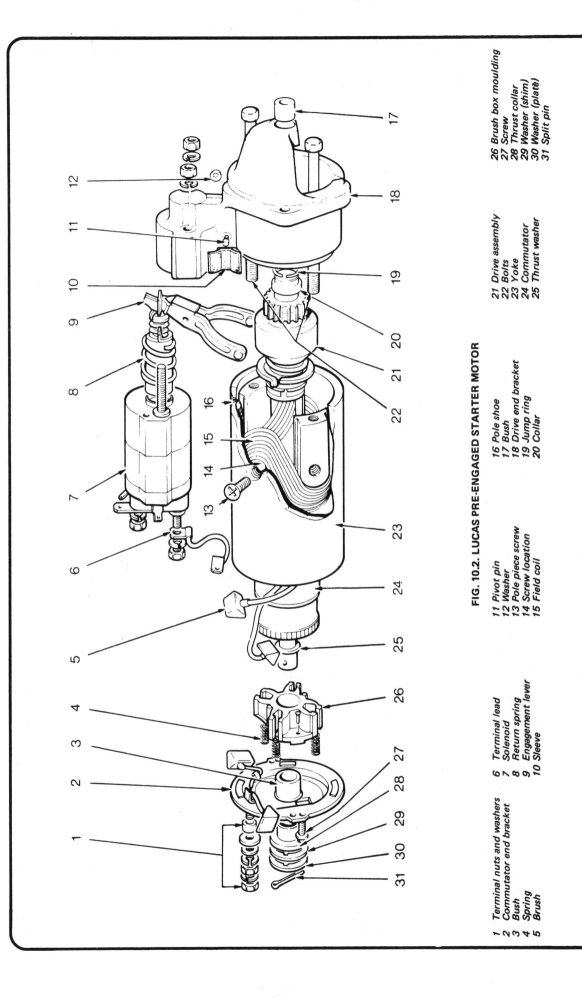

FIG. 10.2. LUCAS PRE-ENGAGED STARTER MOTOR

1 Terminal nuts and washers
2 Commutator end bracket
3 Bush
4 Spring
5 Brush

6 Terminal lead
7 Solenoid
8 Return spring
9 Engagement lever
10 Sleeve

11 Pivot pin
12 Washer
13 Pole piece screw
14 Screw location
15 Field coil

16 Pole shoe
17 Bush
18 Drive end bracket
19 Jump ring
20 Collar

21 Drive assembly
22 Bolts
23 Yoke
24 Commutator
25 Thrust washer

26 Brush box moulding
27 Screw
28 Thrust collar
29 Washer (shim)
30 Washer (plate)
31 Split pin

2   Disconnect the two battery terminals.

3   Make a note of the electrical connections at the rear of the solenoid and disconnect the top heavy duty cable. Also release the two Lucar terminals situated below the heavy duty cable. There is no need to undo the lower heavy duty cable at the rear of the solenoid.

4   Undo and remove the two bolts which hold the starter motor in place and lift away upwards through the engine compartment.

5   Generally, replacement is a straightforward reversal of the removal sequence. Check that the electrical cable connections are clean and firmly attached to their respective terminals.

15 Starter motor (Lucas) - dismantling, overhaul and reassembly

1   Detach the heavy duty cable linking the solenoid STA terminal to the starter motor terminal, by undoing and removing the securing nuts and washers (Fig. 10.2).

2   Undo and remove the two nuts and spring washers securing the solenoid to the drive end bracket.

3   Carefully withdraw the solenoid coil unit from the drive end bracket.

4   Lift off the solenoid plunger and return spring from the engagement lever.

5   Remove the rubber sealing block from the drive end bracket.

6   Remove the retaining ring (spire nut) from the engagement lever pivot pin and withdraw the pin.

7   Unscrew and remove the two drive end bracket securing nuts and spring washers and withdraw the bracket.

8   Lift away the engagement lever from the drive operating plate.

9   Extract the split pin from the end of the armature and remove the shim washers and thrust plate from the commutator end of the armature shaft.

10 Remove the armature together with its internal thrust washer.

11 Withdraw the thrust washer from the armature.

12 Undo and remove the two screws securing the commutator end bracket to the starter motor body yoke.

13 Carefully detach the end bracket from the yoke, at the same time disengaging the field brushes from the brush gear. Lift away the end bracket.

14 Move the thrust collar clear of the jump ring and then remove the jump ring. Withdraw the drive assembly from the armature shaft.

15 At this stage if the brushes are renewed, their flexible connectors must be unsoldered and the connectors of new brushes soldered in their place. Check that the new brushes move freely in their holders as detailed above. If cleaning the commutator with petrol fails to remove all the burnt areas and spots, then wrap a piece of glass paper round the commutator and rotate the armature.

16 If the commutator is very badly worn, remove the drive gear as detailed in the following Section. Then mount the armature in a lathe and, with the lathe turning at high speed, take a very fine cut out of the commutator and finish the surface by polishing with glass paper. DO NOT UNDERCUT THE MICA INSULATORS BETWEEN THE COMMUTATOR SEGMENTS.

17 With the starter motor dismantled, test the four field coils for an open circuit. Connect a 12 volt battery with a 12 volt bulb in one of the leads between the field terminal post and the tapping point of the field coils to which the brushes are connected. An open circuit is proved by the bulb not lighting.

18 If the bulb lights, it does not necessarily mean that the field coils are in order, as there is a possibility that one of the coils will be earthed to the starter yoke or pole shoes. To check this, remove the lead from the brush connector and place it against a clean portion of the starter yoke. If the bulb lights, the field coils are earthing. Replacement of the field coils calls for the use

of a wheel operated screwdriver, a soldering iron, caulking and riveting operations, and is beyond the scope of the majority of owners. The starter yoke should be taken to a reputable electrical engineering works for new field coils to be fitted. Alternatively, purchase an exchange Lucas starter motor.

19 If the armature is damaged this will be evident after visual inspection. Look for signs of burning, discolouration, and for conductors that have lifted away from the conductor. Reassembly is a straightforward reversal of the dismantling procedure.

20 If a bearing is worn so allowing excessive side play of the armature shaft, the bearing bush must be renewed. Drift out the old bush with a piece of suitable diameter rod, preferably with a shoulder on it to stop the bush collapsing.

21 Soak a new bush in engine oil for 24 hours or, if time does not permit, heat in an oil bath at 100°C for two hours prior to fitting.

22 As new bushes must not be reamed after fitting, it must be pressed into position using a small mandrel of the same internal diameter as the bush and with a shoulder on it. Place the bush on the mandrel and press into position using a bench vice.

23 Use a test light and battery to test the continuity of the coil windings between terminal STA and a good earth point on the solenoid body. If the light fails to come on, the solenoid should be renewed.

24 To test the solenoid contacts for correct opening and closing, connect a 12 volt battery and a 60 watt test light between the main unmarked Lucar terminal and the STA terminal. The light should not come on.

25 Energise the solenoid with a separate 12 volt supply connected to the small unmarked Lucar terminal and a good earth on the solenoid body.

26 As the coil is energised the solenoid should be heard to operate and the test lamp should light with full brilliance.

27 The contacts may only be renewed as a set, i.e moving and fixed contacts. The fixed contacts are part of the moulded cover.

28 To fit a new set of contacts, first undo and remove the moulded cover securing screws.

29 Unsolder the coil connections from the cover terminals.

30 Lift away the cover and moving contact assembly.

31 Fit a new cover and moving contact assembly, soldering the connections to the cover terminals.

32 Refit the moulded cover securing screws.

33 Whilst the motor is apart, check the operation of the drive clutch. It must provide instantaneous take up of the drive in one direction and rotate easily and smoothly in the opposite direction.

34 Make sure that the drive moves freely on the armature shaft splines without binding or sticking.

35 To reassemble the starter motor is the reverse sequence to dismantling. The following additional points should be noted:

36 When assembling the drive always use a new retaining ring (spire nut) to secure the engagement lever pivot pin.

37 Make sure that the internal thrust washer is fitted to the commutator end of the armature shaft before the armature is fitted.

38 Make sure that the thrust washers and plate are assembled in the correct order and are prevented from rotating separately, by engaging the collar pin with the locking piece on the thrust plate.

16 Starter motor (Bosch) - dismantling, overhaul and reassembly

The principle of operation is basically identical to that for the Lucas starter motor as described in Section 12. For servicing this starter refer to Fig. 10.3 to Fig. 10.7 also information given in Section 15.

17 Headlight bulb - removal and refitting

1 Undo and remove the two headlight bezel securing nuts located behind the front wing panel.
2 Undo and remove the two upper headlight bezel securing screws and lift away the bezel.
3 Draw the relevant light unit forwards and detach the multi pin connector from the rear of the bulb.
4 Release the spring clip holding the retaining ring and lift away the retaining ring. Detach the bulb.
5 Refitting is the reverse sequence. It is recommended that whenever a bulb is renewed the headlight alignment be checked. Further information will be found in Section 18.

18 Headlight alignment

Because twin headlight units are used it is only possible to obtain an accurate setting using specialist equipment. This is therefore, a job for the local garage. The car should be loaded (or unloaded) as it would be used during the hours of darkness whilst the adjustments are being made.

19 Headlight dip switch - removal and replacement

1 The switch is part of the combination switch mounted on the steering column controlling the direction indicator switch and horn button.
2 Disconnect the battery for safety reasons.
3 Undo and remove the bolts that secure the steering column to the underside of the instrument panel. Lower the steering column.
4 Undo and remove the two screws that secure the steering column half shrouds and lift away the two parts. It may be necessary to use a knife to separate the two halves before removal.
5 Undo and remove the two screws and shakeproof washers located on the lever side of the switch and detach the switch assembly from the steering column.
6 Disconnect the multi-pin plug from the switch cable harness and lift away the switch.
7 Refitting the switch is the reverse sequence to removal. Before the shroud is refitted check that the switch and self cancel system operates correctly. For this the battery will have to be reconnected.

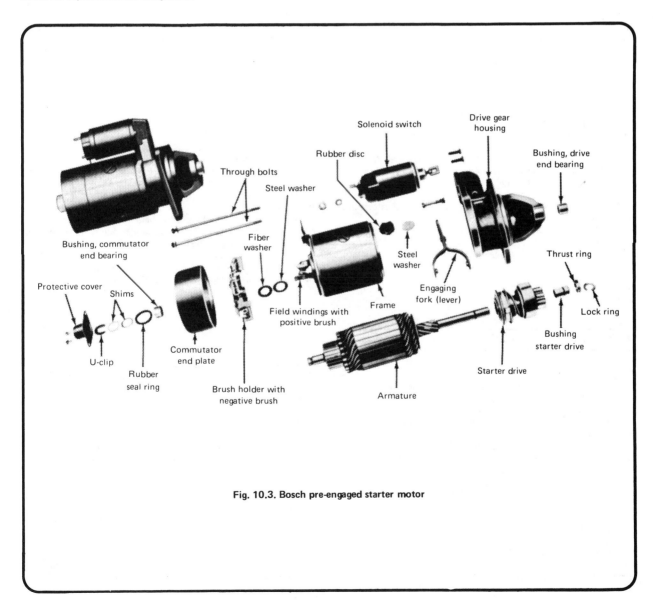

Fig. 10.3. Bosch pre-engaged starter motor

20 Headlight switch - removal and replacement

1 For safety reasons disconnect the battery.
2 Working behind the instrument panel detach the multi pin connector from the rear of the headlight switch.
3 Depress the two switch retaining clips and push the switch out of the panel.
4 To refit the switch push into the panel until the clips spring out thereby retaining it. Reconnect the multi pin connector and finally the battery.

21 Front and rear lights - removal and replacement

Front parking and direction indicator lights
1 Undo and remove the five screws that secure the radiator opening panel.
2 Detach the bulb socket and then undo and remove the two nuts securing the light body. Lift away the light unit.
3 If it is only necessary to renew a bulb or lens undo and remove the two Phillips head screws securing the lens. Lift away the lens. The relevant bulb may now be removed.
4 Refitting or reassembly is the reverse sequence to removal.

Rear, stop and direction indicator lights
1 Working inside the luggage compartment undo and remove the two nuts and bracket that secure the light unit to the body. Lift away the light unit.
2 To fit a new bulb detach the battery earth terminal. Working inside the luggage compartment undo and remove the nuts and one bolt securing the rear light trim cover. Lift away the trim cover.
3 Pull out the spring loaded rear or direction indicator bulb holders and remove the relevant bulb.
4 Refitting or reassembly is the reverse sequence to removal.

22 Marker and number plate lights - removal and replacement

Front
1 Working behind the wing panel undo and remove the two securing nuts. Lift away the clamps and plain washers.
2 The unit may now be drawn away from the wing.
3 Slide back the rubber sleeve on the rear of the light bezel and detach the bulb holder.
4 If it is only necessary to renew the bulb, pull back the rubber sleeve from the bulb holder. Turn the bulb holder anti clockwise slightly and pull from the light body. The bulb may be pulled from the holder.
5 Refitting or reassembly is the reverse sequence to removal.

Rear
1 Working inside the luggage compartment undo and remove the two nuts securing the protective bracket.
2 Lift away the bracket and then the bulb socket. Remove the light body assembly.
3 If it is only necessary to renew the bulb, carry out the

sequence in paragraph 1, then holding the light body turn the bulb holder anti clockwise slightly and pull from the light body. The bulb may be pulled from the holder.
4 Refitting or reassembly is the reverse sequence to removal.

Number plate light
1 For safety reasons disconnect the battery earth terminal.
2 Disconnect the earth and feed cables inside the luggage compartment and pull the cables through the hole in the floor.
3 Carefully press the retaining levers inwards working under the bumper and lift away the assembly. The bulb may now be removed.
4 Refitting the light is the reverse sequence to removal.

23 Reverse light - removal and replacement

1 To remove the light body first detach the lead from the unit and then undo and remove the nut securing the light body to the bracket.
2 Lift away the light body.
3 If it is only necessary to renew the lens or bulb undo and remove the two screws that secure the lens to the body and lift away the lens. The bulb may now be removed.
4 Refitting or reassembly is the reverse sequence to removal.

24 Reverse light switch - adjustment

This section is only applicable to models fitted with manual transmission.
The angular switch bracket is held to the gear change lever housing by one screw. If it is necessary to adjust the position of the switch first slacken the screw and move the gear change lever into the reverse position.
Carefully move the switch towards the gear change lever until the lights come on. Tighten the retaining screw.

25 Hazard flasher switch and unit - removal and replacement switch

Switch
1 For safety reasons disconnect the battery earth terminal.
2 Refer to Section 27 or 28 as applicable and draw the instrument cluster rearwards so as to gain access to the back.
3 Disconnect the terminal connector from the rear of the switch.
4 Carefully depress the two switch retaining clips and push the switch out of the panel.
5 Refitting the switch is the reverse sequence to removal.

Flasher unit
1 For safety reasons disconnect the battery earth terminal.
2 Refer to Section 27 or 28 as applicable and draw the instrument cluster rearwards so as to gain access to the flasher unit.

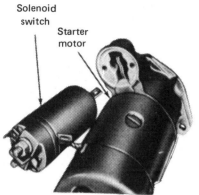

Solenoid switch

Starter motor

Fig. 10.4. Solenoid switch removal (Bosch)

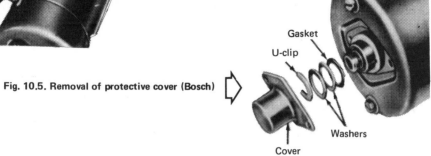

Fig. 10.5. Removal of protective cover (Bosch)

Gasket

U-clip

Washers

Cover

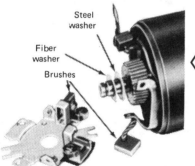

Steel washer

Fiber washer

Brushes

Fig. 10.6. Brush removal (Bosch)

Engaging lever

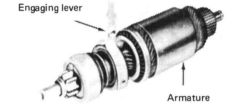

Armature

Fig. 10.7. Armature with engaging lever correctly located (Bosch)

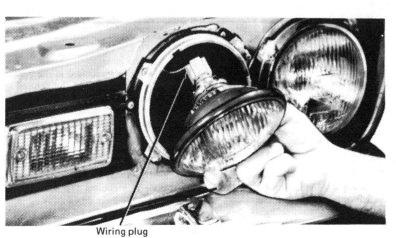

Fig. 10.8. Headlamps – light unit removal

Wiring plug

3 Undo and remove the unit securing screw and washer.
4 Detach the terminals from the flasher unit and lift away the unit.
5 Refitting the flasher unit is the reverse sequence to removal.

---

26 Courtesy light and map light - removal and replacement

Courtesy light bulb or switch

To gain access to the bulb or switch carefully ease the lens from the light body. Remove the bulb or switch as applicable. If the switch is to be removed it is recommended that the battery earth cable be detached as a safety precaution.

Courtesy light door pillar switch

1 Disconnect the battery earth terminal.
2 Using a screwdriver carefully ease the switch from the aperture in the body (Fig. 10.12).
3 Detach the terminal from the back of the switch and lift away the switch.
4 Refitting is the reverse sequence to removal.

Map light bulb

To renew the bulb carefully push the housing back and remove the bulb. Fit the new bulb and housing.

Map light switch

1 Disconnect the battery earth terminal.
2 Undo and remove the two screws that secure the switch to the panel.
3 Draw the switch from the panel and detach the two leads.
4 Refitting is the reverse sequence to removal.

---

27 Instrument cluster (standard) - removal and replacement

1 Disconnect the battery earth terminal.
2 Undo and remove the two bolts that secure the steering column to the underside of the dash panel. Carefully lower the column.
3 Undo and remove the five Phillips head screws that secure the cluster and pad assembly to the instrument panel.
4 Carefully draw the cluster and pad assembly forwards by a sufficient amount to gain access to the connections at the rear of the panel.
5 Make a note of the cable connections at the rear of the gauges and switches and then detach the cables.
6 Disconnect the speedometer cable from the rear of the instrument.
7 The cluster and pad assembly may now be removed from the car.
8 Undo and remove the four screws that secure the cluster to the pad and lift away the cluster assembly.
9 Refitting the cluster and pad is the reverse sequence to removal.

---

28 Instrument cluster (GT) - removal and replacement

1 Disconnect the battery earth terminal.
2 Detach the two heater control knobs.

---

3 Undo and remove the four screws that secure the access cover at the right of the instrument panel. Lift away the cover.
4 Undo and remove the three screws and ONLY slacken the one nut securing the instrument cluster and pad assembly to instrument panel.
5 Undo and remove the two fuse panel securing screws and lower the fuse panel.
6 Carefully pull the cluster and pad assembly rearward by a sufficient amount to gain access to the connections at the rear of the panel.
7 Make a note of the cable connections at the rear of the gauges and switches and then detach the cables.
8 Disconnect the speedometer cable from the rear of the instrument.
9 Disconnect the oil pressure gauge tube at the rear of the gauge. It is very important that the tube is not bent or twisted.
10 The cluster and pad assembly may now be removed from the car.
11 Undo and remove the four screws that secure the cluster to the pad and lift away the cluster assembly.
12 Refitting the cluster and pad is the reverse sequence to removal.

---

29 Speedometer or tachometer - removal and replacement

1 Refer to Section 27 or 28 as applicable and remove the instrument cluster.
2 On GT models remove the odometer reset knob.
3 Undo and remove the six screws that secure the mask and lens to the cluster housing. Lift away the cluster housing.
4 Undo and remove the two screws that secure the speedometer or tachometer and lift away the instrument.
5 Refitting the speedometer or tachometer is the reverse sequence to removal.

---

30 Speedometer cable - removal and replacement

1 Chock the front wheels, jack up the rear of the car and support on firmly based stands.
2 Working under the car carefully remove the snap ring that secures the speedometer cable to the transmission. Detach the cable.
3 Now working in the engine compartment remove the speedometer cable clip located on the engine bulkhead.
4 Ease the speedometer cable rubber grommet from the engine bulkhead.
5 Refer to Section 27 or 28 as applicable and move the instrument cluster rearwards by a sufficient amount to gain access to the rear of the speedometer.
6 Detach the cable from the rear of the speedometer.
7 Refitting is the reverse sequence to removal. For reliable operation it is very important that there are no sharp bends in the cable run.

---

31 Clock - removal and replacement

1 Disconnect the battery earth terminal.
2 With a small screwdriver or knife carefully prise the wood grain panel and clock assembly away from the console.

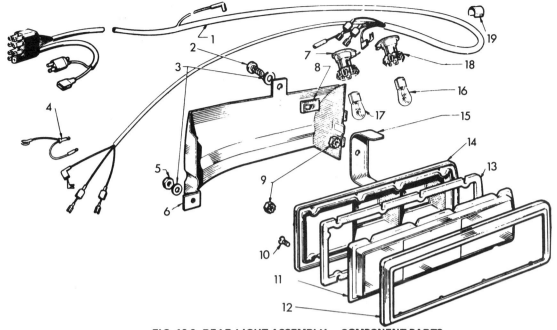

FIG. 10.9. REAR LIGHT ASSEMBLY — COMPONENT PARTS

1	Wiring	6	Trim cover	11	Lens
2	Screw	7	Bulb holder	12	Bezel
3	Washer	8	Screw clip	13	Gasket
4	Connector	9	Nuts and washers	14	Frame
5	Nut	10	Screw	15	Bracket

16	Bulb
17	Bulb
18	Bulb holder
19	Clip

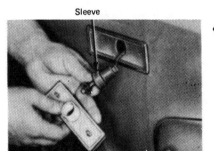

Sleeve

Fig. 10.10. Front marker light removal

Fig. 10.11. Number plate light removal

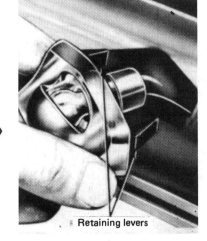

Retaining levers

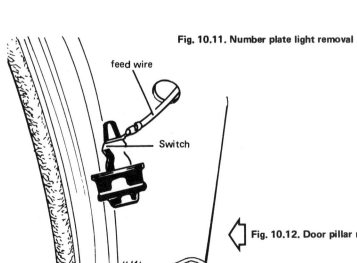

feed wire

Switch

H.141

Fig. 10.12. Door pillar mounted courtesy light switch removal

3 Detach the electric cables and bulb socket from the rear of the instrument.
4 To release the clock from the panel depress the three retaining clips and withdraw the clock.
5 Should adjustment be necessary, rotate the adjustment screw in the required direction.
6 Refitting the clock is the reverse sequence to removal.

32 Fuel, temperature, oil pressure and battery indicator gauge - removal and replacement

1 Refer to Section 27 or 28 as applicable and remove the instrument cluster.
2 On GT models remove the odometer reset knob.
3 Undo and remove the six screws that secure the mask and lens to the cluster housing. Lift away the cluster housing.
4 Undo and remove the securing nuts or screws applicable to the instrument being removed. Lift the instrument from the rear of the cluster.
5 Refitting an instrument is the reverse sequence to removal.

33 Instrument illumination and warning light bulb - removal and replacement

1 Refer to Section 27 or 28 as applicable and remove the instrument cluster.
2 Release the bulb holder from its socket and remove the bulb from the holder.
3 Refitting the bulb, holder and cluster is the reverse sequence to removal.

34 Instrument voltage regulator - removal and replacement

1 Refer to Section 27 or 28 as applicable and remove the instrument cluster.
2 Undo the one screw that secures the instrument voltage regulator to the rear of the cluster and withdraw the regulator.
3 Refitting is the reverse sequence to removal.

35 Switches - removal and replacement

1 For information on removal of the headlight switch refer to Section 20.
2 Refer to Section 27 to 28 as applicable and draw the instrument cluster rearwards sufficiently to gain access to the rear.
3 Detach the connector from the rear of the headlight switch.
4 Depress the two switch retaining clips and push the switch out of the panel.
5 Refitting the switch is the reverse sequence to removal.

36 Ignition switch - removal and replacement

1 Disconnect the battery earth terminal.
2 Undo and remove the two steering column shroud securing screws and lift away the two parts. It may be necessary to use a knife to separate the two halves before removal.
3 Set the ignition key to the 'O' position.
4 Note the location of the cables at the ignition switch and then detach the cables.
5 Undo and remove the two screws that secure the ignition switch to the lock. Lift away the switch.
6 Refitting the ignition switch is the reverse sequence to removal.

37 Steering lock - removal and replacement

1 Disconnect the battery earth terminal.
2 Undo and remove the two steering column shroud securing screws and lift away the two parts. It may be necessary to use a knife to separate the two halves before removal.
3 Undo and remove the two screws that secure the upper steering column support bracket.
4 Turn the column until it is possible to gain access to the headless bolts.
5 Note the location of the cables to the ignition switch and lock body and then detach the cables.
6 Using a suitable diameter drill remove the headless bolts that clamp the lock to the steering column. Alternatively use a centre punch to rotate the bolts.
7 Lift away the lock assembly and clamp bracket.
8 Refitting the lock assembly is the reverse sequence to removal. Make sure that the pawl enters the steering shaft. It will be necessary to use new shear bolts which must be tightened equally before the heads are separated by the shank.

38 Fuses - general

If a fuse blows always trace the cause and rectify before renewing the fuse of the instrument cluster having disconnected the battery.
The fuse panel is located below the instrument cluster and contains seven fuses which protect the circuits.
To remove the fuse panel and mounting pad assembly proceed as follows:
1 Undo and remove the two screws that secure the upper end of the fuse panel and mounting pad assembly to the lower edge of the instrument cluster.
2 Slide the tabs at the lower end of the mounting pad from the slots in the parcel tray.
3 Detach the four harness connectors from the fuse panel.
4 Remove the plastic cover. Undo and remove the two panel mounting screws and finally separate the fuse panel from the mounting pad.
5 Refitting the fuse panel and mounting pad assembly is the reverse sequence to removal.

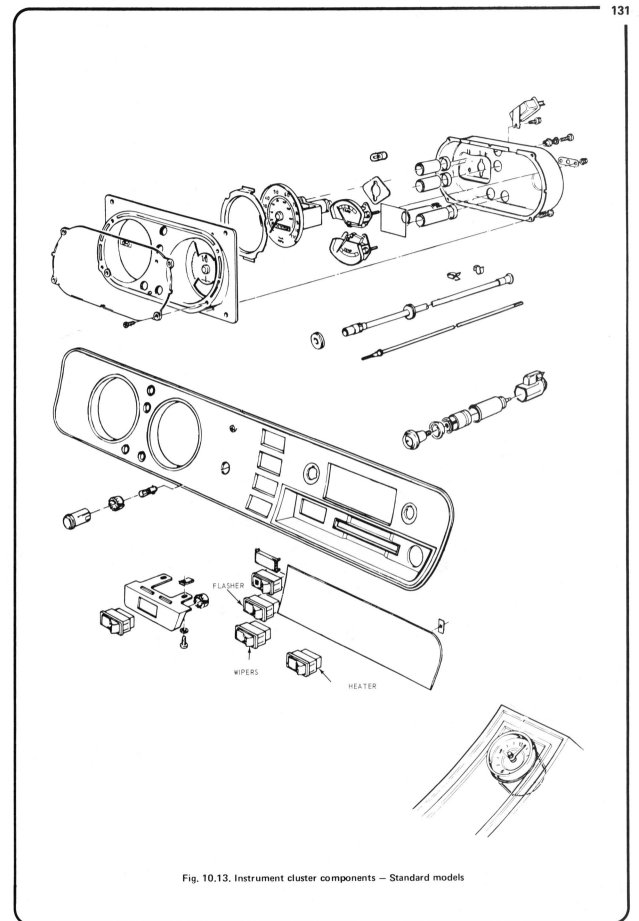

Fig. 10.13. Instrument cluster components — Standard models

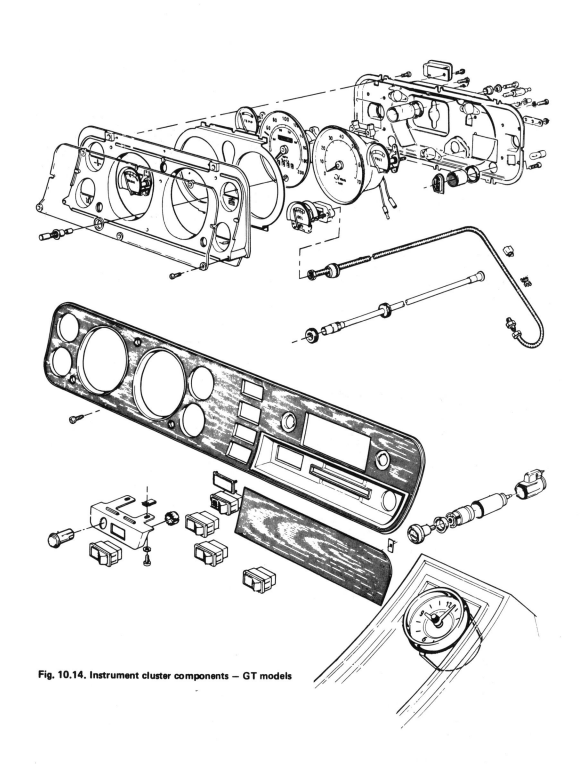

Fig. 10.14. Instrument cluster components — GT models

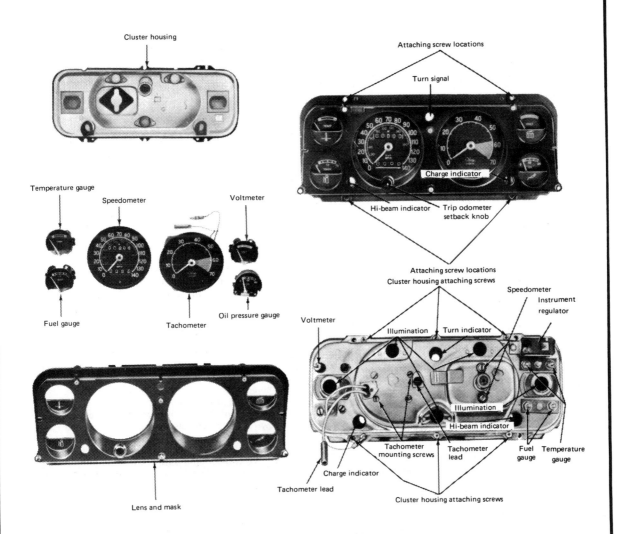

Fig. 10.15. GT cluster assembly

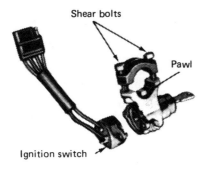

Fig. 10.16. Ignition switch and steering lock

39 Horn - fault tracing and rectification

1　If the horn works badly or fails completely, check the wiring leading to the horn plug which is located on the body panel next to the horn itself. Also check that the plug is properly pushed home and is in a clean condition free from corrosion etc.
2　Check that the horn is secure on its mounting and that there is nothing lying on the horn body.
3　If the fault is not an external one, remove the horn cover and check the leads inside the horn. If these are sound, check the contact breaker contacts. If these are burnt or dirty clean them with a fine file and wipe all traces of dirt and dust away with a petrol moistened rag.

40 Windscreen wiper blades - removal and replacement

1　Lift the wiper arm away from the windscreen and remove the old blade by turning it in towards the arm and then disengage the arm from the slot in the blade.
2　To fit a new blade, slide the end of the wiper arm into the slotted spring fastening in the centre of the blade. Push the blade firmly onto the arm until the raised portion of the arm is fully home in the hole in the blade.

41 Windscreen wiper arm - removal and replacement

1　Before removing a wiper arm, turn the windscreen wiper switch on and off to ensure the arms are in their normal parked position parallel with the bottom of the windscreen.
2　To remove an arm pivot the arm back and pull the wiper arm head off the splined drive. If the arm proves difficult to remove, a screwdriver with a large blade can be used to lever the wiper arm head off the splines. Care must be taken not to damage the splines.
3　When replacing an arm position it so it is in the correct relative parked position and then press the arm head onto the splined drive until it is fully home on the splines.

42 Windscreen wiper mechanism - fault diagnosis and rectification

1　Should the windscreen wipers fail, or work very slowly, then check the terminals on the motor for loose connections, and make sure the insulation of all the wiring is not cracked or broken thus causing a short circuit. If this is in order then check the current the motor is taking by connecting an ammeter in the circuit and turning on the wiper switch. Consumption should be between 2.3 to 3.1 amps.
2　If no current is passing through the motor, check that the switch is operating correctly.
3　If the wiper motor takes a very high current check the wiper blades for freedom of movement. If this is satisfactory check the gearbox cover and gear assembly for damage.

4　If the motor takes a very low current ensure that the battery is fully charged. Check the brush gear and ensure the brushes are bearing on the commutator. If not, check the brushes for freedom of movement and, if necessary, renew the tension springs. If the brushes are very worn they should be replaced with new ones. Check the armature by substitution if this unit is suspect.

43 Windscreen wiper motor and linkage - removal and replacement

1　Disconnect the battery by removing the negative earth lead and then remove the wiper blades and arms as described in Section 41.
2　Undo and remove the two nuts holding the wiper spindles to the bodywork in front of the windscreen.
3　Remove the parcel shelf as described in Chapter 12.
4　To gain better access to the wiper motor disconnect the flexible hoses from the heater to the demister vents above the dash and also the aeroflow flexible pipes.
5　Disconnect the two control cables on the heater at the heater end, making a careful note of their correct fitting in relation to the positions of the heater controls on the facia. Tuck the cables out of the way under the facia.
6　Remove the single screw holding the wiper motor to its mounting bracket and lower the motor and linkage just enough to be able to see the wires running to the motor.
7　Disconnect the wires at their connectors on the motor making a note of their relative positions for reassembly purposes.
8　Now lower the complete wiper motor and linkage assembly down in front of the heater and remove it from the car.
9　Reassembly is a direct reversal of the removal procedure, but the screw securing the wiper motor to its mounting bracket should not be fully tightened down until the wiper spindle nuts have been replaced thus ensuring correct alignment of the linkage.

44 Windscreen wiper motor - dismantling, inspection and reassembly

1　Start by removing the linkage mechanism from the motor. Carefully prise the short wiper link off the motor operating arm and remove the plastic pivot bush.
2　Undo the three screws which hold the linkage to the wiper motor and separate the two.
3　Unscrew the two bolts which hold the motor case to the gearbox housing and withdraw the motor case complete with the armature.
4　Take the brushes out of their holders and remove the brush springs.
5　Undo the three screws which hold the brush mounting plate to the wiper gearbox and withdraw the brush mounting plate.
6　Remove the earth wire on the gearbox cover plate by undoing the screw nearest the motor case. Undo the other screw on the gearbox cover plate and remove the cover plate and switch assembly.
7　Pull the spring steel armature stop out of the gearbox casing.

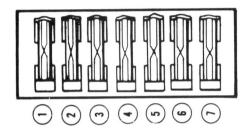

PLASTIC COVER - FUSE BOX

FIG. 10.17. LOCATION OF FUSE BOX AND FUSE IDENTIFICATION

1 (8 amp) Interior lights, cigar lighter, hazard flasher
2 (8 amp) Left side marker lights, left tail light, instrument panel illumination bulbs
3 (8 amp) Right side marker lights, right tail light, license plate light
4 (8 amp) Headlights - high beam
5 (8 amp) Headlights - low beam
6 (8 amp) Stop lights, heater, turn signal, gauges and back-up lights
7 (8 amp) Windshield wiper

Then remove the spring clip and washer which retain the wiper pinion gear in place and withdraw the gear and washer.

8 Undo the nut securing the wiper motor operating arm and remove the lockwasher, arm, wave washer and flat washer in that order.

9 Having removed the operating arm withdraw the output gear, park switch assembly and washer from the gearbox casing.

10 Carefully examine all parts for signs of wear or damage and replace as necessary.

11 Reassembly is a direct reversal of the above procedure.

---

45 Flasher circuit - fault tracing and rectification

If the flasher unit fails to operate, or works very slowly or rapidly, check out the flasher indicator circuit as detailed below, before assuming that there is a fault in the unit.

a) Examine the direction indicator bulbs both front and rear for broken filaments.

b) If the external flashers are working but either of the internal flasher warning lights have ceased to function, check the filaments in the warning light bulbs and replace with a new bulb if necessary.

c) If a flasher bulb is sound but does not work check all the flasher circuit connections with the aid of the wiring diagram found at the end of this chapter.

d) With the ignition switched on check that the current is reaching the flasher unit by connecting a voltmeter between the 'plus' terminal and earth. If it is found that current is reaching the unit connect the two flasher unit terminals together and operate the direction indicator switch. If one of the flasher warning lights comes on this proves that the flasher unit itself is at fault and must be replaced as it is not possible to dismantle and repair it.

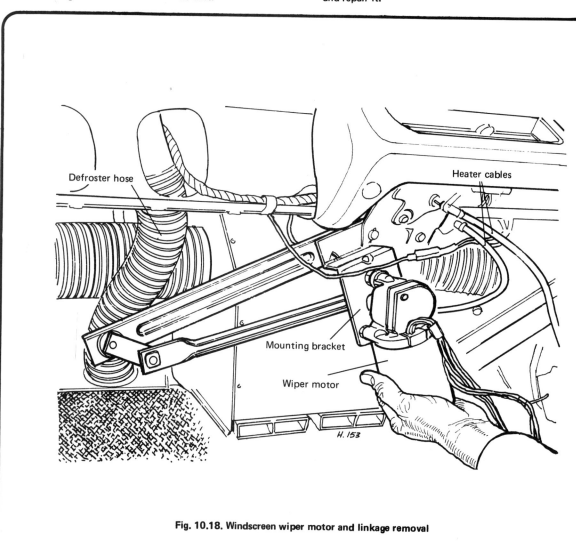

Defroster hose

Heater cables

Mounting bracket

Wiper motor

H. 153

Fig. 10.18. Windscreen wiper motor and linkage removal

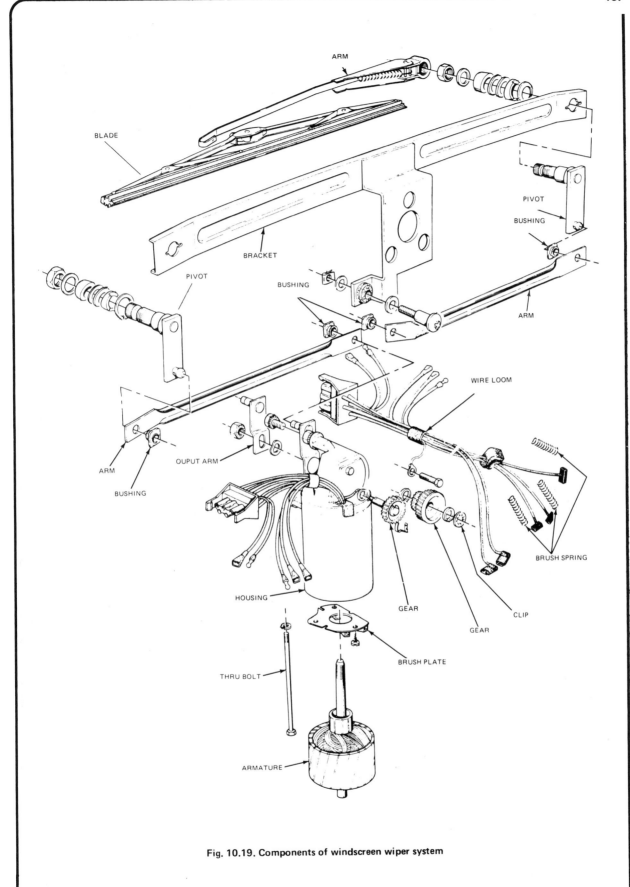

Fig. 10.19. Components of windscreen wiper system

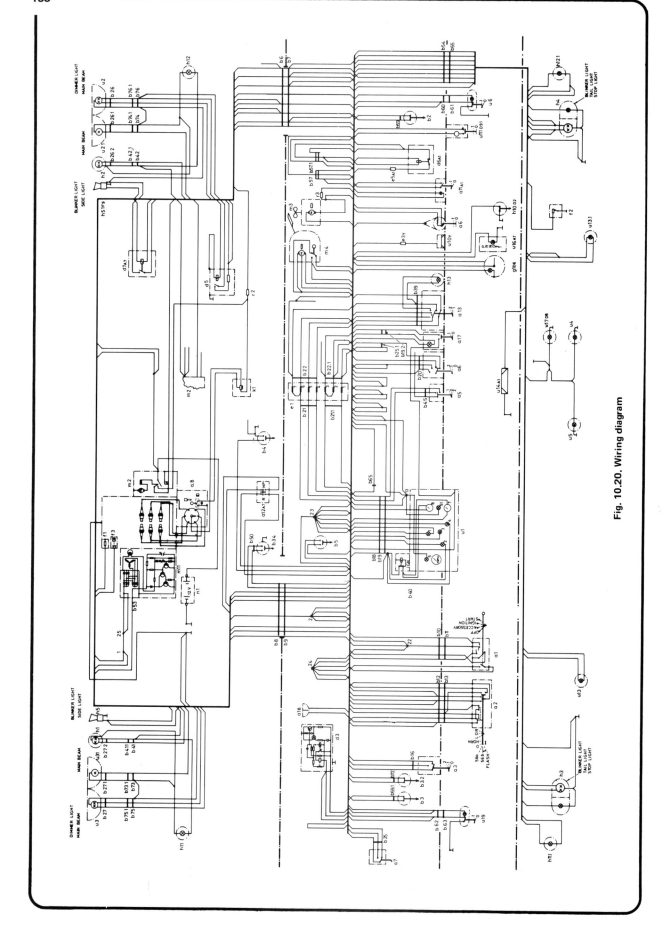

Fig. 10.20. Wiring diagram

a1   Steering ignition lock
a2   Blinker switch
a3   Light switch
a4   Windshield wiper motor switch - two stage
a5   Heating blower switch - two stage
a6   Cigar lighter
a7   Foot operated switch windshield wiper motor
a8   Ignition distributor
a13   Blinker switch warning system
a17   Switch-control-light - two circuit brake system
a18   Buzzer
b2   Door contact interruptor RH interior light
b3   Door contact interruptor LH interior light
b3.2   Door contact interruptor buzzer
b4   Back-up light switch
b5   Stop light switch
b6   Multiple connector - dash board, R
b7   Multiple connector - dash board, R
b8   Multiple connector - dash board, L
b9   Multiple connector - dash board, L
b10   Multiple connector - steering/ignition lock
b11   Multiple connector - steering/ignition lock
b12   Multiple connector - blinker switch
b13   Multiple connector - blinker, switch
b16   Multiple connector - light switch
b18   Multiple connector - instrument cluster
b18.1   Multiple connector - switch - control light - two circuit brake system
b19   Multiple connector - instrument cluster
b19.2   Multiple connector - switch-control light - two circuit brake system
b20   Multiple connector - windshield wiper motor switch
b21   Multiple connector - fuse box
b21.1   Multiple connector - fuse box
b22   Multiple connector - fuse box
b22.1   Multiple connector - fuse box
b25   Multiple connector foot operated switch windshield wiper motor
b25.1   Multiple connector wiper wash system
b26   Multiple connector main beam headlight, R
b26.1   Multiple connector remote headlight, R
b26.2   Multiple connector blinker - side light, R
b27   Multiple connector main beam headlight, L
b27.1   Multiple connector remote headlight, L
b41.1   Multiple connector blinker - side light, L
b42   Multiple connector blinker - side light, R
b42.1   Multiple connector blinker - side light, R
b45   Multiple connector heating blower switch
b50   Multiple connector warning light switch - two circuit

brake system
b53   Multiple connector alternator
b54   Multiple connector - instrument panel, R
b55   Multiple connector - instrument panel, R
b57   Multiple connector
b57.1   Multiple connector
b59   Door contact switch, R
b59.1   Door contact switch, L
b60   Multiple connector - interior light, R
b61   Multiple connector - interior light, R
b62   Multiple connector - interior light, L
b63   Multiple connector - interior light, L
b65   Connector wire 15
b72   Multiple connector buzzer switch
b73   Multiple connector remote headlight, L
b73.1   Multiple connector remote headlight, L
b74   Multiple connector remote headlight, R
b74.1   Multiple connector remote headlight, R
b75   Multiple connector main beam headlight, L
b75.1   Multiple connector main beam headlight, L
b76   Multiple connector main beam headlight, R
b76.1   Multiple connector main beam headlight, R
d3   Blinker unit
d5   Relay remote headlights
e1   Fuse box
f1   Transmitter water temperature gauge
f2   Transmitter fuel gauge
f3   Oil pressure control switch
h1   Blinker - side light, L
h2   Blinker - side light, R
h3   Combined tail light, L
h4   Combined tail light, R
h5   Horn, L
h11   Side marker front, L
h11.1   Side marker back, L
h12   Side marker front, R
h12.1   Side marker back, R
h13   Warning indicator - control light
k1   Ignition coil
m1.1   Alternator
m2   Starter
m3   Heating blower motor
m4   Windshield wiper motor
n1   Battery
r2   Series resistance wire ignition
r3   Series resistor heating blower
u1   Instrument cluster
u2   Main beam headlight, R
u2.1   Remote headlight, R
u3   Main beam headlight, L
u3.1   Remote headlight, L
u4   License plate light, R
u5   License plate light, L
u6   Interior light, R
u13   Back up light, L
u13.1   Back up light, R
u19   Interior light, L
a11   Heating plate switch
d6   Working current relay heating plate
e5   Fuse heating plate
u14   Heating plate
a12   Blocking - switch automatic transmission
u16   Transmission control selector

dial
d7   Working current relay automatic transmission
h10   Hand brake warning switch
g1   Clock
u17   Luggage compartment light
u11.1   Reading light
h5.1   Horn, R
e3   Fuse radio
u10   Radio
b27.2   Multiple connector blinker - side light, L
b34   Warning light switch two circuit brake system
b39   Multiple connector blinker switch warning system
b40   Voltage divider
b41   Multiple connector blinker - side light, L
30   Interior lights
      Reading lights
      Four way hazard flasher
      Clock
      Buzzer
      Cigar lighter
58   Tail light, L
      Side light front and back, L
      Illumination - instrument cluster
      Illumination - cigar lighter
      Illumination - transmission control selector dial
      Illumination - clock
      Tail light, R
      Side light front and back, R
      Luggage compartment lights
      License plate lights
56a   Main beam
      Relay remote headlights
56b   Low beam
15   Back-up lights
      Heating blower motor
      Blinker system
      Stop light
      Voltage divider
      Control light - two circuit brake system
      Control light charging current
      Control light oil pressure
15   Windshiwld wiper motor
      Current circuit heating plate
      Interior wiring diagram and symbol according to DIN. A. IEC.
A1   In combination with heating plate
A7   In combination with automatic gear
D2   In combination with two circuit brake system
D6   In combination with clock
D8   In combination with luggage compartment light
D9   In combination with interior light, L
D9.1   In combination with reading light
F9   In combination with horn, R
Y   In combination with radio

R....   Red
Bk...   Black
Bi...   Blue
W...   White
Br.   Brown
G...   Green
Y...   Yellow
LG..   Light Green
P...   Purple
O...   Orange
Pk..   Pink

Key to Fig. 10.21 - Wiring diagram for 1972 models

Component	Grid location	Component	Grid location
Alternator		Map (light & switch)	B-80 (RPO)
Alternator regulator	G-3	Parking	E-54/J-54
Alternator/w. regulator	C-3	Rear (tail, stop & turn)	G-58
Battery	A-2	Side - marker - front (2 lamps)	J-56
Buzzer (headlamp 'on') & key warning	G-78	rear (2 lamps)	G-56
Cigar lighter	C-74	Motors	
Clock	C-79	Starting	E-6
Distributor	G-14	Windshield wiper	C-17
Emission vacuum	G-21	Radios	D-11
Engine governor	D-14	AM radio	
Flashers	C-60	AM-FM radio	
Emergency warning		Relays	
Direction indicator		Starting motor	F-6
Gauges		Headlamp on	E-51
Ammeter	C-35	Senders	
Fuel	C-39	Fuel gauge	F-39
Instrument voltage regulator	C-41	Oil pressure gauge	F-35
Oil pressure	C-36	Water temperature gauge	G-40
Tachometer	C-12	Spark control unit (emission control)	E-21
Temperature	D-40	Speakers	D-12
Heater, A/C blower resistor	B-43	Front	
Horns	D-16	Speed sensor (emission control)	E-23
Ignition coils	F-13	Switches	
Illumination lamps		Ambient tempersture sensor (emission control)	C-20
Cigar lighter	H-46	Reverse light	F-25
Clock (console)	D-55	Door jamb courtesy light - front R.H.	D-76
Gauge cluster	H-45	L.H.	D-78
Headlamp switch	B-45	Dual brake warning	G-37
Indicator lamps		Hazard warning	C-67
Alternator	D-34	Headlight dimmer	E-45
Dual brake warning	D-37	Heater blower	F-44
High beam	F-47	Ignition	B-9
Hi-water temperature	G-40	Light (headlamp)	B-45
Turn-signal indicator	D-74	Low oil pressure	H-35
Low oil pressure	C-36	Stop light	A-55
Parking brake	H-38	Hi-water temperature	G-40
Lights		Direction indicators	C-64
Engine compartment (light & switch)	(Not available)	Key reminder	J-80
Reverse L.H.	C-22	Windshield wiper 2-speed	G-17
Reverse R.H.	C-25	'Park' - 'Neutral' start (auto. trans. only)	J-17
Headlights	G-48	Map (switch & lamp)	C-80
PRND21 (automatic transmission)	B-52	Horn	C-14
Licence plate	J-58	Transmission (emission control)	E-20

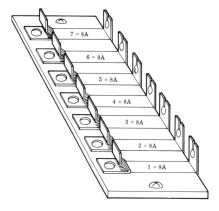

Fuse block

The fuse block is located under the instrument panel to the left of the ashtray. To replace a fuse, snap out the protective cover and pull it away from between the two spring clips. The fuses are identified as follows:

8A	Interior lights, cigar lighter, emergency flasher	8A	High beam
8A	Side lights LH, tail lights LH, instrument cluster illumination	8A	Low beam
8A	Side lights, RH, tail lights RH, rear license plate light	8A	Stop lights, heater blower, turn indicator lights, gauges, back-up lights

Fig 10.21 Wiring diagram 1972 models

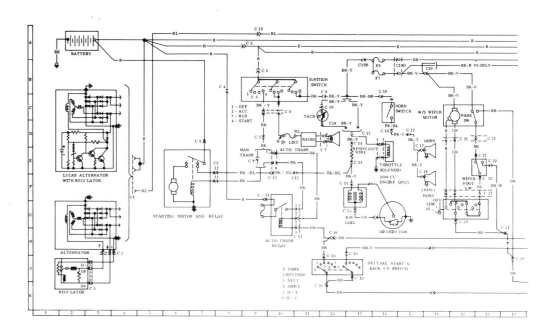

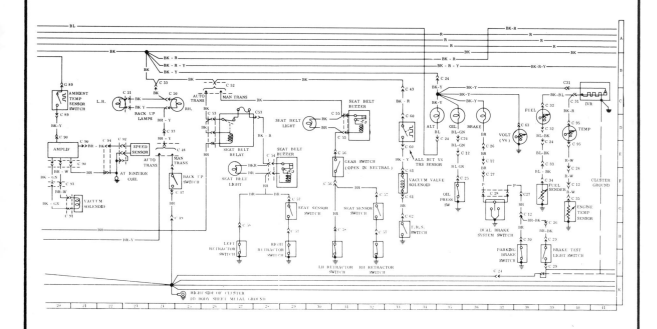

continued overleaf

Fig 10.21 Wiring diagram 1972 models (continued)

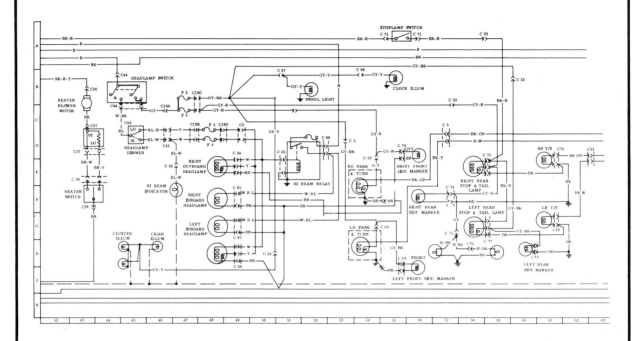

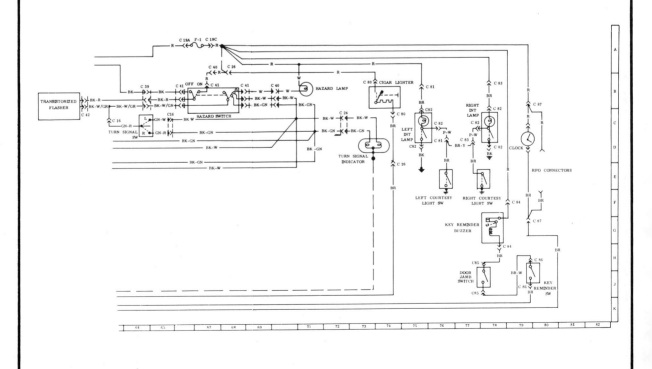

Symptom	Reason/s	Remedy
No electricity at starter motor	Battery discharged	Charge battery
	Battery defective internally	Fit new battery
	Battery terminal leads loose or earth lead not securely attached to body	Check and tighten leads
	Loose or broken connections in starter motor circuit	Check all connections and tighten any that are loose
	Starter motor switch or solenoid faulty	Test and replace faulty components with new
Electricity at starter motor: faulty motor	Starter motor pinion jammed in mesh with flywheel gear ring	Disengage pinion by turning squared end of armature shaft
	Starter brushes badly worn, sticking or brush wire loose	Examine brushes, replace as necessary, tighten down brush wires
	Commutator dirty, worn or burnt	Clean commutator, recut if badly burnt
	Starter motor armature faulty	Overhaul starter motor, fit new armature
	Field coils earthed	Overhaul starter motor
Electrical defects	Battery in discharged condition	Charge battery
	Starter brushes badly worn, sticking, or wires loose	Examine brushes, replace as necessary, tighten down brush wires
	Loose wires in starter motor	Check wiring and tighten as necessary
Dirt or oil on drive gear	Starter motor pinion sticking on the screwed sleeve	Remove starter motor, clean starter motor drive
Mechanical damage	Pinion or flywheel gear teeth broken or worn	Fit new gear ring to flywheel, and new pinion to starter motor drive
Lack of attention or mechanical damage	Pinion or flywheel gear teeth broken or worn	Fit new gear teeth to flywheel, or new pinion to starter motor drive
	Starter drive main spring broken	Dismantle and fit new main spring
	Starter motor retaining bolts loose	Tighten starter motor securing bolts Fit new spring washer if necessary
Wear or damage	Battery defective internally	Remove and fit new battery
	Electrolyte level too low or electrolyte too weak due to leakage	Top up electrolyte level to just above plates
	Plate separators no longer fully effective	Remove and fit new battery
	Battery plates severely sulphated	Remove and fit new battery
Insufficient current flow to keep battery	Fan belt slipping	Check belt for wear, replace if necessary and tighten
	Battery terminal connections loose or corroded	Check terminals for tightness, and remove all corrosion
	Alternator not charging properly	See next sub section
	Short in lighting circuit causing continual battery drain	Trace and rectify
	Regulator unit not working correctly	See next sub section
Alternator not charging	Loose or dirty cable connections	Check all electrical connections for tightness and good contact
	Fan belt very loose or even missing	Check belt for wear, replace if necessary and adjust

If all appears to be well but the alternator is still not charging take the car to an automobile electrician for checking of the regulator and alternator

Symptom	Reason/s	Remedy
Fuel gauge gives no reading	Fuel tank empty!	Fill fuel tank
	Electric cable between tank sender unit and gauge earthed or loose	Check cable for earthing and joints for tightness
	Fuel gauge case not earthed	Ensure case is well earthed
	Fuel gauge supply cable interrupted	Check and replace cable if necessary
	Fuel gauge unit broken	Replace fuel gauge
Fuel gauge registers full all the time	Electric cable between tank unit and gauge broken or disconnected	Check over cable and repair as necessary
Horn operates all the time	Horn push either earthed or stuck down	Disconnect battery earth. Check and rectify source of trouble
	Horn cable to horn push earthed	Disconnect battery earth. Check and rectify source of trouble

Symptom	Reason/s	Remedy
Horn fails to operate	Blow fuse	Check and renew if broken. Ascertain cause
	Cable or cable connection loose, broken or disconnected	Check all connections for tightness and cables for breaks
	Horn has an internal fault	Remove and overhaul horn
Horn emits intermittent or unsatisfactory noise	Horn incorrectly adjusted	Adjust horn until best note obtained
Lights do not come on	If engine not running, battery discharged	Push-start car, charge battery
	Light bulb filament burnt out or bulbs broken	Test bulbs in live bulb holder
	Wire connections loose, disconnected or broken	Check all connections for tightness and wire cable for breaks
	Light switch shorting or otherwise faulty	By-pass light switch to ascertain if fault is in switch and fit new switch as appropriate
Lights come on but fade out	If engine not running battery discharged	Push-start car, and charge battery
Lights give very poor illumination	Lamp glasses dirty	Clean glasses
	Reflector tarnished or dirty	Fit new reflectors
	Lamps badly out of adjustment	Adjust lamps correctly
	Incorrect bulb with too low wattage fitted	Remove bulb and replace with correct grade
	Existing bulbs old and badly discoloured	Renew bulb units
	Electrical wiring too thin not allowing full current to pass	Re-wire lighting system
Lights work erratically - flashing on and off, especially over bumps	Battery terminals or earth connection loose	Tighten battery terminals and earth connection. Examine and rectify.
	Lights not earthing properly	
	Contacts in light switch faulty	By-pass light switch to ascertain if fault is in switch and fit new switch as appropriate
Wiper motor fails to work	Blown fuse	Check and replace fuse if necessary
	Wire connections loose, disconnected, or broken	Check wiper wiring. Tighten loose connections.
	Brushes badly worn	Remove and fit new brushes
	Armature worn or faulty	If electricity at wiper motor remove and Overhaul and fit replacement armature.
	Field coils faulty	Purchase reconditioned wiper motor
Wiper motor works very slowly and takes excessive current	Commutator dirty, greasy or burnt	Clean commutator thoroughly
	Drive to wheelboxes too bent or unlubricated	Examine drive and straighten out severe curvature. Lubricate
	Wheelbox spindle binding or damaged	Remove, overhaul, or fit replacement
	Armature bearings dry or unaligned	Replace with new bearings correctly aligned
	Armature badly worn or faulty	Remove, overhaul, or fit replacement armature
Wiper motor works slowly and takes little current	Brushes badly worn	Remove and fit new brushes
	Commutator dirty, greasy or burnt	Clean commutator thoroughly
	Armature badly worn or faulty	Remove and overhaul armature or fit replacement
Wiper motor works but wiper blades	Drive disengaged or faulty	Examine and if faulty, replace
	Wheelbox spindle damaged or worn	Examine and if faulty, replace
	Wiper motor gearbox parts badly worn	Overhaul or fit new motor

Chapter 11 Suspension and steering

Contents

Specifications

Front suspension type ... ... Independent, Mac Pherson strut

Coil springs
Identification:
    Standard ... ... Red
    Heavy duty ... . Red/white

    mean load ... ... 707 lb (320.7 kg)
    mean rate ... ... 122 lb/in (21.8 kg f cm)
    Coil diameter ... ... 5.31 in (134.9 mm)
    Wire diameter:
        Standard ... ... 0.465 in (11.81 mm)
        Heavy duty ... ... 0.472 in (11.99 mm)

Suspension unit identification
Standard ... ... Violet
Heavy duty ... ... Green/white

Rear suspension type ... ... Semi elliptic leaf spring
Identification:
    Heavy duty ... ... Blue
    Number of leaves 3
    Spring length between eye centres ... ... 47 in (114.4 cm)
    Width of leaves ... ... 2.0 in (51 mm)
    Length between radius arm bush centres ... ... 9.91 in (251.7 mm)

Dampers
Type ... ... Telescopic - double acting
Identification:
    Standard ... ... Red
    Heavy duty ... ... Brown/white

Steering gear
Type ... ... Rack and pinion
Rack travel (lock to lock) ... ... 4.92 in (12.5 cm)
Teeth on pinion 6
Lubricant capacity ... ... 0.3 US pint (0.15 litre)
Lubricant type ... ... Castrol Hypoy (EP 90)
Pinion bearing pre-load adjustment ... ... Selective shims
Rack damper adjustment ... ... Selective shims
Caster ... ... - ½º to +1 to 1½º
Camber ... ... - ¼º to -¾º
King pin inclination ... ... 7º 30' to 8º 30'

Max. wheel lock angles:
    back ... ... 41º 36'
    front ... ... 39º 15'

Front lock setting:

at 20º back	18º 15' to 19º 45'	
at 35º back	32º 15' to 33º 45'	
Toe in	0 in to ¼ in (0 to 6.35 mm)	
Turning circle	31.5 ft (9.6 m)	

Wheels and tyres

Standard	165 SR - 13 radial ply	
Optional	185/70 SR - 13	
or	185/70 HR - 13	

Tyre pressures*

	lb/sq in	kg/sq cm
165 SR - 13 front	27	1.9
rear	31	2.2
185/70 SR - 13 front	24	1.7
rear	29	2.04
185/70 HR - 13 front	24	1.7
rear	28	2.0

Note. The recommended pressures should be taken when the tyre is cold as a hot tyre normally shows a higher pressure.

* For full load or high speed motoring refer to the drivers handbook or tyre specialist.

Torque wrench settings:

	lb f ft	kg fm
Wheel nuts	50 to 55	7.0 to 7.7
Suspension unit upper mounting bolts	15 to 18	2.07 to 2.49
Track control arm ball stud	30 to 35	4.15 to 4.85
Torsion bar front clamps	15 to 18	2.07 to 2.49
Torsion bar to track control arm	25 to 30	3.46 to 4.15
Track control arm inner bushing	22 to 27	3.04 to 3.73
Radius arms to axle housing	25 to 30	3.46 to 4.15
Radius arms to body	25 to 30	3.46 to 4.15
Shock absorber to axle	40 to 45	5.54 to 6.22
Shock absorber to body	15 to 20	2.07 to 2.76
Rear spring 'U' bolts	25 to 30	3.46 to 4.15
Rear spring front hanger	27 to 32	3.73 to 4.42
Rear spring rear shackle nuts	8 to 10	1.11 to 1.38
Steering arms to suspension unit	30 to 34	4.2 to 4.7
Steering gear to crossmember	15 to 18	2.1 to 2.4
Track rod end to steering arm	18 to 22	2.5 to 3.0
Flexible coupling to pinion spline	12 to 15	1.7 to 2.1
Universal joint to steering shaft	12 to 15	1.7 to 2.1
Steering wheel nut	20 to 25	2.8 to 3.4

1 General description

Each of the independent front suspension Macpherson strut units consists of a vertical strut enclosing a double acting damper surrounded by a coil spring. The upper end of each strut is secured to the top of the wing valance under the bonnet by rubber mountings.

The wheel spindle carrying the brake assembly and wheel hub is forged integrally with the suspension unit foot.

The steering arms are connected to each unit which are in turn connected to track rods and thence to the rack and pinion steering gear.

The lower end of each suspension unit is located by a track control arm. A stabilising torsion bar is fitted between the outer ends of each track control arm and secured at the front to mountings on the body front member.

A rubber rebound stop is fitted inside each suspension unit thus preventing the spring becoming over-extended and jumping out of its mounting plates. Upward movement of the wheel is limited by the spring becoming fully compressed but this is damped by the addition of a rubber bump stop fitted around the suspension unit piston rod which comes into operation before the spring is fully compressed.

Whenever repairs have been carried out on a front suspension unit it is essential to check the wheel alignment as the linkage could be altered which will effect the correct front wheel settings.

Every time the car goes over a bump vertical movement of a front wheel pushes the damper body upwards against the combined resistance of the coil spring and the damper piston.

Hydraulic fluid in the damper is displaced and it is then forced through the compression valve into the space between the inner and outer cylinder. On the downward movement of the suspension, the road spring forces the damper body downward against the pressure of the hydraulic fluid which is forced back again through the rebound valve. In this way the natural oscillations of the spring are damped out and a comfortable ride is obtained.

On the front uprights it is worth noting that there is a shroud inside the coil spring which protects the machined surface of the piston rod from road dirt.

The steering gear is of the rack and pinion type and is located on the front crossmember by two 'U' shaped clamps. The pinion is connected to the steering column by a flexible coupling. Above the flexible coupling the steering column is split by a universal joint designed to collapse on impact thus minimising injury to the driver in the event of an accident.

Turning the steering wheel causes the rack to move in a lateral direction and the track rods attached to either end of the rack pass this movement to the steering arms on the suspension/axle units thereby moving the road wheels.

Two adjustments are possible on the steering gear, namely rack damper adjustment and pinion bearing pre-load adjustment, but the steering gear must be removed from the car to carry out these adjustments. Both adjustments are made by varying the thickness of shim-packs.

At the rear the axle is located by two inverted 'U' bolts at each end of the casing to underslung semi-elliptical leaf springs which provide both lateral and longitudinal location. Lateral movement of the rear axle is further controlled by the fitting of radius arms which are angled inwards to the axle casing from their body mounting points.

Double acting telescopic shock absorbers are fitted between the spring plates on the rear axles and reinforced mountings in the boot of the car. These shock absorbers work on the same principle as the front shock absorber.

In the interests of lessening noise and vibration the springs and dampers are mounted on rubber bushes. A rubber spacer is also incorporated between the axle and the springs.

2 Front hub bearings - maintenance, removal and replacement

1 After jacking up the car and removing the front road wheel, disconnect the hydraulic brake pipe at the union on the suspension unit and either plug the open ends of the pipes, or have a jar handy to catch the escaping fluid.
2 Bend back the locking tabs on the two bolts holding the brake caliper to the suspension unit, undo the bolts and remove the caliper.
3 By judicious tapping and levering remove the dust cap from the centre of the hub (Fig. 11.4).
4 Remove the split pin from the nut retainer and undo the larger adjusting nut from the stub axle.
5 Withdraw the thrust washer and the outer tapered bearing.
6 Pull off the complete hub and disc assembly from the stub axle.
7 From the back of the hub assembly carefully prise out the grease seal and remove the inner tapered bearing.
8 Carefully clean out the hub and wash the bearings with petrol making sure that no grease or oil is allowed to get onto the brake disc.
9 Working the grease well into the bearings fully pack the bearing cages and rollers with Castrol LM Grease. NOTE: Leave the hub and grease seal empty to allow for subsequent expansion of the grease.
10 To reassemble the hub assembly first fit the inner bearing and then gently tap the grease seal back into the hub. If the seal was at all damaged during removal a new one must be fitted.
11 Replace the hub and disc assembly on the stub axle and slide on the outer bearing and the thrust washer.
12 Tighten down the centre adjusting nut to a torque of 27 lb ft (3.73 kg m) whilst rotating the hub and disc to ensure free movement then slacken the nut of 90° and fit the nut retainer and new split pin but at this stage do not bend back the split pin.
13 At this stage it is advisable, if a dial gauge is available to

check the disc for run-out. The measurement should be taken as near to the edge of the worn, smooth part of the disc as possible and must not exceed 0.0035 inch (0.089 mm). If this figure is found to be excessive check the mating surfaces of the disc and hub for dirt or damage and also check the bearings and cups for excessive wear or damage.
14 If a dial gauge is not available refit the caliper to the suspension unit, using new locking tabs, and tighten the securing bolts to a torque of 45 to 50 lb ft (6.22 to 6.94 kg m).
15 The brake disc run-out can now be checked by means of a feeler gauge or gauges between the casting of the caliper and the disc. Establish a reasonably tight fit with the gauges between the top of the casting and the disc and rotate the disc and hub. Any high or low spot will immediately become obvious by the extra tightness of looseness of the fit of the gauges, and the amount of run-out can be checked by adding or subtracting gauges as necessary. It is only fair to point out that this method is not as accurate as when using a dial guage owing to the rough nature of the caliper casting.
16 Once the disc run-out has been checked and found to be correct, bend the ends of the split pin back and replace the dust cap.
17 Reconnect the brake hydraulic pipe and bleed the brakes as described in Chapter 9.

3 Front hub bearings - adjustment

1 To check the condition of the hub bearings, jack up the front end of the car and grasp the road wheel at two opposite points to check for any rocking movement in the wheel hub. Watch carefully for any movement in the steering gear, which can easily be mistaken for hub movement.
2 If a front wheel hub as excessive movement, this is adjusted by removing the hub cap and then levering off the small dust cap. Remove the split pin through the stub axle and take off the adjusting nut retainer.
3 If a torque wrench is available tighten the centre adjusting nut down to a torque of 27 lb ft (3.73 kg m) and then slacken it off 90° and replace the nut retainer and a new split pin.
4 Assuming a torque wrench is not available however, tighten up the centre nut until a slight drag is felt on rotating the wheel. Then loosen the nut very slowly until the wheel turns freely again and there is just a perceptible end float.
5 Now replace the nut retainer, a new split pin and the dust cap.

4 Front hub - removal and replacement

1 Follow the instructions given in Section 2 of this Chapter up to, and including paragraph 7.
2 Bend back the locking tabs and undo the four bolts holding the hub to the brake disc.
3 If a new hub assembly is being fitted it is supplied complete with new bearing cups and bearings. The bearing cups will already be fitted in the hub. It is essential to check that the cups and bearings are of the same manufacture; this can be done by reading the name on the bearings.
4 Clean with care the mating surfaces of the hub and check for blemishes or damage. Any dirt or blemishes will almost certainly give rise to disc run-out. Using new locking tabs bolt the disc and

the hub together and tighten the bolts to a torque of 30 to 34 lb ft (4.15 to 4.70 kg m).

5 To grease and reassemble the hub assembly follow the instructions given in Section 2, paragraphs 9 on.

5   Front suspension unit - removal and replacement

1 It is difficult to work on the front suspension of the Capri without one or two special tools, the most important of which is a set of adjustable spring clips, (USA number T70P - 5045). This tool, or similar clips are vital and any attempt to dismantle the units without them may result in personal injury.

2 Get someone to sit on the wing of the car and with the spring partially compressed in this way, securely fit the spring clips.

3 Jack up the car and remove the road wheel, then disconnect the brake pipe at the bracket on the suspension leg and plug the pipes or have a jar handy to catch the escaping hydraulic fluid.

4 Disconnect the track rod from the steering arm by pulling out the split pin and undoing the castellated nut, thus leaving the steering arm attached to the suspension unit.

5 Remove the outer end of the track control arm from the base of the suspension unit by pulling out the split pin and undoing the castellated nut.

6 Working under the bonnet undo the three bolts holding the top end of the suspension unit to the side panel and lower the unit complete with the brake caliper away from the car.

7 Replacement is a direct reversal of the removal sequence, but remember to use new split pins on the steering arm to track rod nut and also on the track control arm to suspension unit nut.

8 The top suspension unit mounting bolts should be tightened to a torque of 15 to 18 lb ft (2.1 to 2.5 kg m), the track control arm to suspension unit nut to a torque of 30 to 35 lb ft (4.2 to 4.8 kg m) and the steering arm to track rod nut to a torque of 18 to 22 lb ft (2.5 to 3.0 kg m).

6   Front coil spring - removal and replacement

1 Get someone to sit on the front wing of the car and with the spring partially compressed in this way securely fit spring clips or if available, adjustable spring restrainer tool (USA number T70P - 5045).

2 Jack up the front of the car, fit stands and remove the road wheel.

3 Working under the bonnet, remove the nut and the angled retainer.

4 Undo and remove the three bolts securing the top of the suspension unit to the side panel.

5 Push the piston rod downwards as far as it will go. It should now be possible to remove the top mounting assembly, the dished washer and the upper spring seat from the top of the spring.

6 The spring can now be lifted off its bottom seat and removed over the piston assembly.

7 If a new spring is being fitted check extremely carefully that it is of the same rating as the spring on the other side of the car. The colour coding of the springs can be found in a specifications at the beginning of this chapter.

8 Before fitting a new spring it must be compressed with the adjustable restrainers and make sure that the clips are placed on the same number of coils, and in the same position as on the spring that has been removed.

9 Place the new spring over the piston and locate it on its bottom seat, then pull the piston upwards and fit the upper spring seat so that it locates correctly on the flats cut on the piston rod.

10 Fit the dished washer to the piston rod ensuring that the convex side faces upwards.

11 Now fit the top mount assembly. With the steering in the straight ahead position fit the angled retainer facing inwards at 90° to the wheel angles and the piston rod nut having previously applied Loctite or similar compound to the thread. Do not fully tighten down the nut at this stage.

12 If necessary pull the top end of the unit upwards until it is possible to locate correctly the top mount bracket and fit the three retaining bolts from under the bonnet. These nuts must be tightened down to a torque of 15 to 18 lb ft (2.1 to 2.5 kg m).

13 Remove the spring clips, fit the road wheel and lower the car to the ground.

14 Finally, slacken off the piston rod nut, get an assistant to hold the upper spring seat to prevent it turning, and retighten the nut to a torque of 28 to 30 lb ft (3.9 to 4.4 kg m).

7   Front stabilizer bar - removal and replacement

1 Jack up the front of the car, support the car on suitable stands and remove both front road wheels.

2 Working under the car at the front, knock back the locking tabs on the four bolts securing the two front clamps that hold the stabilizer bar to the frame and then undo the four bolts and remove the clamps and rubber insulators.

3 Remove the split pins from the castellated nuts retaining the stabilizer bar to the track control arms then undo the nuts and pull off the large washers, carefully noting the way in which they are fitted.

4 Pull the stabilizer bar forwards out of the two track control arms and remove it from the car.

5 With the stabilizer bar out of the car remove the sleeve and large washer from each end of the bar again noting the correct fitting positions.

6 Reassembly is a reversal of the above procedure, but new locking tabs must be used on the front clamp bolts and new split pins on the castellated nuts. The nuts on the clamps and the castellated nuts on each end of the stabilizer bar must not be fully tightened down until the car is resting on its wheels.

7 Once the car is on its wheels the castellated nuts on the ends of the stabilizer bar should be tightened down to a torque of 25 to 30 lb ft (3.46 to 4.15 kg m) and the new split pins fitted. The four clamp bolts on the front mounting points must be tightened down to a torque of 15 to 18 lb ft (2.07 to 2.47 kg m) and the locking tabs knocked up.

8   Track control arm - removal and replacement

1 Jack up the front of the car, support the car on suitable stands and remove the front wheel.

2 Working under the car remove the split pin and unscrew the castellated nut that secures the track control arm to the stabilizer bar.

3 Lift away the large dished washer noting which way round it is fitted.

4 Remove the self lock nut and flat washer from the back of the track control arm pivot bolt. Release the inner end of the track control arm.

5 Withdraw the split pin and unscrew the nut that secures the track control arm ball joint to the base of the suspension unit. Separate the joint.

6   To refit the track control arm first assemble the track control arm ball stud to the base of the suspension unit.

7   Refit the nut and tighten to a torque wrench setting of 30 to 35 lb ft (4.15 to 4.8 kg m). Secure with a new split pin.

8   Place the track control arm so that it correctly locates over the stabilzer bar and then secure the inner end.

9   Slide the pivot bolt into position from the front and secure with the flat washer and a new self locking nut. The nut must be to the rear. Tighten the nut to a torque wrench setting of 22 to 27 lb ft (3.04 to 3.7 kg m) when the car is on the ground.

10 Fit the dished washer to the end of the stabilizer bar making sure it is the correct way round and secure with the castellated nut. This must be tightened to a torque wrench setting of 15 to 45 lb ft (2.07 to 6.22 kg m) when the car is on the ground. Lock the castellated nut with a new split pin.

9   Rear damper - removal and replacement

1   Chock the front wheels to prevent the car moving, then jack up the rear of the car and for convenience sake remove the road wheels.

2   Working inside the boot, hold the top of the piston and prevent it turning by holding a small spanner across the flats provided and then with an open ended spanner remove the further rubber bush and steel washer from the top of the piston rod.

3   Lift off the large steel washer and the rubber bush.

4   Working under the car, remove the nut, lock washer and bolt that retain the lower end of the damper to the axle casing.

5   Lower the damper from the car, then remove the further rubber bush and steel washer from the top of the piston rod.

6   Replacement is a reversal of the above procedure.

7   The nut on the bolt securing the lower end of the damper must be tightened down to a torque of 40 to 50 lb ft (5.54 to 6.22 kg m).

8   The main nut on the top mounting must be tightened to a torque of 20 to 25 lb ft (2.76 to 3.46 kg m) but the piston must be prevented from rotating during this operation. Most torque wrenches will not allow the flats on the piston rod to be held to prevent turning so it is better to get an assistant to hold the upper half of the damper from under the car.

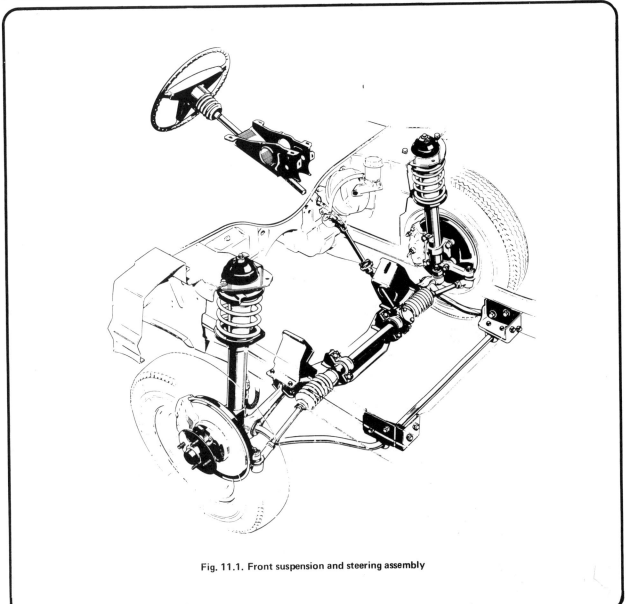

Fig. 11.1. Front suspension and steering assembly

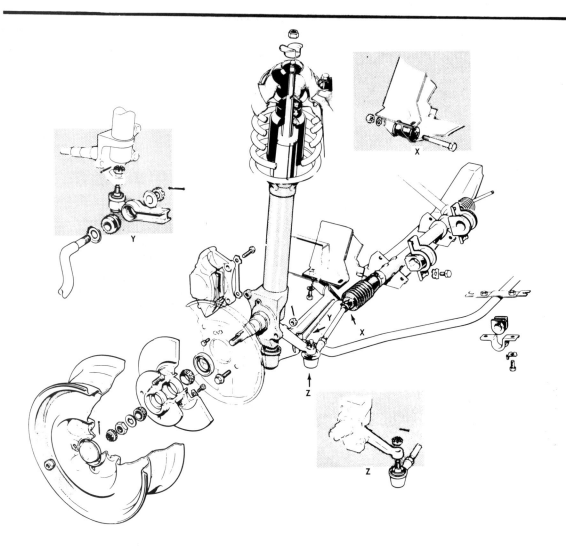

Fig. 11.2. Front suspension and steering attachments

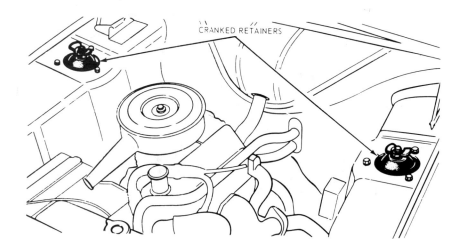

Fig. 11.3. Location of front suspension units in engine compartment. Note position of cranked retainers

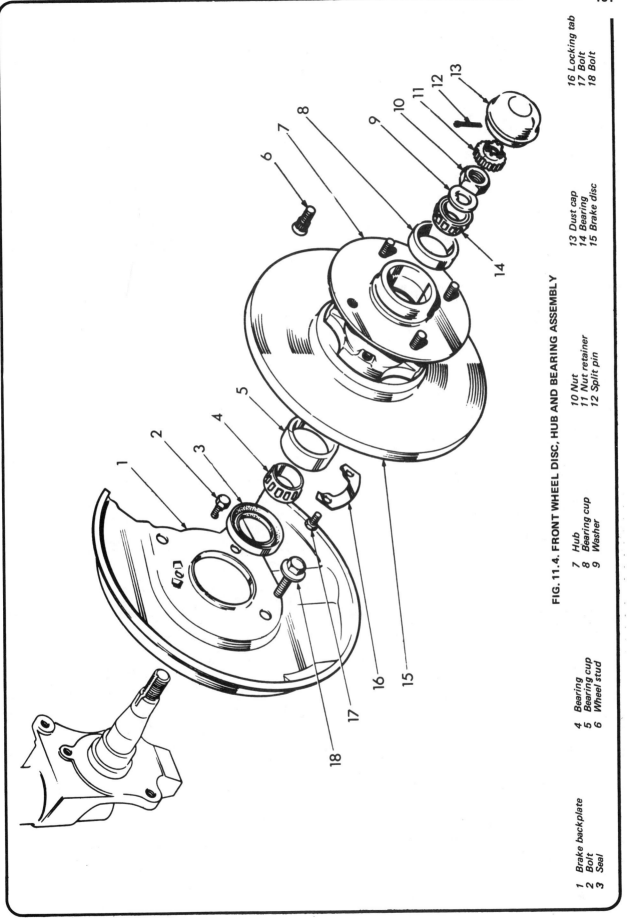

FIG. 11.4. FRONT WHEEL DISC, HUB AND BEARING ASSEMBLY

1 Brake backplate
2 Bolt
3 Seal

4 Bearing
5 Bearing cup
6 Wheel stud

7 Hub
8 Bearing cup
9 Washer

10 Nut
11 Nut retainer
12 Split pin

13 Dust cap
14 Bearing
15 Brake disc

16 Locking tab
17 Bolt
18 Bolt

10 Rear spring - removal and replacement

1   Chock the front wheels to prevent the car moving, then jack up the rear of the car and support it on suitable stands. To make the springs more accessible remove the road wheels.

2   Then place a trolley jack underneath the differential housing to support the rear axle assembly when the springs are removed. Do not raise the jack under the differential housing so that the springs are flattened, but raise it just enough to take the full weight of the axle with the springs fully extended.

3   Undo the rear shackle nuts and remove the combined shackle bolt and plate assemblies. Then remove the rubber bushes.

4   Undo the nut from the front mounting and take out the bolt running through the mounting.

5   Undo the nuts on the ends of the four 'U' bolts and remove the 'U' bolts together with the attachment plate and rubber spring insulators.

6   Replacement is a direct reversal of the above procedure. The nuts on the 'U' bolts, spring front mounting and rear shackles must be torqued down to the figures given in the specifications at the beginning of this chapter only AFTER the car has been lowered onto its wheels.

11 Radius arm - removal and replacement

1   Chock the front wheels to prevent the car moving, then jack up the rear of the car and support it on suitable stands.

2   Undo the nut and remove the bolt holding the rear end of the radius arm to the axle casing.

3   To take the tension off the radius arm it may be necessary to slightly raise the axle casing with a jack.

4   Repeat this procedure on the front mounting nut and bolt and remove the radius arm from the car.

5   Replacement is a reversal of the above procedure but the nuts should be torqued down to the figures given in the specifications at the beginning of this chapter AFTER the car has been lowered onto its wheels.

12 Rear spring and radius arm bush - removal and replacement

The bushes fitted to the rear spring eyes and ends of the radius arms are a press fit. They may be removed and new ones fitted using a large bench vice and suitable diameter tubes.

13 Rack and pinion steering gear - removal and replacement

1   Before starting this job, set the front wheels in the straight ahead position. Then jack up the front of the car and place blocks under the wheels; lower the car slightly on the jack so that the track rods are in a near horizontal position.

2   Remove the nut and bolt from the clamp at the front of the flexible coupling on the steering column. This clamp holds the coupling to the pinion splines.

3   Working on the front crossmember, knock back the locking tabs on the two nuts on each 'U' clamp, undo the nut and remove the locking tabs and clamps (Fig. 11.10).

4   Remove the split pins and castellated nuts from the ends of each track rod where they join the steering arms. Separate the track rods from the steering arms and lower the steering gear downwards out of the car.

5   Before replacing the steering gear make sure that the wheels have remained in the straight ahead position. Also check the condition of the mounting rubbers round the housing and if they appear worn or damaged renew them.

6   Check that the steering gear is also in the straight ahead position. This can be done by ensuring that the distances between the ends of both track rods and the steering gear housing on both sides are the same.

7   Place the steering gear in its location on the crossmember and at the same time mate up the splines on the pinion with the splines in the clamp on the steering column flexible coupling.

8   Replace the two 'U' clamps using new locking tabs under the bolts, tighten down the bolts to a torque of 12 to 15 lb ft (1.7 to 2.0 kg m) and bend up the locking tabs.

9   Refit the track rod ends into the steering arms, replace the castellated nuts and tighten them to a torque of 18 to 22 lb ft (2.5 to 3.0 kg m). Use new split pins to retain the nuts.

10 Tighten the clamp bolt on the steering column flexible coupling to a torque of 12 to 15 lb ft (1.7 to 2.1 kg m) having first made sure that the pinion is correctly located in the splines.

11 Jack up the car, remove the blocks from under the wheels and lower the car to the ground. It is advisable at this stage to take your car to your local dealer and have the toe-in checked.

14 Rack and pinion steering gear - adjustments

1   For the steering gear to function correctly, two adjustments are necessary. These are pinion bearing pre-load and rack damper adjustment.

2   To carry out these adjustments, remove the steering gear from the car as described in the previous Section, then mount the steering gear in a soft jawed vice so that the pinion is in a horizontal position and the rack damper cover plate to the top.

3   Remove the rack damper cover plate by undoing the two retaining bolts, then take off the gasket and shims from under the plate. Also remove the small spring and the recessed yoke which bears on the rack.

4   Now remove the pinion bearing pre-load cover plate from the base of the pinion, by undoing the two bolts. Then take off the gasket and shim pack.

5   To set the pinion bearing pre-load correctly, replace the cover plate without the gasket and shims and tighten down the bolts evenly until the cover plate is just touching the pinion bearing.

6   Using feeler gauges, measure the gap between the cover plate and the steering gear casing. To be sure that the cover plate has been evenly tightened, take a reading adjacent to each bolt. These readings should be the same. If they are not, loosen the cover plate and retighten it more evenly.

7   Assemble a shim pack with a gasket on either side of the shims which is 0.002 inch to 0.004 inch (0.05 to 0.10 mm) less than the gap previously measured. The thickness of the shim pack includes the two gaskets. Shim thicknesses available are listed below.

Steel	0.010 in. (0.054 mm)
Steel	0.005 in. (0.127 mm)
Steel	0.002 in. (0.051 mm)
Paper	0.005 in. (0.127 mm)

8 Remove the cover plate again, fit the assembled shim pack and gasket, with the gasket next to the cover plate, refit the cover plate, and having applied Loctite or similar sealer on the threads of the bolts, tighten them down with a torque of 6 to 8 lb ft (0.9 to 1.1 Kg m).

9 To set the rack damper adjustment, replace the yoke in its location on the rack and make sure it is fully home. Then measure the distance between the bottom of the recess in the yoke and the top of the steering gear casing.

10 Assemble a shim pack with a gasket on either side of the shims which is between .0005 to .0035 inch greater than the dimension measured in the previous paragraph. Shim thicknesses available are as listed below.

Material	Thickness
Steel	0.010 in. (0.254 mm)
Steel	0.005 in. (0.127 mm)
Steel	0.002 in. (0.051 mm)
Paper	0.005 in. (0.127 mm)

11 Refit the spring into its recess in the yoke and fit the shim pack and gaskets. Replace the cover plate having first applied Loctite or similar sealing compound to the bolt threads. Then tighten down the bolts with a torque of 6 to 8 lb ft (0.9 to 1.1 kg m).

---

15 Rack and pinion gear - dismantling and reassembly

---

1 Remove the steering gear from the car as described in Section 13.

2 Unscrew the ball joints and locknuts from the end of each track rod, having previously marked the threads to ensure correct positioning on reassembly. Alternatively the number of turns required to undo the ball joint can be counted and noted.

3 Slacken off the clips securing the rubber bellows to each track rod and the steering gear housing then pull off the bellows. Have a quantity of rag handy to catch the oil which will escape when the bellows are removed.

4 To dismantle the steering gear, it is only necessary to remove the track rod which is furthest away from the pinion on either right or left hand drive cars.

5 To remove the track rod place the steering gear in a soft jawed vice. Working on the track rod ball joint carefully drill out the pin that locks the ball housing to the locknut. Great care must be taken not to drill too deeply or you will drill into the threads on the rack thus causing irrepairable damage. The hole should be about 3/8th inch deep.

6 Hold the locknut with a spanner, then grip the ball housing with a mole wrench and undo it from the threads on the rack.

7 Take out the spring and ball seat from the recess in the end of the rack and then unscrew the locknut from the threads on the rack. The spring and ball seat must be replaced by new components on reassembly.

8 Carefully prize out the pinion dust seal then withdraw the pinion together with the bearing assembly nearest the flexible coupling. As the bearings utilise bearing tracks and loose balls (14 in each bearing) care must be taken not to lose any of the balls or drop them into the steering gear on reassembly.

9 With the pinion removed, withdraw the complete rack assembly with one track rod still attached from the pinion end of the casing, having first removed the rack damper cover, gasket, shims, springs and yoke as described in Section 14, paragraph 3.

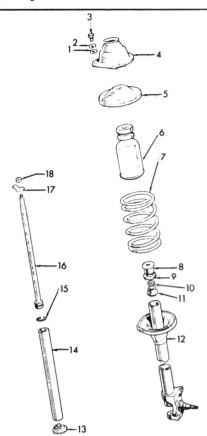

FIG. 11.5. EXPLODED VIEW OF FRONT SUSPENSION UNIT

1 Washer	10 Rod gland
2 Spring washer	11 Rod bush and guide
3 Bolt	12 Tube & spindle assembly
4 Upper mounting	13 Compression valve
5 Upper spring seat	14 Cylinder
6 Bump stop	15 Ring
7 Coil spring	16 Piston
8 Piston rod gland cap	17 Cranked retainer
9 Oil seal ring	18 Nut

10 Now remove the remaining pinion bearing assembly from the rack casing.

11 It is always advisable to withdraw the rack from the pinion end of the casing. This avoids passing the rack teeth through the bush at the other end of the casing and causing possible damage.

12 Carefully examine all parts for signs of wear or damage. Check the condition of the rack support bush at the opposite end of the casing from the pinion. If this is worn renew it. If the rack or pinion teeth are in any way damaged a completely new steering gear will have to be fitted.

13 Take the pinion oil seal off the top of the casing and replace it with a new seal.

14 To commence reassembly fit the lower pinion bearing and thrust washer into their recess in the casing. The loose balls can be held in place by a small amount of grease.

15 Replace the rack in the casing from the pinion end and position it in the straight ahead position by equalising the amount it protrudes at either end of the casing.

16 Replace the remaining pinion bearing and thrust washer onto the pinion and fit the pinion into the casing so that the larger master spline on the pinion shaft is parallel to the rack and on the right hand side of the pinion. This applies to both right and left hand drive cars.

17 Replace the rack damper yoke, springs, shims, gasket and cover plate.

18 To replace the track rod that has been removed, start by fitting a new spring and ball seat to the recess in the end of the rack shaft and replace the locknut onto the threads of the rack.

19 Lubricate the ball, ball seat and ball housing with a small amount of SAE 90 EP oil. Then slide the ball housing over the track and screw the housing onto the rack threads keeping the track rod in the horizontal position until the track rod starts to become stiff to move.

20 Using a normal spring balance hook it round the track rod half an inch from the end and check the effort required to move

it from the horizontal position.

21 By adjusting the tightness of the ball housing on the rack threads the effort required to move the track rod must be set at 5 lbs. (2.8 kg).

22 Tighten the locknut up to the housing and then recheck that the effort required to move the track rod is still correct at 5 lb. (2.8 kg).

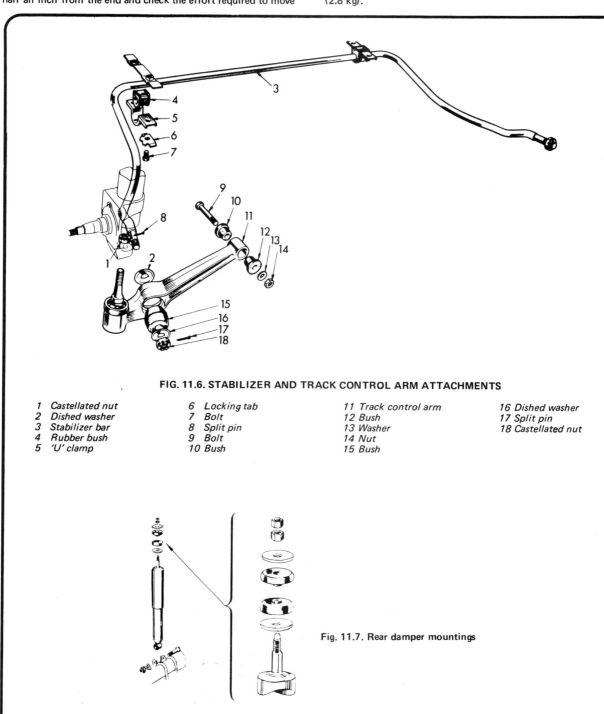

FIG. 11.6. STABILIZER AND TRACK CONTROL ARM ATTACHMENTS

1 Castellated nut	6 Locking tab	11 Track control arm	16 Dished washer
2 Dished washer	7 Bolt	12 Bush	17 Split pin
3 Stabilizer bar	8 Split pin	13 Washer	18 Castellated nut
4 Rubber bush	9 Bolt	14 Nut	
5 'U' clamp	10 Bush	15 Bush	

Fig. 11.7. Rear damper mountings

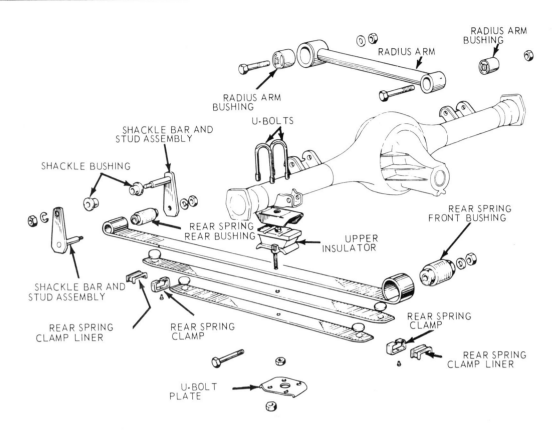

Fig. 11.8. Exploded view of rear suspension and attachments

RADIUS ARM

RADIUS ARM
BUSHING

RADIUS ARM
BUSHING

U-BOLTS

SHACKLE BAR AND
STUD ASSEMBLY

SHACKLE BUSHING

REAR SPRING
FRONT BUSHING

REAR SPRING
REAR BUSHING

UPPER
INSULATOR

SHACKLE BAR AND
STUD ASSEMBLY

REAR SPRING
CLAMP

REAR SPRING
CLAMP LINER

REAR SPRING
CLAMP

REAR SPRING
CLAMP LINER

U-BOLT
PLATE

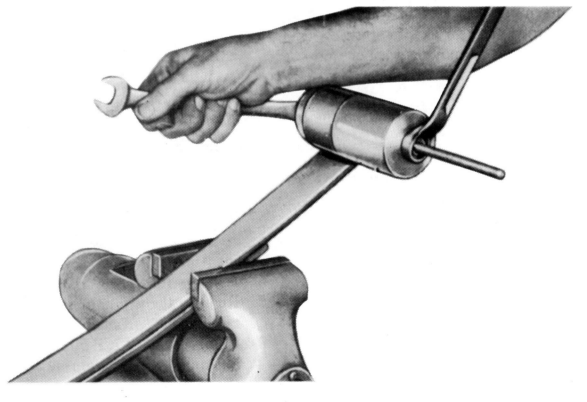

Fig. 11.9. Alternative method of removing spring bushes

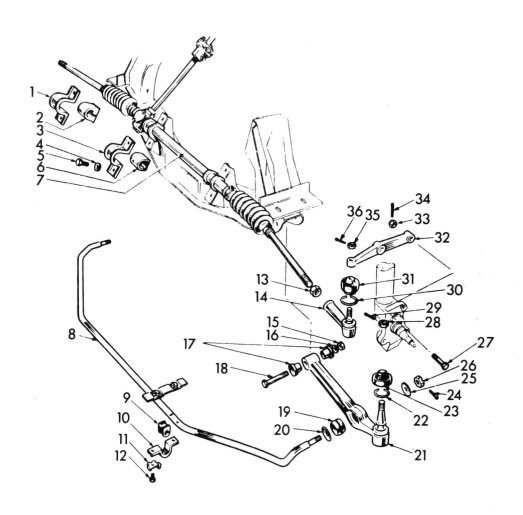

FIG. 11.10. RACK AND PINION AND TRACK CONTROL ASSEMBLIES

1 'U' clamp	10 Clamp	19 Bush	28 Castellated nut
2 Rubber bush	11 Locking tab	20 Washer	29 Split pin
3 'U' clamp	12 Bolt	21 Track control arm	30 Ring
4 Washer	13 Locknut	22 Ring'	31 Bush
5 Bolt	14 Track rod end	23 Seal	32 Steering arm
6 Bush	15 Nut	24 Split pin	33 Nut
7 Rack housing	16 Washer	25 Washer	34 Split pin
8 Torsion bar	17 Bush	26 Castellated nut	35 Castellated nut
9 Rubber bush	18 Bolt	27 Bolt	36 Split pin

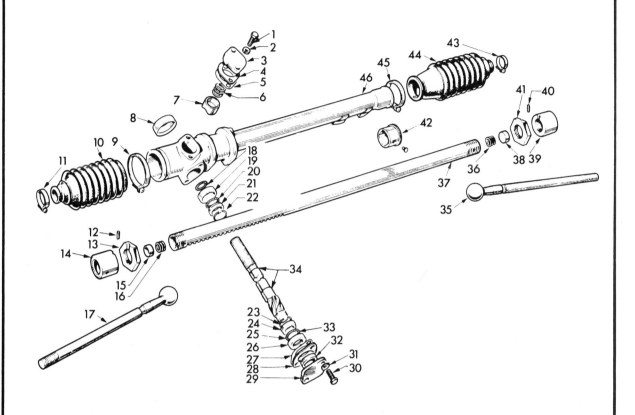

FIG. 11.11. RACK AND PINION INTERNAL COMPONENTS

1 Bolt	13 Nut	25 Balls	37 Rack
2 Washer	14 Ball joint housing	26 Bearing	38 Bearing
3 Cover	15 Bearing	27 Shim	39 Ball joint housing
4 Gasket	16 Spring	28 Gasket	40 Pin
5 Shim	17 Track rod	29 Cover	41 Nut
6 Spring	18 Oil seal	30 Bolt	42 Bush
7 Rack slipper	19 Bearing	31 Washer	43 Clip
8 Seal	20 Balls	32 Spacer	44 Bellows
9 Clip	21 Race	33 Balls	45 Clip
10 Bellows	22 Circlip	34 Pinion	46 Rack housing
11 Clip	23 Circlip	35 Track rod	
12 Pin	24 Race	36 Spring	

23 On the line where the locknut and ball housing meet, drill a 0.125 inch, (3.18 mm) diameter hole which must be 0.375 inch (9.52 mm) deep. Even if the two halves of the old hole previously drilled out align a new hole must be drilled.

24 Tap a new retaining pin into the hole and peen the end over to secure it.

25 Replace the rubber bellows and the track rod ends ensuring that they are replaced in exactly the same position from which they were removed.

26 Remove the rack damper cover plate and pour in 0.25 pint (0.3 US pints, 0.15 litre) of SAE 90 EP oil. Then carry out both steering gear adjustments as detailed in the previous Section.

27 After replacing the steering gear on the car as described in Section 10, it is strongly recommended that you take the car to your nearest Capri dealer and have the toe-in correctly adjusted.

16 Steering wheel and column - removal and replacement

1 Place the car with its wheels in the straight ahead position, disconnect the battery by removing the negative earth lead and disconnect the choke cable from the carburettor.

2 Working under the bonnet undo the clamp bolt on the top of the steering column universal joint.

3 Moving inside the car, prize out the centre emblem on the steering wheel, knock back the locking tab on the centre nut and undo the nut. Remove the locking tab and pull the steering wheel off its splines.

4 Undo the two screws securing the steering column shrouds to the column. Then remove the two bolts securing the bottom of the shroud and the column to the underside of the facia. Lift the indicator cancelling cam and its spring off the shaft, noting the position in which they are fitted in relation to the switch.

5 Pull off the multi-pin connectors to the indicator switch and ignition switch, then remove the indicator switch assembly from the top of the column by undoing the two small retaining screws.

6 Withdraw the steering column into the car taking care not to damage the grommet where the column passes through the floor of the car.

7 Replacement is a direct reversal of the above procedure. Note that the clamp bolt on the universal joint must be tightened to a torque of 12 to 15 lbf.ft. (1.7 to 2.1 kgf.m) and the steering wheel retaining nut to a torque of 20 to 25 lbf.ft. (2.8 to 3.4 kgf.m). Before replacing this nut ensure that the indicators cancel correctly.

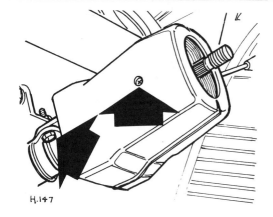

H.147

Fig. 11.14(a) View of left and right-hand screws and bolts to be removed to release shroud and steering column

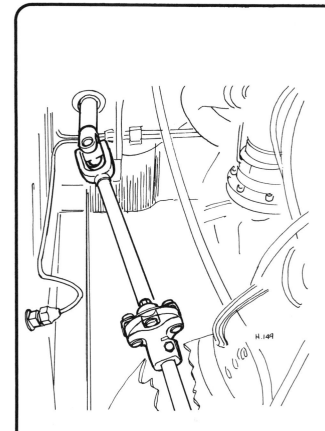

H.149

Fig. 11.12. Steering column universal joint and flexible coupling

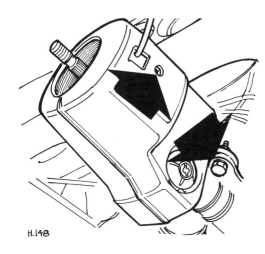

H.148

Fig. 11.14(b) View of left and right-hand screws and bolts to be removed to release shroud and steering column

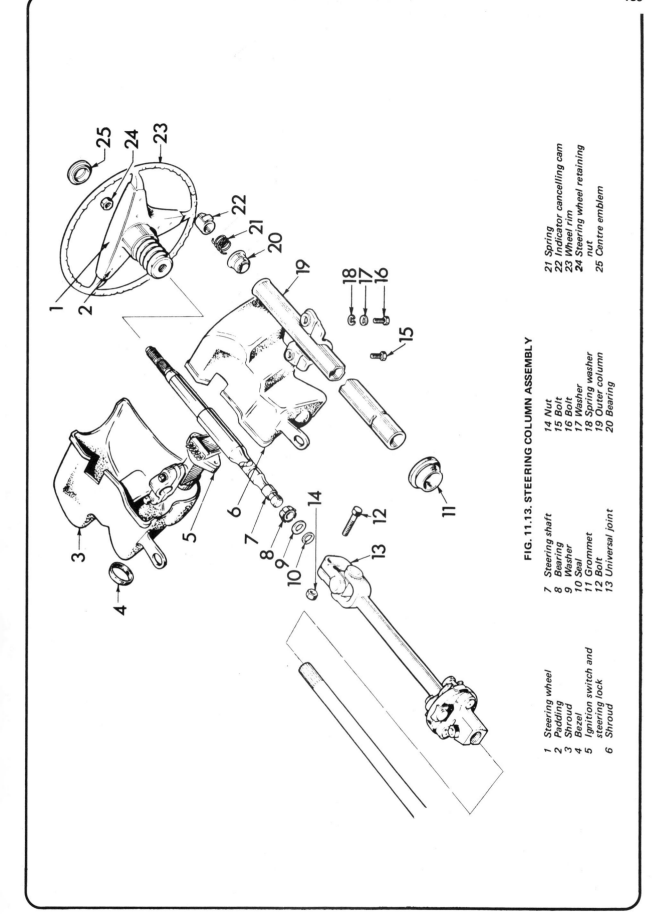

FIG. 11.13. STEERING COLUMN ASSEMBLY

1 Steering wheel
2 Padding
3 Shroud
4 Bezel
5 Ignition switch and
   steering lock
6 Shroud

7 Steering shaft
8 Bearing
9 Washer
10 Seal
11 Grommet
12 Bolt
13 Universal joint

14 Nut
15 Bolt
16 Bolt
17 Washer
18 Spring washer
19 Outer column
20 Bearing

21 Spring
22 Indicator cancelling cam
23 Wheel rim
24 Steering wheel retaining
   nut
25 Centre emblem

Before diagnosing faults from the following chart, check that any irregularities are not caused by:-

1. Binding brakes.
2. Incorrect 'mix' of radial and cross-ply tyres.
3. Incorrect tyre pressures.
4. Misalignment of the body frame

Symptom	Reason/s	Remedy
Steering wheel can be moved considerably before any sign of movement of the wheel is apparent	Wear in the steering linkage, gear and column coupling	Check movement in all joints and steering gear and overhaul and renew as required.
Vehicle difficult to steer in a consistent straight line - wandering	As above Wheel alignment incorrect (indicated by excessive or uneven tyre wear).	As above. Check wheel alignment.
	Front wheel hub bearings loose or worn	Adjust or renew as necessary.
	Worn ball joints or suspension arms	Renew as necessary.
Steering stiff and heavy	Incorrect wheel alignment (indicated by excessive or uneven tyre wear).	Check wheel alignment.
	Excessive wear or seizure in one or more of the joints in the steering linkage or suspension arm ball joints	Renew as necessary or grease the suspension unit ball joints.
	Excessive wear in the steering gear unit	Adjust if possible or renew.
Wheel wobble and vibration	Road wheels out of balance.	Balance wheels.
	Road wheels buckled	Check for damage.
	Wheel alignment incorrect	Check wheel alignment.
	Wear in the steering linkage, suspension arm ball joints or suspension arm pivot bushes	Check and renew as necessary.
	Broken front spring	Check and renew as necessary.
Excessive pitching and rolling on corners and during braking	Defective dampers and/or broken spring	Check and renew as necessary.

Chapter 12 Bodywork and underframe

Contents

1 General description

The combined body and underframe is of an all steel welded construction. This makes a very strong and torsionally ridged shell.

The Capri is only available in two door form. The door hinges are welded to the doors and securely bolted to the body. To prevent the doors opening too wide and causing damage check straps are fitted. The driver's door is locked from the outside by means of a key, the other door being locked from the inside.

Toughened safety glass is fitted to all windows; as an additional safety precaution the windscreen glass has a specially toughened 'Zone' in front of the driver. In the event of the windscreen shattering this 'Zone' breaks into much larger pieces than the rest of the screen thus giving the driver much better vision than would otherwise be possible.

The Capri uses the Aeroflow type of ventilation system. Air being drawn in through a grille on the scuttle can either be heated or pass straight into the car. Used air passes out through a grille at the base of the rear window.

All models are fitted with bucket type front seats with seat belts as standard. The rear seats are also fitted with anchor points for belts which can be obtained as an optional extra.

2 Maintenance - bodywork and underframe

1 The condition of your car's bodywork is of considerable importance as it is on this that the second-hand value of the car will mainly depend. It is very much more difficult to repair neglected bodywork than to renew mechanical assemblies. The hidden portions of the body, such as the wheel arches and the underframe and the engine compartment are equally important, through obviously not requiring such frequent attention as the immediately visible paintwork.

2 ... visit your local dealer and have the underside of the body steam cleaned. This will take about 1½ hours. All traces of dirt and oil will be removed and the underside can then be inspected carefully for rust, damaged hydraulic pipes, frayed electrical wiring and similar maladies. The car should be greased on completion of this job.

3 At the same time the engine compartment should be cleaned in the same manner. If steam cleaning facilities are not available then brush 'Gunk' or a similar cleanser over the whole engine and engine compartment with a stiff paint brush, working it well in where there is an accumulation of oil and dirt. Do not paint the ignition system but protect it with oily rags when the Gunk is washed off. As the Gunk is washed away it will take with it all traces of oil and dirt, leaving the engine looking clean and bright.

4 The wheel arches should be given particular attention as under-sealing can easily come away here and stones and dirt thrown up from the road wheels can soon cause the paint to chip and flake, and so allow rust to set in. If rust is found, clean down to the bare metal with wet and dry paper, paint on an anti-corrosive coating such as Kurust, or if preferred, red lead, and renew the paintwork and undercoating.

5 The bodywork should be washed once a week or when dirty. Thoroughly wet the car to soften the dirt and then wash the car down with a soft sponge and plenty of clean water. If the surplus dirt is not washed off very gently, in time it will wear the paint down as surely as wet and dry paper. It is best to use a hose if this is available. Give the car a final wash down and then dry with a soft chamois leather to prevent the formation of spots.

6 Spots of tar and grease thrown up from the road can be removed with a rag dampened with petrol.

7 Once every six months, or every three months if wished, give the bodywork and chromium trim a thoroughly good wax polish, if a chromium cleaner is used to remove rust on any of the car's plated parts remember that the cleaner also removes part of the chromium so use sparingly.

3 Maintenance - upholstery and carpets

1 Remove the carpets and thoroughly vacuum clean the interior of the car every three months or more frequently if necessary.
2 Beat out the carpets and vacuum clean them if they are very dirty. If the headlining or upholstery is soiled apply an upholstery cleaner with a damp sponge and wipe off with a clean dry cloth.

4 Maintenance - PVC external roof covering

Under no circumstances try to clean any external PVC roof covering with detergents, caustic soaps or spirit cleaners. Plain soap and water is all that is required with a soft brush to clean dirt that may be ingrained. Wash the covering as frequently as the rest of the car.

5 Minor body repairs

1 At some time during your ownership of your car it is likely that it will be bumped or scraped in a mild way, causing some slight damage to the body.
2 Major damage must be repaired by your local dealer, but there is no reason why you cannot successfully beat out, repair, and respray minor damage yourself. The essential items which the owner should gather together to ensure a really professional job are:—
a) A plastic filler.
b) Paint whose colour matches exactly that of the bodywork, either in a can for application by a spray gun, or in an aerosol can.
c) Fine cutting paste.
d) Medium and fine grade wet and dry paper.
3 Never use a metal hammer to knock out small dents as the blows tend to scratch and distort the metal. Knock out the dent with a mallet or rawhide hammer and press on the underside of the dented surface a metal dolly or smooth wooden block roughly contoured to the normal shape of the damaged area.
4 After the worst of the damaged area has been knocked out, rub down the dent and surrounding area with medium wet and dry paper and thoroughly clean away all traces of dirt.
5 The plastic filler comprises a paste and a hardener which must be thoroughly mixed together. Mix only a small portion at a time as the paste sets hard within five to fifteen minutes depending on the amount of hardener used.
6 Smooth on the filler with a knife or stiff plastic to the shape of the damaged portion and allow to thoroughly dry — a process which takes about six hours. After the filler has dried it is likely that it will have contracted slightly so spread on a second layer of filler if necessary.
7 Smooth down the filler with fine wet and dry paper wrapped round a suitable block of wood and continue until the whole area is perfectly smooth and it is impossible to feel where the filler joins the rest of the paintwork.
8 Spray on from an aerosol can, or with a spray gun, an anti-rust undercoat, smooth down with wet and dry paper, and then spray on two coats of the final finishing using a circular motion.
9 When thoroughly dry polish the whole area with a fine cutting paste to smooth the resprayed area into the remainder of the body and to remove the small particles of spray paint which

will have settled round the area.
10 This will leave the body looking perfect with not a trace of the previous unsightly dent.

6 Major body repairs

1 Because the body is built on the monocoque principle and is integral with the underframe, major damage must be repaired by competent mechanics with the necessary welding and hydraulic straightening equipment.
2 If the damage has been serious it is vital that the body is checked for correct alignment, as otherwise the handling of the car will suffer and many other faults such as excessive tyre wear and wear in the transmission and steering may occur. A special alignment jig is available to repair dealers; a repaired car should always be checked on this jig.

7 Maintenance - locks and hinges

Once every six months or 6,000 miles, the door, bonnet and boot hinges should be oiled with a few drops of engine oil from an oil can. The door striker plates can be given a thin smear of grease to reduce wear and ensure free movement.

8 Front bumper - removal and replacement

1 Undo the single retaining bolt on either end of the bumper from inside the front wings.
2 Working at the back of the bumper remove the nuts from the two chrome headed bolts, withdraw the bolts and lift the bumper away.
3 Replacement is a reversal of the above procedure, but before replacing the two bolts from inside the wings ensure that the bumper is correctly located. To make sure this is correct it is advisable not to tighten the centre nuts fully down until the end bolts have been located.

9 Rear bumper - removal and replacement

1 From behind the bumper bar remove the nuts from the four chrome headed bolts, withdraw the bolts and lift the bumper away.
2 Replacement is a direct reversal of the removal procedure, but it is advisable not to fully tighten down the nuts until it is certain that the bumper is perfectly straight and correctly located.

10 Windscreen glass - removal and replacement

1 If you are unfortunate enough to have a windscreen shatter, or should you wish to renew your present windscreen, fitting a replacement is one of the few jobs which the average owner is advised to leave to a professional. For the owner who wishes to attempt the job himself the following instructions are given.

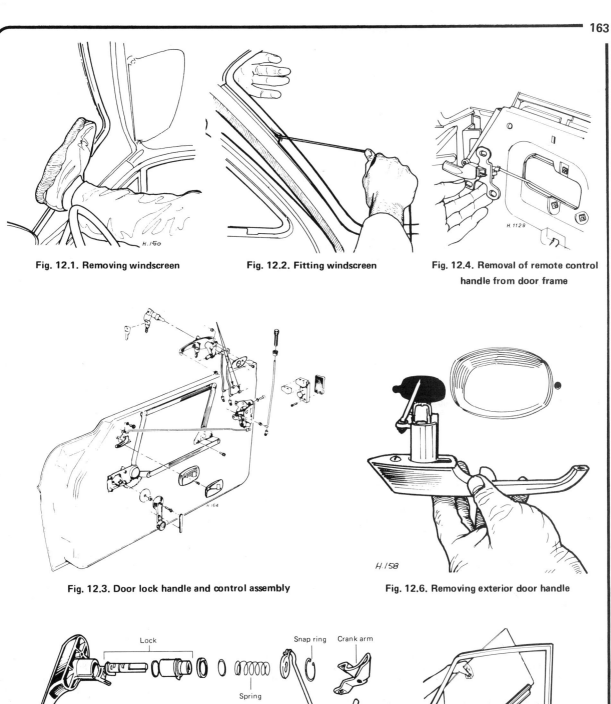

Fig. 12.1. Removing windscreen

Fig. 12.2. Fitting windscreen

Fig. 12.4. Removal of remote control handle from door frame

Fig. 12.3. Door lock handle and control assembly

Fig. 12.6. Removing exterior door handle

Lock

Snap ring   Crank arm

Spring

Door handle

Rod

Pivot pin

Fig. 12.5. Door handle and lock assembly

Fig. 12.7. Removal of door window glass

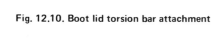

Fig. 12.10. Boot lid torsion bar attachment

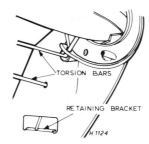

TORSION BARS

RETAINING BRACKET

2 Cover the bonnet with a blanket or cloth to prevent accidental damage and remove the windscreen wiper blades and arms as detailed in Chapter 10, Section 41.

3 Put on a pair of lightweight shoes and get into one of the front seats. With a piece of soft cloth between the soles of your shoes and the windscreen, place both feet in one top corner of the windscreen and push firmly.

4 When the weatherstrip has freed itself from the body flange in that area repeat the process at frequent intervals along the top edge of the windscreen until, from outside the car the glass and weatherstrip can be removed together.

5 If you are having to replace your windscreen due to a shattered screen, remove all traces of sealing compound and broken glass from the weatherstrip and body flange.

6 Move the heater controls to 'Hot' and 'Defrost' and switch on the blower motor. This will remove any glass fragments in the ducting. Be careful about flying glass so take necessary precautions.

7 Gently prize out the clip which covers the joint of the chromium finisher strip and pull the finisher strip out of the weatherstrip. Then remove the weatherstrip from the glass or if it is still on the car, as in the case of a shattered screen, remove it from the body flange.

8 To fit a new windscreen start by fitting the weatherstrip around the new windscreen glass.

9 Apply a suitable sealer such as Ford C5AZ—19554—A to the weatherstrip to body groove. In this groove then fit a fine but strong piece of cord right the way round the groove allowing an overlap of about six inches at the joint.

10 From outside the car place the windscreen in its correct position making sure that the loose end of the cord is inside the car.

11 With an assistant pressing firmly on the outside of the windscreen get into the car and slowly pull out the cord thus drawing the weatherstrip over the body flange.

12 Apply a further layer of sealer to the underside of rubber to glass groove from outside the car.

13 Replace the chromium finisher strip into its groove in the weatherstrip and replace the clip which covers its joint.

14 Carefully clean off any surplus sealer from the windscreen before it has a chance to harden and then replace the windscreen wiper arms and blades.

11 Door rattles - tracing and rectification

1 The most common case of door rattle is a misaligned, loose, or worn striker plate, however, other causes may be:—
a) Loose door or window winder handles.
b) Loose, or misaligned door lock components.
c) Loose or worn remote control mechanism.

2 It is quite possible for door rattles to be the result of a combination of the above faults so a careful examination should be made to determine the exact cause of the rattle.

3 If striker plate wear or misalignment is the cause of the rattle the plate should be renewed or adjusted as necessary. The procedures for these tasks are detailed in Section 12.

4 Should the window winder handle rattle, this can be easily rectified by inserting a rubber washer between the escutcheon and door trim panel.

5 If the rattle is found to be emanating from the door lock it will in all probability mean that the lock is worn and therefore should be replaced with a new unit as described in Section 14.

6 Lastly, if it is worn hinge pins causing the rattle they should be renewed. This is not a D.I.Y. job as a special tool is required for their removal and replacement.

12 Door striker plate - removal, replacement and adjustment

1 Striker plate removal and adjustment are not really D.I.Y. tasks as a special tool is required to turn the plate retaining screws. An ordinary screwdriver will not fit. However, if the tool (Churchill No. RIBE M6 special screwdriver) can be hired or loaned from your local dealers, proceed as follows;

2 If it is wished to renew a worn striker plate mark its position on the door pillar with a pencil. This will enable the new plate to be fitted in exactly the same position.

3 To remove the plate, simply undo the four special screws which hold the plate and anti-slip shim in position. Replacement is equally straightforward.

4 To adjust the striker plate slacken the retaining screws until the plate can just be moved, gently close the door, with the outside push button depressed, to the fully closed position. Release the button.

5 Move the door in and out until it is flush with the surrounding bodywork. Then fully depress the button and gently open the door.

6 Check that the striker plate is vertical and tighten down the four special screws. Adjustment is now completed.

13 Door trim panel - removal and replacement

1 Carefully prise the black plastic trim from its recess in the window winder handle. This will expose the handle retaining screws. Remove the screw, handle and escutcheon.

2 Unscrew the screw securing the escutcheon in position. Remove the escutcheon.

3 Unscrew and remove the black plastic knob on the interior door lock. Carefully prise the escutcheon beneath it out of the trim.

4 Remove the two screws securing the lower part of the armrest. Move the armrest towards the top front corner of the door. This will release the retaining lug. Remove the armrest complete.

5 Insert a thin strip of metal with all the sharp edges removed (a six inch steel rule is ideal) between the door and the recessed trim panel. This will release one or two of the panel retaining clips without damaging the trim. The panel can now be gently eased off by hand. Removal is now complete.

6 Replacement is generally a reversal of the removal procedure. NOTE: When replacing the panel ensure that each of the panel retaining clips is firmly located in its hole by sharply striking the panel in the approximate area of each clip with the palm of the hand. This will eliminate the possibility of the trim rattling.

14 Door lock assembly - removal and replacement

1 Remove the door trim panel as described in Section 13.

2 Temporarily replace the window winder handle and wind the window up. Remove the polythene sheet covering the interior of the door by cutting through the adhesive around its periphery with a sharp blade.

3 Disconnect the remote control rod by freeing it from the clip at the remote handle end.

4 Disconnect the push button rod, exterior operating rod and locking rod from the lock by releasing their clips.

5 Unscrew and remove the two screws securing the window channel.

6 Remove the three screws securing the lock to the door, the lock can now be withdrawn. Remove the four rod connecting clips from the lock. Removal is now complete.

7 Replacement: Replace the four rod connecting clips on the lock.

8 Reposition the lock assembly in the door recess and secure it with the three screws. Replace the two window channel retaining screws.

9 Reconnect all operating rods, and check the operation of the lock.

10 Replace the polythene sheet over the door apertures, using a suitable adhesive, followed by the door trim panel and fitments.

15 Door lock interior remote control handle - removal and replacement

1 Remove the door trim panel as described in Section 13, followed by the polythene sheet covering the door apertures.

2 Disconnect the spring clip securing the remote control operating rod to the lock mechanism.

3 Remove the three screws securing the remote control assembly to the door inner panel. Push out the anti-rattle clip around the remote control operating rod and remove the remote control assembly through the door access hole. Removal is now complete.

4 Replacement is a straightforward reversal of the removal procedure.

16 Door glass - removal and replacement

1 First remove the door trim panel and window regulator assembly as described in Sections 13 and 20 respectively.

2 The window glass can now be rotated through 90⁰ and remove through the top of the door.

3 Replacement is a straightforward reversal of the removal procedure.

17 Door outer belt weatherstrip - removal and replacement

1 Wind the window down to its fullest extent. Carefully prise the weatherstrip out of the groove in the door outer bright metal finish moulding.

2 Replacement: Correctly position the weatherstrip over its groove. With the thumbs, carefully press the strip fully into the groove.

3 Wind the window up and check that the weatherstrip is correctly fitted.

18 Bonnet - removal and replacement

1 Open the bonnet lid and prop it in the open position with its stay.

2 Using a suitable sharp implement scribe a line around the exterior of the hinges in the bonnet. Unscrew and remove the two nuts and washers on each side, followed by the bolt plates.

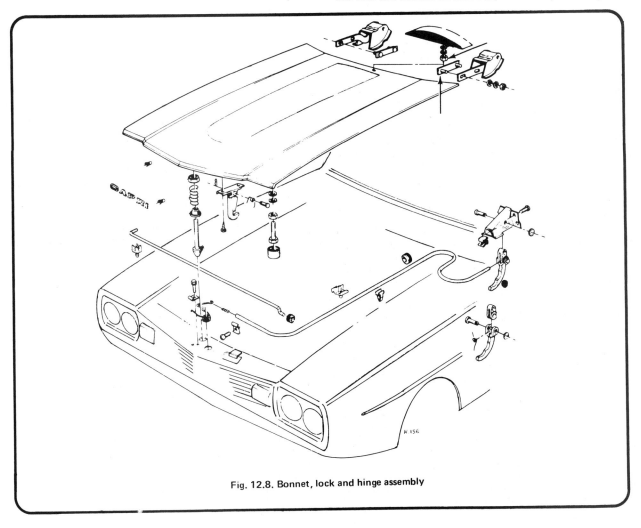

Fig. 12.8. Bonnet, lock and hinge assembly

With the help of an assistant the bonnet can now be lifted off, after releasing the stay.

3   Replacement is a reversal of the removal procedure. However, before finally tightening the nuts which secure the bonnet ensure that the hinges are correctly aligned with the scribed lines. This will ensure correct bonnet/body alignment.
.

19 Boot lid - removal and replacement

1   Open the boot lid to its fullest extent. Using a suitable implement scribe a line around the exterior of the hinges.
2   Remove the two bolts and washers on each side securing the boot lid to its hinges. With assistance the boot lid can now be lifted off.
3   Replacement is a reversal of the removal procedure, however, before fully tightening the boot lid securing bolts ensure that the hinges are aligned with the scribed marks in the lid. This will ensure correct boot lid/body alignment.

20 Window regulator - removal and replacement

1   Remove the door trim panel as described in Section 13. Carefully peel off the polythene sheet over the door apertures.
2   Temporarily replace the window regulator handle and wind the window down. Remove the seven screws securing the regulator assembly to the door.
3   Carefully draw the regulator assembly towards the rear of the door, this will disengage it from the rubber in the base of the window glass.
4   Push the window glass up and support it in the raised position with a wedge. The regulator assembly can now be withdrawn through the access hole in the door.
5   Refitting the regulator is the reverse sequence to removal. Lubricate all moving parts.

21 Heater assembly - removal and replacement

1   Remove the earth terminal connection from the battery. Remove the radiator cap, open the cooling system drain taps and allow all of the coolant to drain. NOTE: If the coolant contains anti-freeze, drain it into a suitable container, this will allow the coolant to be re-used.
2   Next remove the seven cross-head screws securing the under-dash cowl panel, followed by the four parcel shelf securing trim clips, two each side. Remove the two screws on the passenger side, and one on the driver's side, and withdraw the parcel shelf.
3   Slacken the two wire clips and disconnect the two heater pipes from their unions on the bulkhead. This is done from inside the engine compartment.
4   Still in the engine compartment, remove the two screws holding the heater pipe plate and sealing gasket to the bulkhead. Detach the plate and gasket from the bulkhead.
5   Remove the ashtray and pull off the heater control knobs. Detach the heater control quadrant from the dashboard, by removing its two securing screws. Withdraw the control quadrant

from beneath the dashboard.
6   Remove the temperature control and direction control outer cable clips from the quadrant plate and detach the two inner cables from the control levers.
7   Note the wiring positions and detach the wires from the heater blower motor.
8   Working under the facia pull the air supply pipe from the face level vent. Remove the belt rail finishing strip by unscrewing the three securing screws. The face level vent assembly can then be removed after undoing its three securing screws. To gain access to one of the mounting screws at the left side of the heater assembly the windscreen wiper motor must be removed. Refer to Chapter 10, Section 43.
9   If a floor console is fitted this must next be removed. Otherwise proceed to paragraph 16.
10 Using a small screwdriver ease up the wood grain panel in front of the handbrake lever. Lift away the panel. Undo and remove the two screws securing the forward end of the console to the floor.
11 Carefully lift the gear change lever rubber boot up and remove the two screws at the rear end.
12 With a screwdriver ease up the rear panel and remove the two screws.
13 Carefully prise up the clock wood grain panel and disconnect the two electrical connectors and one illumination bulb.
14 Undo and remove the main securing screw at the rear end under the clock panel.
15 Slide the plastic brace below the handbrake lever forwards and remove it. The console may now be lifted away from inside the car.
16 Finally remove the four retaining bolts and withdraw the heater assembly.
17 Replacement is generally a reversal of the removal procedure. NOTE: When the heater assembly is reinstalled it will probably be necessary to adjust the heater control cables as detailed in Section 24.

22 Heater motor - removal and replacement

1   Remove the heater assembly as described in Section 21.
2   Release the eight clips that hold the two halves of the heater assembly together.
3   Release the retaining clips from the temperature control flap shaft and withdraw the shaft.
4   Lift away the heater radiator tube gasket.
5   Detach the electric cables from the resistor pack and separate the upper half of the assembly from the lower half.
6   Disconnect the two cables from the motor and then release the four clips that hold the motor to the centre hub.
7   Carefully lift away the motor and fan assembly.
8   Reassembly of the motor and casing is the reverse sequence to removal.

23 Heater radiator - removal and replacement

1   Remove the heater assembly as described in Section 21.
2   Separate the two halves of the assembly as described in Section 22, paragraphs 2 to 5 inclusive.
3   The radiator may now be withdrawn from the lower half of the heater.
4   Refitting the radiator and reassembly is the reverse sequence to removal.

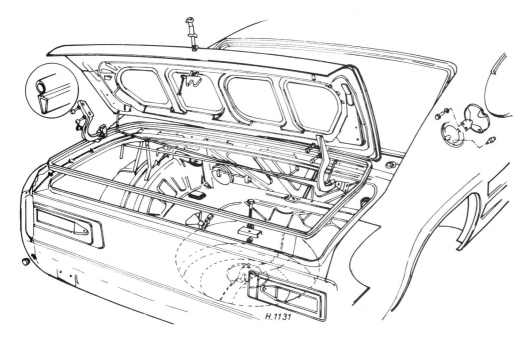

Fig. 12.9. Luggage compartment fittings

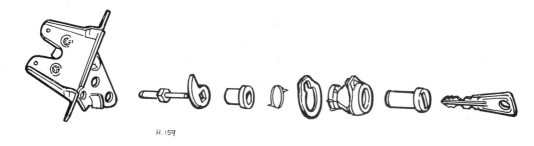

Fig. 12.11. Boot lid lock assembly

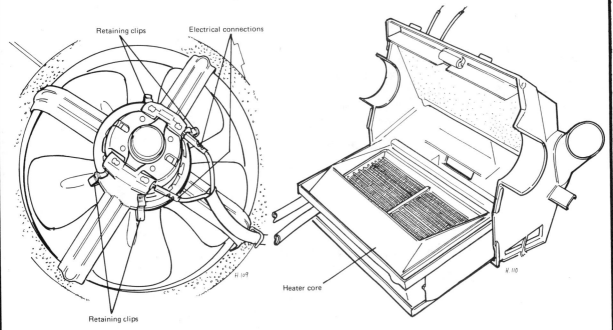

Retaining clips   Electrical connections

Retaining clips

Heater core

Fig. 12.14. Heater motor and fan assembly   **Fig. 12.15. Removal of heater unit radiator**

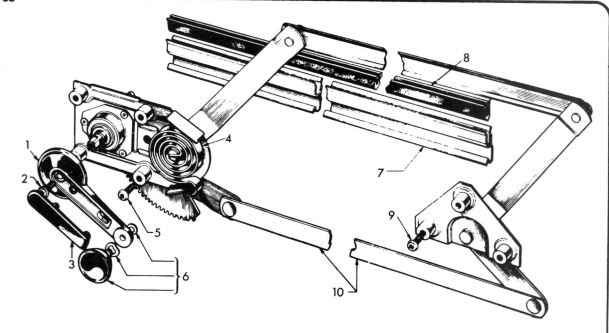

FIG. 12.12. WINDOW CONTROL ASSEMBLY

1 Escutcheon	4 Spring	7 Channel	10 Regulator assembly
2 Retaining screw	5 Screw	8 Sealing strip	
3 Insert	6 Handle assembly	9 Screw	

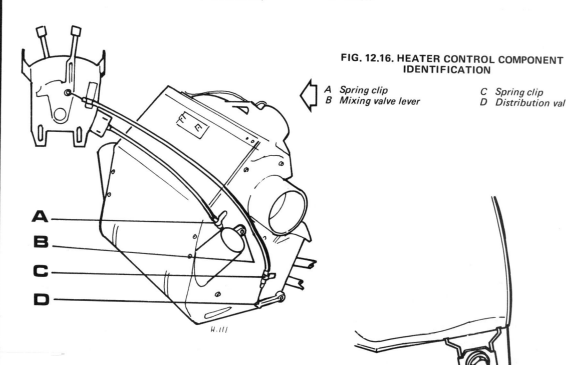

FIG. 12.16. HEATER CONTROL COMPONENT IDENTIFICATION

A Spring clip   C Spring clip
B Mixing valve lever   D Distribution valve lever

Fig. 12.17. Rear seat securing bolt

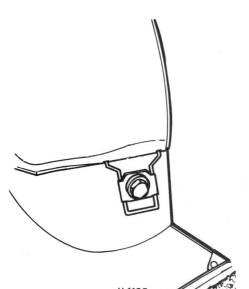

H.1125

24 Heater control cables - adjustment

1 Control cable adjustment should be carried out whenever the control cables have been disconnected from the heater, or if the heater cannot be operated correctly.

2 Move the lower control lever to the extreme left position and release the spring clip that secures the direction control cable to the heater body.

3 Move the floor-defrost door to the off position by rotating the lever up to the end of its travel.

4 Slide the end of the outer cable to the floor defrost lever and secure to the heater body with the spring clip.

5 To adjust the temperature control cable move the upper control lever to the extreme left position.

6 Release the spring clip that secures the temperature control cable to the heater.

7 Move the temperature blend door firmly to the maximum heat position by rotating the door lever up to the end of its travel.

8 Slide the end of the outer cable to the temperature blend door lever and secure to the heater body with the spring clip.

25 Front seat - removal and replacement

1 Undo and remove the two bolts and spring washers that secure the front ends of the seat mounting brackets to the box member on the front panel.

2 Release the seat locking catch and tip the seat forwards. Undo and remove the two bolts and washers that secure the rear ends of the seat mounting brackets to the floor panel.

3 Carefully lift away the seat and mounting brackets.

4 Refitting the front seat is the reverse sequence to removal. Lubricate all moving parts to ensure ease of operation.

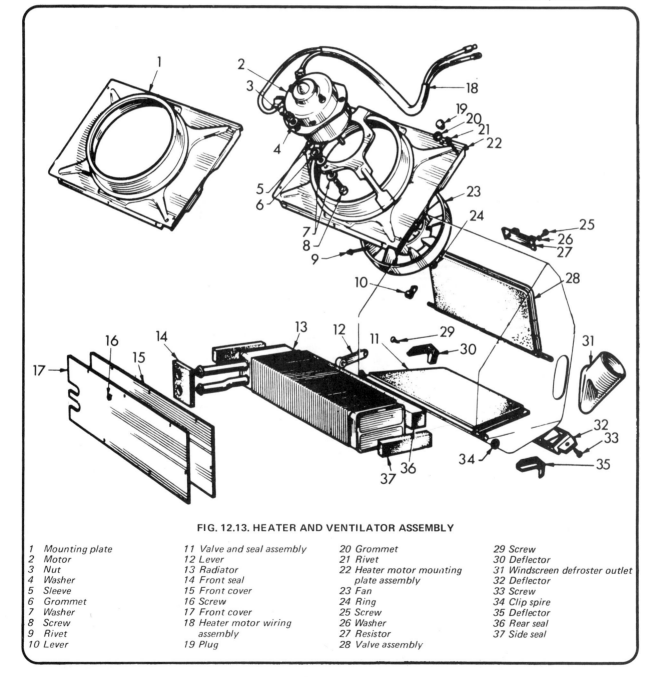

FIG. 12.13. HEATER AND VENTILATOR ASSEMBLY

1	Mounting plate	11	Valve and seal assembly	20	Grommet	29 Screw
2	Motor	12	Lever	21	Rivet	30 Deflector
3	Nut	13	Radiator	22	Heater motor mounting	31 Windscreen defroster outlet
4	Washer	14	Front seal		plate assembly	32 Deflector
5	Sleeve	15	Front cover	23	Fan	33 Screw
6	Grommet	16	Screw	24	Ring	34 Clip spire
7	Washer	17	Front cover	25	Screw	35 Deflector
8	Screw	18	Heater motor wiring	26	Washer	36 Rear seal
9	Rivet		assembly	27	Resistor	37 Side seal
10	Lever	19	Plug	28	Valve assembly	

26 Rear seat - removal and replacement

1   Unscrew and remove the two crosshead screws located at the lower edge of the cushion. Lift away the cushion.
2   Open the boot lid and from inside the boot compartment turn the seat pegs with a screwdriver so as to release them from the two spring clips that secure the top of the rear backrest.
3   Unscrew the two bolts located one each side at the lower corner and lift away the bracket from inside the car.
4   Refitting the rear seat backrest and cushion is the reverse sequence to removal.

27 Front parcel shelf - removal and replacement

1   Undo and remove the two screws and two nuts and washers that secure the parcel shelf in the area around the bonnet release catch handle.
2   Undo and remove the two screws and washers that secure the fuse panel and carefully move to one side.
3   Undo and remove the four access trim panel attaching screws and washers and also the map light retaining clip.
4   Undo and remove the two screws that secure the map light.
5   Undo and remove the two screws that secure the map light bracket.
6   Undo and remove the one nut and washer located on the right hand inside of the parcel shelf compartment.
7   Release the two plastic pins each side of the parcel shelf and then lift away the parcel shelf from inside the car.
8   Refitting the parcel shelf is the reverse sequence to removal.

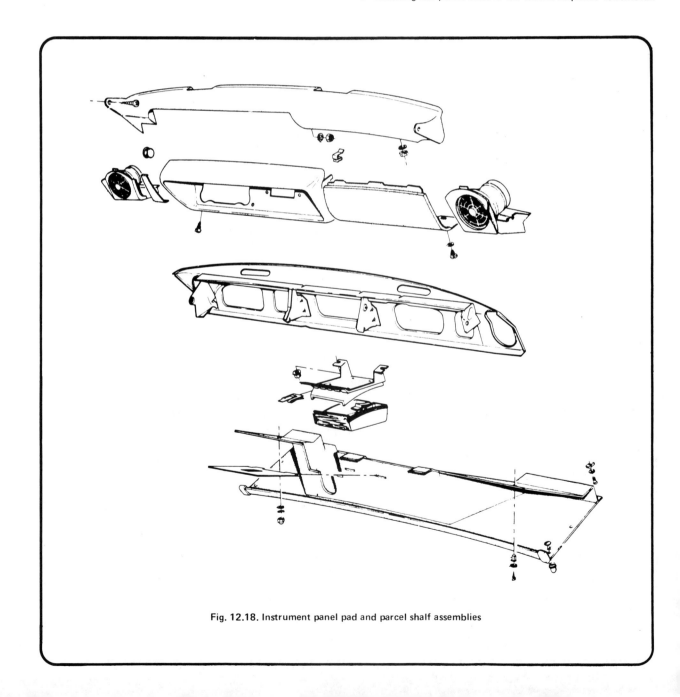

Fig. 12.18. Instrument panel pad and parcel shalf assemblies

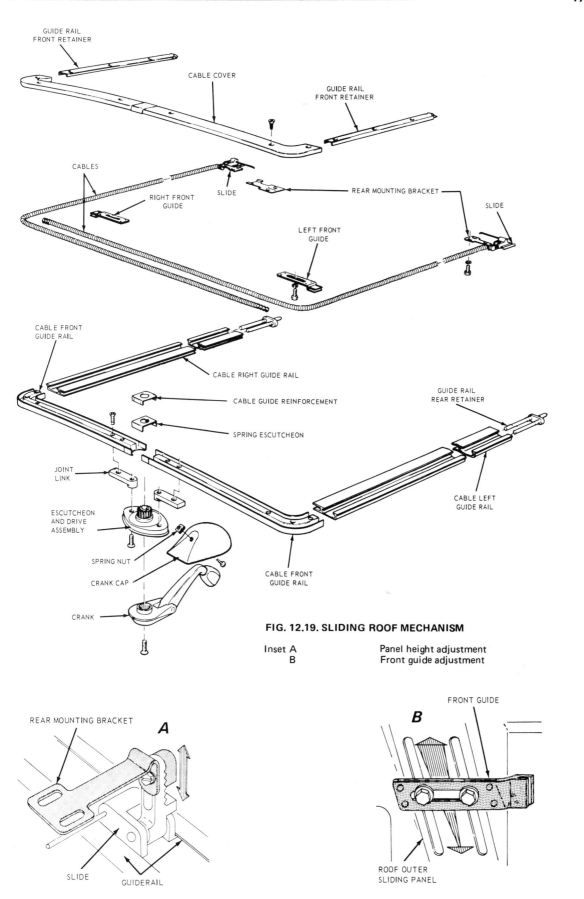

FIG. 12.19. SLIDING ROOF MECHANISM

Inset A   Panel height adjustment
     B   Front guide adjustment

28 Floor console - removal and replacement

1   Using a small screwdriver ease up the wood grain panel in front of the handbrake lever. Lift away the panel.
2   Undo and remove the two screws securing the forward end of the console to the floor.
3   Carefully lift the gear change lever rubber boot up and remove the two screws at the rear end.
4   With a screwdriver ease up the rear panel and remove the two screws.
5   Carefully prise up the clock wood grain panel and disconnect the two electrical connectors and one illumination bulb.
6   Undo and remove the main securing screw at the rear end under the clock panel.
7   Slide the plastic brace below the hand brake lever forwards and remove it. The console may now be lifted away from inside the car.

8   Refitting the console is the reverse sequence to removal.

29 Instrument panel pad - removal and replacement

1   Undo and remove the two screws that secure the left and right 'A' pillar post garnish mouldings.
2   Undo and remove each corner screw which will be visible once the garnish mouldings have been removed.
3   Refer to Chapter 10 and remove the instrument cluster panel pad assembly.
4   Undo and remove the two nuts and washers which are located immediately above the instrument cluster opening.
5   Undo and remove the one remaining nut and washer which is located on the right hand side of the instrument panel pad.
6   Carefully draw the instrument panel pad away from the instrument panel assembly.
7   Refitting the instrument panel pad is the reverse sequence to removal.

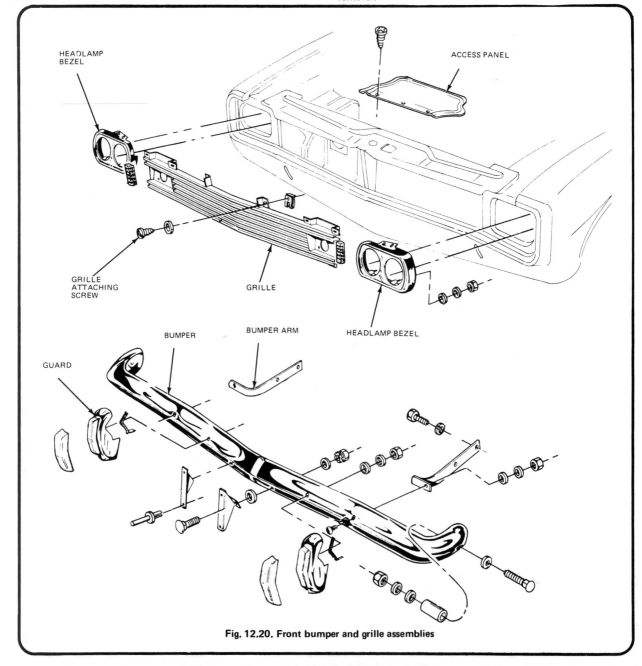

HEADLAMP BEZEL

ACCESS PANEL

GRILLE ATTACHING SCREW

GRILLE

HEADLAMP BEZEL

GUARD

BUMPER

BUMPER ARM

Fig. 12.20. Front bumper and grille assemblies

30 Sun roof panel - adjustment, removal and replacement

The slide and control assembly is shown in Fig. 12.18 and it will be seen that the roof panel is able to slide forwards and rearwards on guide rails when the crank handle is operated. The handle is splined to a little pinion which drives two flexible cables, these being attached to a slide which move rearwards or forwards in one of the two guide rails.

The left and right hand slides are attached to rear brackets which are secured to the rear of the sliding panel at the left and right hand sides. The left and right front guides are attached to the front of the sliding panel also slide on the left and right guide rails respectively.

Because the interior trim panels have to be removed for access to the sun roof panel it is recommended that these jobs be left to the local Capri Agent or body specialist.

31 Front grille - removal and replacement

1   Undo and remove the two lower nuts and washers that secure each headlamp bezel to the body. Access to these is gained from the rear of each headlight unit.
2   Undo and remove the two upper screws that secure each headlight bezel.
3   Undo and remove the ten screws that secure the grille to the body. Draw the grille downwards and detach the parking light bulbs.
4   Each parking light unit may be removed once the two securing nuts and washers have been removed.
5   Refitting the front grille is the reverse sequence to removal.

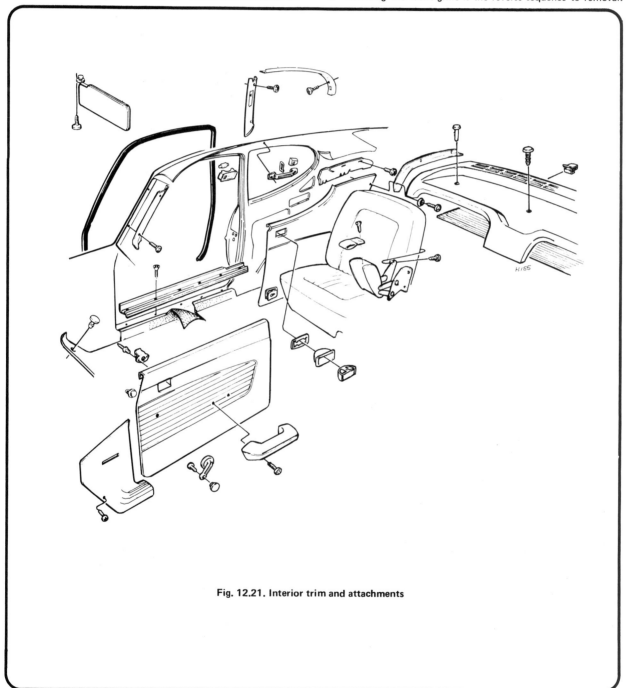

Fig. 12.21. Interior trim and attachments

Chapter 13 Supplement for 171 cu in (2792 cc) models

Contents

Specifications (where different from those previously given)

Engine
General
Bore	3.66 in.	92.961 mm
Stroke	2.70 in.	68.58 mm
Cubic capacity	170.8 cu in.	2800 cc
Oil pressure (hot at 1500 rpm)	40 lb/in.^{2} minimum	

Cylinder block
Bore diameter* (standard):
Class 1	3.6616 in.	(93.0046 mm)
Class 2	3.6620 in.	(93.0148 mm)
Class 3	3.6624 in.	(93.0250 mm)
Class 4	3.6630 in.	(93.0402 mm)

*All dimensions ± 0.0002 in. (0.005 mm)
Bore diameter* (oversize):
0.020 service	3.6821 in.	(93.5253 mm)
0.040 service	3.7018 in.	(94.0257 mm)

*All dimensions ± 0.0002 (0.005 mm)

Pistons

Piston clearance	0.001 to 0.0025 in. (0.025 to 0.038 mm)
Piston diameter:	
Standard	3.6605 to 3.6614 in. (92.9767 to 93.00 mm)
Oversize (0.020 in.)	3.6802 to 3.6812 in. (93.477 to 93.5025 mm)
Oversize (0.040 in.)	3.6999 to 3.7009 in. (93.9775 to 94.003 mm)

Cylinder head

Valve clearance (cold-only):	
Inlet	0.014 in. (0.36 mm)
Exhaust	0.016 in. (0.4 mm)

Torque wrench settings

	lb ft	Kg m
Support bracket to engine	40 to 45	(5.5 to 6.2)
Support bracket to insulator	17 to 27	(2.35 to 3.73)
Insulator to frame	17 to 27	(2.35 to 3.73)
Crossmember to frame bracket	10 to 13	(1.38 to 1.8)
Insulator to crossmember	12 to 15	(1.66 to 2.07)
Insulator to transmission bracket	13 to 16	(1.8 to 2.21 kg m)
Transmission bracket securing bolt	37 to 42	(5.1 to 5.8)
Flywheel	47 to 52	(6.45 to 7.12)
Front cover	12 to 15	(1.66 to 2.1)
Water pump	6 to 9	(0.83 to 1.24)
Rocker shaft supports	43 to 49	(5.9 to 6.76)
Rocker arm covers	2 to 5	(0.28 to 0.69)
Spark plugs	15 to 22	(2.1 to 3)
Vibration damper bolt	92 to 104	(12.7 to 14.4)

Cooling system
Viscous drive fan assembly now fitted

Fuel system and carburation
Fuel pump

Delivery pressure	3.5 to 5.5 lb/in^2 (0.245 to 0.385 kg/cm^2)
Flow rate	1 pt/15 seconds (0.43 litres/15 seconds)
Lift	0.193 to 0.213 in. (4.9 to 5.4 mm)

Emission control systems
Revised specification (see text)

Ignition system
Distributor

Type:	
Manual - Ford Part Number	74TF - 12100 - NA
Automatic - Ford Part number	74TF - 12100 - RA
Contact breaker points gap	0.023 to 0.027 in. (0.58 to 0.69 mm)
Dwell angle	37 to 410

Propeller shaft and universal joints
Constant velocity type centre coupling now used on some models

Braking system
Rear brake:

Lining width	2.70 in. (55.4 mm)
Total swept area	123 sq in. (795 sq cm)

Electrical system
Alternator

Speed (ratio to engine)	2.2 : 1

Regulator

Voltage setting	13.7 to 14.4 volts

Fuse unit

		Fuse number	Fuse rating
Number of fuses	7		
Circuits protected:			
Cigar lighter, clock, interior light		1	16 amp
Number plate, instrument cluster lamps		2	8 amp
Right-hand front and tail lights		3	8 amp
Left-hand front and tail lights		4	8 amp
Heater blower, horn		5	16 amp
Reverse light, wiper motor, instruments		6	16 amp
Stop lights, direction indicators		7	16 amp

Suspension and steering

Rear suspension

Type	Semi elliptic rear springs with stabilizer bar

Steering gear

Maximum wheel lock angles (theoretical):

back	37°
front	34°30'

Torque wrench settings

	lb ft	kg m
Rear spring 'U' bolts	18 to 26	2.5 to 3.6
Stabilizer bar brackets to rear axle	29 to 37	4 to 5.1
Stabilizer bar bushing fitting to body	33 to 37	4.6 to 5.1
Locknuts on stabilizer bar bushing fitting	26 to 30	3.6 to 4.1

Bodywork and underframe

Air conditioning system

Type	Ford, integral

Drivebelt tension (cold) using tool number 'T63L-8620-A'

New belt	140 lb
Used belt	110 lb
Allowable compressor clutch runout	1/32 in. (0.8 mm) max.

Torque wrench settings

	lb ft	kg m
Back plate	9 to 17	1.24 to 2.35
Base plate	14 to 22	1.93 to 3.04
Clutch mounting	20 to 30	2.76 to 4.14
Cylinder head	15 to 23	2.07 to 3.17
Front seal plate	7 to 13	0.97 to 1.79
Mounting bolt	20 to 30	2.76 to 4.14
Oil filter plug	4 to 11	0.55 to 1.52

Introduction

This supplement to the Owners' Workshop Manual has been added to cover the production modifications for 1974 onward models. The most important of these modifications are:

1 Engine capacity increased from 2600 (155 cu in) to 2800 cc (171 cu in)
2 The addition of a viscous drive cooling fan assembly.
3 A modified emission control system to meet the requirements of the 1974 Federal emissions standards with regard to crankcase, exhaust and evaporative pollutants.
4 A constant velocity type centre propeller shaft bearing on some models.
5 An increase in lining width for the rear brakes.
6 A modified rear suspension which incorporates a stabilizer bar instead of two radius arms.
7 Impact resistant front and rear bumpers.
8 An optional fitment air conditioning pack.
9 An electrically assisted, water heated, automatic choke.
10 A starter interlock seat belt system.
11 A modified facia layout.

Although there have been comparatively few changes for these later models, there are some instances where torque values and certain other information have been altered. It is therefore very important that the reader refers to the appropriate Section before commencing any repair work or adjustment.

Chapter 13 is divided in Sections which each relate to one of the preceding 12 Chapters in the manual. There Sections detail the differences between components and working procedures for 1974 onward model. If a component or procedure is not specifically mentioned it can be assumed that it remains the same as for earlier models - and is covered by one of the first 12 Chapters in this manual.

Each Section is broken down into sub-Sections (headed in italic type). The sub-Sections detail working procedures for a particular component or mechanism within the system encompassed by the Section.

Routine maintenance

In addition to the Routine Maintenance schedule given at the beginning of the manual, the following items are now applicable for 1974 onward models.

Every 6000 miles (10000 km) or 6 months

1 Renew the fuel filter in the carburettor (first 6000 miles

only).

2   Check the tightness of inlet manifold bolts.

3   Inspect all the drivebelts for deterioration and adjust as necessary.

4   Arrange for your local Ford dealer to inspect/adjust **all** the items in the emission control systemss.

Every 12000 miles (20000 km) or 12 months)

1   Remove the oil filler cap from the rocker housing, swill the complete item in petrol, shake it dry, inspect it for damage, then refit it to the car (or renew it if damaged).

1   Engine

1   General description

Apart from the increased cylinder bore and piston stroke, the engine is similar to the 2600 cc (155 cu in) version described in Chapter 1.

2   Engine - removal without gearbox

The procedure for removal of the engine without the gearbox is similar to that described in Chapter 1 for the 2600 cc (155 cu in) engine. However, if a 'thermactor' system is fitted, pipes and/or parts must first be removed to provide adequate clearance as the engine is being lifted out. If an air conditioning system is fitted to the car, the refrigerant charge must be drained before the pipes are disconnected. (See Section 8.10).

3   Engine ancilliaries - removal

1   In addition to the items listed in Section 9, of Chapter 1, the following items should also be included, where appropriate:

1   The items applicable to the emission control system.

2   The air conditioning compressor and associated equipment.

4   Engine reassembly - general note

The procedures given for engine reassembly, in Chapter 1, are applicable to the 2800 cc engine but the following points should be noted:

a)   The sump bolts should be tightened in the sequence shown in Fig 13.2.

b)   The inlet manifold bolts should be tightened in the sequence shown in Fig 13.3.

c)   The cylinder head bolts should be tightened in the sequence shown in Fig 13.4.

d)   No gaskets are used on the exhaust manifolds when fitting to the block. The sealing faces should be lightly smeared with a graphited grease before being fitted. After fitting the right-hand exhaust manifold the manifold shroud must be fitted.

e)   The items of equipment in the emission control system and the air conditioning compressor (as applicable) must also be refitted.

5   Engine - replacement without gearbox

The procedure for engine replacement is similar to that described in Chapter 1, but it will also be necessary to refit any pipes to the emission control system and air conditioning system. Where applicable, the air conditioning system will require evacuating and recharging as described in Section 8.10

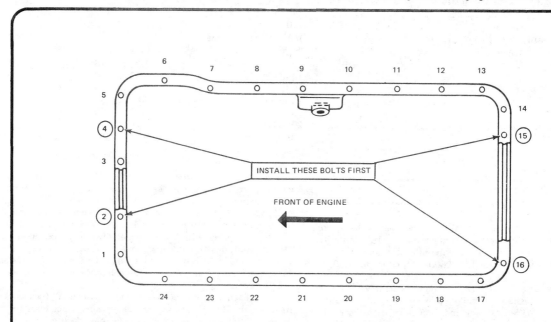

Fig. 13.2. The tightening sequence for the sump (oil pan) bolts

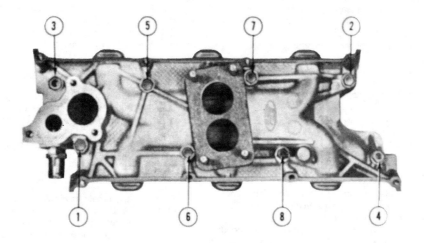

Fig. 13.3. The tightening sequence for the inlet manifold bolts

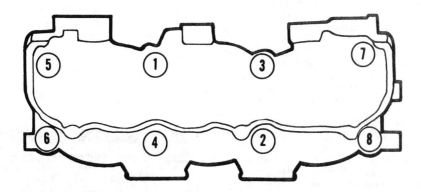

Fig. 13.4. The tightening sequence for the cylinder head bolts

2 Cooling system

1 Viscous drive fan assembly - general description

1 On 1974 onward mdoels a viscous drive unit is fitted to the cooling fan. This is designed to operate at reduced speed when the engine is rotating at high speed and therefore absorb less power and produces less noise.
2 The drive unit works on the principle of a torque ocnverter and acts in a manner similar to a slipping clutch once a predetermined engine speed has been reached.

2 Viscous drive fan assembly - removal and refitting

1 Remove the radiator, as described in Section 2.2.
2 Loosen the centre bolt of the viscous drive coupling.
3 Undo and remove the four nuts and bolts attaching the coupling to the fan, then separate the fan and coupling.
4 When refitting, attach the coupling to the fan with the four bolts and nuts.
5 Position the assembly on the water pump extension shaft and fit the centre bolt. Tighten the bolt to the specified torque.
6 Refit the radiator (see Section 2.2 if necessary).

3 Radiator - removal and refitting

1 On 1974 onward models, a radiator/fan shroud is fitted between the radiator and the fan.
2 The procedure for removal of the radiator, which is given in

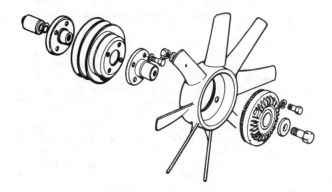

Fig. 13.5. The viscous drive fan assembly

Chapter 2, Section 5, is still applicable; but before the radiator retaining bolts can be removed it is necessary to remove the four screw and washer assemblies which secure the shroud, then slide the shroud back over the fan.

3   Refitting is a reverse of the removal procedure.

3   Fuel system and carburation

1   General description

The fuel system for 1974 onward models is still essentially the same as for earlier models. However, due to revised Federal emissions standards, modifications have been made to the emission control systems and have necessitated the modification of the choke control so that it is electrically assisted in its operation.

All 1974 onward cars are equipped with a decal label containing emission control data for that particular engine. The details on the label must be complied with.

Two deceleration valves are now used to provide enriched mixture during engine deceleration. As this occurs with a closed throttle, the valves provide a momentary fuel/air flow into the inlet manifold, bypassing the carburettor. Whereas, only one valve was previously used, the second valve is modified for control by a temperature sensitive ported vacuum switch (PVS) valve.

The electrically assisted choke comprises a positive temperature coefficient (PTC) device, powered from the centre tapping of the alternator, and installed between the choke thermostatic spring and choke casting. It is energised at all times whilst the engine is running.

To provide closer control over ignition advance and retard, a spark delay valve (SDV) is fitted. This slows down air flow in the distributor vacuum line.

The engine is fitted with a closed crankcase emission control system which features a ventilated crankcase filler cap and vacuum operated positive crankcase ventilation (PCV) valve. This permits engine fumes to recirculate into the inlet manifold and allows fresh air into the crankcase through the filler cap.

In order to reduce the carbon monoxide and hydrocarbon content passed to the atmosphere in exhaust gases, a Thermactor Exhaust Emission Control System is added. This pumps fresh air into the hot exhaust gas stream through a port near the exhaust valve, and has the effect of adding oxygen to the gases which are then mainly converted to carbon dioxide and steam. This system comprises an engine driven air supply pump, an air bypass valve which dumps some of the fresh air back to the atmosphere during over - run to prevent backfiring, an exhaust check valve which prevents the reverse flow of exhaust gases in the event of low pressure or faulty pump operation, and the associated interconnecting pipes.

A further aid to the control of exhaust emissions is the Exhaust Gas Recirculation (EGR) System which reduces the generation of nitrous oxides by re-introducing small amounts of exhaust gas into the combustion cycle. The amount of exhaust gas which is re-introduced and the timing of the cycle are controlled by such factors as engine vacuum, temperature and vehicle speed.

The exhaust gas recirculation valve (EGR) valve is vacuum operated and fitted to a spacer beneath the carburettor. A venturi vacuum amplifier uses the weak vacuum signal in the carburettor throat to develop a strong signal to operate the EGR valve. The amplifier comprises a vacuum reservoir and check valve to maintain adequate vacuum regardless of engine manifold vacuum. A relief valve is used to dump the EGR signal when the venturi vacuum signal is equal to a greater than the inlet manifold vacuum. Therefore at, or near, full throttle conditions the EGR valve is allowed to close when maximum engine power is required.

2   Emission control systems - adjustments

In view of the complexities of the systems it is most unwise to attempt to adjust or dismantle any of the items. In the event of malfunction of the carburation system, whether it be an irregular idling speed, petrol fumes, exhaust smoke or engine running on after the ignition is switched off, it is imperative that the local Ford dealer is consulted.

3   Carburettor with electrically assisted choke - general note

The instructions given in Sections 12 and 13, of Chapter 3, are equally applicable to the later carburettor except that the electrical lead must be disconnected when removing the carburettor from the car, and the gasket which lies between the thermostatic housing and choke housing is replaced by the electric choke heater.

4   Accelerator cable - adjustment

1   To adjust the accelerator cable where manual transmission is fitted, hold the throttle pedal down with a suitable weight and reposition the accelerator cable in the retaining clip as necessary.

2   Where automatic transmission is fitted, adjust the accelerator cable as described in the preceeding paragraph, then place the transmission lever in full 'kick-down' position. Referring to Fig. 13.20. adjust nuts 'A' and 'B' to give the specified clearance between the throttle operating rod and the carburettor linkage 'kick-down' lever.

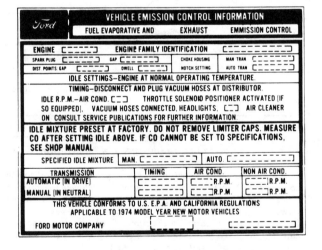

Fig. 13.6. Typical emission control decal

EMISSION CONTROL SYSTEM COMPONENT APPLICATION

	DUAL DIAPHRAGM DISTRIBUTOR	EGR	DECEL VALVE	VACUUM RESERVOIR	THERMACTOR
2800 cc MANUAL	CALIFORNIA ONLY *	YES	YES	CALIFORNIA ONLY	YES
2800 cc AUTOMATIC	CALIFORNIA ONLY *	YES	NO	CALIFORNIA ONLY	YES

*VEHICLES SOLD OUTSIDE CALIFORNIA WILL BE FITTED WITH A COMMON DUAL DIAPHRAGM DISTRIBUTOR BUT THE SECONDARY (RETARD) DIAPHRAGM WILL BE OPEN TO ATMOSPHERE

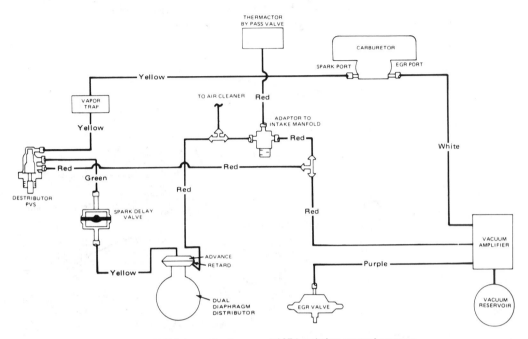

Fig. 13.7 Schematic diagram of 1974 emission control systems

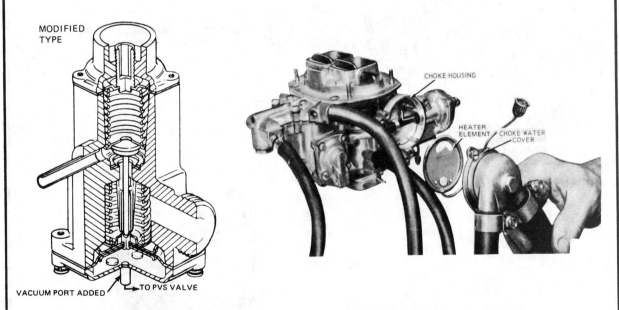

Fig. 13.8. Modified deceleration valve for control by a PVS valve

Fig. 13.9. The electrically assisted choke

182

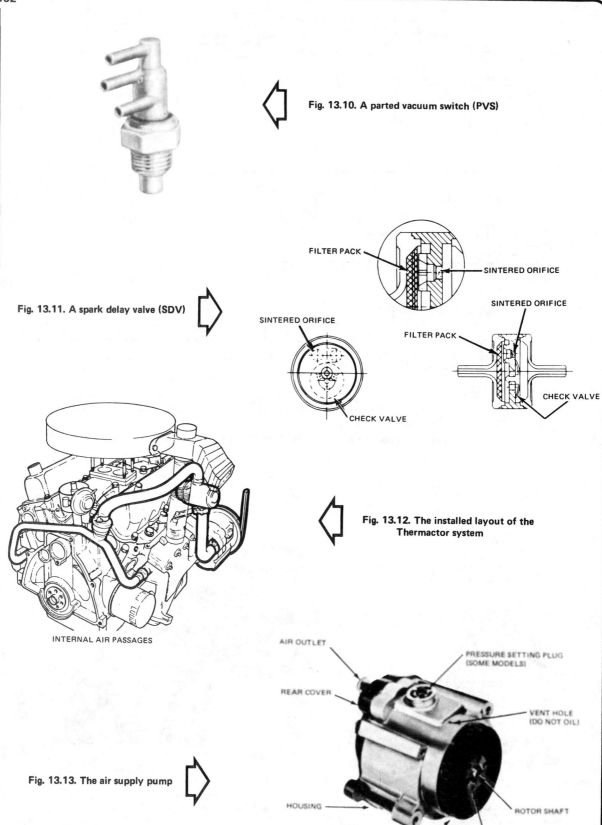

Fig. 13.10. A parted vacuum switch (PVS)

Fig. 13.11. A spark delay valve (SDV)

FILTER PACK

SINTERED ORIFICE

SINTERED ORIFICE

SINTERED ORIFICE

FILTER PACK

CHECK VALVE

CHECK VALVE

Fig. 13.12. The installed layout of the Thermactor system

INTERNAL AIR PASSAGES

AIR OUTLET

PRESSURE SETTING PLUG (SOME MODELS)

REAR COVER

VENT HOLE (DO NOT OIL)

HOUSING

ROTOR SHAFT

Fig. 13.13. The air supply pump

CENTRIFUGAL FILTER FAN

DRIVE HUB

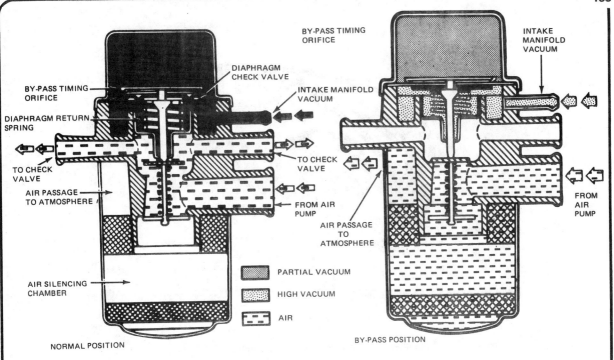

BY-PASS TIMING ORIFICE

DIAPHRAGM CHECK VALVE

INTAKE MANIFOLD VACUUM

BY-PASS TIMING ORIFICE

DIAPHRAGM RETURN SPRING

TO CHECK VALVE

AIR PASSAGE TO ATMOSPHERE

AIR SILENCING CHAMBER

TO CHECK VALVE

FROM AIR PUMP

NORMAL POSITION

INTAKE MANIFOLD VACUUM

AIR PASSAGE TO ATMOSPHERE

FROM AIR PUMP

BY-PASS POSITION

PARTIAL VACUUM

HIGH VACUUM

AIR

Fig. 13.14. A typical air bypass valve

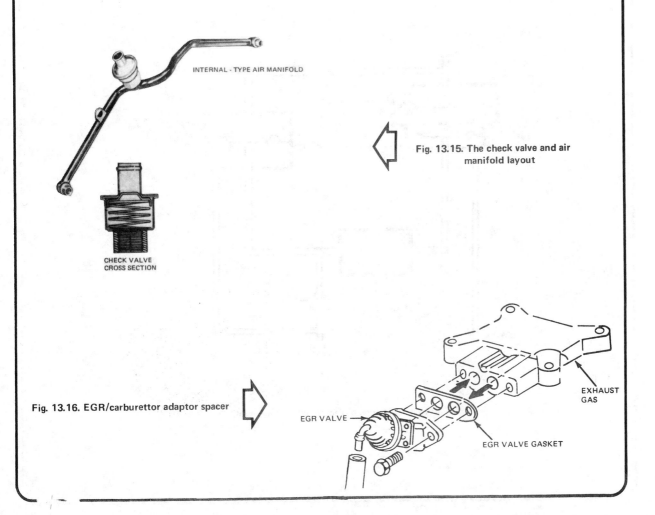

INTERNAL - TYPE AIR MANIFOLD

CHECK VALVE CROSS SECTION

Fig. 13.15. The check valve and air manifold layout

Fig. 13.16. EGR/carburettor adaptor spacer

EXHAUST GAS

EGR VALVE

EGR VALVE GASKET

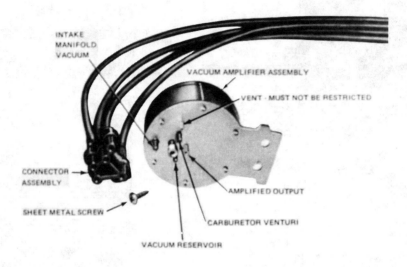

INTAKE MANIFOLD VACUUM

VACUUM AMPLIFIER ASSEMBLY

VENT · MUST NOT BE RESTRICTED

CONNECTOR ASSEMBLY

SHEET METAL SCREW

AMPLIFIED OUTPUT

CARBURETOR VENTURI

VACUUM RESERVOIR

Fig. 13.17. The venturi vacuum amplifier

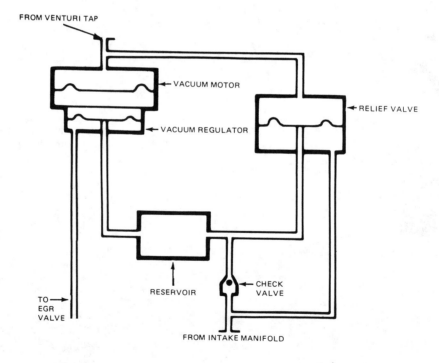

FROM VENTURI TAP

VACUUM MOTOR

RELIEF VALVE

VACUUM REGULATOR

RESERVOIR

CHECK VALVE

TO EGR VALVE

FROM INTAKE MANIFOLD

Fig. 13.18. Schematic diagram of vacuum amplifier

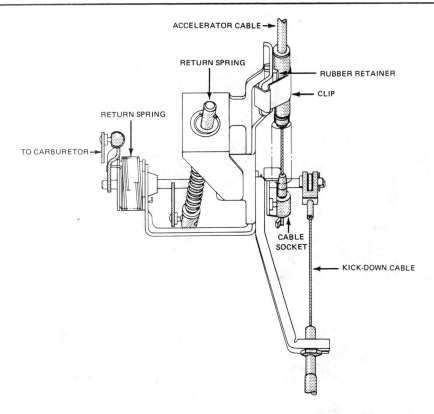

Fig. 13.19. Throttle linkage, rear view

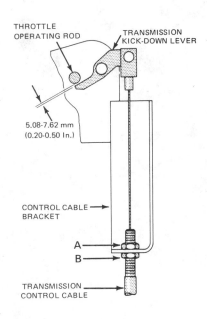

Fig. 13.20. Kick - down cable adjustment

4 Ignition system

1 General description

Apart from the ignition controls which are governed by devices in the emission control system, as outlined in Section 3, the only other alteration to the ignition system is the fitment of a dual diaphragm vacuum advance unit to the distributor.

The outer (primary) diaphragm senses carburettor vacuum just upstream of the throttle butterflies to advance ignition timing; the inner (secondary) diaphragm sences manifold vacuum. Therefore, when the manifold vacuum is high (eg; during deceleration or idling) the secondary diaphragm retards the spark. As soon as the throttle is opened, the primary diaphragm takes control and causes the spark to advance. The purpose of this system is to decrease the emission of unburnt hydrocarbons at low throttle openings.

2 Distributor - removal and replacement

Initially remove the air cleaner assembly then proceed as for the 2600 cc (155 cu in) engine distributor in Sections 7 and 9, of Chapter 4.

3 Distributor - dismantling, overhaul and reassembly

1 Initially release the two spring clips which retain the distributor cap, then pull off the cap followed by the rotor.
2 Remove the lead from the terminal and grommet in the side of the distributor body.
3 Take out the conderser retaining screw and ease the gromment out of the distributor body. Now remove the condenser and lead.
4 Remove the vacuum unit retaining screws and the cam wiper (which is retained by one of these screws).

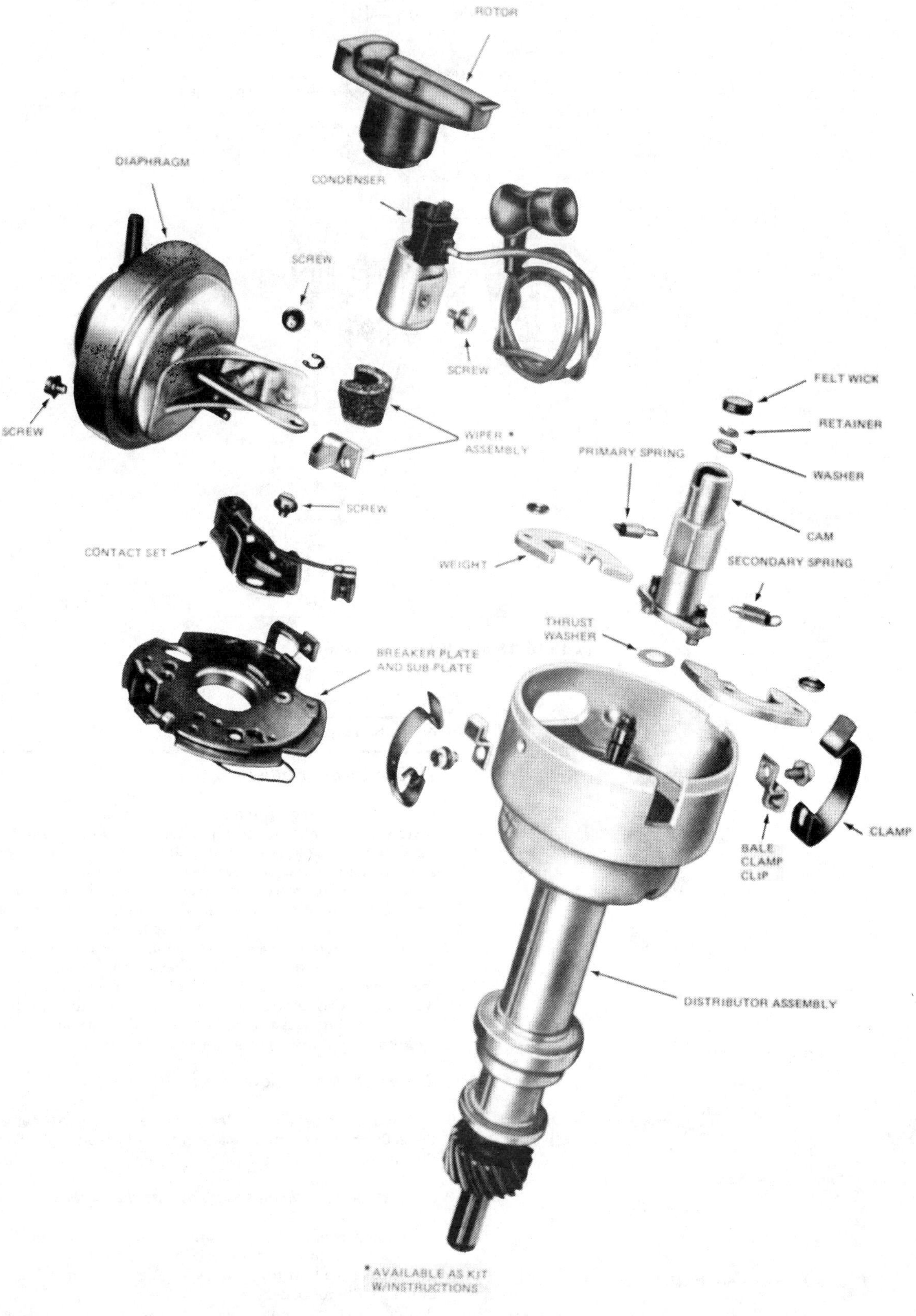

ROTOR

DIAPHRAGM

CONDENSER

SCREW

SCREW

SCREW

FELT WICK

RETAINER

WASHER

WIPER *
ASSEMBLY

PRIMARY SPRING

CAM

SCREW

CONTACT SET

WEIGHT

SECONDARY SPRING

THRUST
WASHER

BREAKER PLATE
AND SUB PLATE

CLAMP

BALE
CLAMP
CLIP

DISTRIBUTOR ASSEMBLY

*AVAILABLE AS KIT
W/INSTRUCTIONS

**Fig. 13.21. The component parts of the distributor
(minus the cap)**

5 Carefully prise off the 'C' clip retaining the vacuum advance link to the breaker plate. Disengage the link from the plate and remove the vacuum unit.

6 Remove the screws securing the cap retaining spring clips on the distributor body. These screws also retain the breaker plate which can now be prised out of the body. Note that this step may be difficult since the body is intentionally distorted during original assembly to hold the plate in position.

7 Use a screwdriver to disassemble the points from the breaker plate.

8 Carefully disengage and remove the primary and secondary centrifugal advance springs then remove the 'C' clips from the weights. Lift off the weights.

9 Carefully prise on the lower edge of the cam using a screwdriver, to disengage the cam retaining ring. Lift off the cam, and lift off the felt wick and loose cam retaining ring.

10 Now follow the procedure given in Chapter 4, Section 8, paragraphs 13 to 21, inclusive.

11 to reassemble, first lubricate the top of the distributor shaft with engine oil and install the cam assembly. Fit the retaining ring in the top of the cam and install the felt wick.

12 Sparingly, coat the pivot pins with a general purpose grease and fit the vacuum weight and new 'C' clips. Fit the primary and secondary springs (see Fig. 13.22.).

13 Position the breaker plate in the distributor body so that the mounting holes are correctly aligned then carefully tap the plate down onto its seating.

14 Fit the vacuum advance unit with the advance link over the post on the breaker plate and fit a new 'C' clip.

15 Position the cam wiper and fit the vacuum unit attaching screw through the distributor body into the cam wiper post. Now fit the remaining vacuum unit securing screw.

16 Install the contact breaker points and lightly secure them with the screw, then set the gap as detailed in Chapter 4, Section

3, paragraphs 4, 5 and 6.

17 Fit the terminal and grommet in the side of the distributor body and position the condenser inside the distributor.

18 Fit the securing screw through the distributor body to retain the condenser. Attach the point lead to the terminal and fit the rotor.

19 Refit the distributor cap.

4 Vacuum control valve (PVS valve) - removal and refitting

1 Partially drain the cooling system into a clean container.

2 Disconnect the hoses from the valve then unscrew it from the thermostat housing.

3 When refitting the valve, ensure that the threads are clean then smear them with a water resistant sealant.

4 Screw in the valve, refit the hoses and top-up the cooling system.

5 Propeller shaft and universal joints

1 General description

Some 1974 onward models are fitted with a 'constant-velocity' type centre joint to reduce vibration at high rotational speeds. This bearing cannot be dismantled and in the event of it requiring attention the entire driveshaft must be renewed.

On all propeller shafts, the use of circlips to retain the bearings and caps has been discontinued. The assemblies are now staked into the yoke which requires the use of special tools to dismantle and reassemble. This operation is considered beyond the scope of the average d-i-y man. If the yoke bearings do fail, it will be necessary to purchase a replacement propeller shaft.

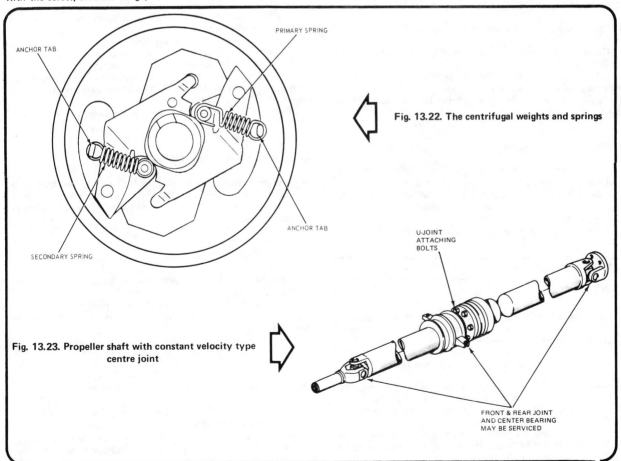

Fig. 13.22. The centrifugal weights and springs

Fig. 13.23. Propeller shaft with constant velocity type centre joint

6 Electrical system

1 General description

The electrical system is essentially unchanged for 1974 onward models with the exception of a revised instrument layout and modified wiring loom. Details of the starter interlock seat belt system will be found in Section 8.

2 Instrument cluster - removal and refitting

1 Disconnect the battery earth lead.
2 Take out the screws securing the steering column shroud; remove the lower half of the shroud and release the shroud upper half retaining lug from its spring clip on the steering column by pulling sharply upwards.
3 Take out the ashtray then withdraw the hazard flasher switch and disconnect the wiring at the cable connector.
4 Take out the screws which retain the direction indicator switch, then leave the switch hanging by the harness.
5 Remove the screws retaining the lower dash trim panel. Pull the panel forwards, and downwards, to gain access to the cigar lighter and clock cable connectors. Disconnect the cables and remove the trim panel.
6 Pull off the knob from the instrument panel illumination control.
7 Remove the lower screws retaining the instrument cluster bezel then release the bezel by pulling it downwards. Disconnect the seat belt warning light at the connector.
8 Unscrew the oil pressure line union.
9 Remove the instrument cluster securing screws, disconnect the speedometer cable and multi-way connector from the rear of the instrument cluster. Remove the complete instrument cluster.
10 Refitting is a reverse of the removal procedure.

3 Ignition switch - removal and refitting

1 Remove the instrument cluster as described in the previous sub-Section.
2 Set the ignition key to the 'O' position then remove the multi-way connector from the ignition switch.
3 Remove the screws which secure the ignition switch to the lock then withdraw the switch.
4 Refitting is a reversal of the removal procedure.

4 Seat belt warning buzzer - removal and refitting

1 Remove the lower dash trim panel by following the procedure of paragraphs 1 to 5 inclusive, in Section 6.2.
2 Undo and remove the screw(s) holding the buzzer unit to the steering column bracket. Disconnect the wiring harness and withdraw the unit.
3 Refitting is the reverse of the removal procedure.

7 Suspension and steering

1 General description

With the exception of the radius arm rear axle location, which has been superseded by a stabilizer bar, the system is unaltered from the previous models.

2 Stabilizer bar - removal, rebushing and refitting

1 Chock the front wheels to prevent the car from moving, then jack-up the rear of the car and support it on suitable stands.
2 Disconnect the handbrake primary cable from the relay lever on the rear axle and withdraw the cable.
3 Remove the two stabilizer bar retaining clamps from the axle housing. Whilst the bolts are being undone it will be advantageous to restrain the stabilizer bar.

4 Remove the through-bolts and nuts from the stabilizer bar/sidemember attachments.
5 If the bushes are to be renewed they can be pressed out of the end assembly. New ones can then be pressed in, chamfered end first.
6 If the mounting bushings are to be renewed, the end assemblies will have to be removed after loosening the locknuts. The mounting bushes can then be slid off and replacements fitted. When the end assemblies are refitted they must be screwed on to the dimension shown in Fig. 13.34.
7 Refitting the stabilizer bar is a reversal of the removal procedure but the following points must be noted:
a) The stabilizer bar/sidemember bolts are fitted with the bolt heads on the inside of the sidemembers.
b) It is essential that the weight of the car is resting on the roadwheels before the mounting nuts and bolts, and the retaining clamp bolts are tightened.

8 Bodywork and underframe

1 General note

Apart from the addition of impact resistant front and rear bumpers, the bodywork for 1974 onward models is virtually unaltered.

However, the seat belts now have a starter interlock system which prevents the car from being started unless a predetermined sequence is followed, and an optional air conditioning system is available.

2 Front bumper - removal and refitting

1 Remove the bumper assembly retaining nuts from the bumper brackets (arms).
2 Take off the number plate brackets.
3 Remove the bolts which retain the bumper reinforcement and separate the reinforcement from the bumper.
4 The replaceable trim strip can be pulled from the bumper if it is well lubricated with water. When refitting a new strip, this too will need lubricating with water.
5 Refitting the bumper to the car is a reversal of the removal procedure.

3 Rear bumper - removal and refitting

1 The procedure for removal and refitting of the rear bumper is similar to that described for the front bumpers except that there are for attachment bolts for the reinforcement at each bumper bracket.

4 Glove box - removal and refitting

1 Remove the lower dash trim panel as described in paragraphs 1 to 5, in Section 6.2.
2 Remove the upper and lower glovebox retaining screws then pull the glovebox forward to gain access to the light cable connector.
3 Disconnect the cable and withdraw the glove box.
4 Refitting is the reverse of the removal procedure.

5 Starter interlock seat belts - general description

The starter interlock seat belt system prevents operation of the vehicle unless the seat belts of all occupied seats are correctly fastened. A warning light and buzzer will operate if the correct sequence is not followed or where the sequence is bypassed after the engine has been started.

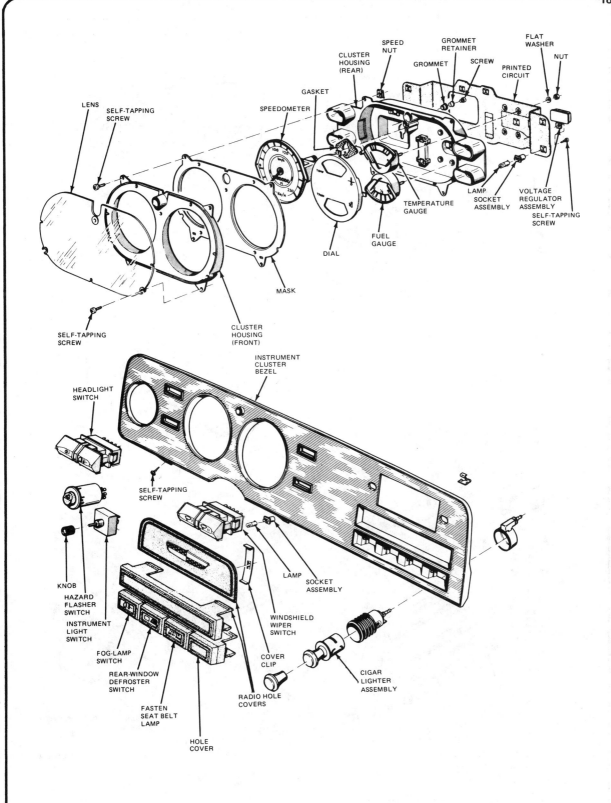

Fig. 13.24. The component parts of the standard instrument cluster

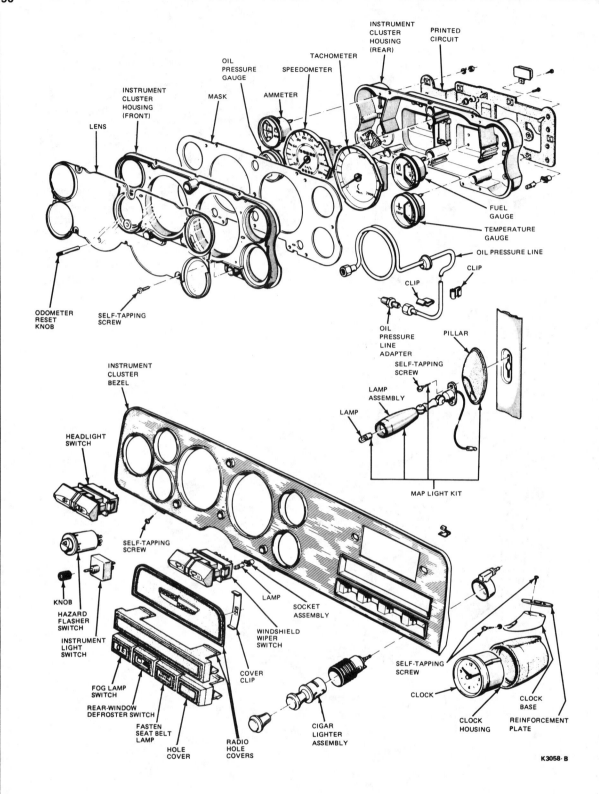

Fig. 13.25. The component parts of the optional instrument cluster

K3058-B

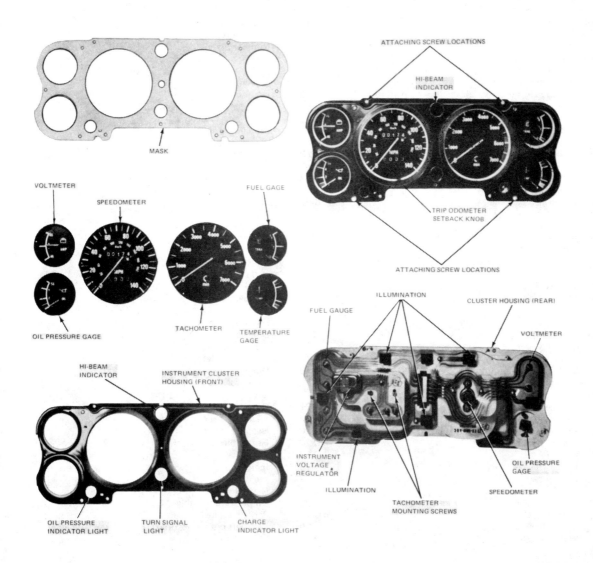

Fig. 13.26. The cluster assembly

Fig. 13.28 Wiring diagram for 1973 models

Alternator and regulator (Lucas)	C-7		Oil pressure	C-11
Alternator (Bosch)	D-1		Seat belt (man. trans.)	D-5
Buzzers			(auto. trans.)	D-4
Key reminder	B-4		Direction indicator	D-26
Seat belt (man. trans.)	D-6		Exterior	
(auto. trans.)	D-4		Reverse	E-13
Cigar lighter	B-28		Head - right	E-18
Clock	B-28		- left	E-17
Constant voltage regulator	C-13		Number plate	C-22
Distributor	E-3		Park and direction indicator (right)	B-23
Emission controls			(left)	D-23
Manual trans.			Side marker (right front)	B-23
Ambient temp. switch	C-8		(left front)	C-23
T.R.S. switch	D-9		(right rear)	B-24
Vacuum solenoid	D-9		(left rear)	D-24
Auto. trans.			Stop light (right)	C-15
Ambient temp. switch	C-8		(left)	C-14
E.S.C. amplifier	D-8		Taillight (right)	B-24
Speed sensor	E-8		(left)	D-24
Vacuum solenoid	E-8		Rear direction indicator (right)	B-24
Flashers			(left)	D-24
Emergency warning	C-28		Relays	
Direction indicator	C-28		Auto. trans.	D-2
Gauges			Dimmer	D-18
Ammeter	A-1		Heated blacklight	C-16
Fuel	C-13		Seat belt	D-4
Tachometer	C-12		Starter motor	C-2
Temperature	C-13		Senders	
Heated backlight	C-16		Fuel	C-13
Heater blower motor	C-5		Temperature	C-13
Horns	D-7		Switches	
Ignition coil	E-3		Reverse lamp	D-13
Ignition resistor	D-3		Dimmer	C-18
Windshield wiper			Door jamb (right)	C-27
Motor	C-10		(left)	C-27
Switch	D-10		Door jamb - key buzzer	B-5
Foot switch	E-10		Dual brake warning	D-12
Instrument panel lights			Gear	D-5
Dimmer control	D-21		Glove box lamp	B-28
Illumination			Hazard flasher	B-26
Ammeter and oil pressure	D-20		Heated backlight	C-15
Blower switch	C-20		Heater blower	C-6
Cigar lighter	C-19		Horn	C-5
Clock	D-19		Ignition	B-3
Flasher switch	D-22		Lighting	B-18
PRNDL (auto. trans.)	C-21		Neutral start	F-2
Lighting switch	D-21		Oil pressure warning	D-11
Tachometer	D-20		Parking brake	D-13
Temp. and fuel gauge	D-20		Seat belt retractor - drivers	
Wiper switch	D-22		(auto. trans.)	E-4
Lamps			(man. trans.)	E-5
Courtesy			Passenger	
Glove box	B-28		(auto. trans.)	D-5
Interior	B-27		(man. trans.)	D-6
Map	B-29		Direction indicator	C-26
Indicator			Seat sensor (auto. trans.)	D-4
Alternator	C-11		(man. trans.)	D-6
Brake warning	C-12		Stop light	D10
High beam	D-19			

Wiring colour key

BK Black   R Red   Y Yellow   BL Blue   W White   GN Green   GY Grey   BR Brown   V Violet

1 =	16A	Cigar lighter, clock, interior light
2 =	8A	Rear license plate light, instrument cluster illumination
3 =	8A	Tail light RH, parking light RH
4 =	8A	Tail light LH, parking light LH
5 =	16A	Horn, heater blower
6 =	16A	Wiper motor, back-up light, instrument cluster
7 =	16A	Turn indicator lights, stop lights

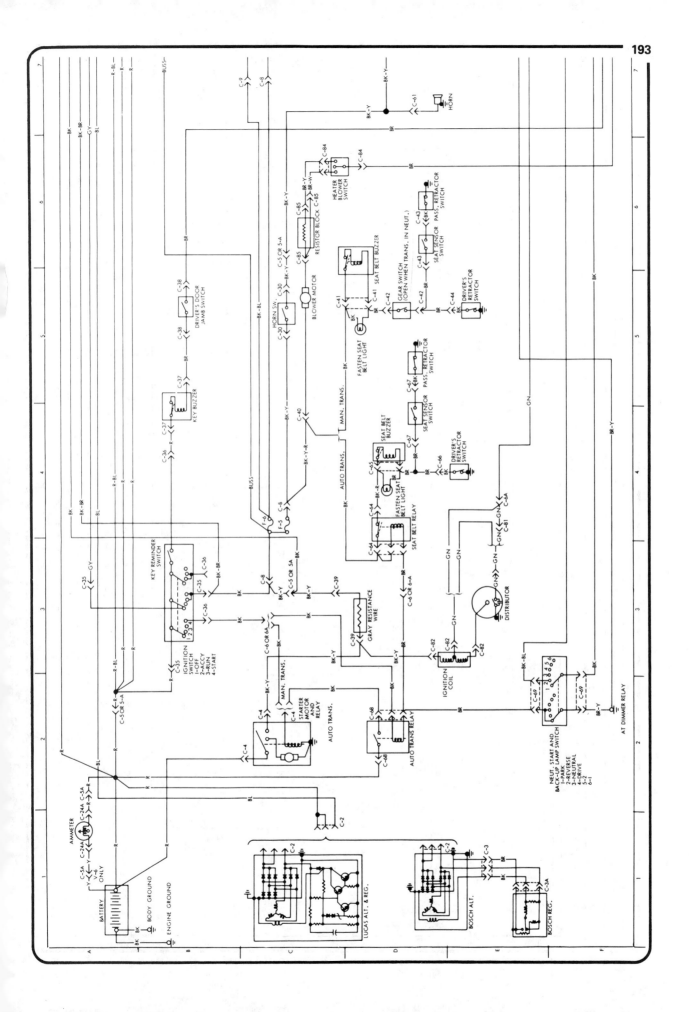

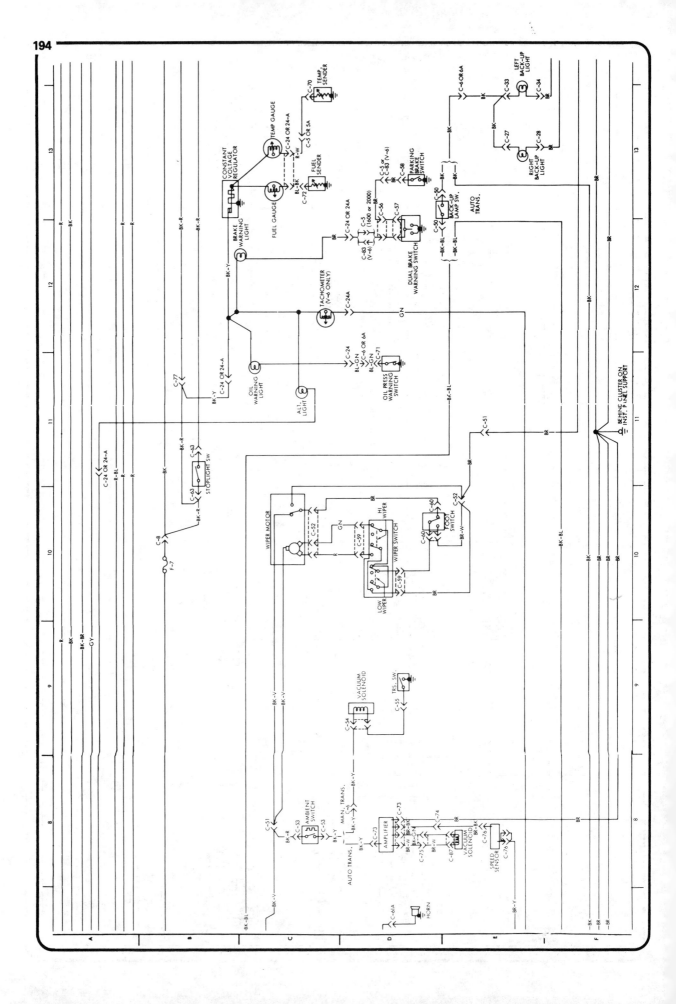

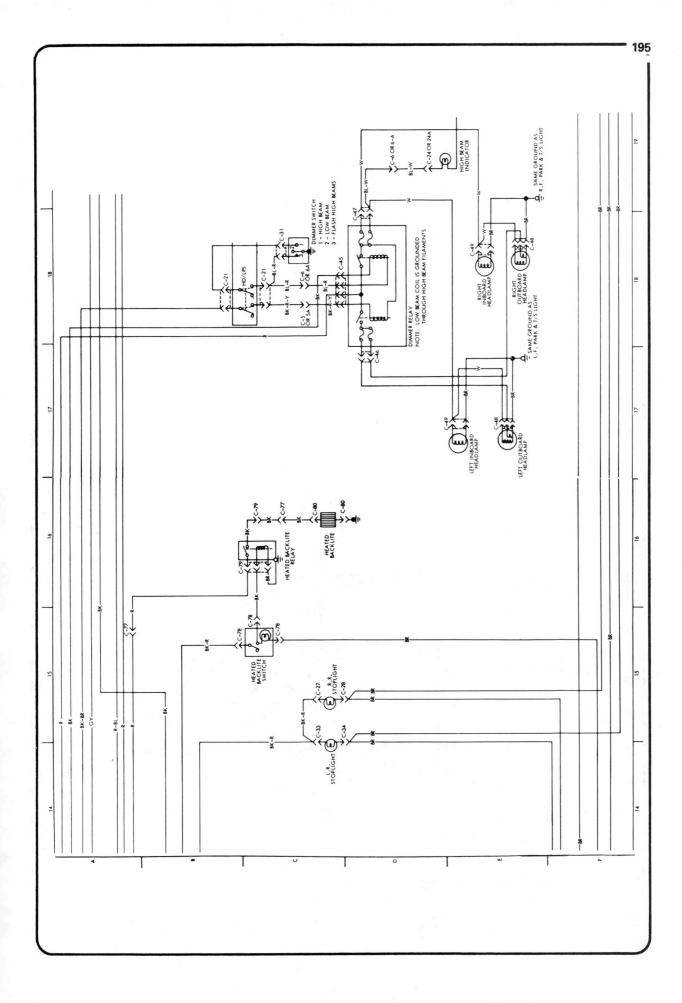

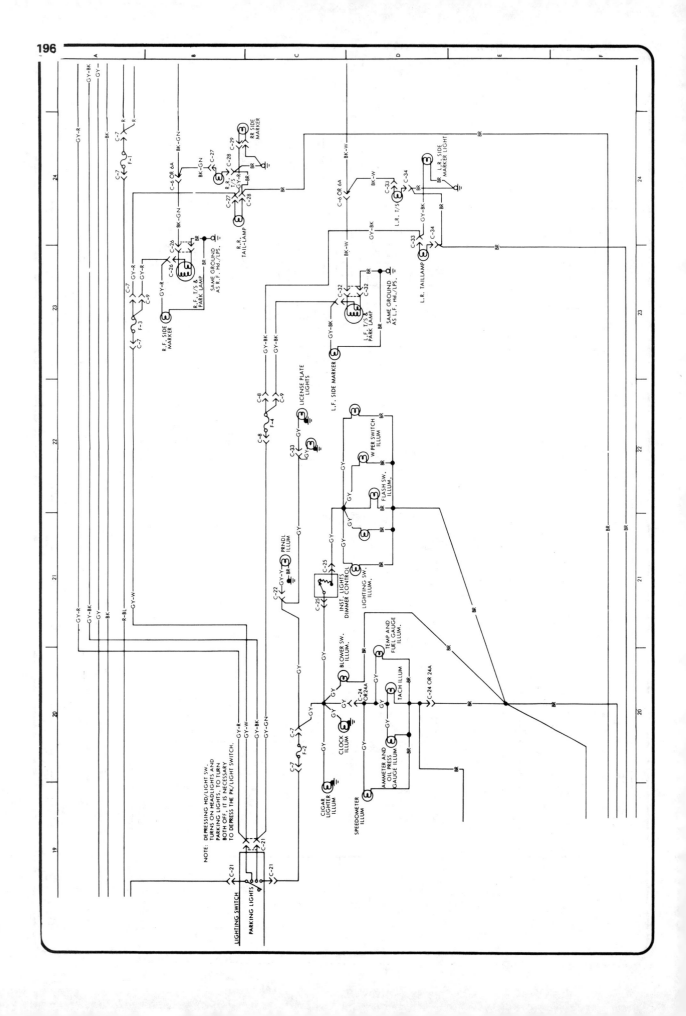

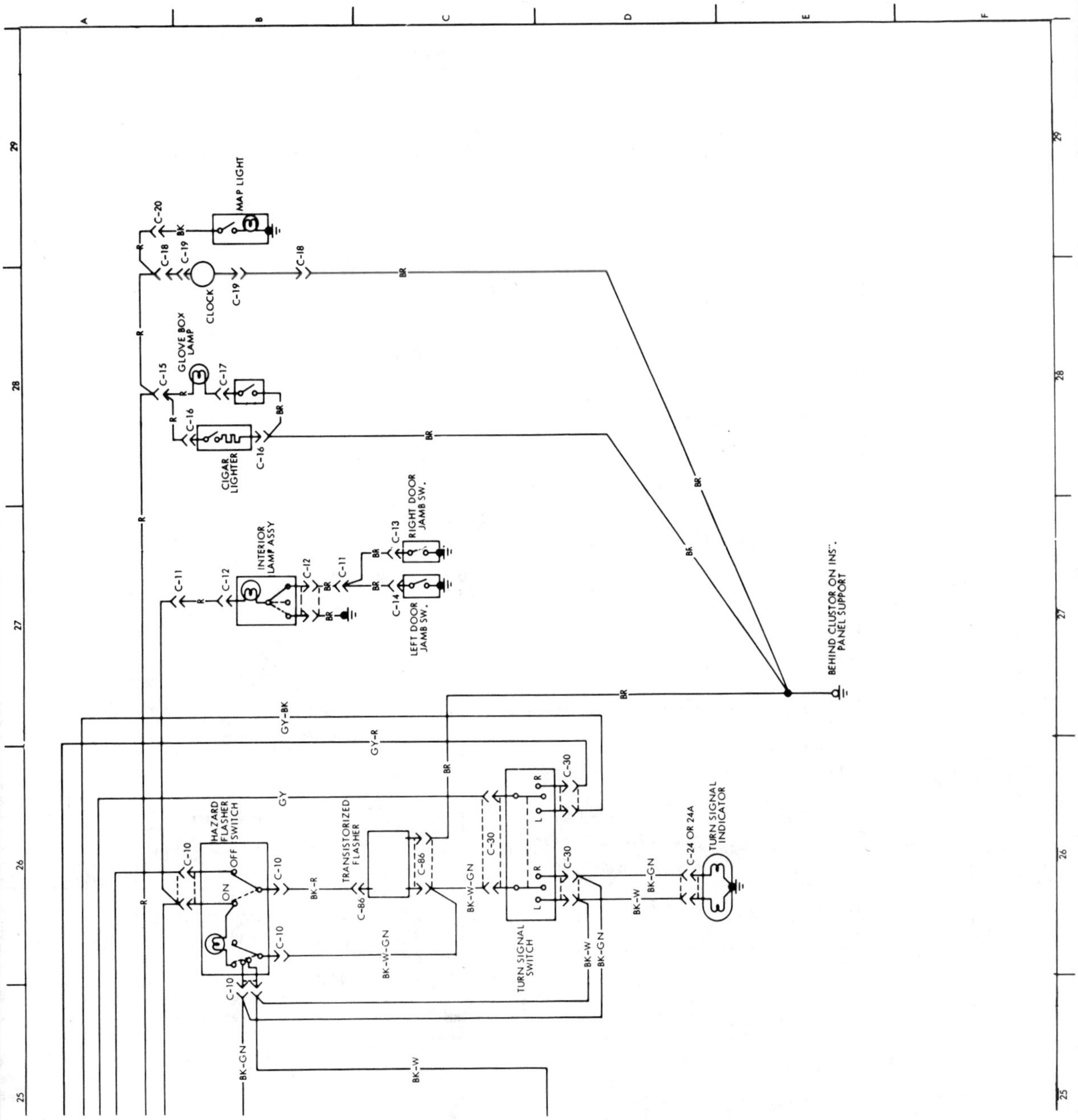

A   B   C   D   E   F

29

MAP LIGHT
C-20
C-18   C-19 BK
C-18
C-19
CLOCK
GLOVE BOX LAMP
C-15
C-16   C-17
CIGAR LIGHTER
C-16

28

BR

BK

INTERIOR LAMP ASSY
C-11
C-12   C-12
C-11   BK
RIGHT DOOR JAMB SW.
C-13
LEFT DOOR JAMB SW.
C-14

BEHIND CLUSTOR ON INST. PANEL SUPPORT

27

BR

GY-BK

GY-R

HAZARD FLASHER SWITCH
C-10
OFF
ON
C-10
C-10

TRANSISTORIZED FLASHER
BK-R
C-86
BK-W-GN
C-86

TURN SIGNAL SWITCH
R   R
L   L
C-30
C-30
C-30

GY

BR

BK-W-GN
BK-W
BK-GN

TURN SIGNAL INDICATOR
C-24 OR 24A

26

R

BK-GN
BK-W

25

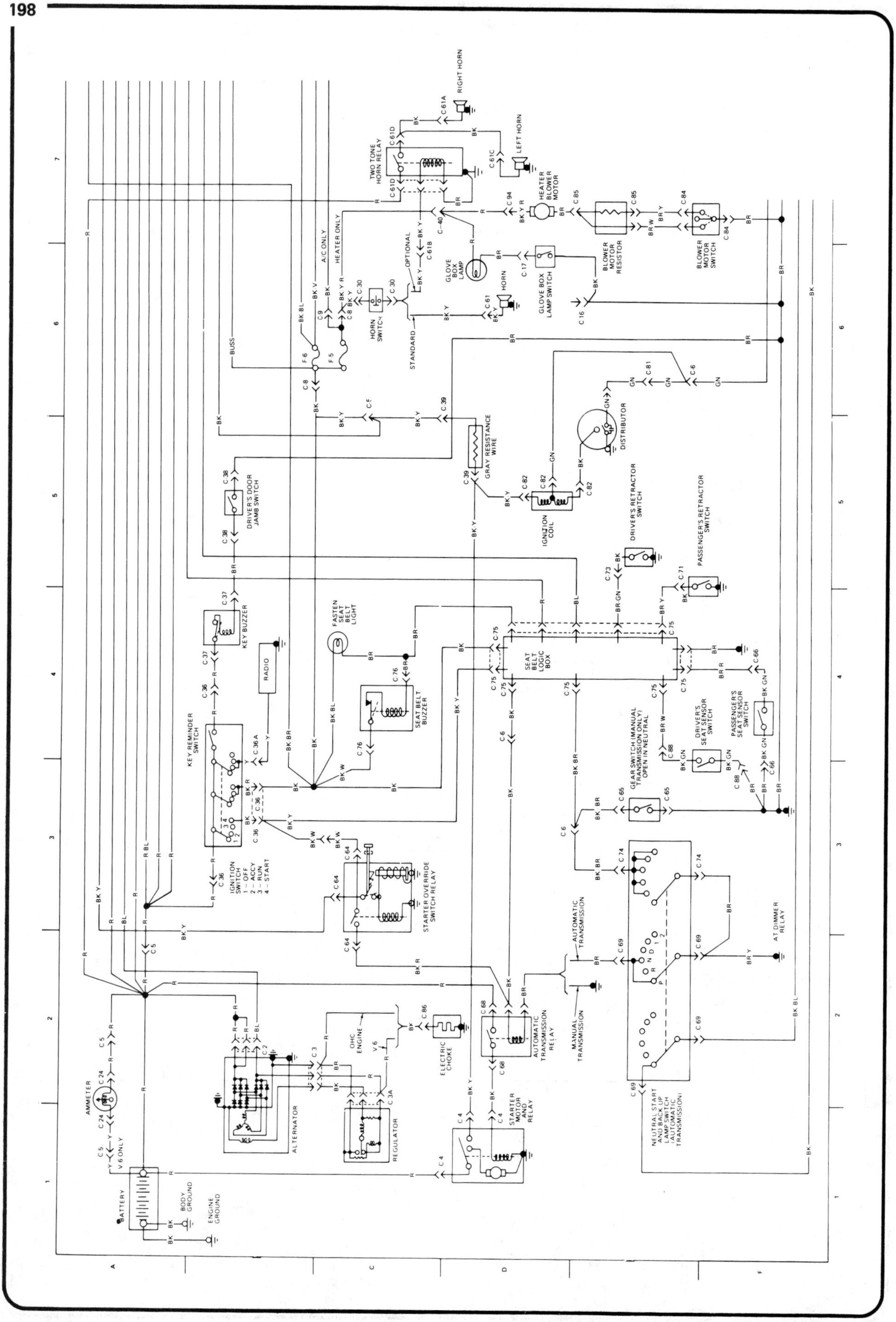
BATTERY
BODY GROUND
ENGINE GROUND
AMMETER
V6 ONLY
ALTERNATOR
REGULATOR
OHC ENGINE
ELECTRIC CHOKE
STARTER MOTOR AND RELAY
AUTOMATIC TRANSMISSION RELAY
MANUAL TRANSMISSION
AUTOMATIC TRANSMISSION
NEUTRAL START AND BACK UP LAMP SWITCH (AUTOMATIC TRANSMISSION)
AT DIMMER RELAY
STARTER OVERRIDE SWITCH RELAY
IGNITION SWITCH
1 – OFF
2 – ACCY
3 – RUN
4 – START
KEY REMINDER SWITCH
RADIO
KEY BUZZER
SEAT BELT BUZZER
FASTEN SEAT BELT LIGHT
SEAT BELT LOGIC BOX
GEAR SWITCH (MANUAL TRANSMISSION ONLY) OPEN IN NEUTRAL
DRIVER'S SEAT SENSOR SWITCH
PASSENGER'S SEAT SENSOR SWITCH
DRIVER'S RETRACTOR SWITCH
PASSENGER'S RETRACTOR SWITCH
DRIVER'S DOOR JAMB SWITCH
IGNITION COIL
GRAY RESISTANCE WIRE
DISTRIBUTOR
BUSS
HORN SWITCH
STANDARD
OPTIONAL
HORN
GLOVE BOX LAMP
GLOVE BOX LAMP SWITCH
BLOWER MOTOR RESISTOR
BLOWER MOTOR SWITCH
HEATER BLOWER MOTOR
A/C ONLY
HEATER ONLY
TWO TONE HORN RELAY
RIGHT HORN
LEFT HORN

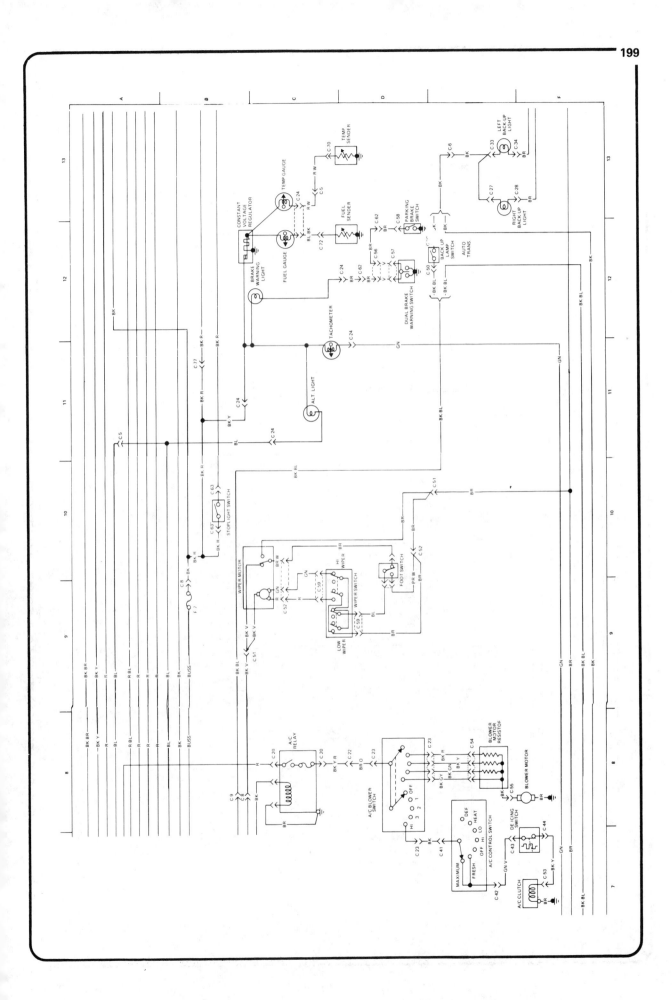

NOTE: DEPRESSING HEADLIGHT SWITCH TURNS ON HEADLIGHTS AND PARKING LIGHTS. TO TURN BOTH OFF, IT IS NECESSARY TO DEPRESS THE PARKING LIGHT SWITCH

GY W GY GN

LIGHTING SWITCH

PARKING LIGHTS

HIGH BEAM INDICATOR

SAME GROUND AS RIGHT FRONT PARK AND TURN SIGNAL LIGHT

DIMMER SWITCH
1 - HIGH BEAM
2 - LOW BEAM
3 - FLASH HIGH BEAMS

DIMMER RELAY
NOTE: LOW BEAM COIL IS GROUNDED THROUGH HIGH BEAM FILAMENTS

RIGHT INBOARD HEADLIGHT

RIGHT OUTBOARD HEADLIGHT

SAME GROUND AS LEFT FRONT PARK AND TURN SIGNAL LIGHT

LEFT INBOARD HEADLIGHT

LEFT OUTBOARD HEADLIGHT

HEATED BACKLITE RELAY

HEATED BACKLITE

HEATED BACKLITE INDICATOR LIGHT

HEATED BACKLITE SWITCH - A/C

HEATED BACKLITE SWITCH (NON A/C)

R.R. STOPLIGHT

L.R. STOPLIGHT

BK-BN BK-Y R BK R-BL R R BK

C 21 C 21 C 6 C 24 C 49 C 48 C 47 C 45 C 46 C 31 C 5 C 77 C 79 C 80 C 95 C 83 C 78 C 27 C 28 C 33 C 34

BK-BR BR BL-R BK-R-Y BK BL-R BK-R-Y R W BL-W BLW BR BK-R BK BR BR-BR

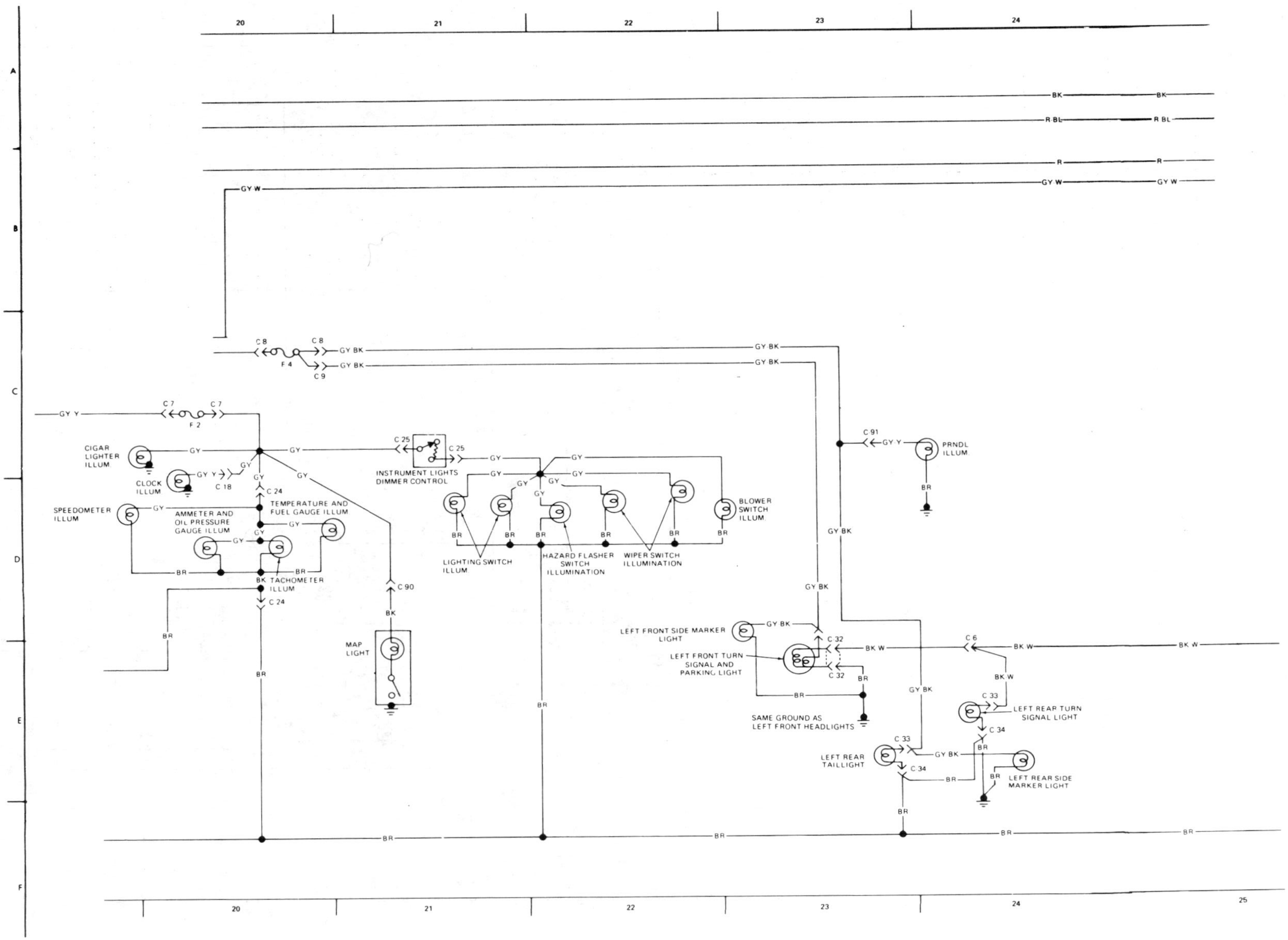

20
21
22
23
24
25
A
B
C
D
E
F
BK
R BL
R
GY W
GY BK
GY Y
GY
BR
BK W
C 7
F 2
C 8
F 4
C 9
C 18
C 24
C 25
C 90
C 91
C 6
C 32
C 33
C 34
CIGAR LIGHTER ILLUM
CLOCK ILLUM
SPEEDOMETER ILLUM
AMMETER AND OIL PRESSURE GAUGE ILLUM
TEMPERATURE AND FUEL GAUGE ILLUM
TACHOMETER ILLUM
MAP LIGHT
INSTRUMENT LIGHTS DIMMER CONTROL
LIGHTING SWITCH ILLUM
HAZARD FLASHER SWITCH ILLUMINATION
WIPER SWITCH ILLUMINATION
BLOWER SWITCH ILLUM
PRNDL ILLUM
LEFT FRONT SIDE MARKER LIGHT
LEFT FRONT TURN SIGNAL AND PARKING LIGHT
SAME GROUND AS LEFT FRONT HEADLIGHTS
LEFT REAR TURN SIGNAL LIGHT
LEFT REAR TAILLIGHT
LEFT REAR SIDE MARKER LIGHT

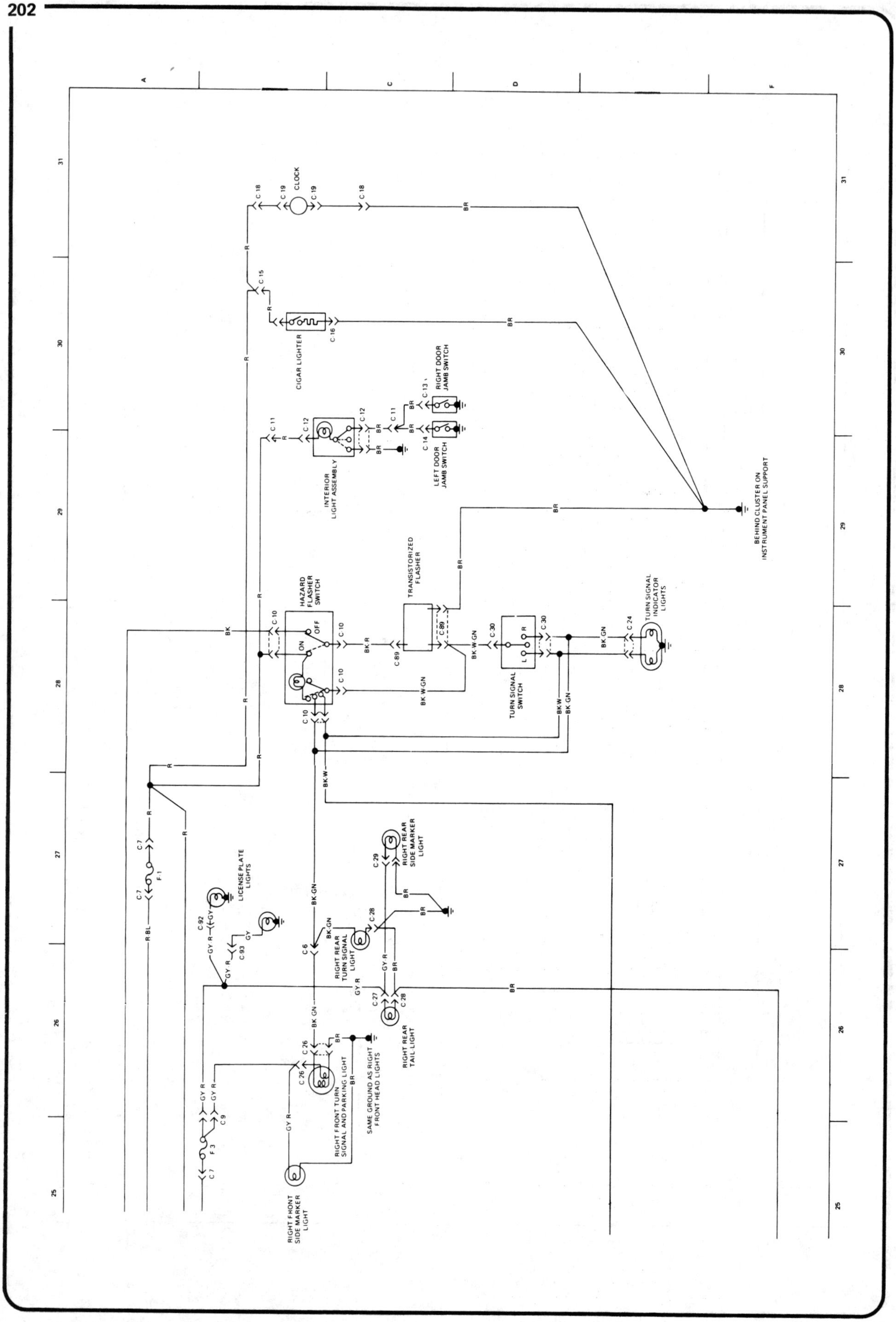

CLOCK

C 18 · C 19 · C 19 · C 18

BR

C 15

R

CIGAR LIGHTER

C 16

BR

RIGHT DOOR JAMB SWITCH

C 13

C 11

BR BR

C 12

C 11

R

INTERIOR LIGHT ASSEMBLY

LEFT DOOR JAMB SWITCH

BR

BEHIND CLUSTER ON INSTRUMENT PANEL SUPPORT

BR

TRANSISTORIZED FLASHER

BK

HAZARD FLASHER SWITCH

OFF

ON

C 10

C 10

C 10

BK·R

C 89

C 89

BK·W·GN

BK·W·GN

C 30

C 30

TURN SIGNAL SWITCH

R

L

C 30

BK·W

BK GN

C 24

BK GN

TURN SIGNAL INDICATOR LIGHTS

R BL

C 7

F·1

R

R

R

LICENSE PLATE LIGHTS

GY R

C 92

GY R

C 93

GY

BK GN

BK GN

C 6

RIGHT REAR TURN SIGNAL LIGHT

C 28

BR

GY R

C 29

BR

RIGHT REAR SIDE MARKER LIGHT

BR

GY R

GY R

C 27

C 28

BR

RIGHT REAR TAIL LIGHT

GY R

C 9

F·3

C 7

GY R

C 26

BR

BR

RIGHT FRONT TURN SIGNAL AND PARKING LIGHT

SAME GROUND AS RIGHT FRONT HEAD LIGHTS

RIGHT FRONT SIDE MARKER LIGHT

Fig. 13.29 Wiring diagram for 1974 models

Components	Location	Components	Location
Air condition clutch	F-7	Right rear	C-27
Alternator	B-1	Stop lights	
Alternator regulator	C-1	Left	C-14
Battery	A-1	Right	C-14
Buzzers		Tail lights	
Key reminder	B-4	Left	E-23
Seat belt	C-4	Right	C-26
Cigar lighter	B-30	Rear direction indicator	
Clock	B-31	Left	E-24
Constant voltage regulator	B-12	Right	C-27
Distributor	E-5	Motors	
Flashers		A/C blower	F-8
Hazard flasher	C-28	Heater blower	D-7
Direction indicator	E-28	Starter	D-1
Gauges		Windshield wiper	B-9
Ammeter	A-2	Radio	
Fuel	C-12	Relays	
Tachometer	C-11	Air conditioning	C-8
Temperature	C-13	Automatic transmission	D-2
Heated backlight	C-16	Dimmer	D-18
Heater blower motor	D-7	Heated backlight	C-16
Heater blower motor resistor	E-7	Starter motor	D-1
Horns	D-6, D-7	Starter override switch	C-3
Ignition coil	D-5	Two-tone horn	C-7
Ignition resistor wire	D-5	Self belt logic box	D-4
Illumination lights		Senders	
Ammeter and oil pressure gauge	D-20	Fuel gauge	C-12
Blower switch	D-23	Water temperature gauge	C-13
Cigar lighter	C-19	Switches	
Clock	D-20	A/C blower	D-8
Dome	B-29	A/C control	E-7
Fuel gauge	C-12	Dimmer	
Glove box	D-6	Instrument panel illumination	C-21
Hazard flasher	D-22	High beam	C-18
Lighting switch	D-21	Door jamb	
Map	E-21	Driver's	B-5, C-29
PRND 12	C-24	Passenger's	C-30
Tachometer	C-11	Door jamb - key buzzer	B-4
Temperature gauge	C-13	Dual brake warning	D-12
Windshield wiper switch	D-22	Gear	E-3
Indicator lights		Glove box lamp	D-6
Alternator	C-11	Hazard flasher	B-28
Brake warning	C-12	Heated backlight	E-15
Heated backlight	E-16	Heater blower	F-7
High beam	E-19	Horn	C-6
Seat belt	C-4	Ignition	B-3
Direction indicator	E-28	Lighting	C-18
Exterior lights		Neutral start	E-2
Reverse	E-13	Parking brake	D-12
Headlights		Seat belt retractor	
Left	E-17	Driver's	E-5
Right	E-18	Passenger's	F-4
Number plate	B-27	Direction indicator	D-28
Park and direction indicator		Seat sensor	
Left	E-23	Driver's	F-3
Right	B-26	Passenger's	F-4
Side marker		Starter override	C-3
Left front	E-23	Stoplight	B-10
Left rear	E-24	Windshield wiper	C-9
Right front	B-25	Foot switch	D-10

Wiring colour code

BK	Black	BL	Blue	GY	Gray	V	Violet
R	Red	W	White	BR	Brown	O	Orange
Y	Yellow	GN	Green				

The following procedure outlines the starting sequence.

1 Seat occupied or weight of 17 to 47 lb placed on the seat cushion. Weight sensing switch closes.
2 Seat belt is fastened on occupied seat which opens the normally closed buckle switch.
3 Key inserted and engine is started.

If the engine fails to start after following the correct procedure, an override switch in the engine compartment can be pressed. This will permit one engine start attempt only to be carried out, following which the switch must be reset if a further attempt is to be made.

6 *Starter interlock seat belts - fault finding preliminary checks*
Note: If a fault cannot be traced from the preliminary checks, reference should be made to the diagnostic sequence charts in the following Section.

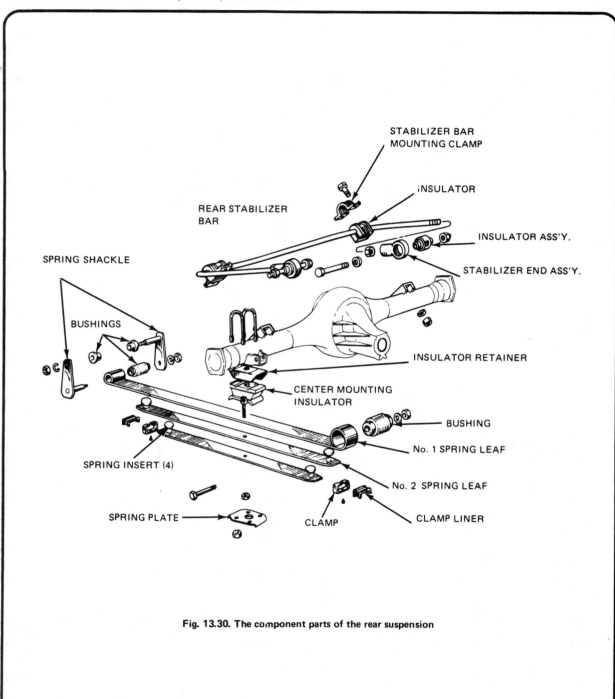

Fig. 13.30. The component parts of the rear suspension

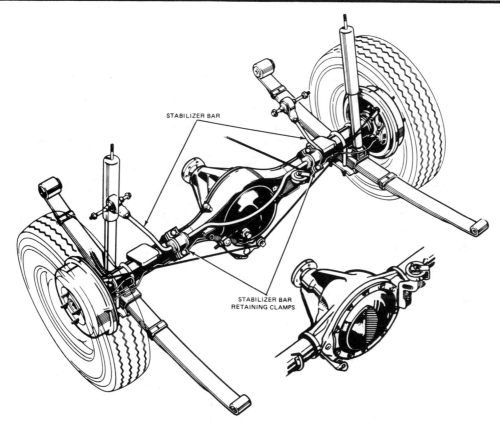

STABILIZER BAR

STABILIZER BAR
RETAINING CLAMPS

Fig. 13.31. The rear axle layout

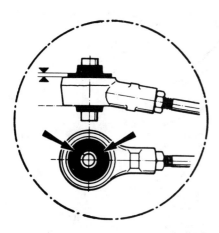

Fig. 13.33. The stabilizer bar bushing and end assembly

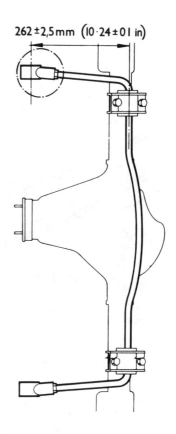

262 ±2,5mm (10·24±0·1 in)

Fig. 13.34 Dimensions for refitting the stabilizer bar

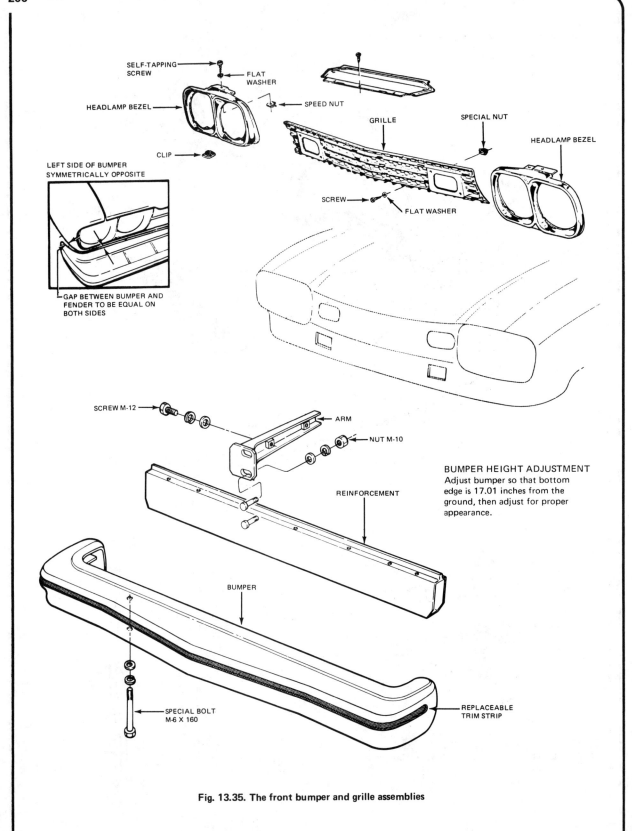

SELF-TAPPING SCREW

FLAT WASHER

HEADLAMP BEZEL

SPEED NUT

GRILLE

SPECIAL NUT

HEADLAMP BEZEL

CLIP

LEFT SIDE OF BUMPER SYMMETRICALLY OPPOSITE

SCREW

FLAT WASHER

GAP BETWEEN BUMPER AND FENDER TO BE EQUAL ON BOTH SIDES

SCREW M-12

ARM

NUT M-10

REINFORCEMENT

BUMPER HEIGHT ADJUSTMENT
Adjust bumper so that bottom edge is 17.01 inches from the ground, then adjust for proper appearance.

BUMPER

SPECIAL BOLT M-6 X 160

REPLACEABLE TRIM STRIP

Fig. 13.35. The front bumper and grille assemblies

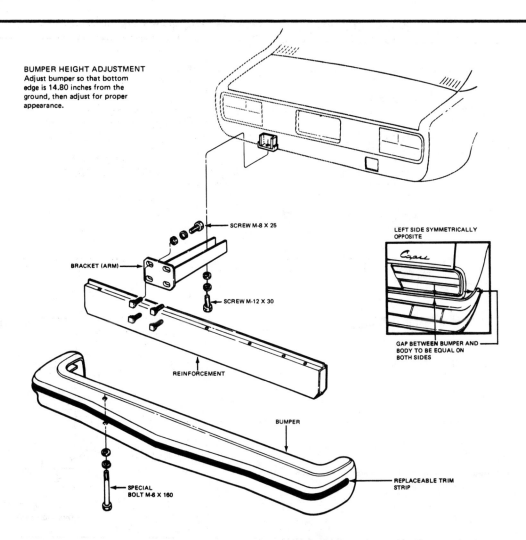

BUMPER HEIGHT ADJUSTMENT
Adjust bumper so that bottom edge is 14.80 inches from the ground, then adjust for proper appearance.

SCREW M-8 X 25

LEFT SIDE SYMMETRICALLY OPPOSITE

BRACKET (ARM)

SCREW M-12 X 30

GAP BETWEEN BUMPER AND BODY TO BE EQUAL ON BOTH SIDES

REINFORCEMENT

BUMPER

REPLACEABLE TRIM STRIP

SPECIAL BOLT M-6 X 160

Fig. 13.36. The rear bumper assembly

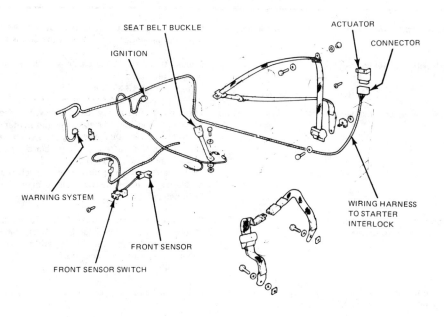

SEAT BELT BUCKLE

ACTUATOR

CONNECTOR

IGNITION

WARNING SYSTEM

FRONT SENSOR

FRONT SENSOR SWITCH

WIRING HARNESS TO STARTER INTERLOCK

Fig. 13.37 Wiring layout for the starter interlock seat belt system

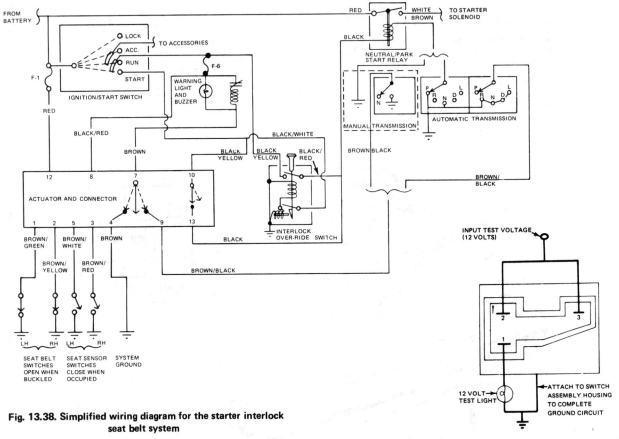

Fig. 13.38. Simplified wiring diagram for the starter interlock seat belt system

Fig. 13.39. Test connections for the override switch

Symptom	Check
Starter will not operate after following the correct sequence	Check for a closed seat belt switch when the belt is unfastened, and open switch when the belt is fastened.
Starter operates with belt unfastened	Check that the seat sensor switch is closed to earth with weight on seat Refer to Figs.13.37 and 13.38.
Starter fails to operate after emergency override switch is pressed	Disconnect emergency override switch from connector, then normalize the switch relays by momentarily connecting blade '3' to the battery then earthing the switch case. Reconnect the battery lead to blade '2' then check that no voltage exists at blade '1'. Push the red override button and check that voltage now exists at blade '1'. If the switch fails to operate satisfactorily it must be renewed.
Warning light and buzzer on when a gear is selected even though the correct sequence has been followed	Check for voltage at number '1' fuse (dome light is powered from number '1' fuse) If satisfactory, check for voltage at pin '12' of actuator module connector. If satisfactory, actuator module is at fault and must be renewed. If no voltage is present, check for an open circuit fuse or lead.
Warning light and buzzer fail to operate when a gear is selected and the ignition is switched on with the belts unfastened.	Check for voltage at number '1' fuse.
Warning light and buzzer on with neutral or park selected	Check for open circuit between selector switch and earth with neutral or park selected, and closed circuit when a gear is selected.

7 Starter interlock seat belts - diagnostic fault sequence chart

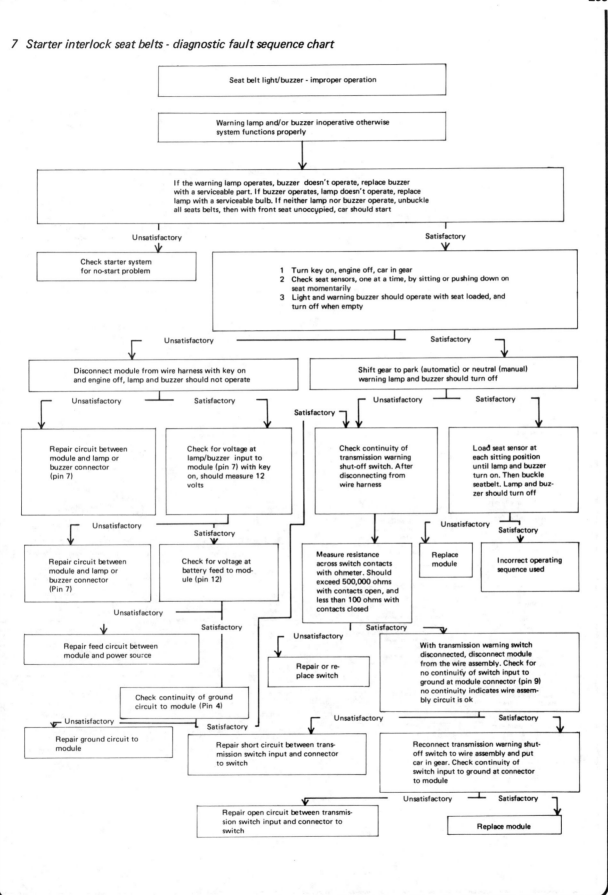

Seat belt light/buzzer - improper operation

Warning lamp and/or buzzer inoperative otherwise system functions properly

If the warning lamp operates, buzzer doesn't operate, replace buzzer with a serviceable part. If buzzer operates, lamp doesn't operate, replace lamp with a serviceable bulb. If neither lamp nor buzzer operate, unbuckle all seats belts, then with front seat unoccupied, car should start

Unsatisfactory

Check starter system for no-start problem

Satisfactory

1. Turn key on, engine off, car in gear
2. Check seat sensors, one at a time, by sitting or pushing down on seat momentarily
3. Light and warning buzzer should operate with seat loaded, and turn off when empty

Unsatisfactory

Disconnect module from wire harness with key on and engine off, lamp and buzzer should not operate

Satisfactory

Shift gear to park (automatic) or neutral (manual) warning lamp and buzzer should turn off

Unsatisfactory

Repair circuit between module and lamp or buzzer connector (pin 7)

Satisfactory

Check for voltage at lamp/buzzer input to module (pin 7) with key on, should measure 12 volts

Satisfactory

Unsatisfactory

Check continuity of transmission warning shut-off switch. After disconnecting from wire harness

Satisfactory

Load seat sensor at each sitting position until lamp and buzzer turn on. Then buckle seatbelt. Lamp and buzzer should turn off

Unsatisfactory

Repair circuit between module and lamp or buzzer connector (Pin 7)

Satisfactory

Check for voltage at battery feed to module (pin 12)

Measure resistance across switch contacts with ohmeter. Should exceed 500,000 ohms with contacts open, and less than 100 ohms with contacts closed

Unsatisfactory

Replace module

Satisfactory

Incorrect operating sequence used

Unsatisfactory

Repair feed circuit between module and power source

Satisfactory

Check continuity of ground circuit to module (Pin 4)

Unsatisfactory

Repair or replace switch

Satisfactory

With transmission warning switch disconnected, disconnect module from the wire assembly. Check for no continuity of switch input to ground at module connector (pin 9) no continuity indicates wire assembly circuit is ok

Unsatisfactory

Repair ground circuit to module

Satisfactory

Unsatisfactory

Repair short circuit between transmission switch input and connector to switch

Satisfactory

Reconnect transmission warning shut-off switch to wire assembly and put car in gear. Check continuity of switch input to ground at connector to module

Unsatisfactory

Repair open circuit between transmission switch input and connector to switch

Satisfactory

Replace module

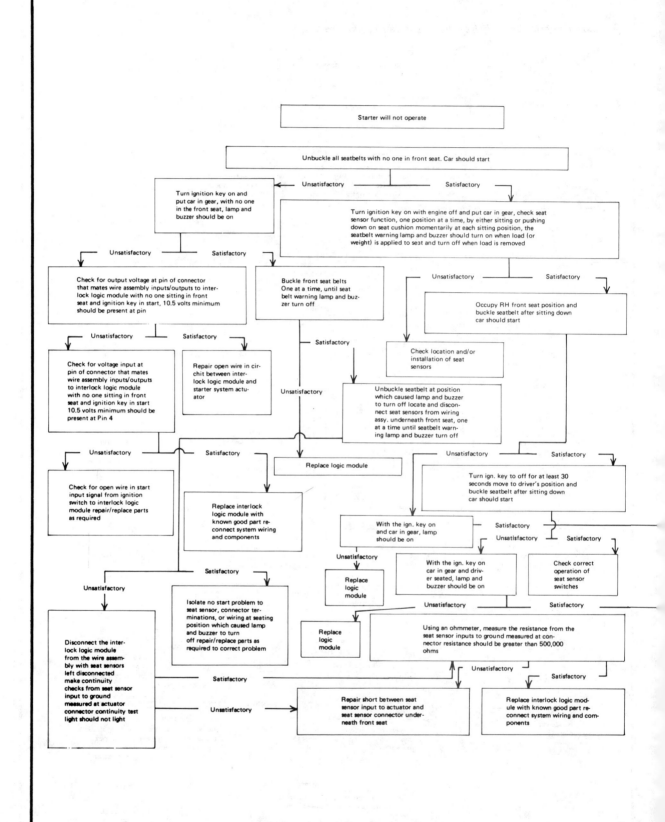

Starter will not operate

Unbuckle all seatbelts with no one in front seat. Car should start

Unsatisfactory — Satisfactory

Turn ignition key on and put car in gear, with no one in the front seat, lamp and buzzer should be on

Turn ignition key on with engine off and put car in gear, check seat sensor function, one position at a time, by either sitting or pushing down on seat cushion momentarily at each sitting position, the seatbelt warning lamp and buzzer should turn on when load (or weight) is applied to seat and turn off when load is removed

Unsatisfactory — Satisfactory

Check for output voltage at pin of connector that mates wire assembly inputs/outputs to interlock logic module with no one sitting in front seat and ignition key in start, 10.5 volts minimum should be present at pin

Buckle front seat belts One at a time, until seat belt warning lamp and buzzer turn off

Unsatisfactory — Satisfactory

Occupy RH front seat position and buckle seatbelt after sitting down car should start

Check for voltage input at pin of connector that mates wire assembly inputs/outputs to interlock logic module with no one sitting in front seat and ignition key in start 10.5 volts minimum should be present at Pin 4

Repair open wire in circhit between interlock logic module and starter system actuator

Satisfactory

Check location and/or installation of seat sensors

Unsatisfactory

Unbuckle seatbelt at position which caused lamp and buzzer to turn off locate and disconnect seat sensors from wiring assy. underneath front seat, one at a time until seatbelt warning lamp and buzzer turn off

Unsatisfactory — Satisfactory

Check for open wire in start input signal from ignition switch to interlock logic module repair/replace parts as required

Replace logic module

Unsatisfactory — Satisfactory

Turn ign. key to off for at least 30 seconds move to driver's position and buckle seatbelt after sitting down car should start

Replace interlock logic module with known good part reconnect system wiring and components

With the ign. key on and car in gear, lamp should be on

Satisfactory

Unsatisfactory — Satisfactory

Unsatisfactory

Replace logic module

With the ign. key on car in gear and driver seated, lamp and buzzer should be on

Check correct operation of seat sensor switches

Satisfactory

Isolate no start problem to seat sensor, connector terminations, or wiring at seating position which caused lamp and buzzer to turn off repair/replace parts as required to correct problem

Replace logic module

Unsatisfactory — Satisfactory

Using an ohmmeter, measure the resistance from the seat sensor inputs to ground measured at connector resistance should be greater than 500,000 ohms

Disconnect the interlock logic module from the wire assembly with seat sensors left disconnected make continuity checks from seat sensor input to ground measured at actuator connector continuity test light should not light

Satisfactory

Unsatisfactory — Satisfactory

Unsatisfactory

Repair short between seat sensor input to actuator and seat sensor connector underneath front seat

Replace interlock logic module with known good part reconnect system wiring and components

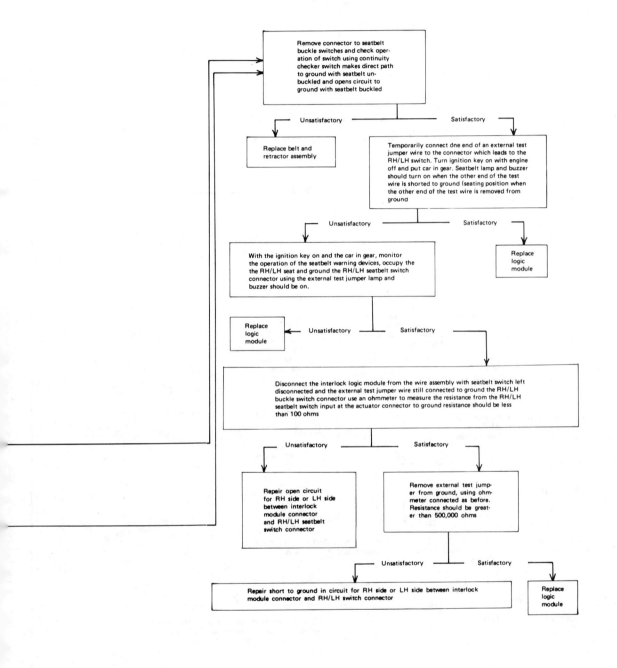

Remove connector to seatbelt buckle switches and check operation of switch using continuity checker switch makes direct path to ground with seatbelt unbuckled and opens circuit to ground with seatbelt buckled

Unsatisfactory → Replace belt and retractor assembly

Satisfactory → Temporarily connect óne end of an external test jumper wire to the connector which leads to the RH/LH switch. Turn ignition key on with engine off and put car in gear. Seatbelt lamp and buzzer should turn on when the other end of the test wire is shorted to ground (seating position when the other end of the test wire is removed from ground

Unsatisfactory → With the ignition key on and the car in gear, monitor the operation of the seatbelt warning devices, occupy the the RH/LH seat and ground the RH/LH seatbelt switch connector using the external test jumper lamp and buzzer should be on.

Satisfactory → Replace logic module

Unsatisfactory → Replace logic module

Satisfactory → Disconnect the interlock logic module from the wire assembly with seatbelt switch left disconnected and the external test jumper wire still connected to ground the RH/LH buckle switch connector use an ohmmeter to measure the resistance from the RH/LH seatbelt switch input at the actuator connector to ground resistance should be less than 100 ohms

Unsatisfactory → Repair open circuit for RH side or LH side between interlock module connector and RH/LH seatbelt switch connector

Satisfactory → Remove external test jumper from ground, using ohmmeter connected as before. Resistance should be greater than 500,000 ohms

Unsatisfactory → Repair short to ground in circuit for RH side or LH side between interlock module connector and RH/LH switch connector

Satisfactory → Replace logic module

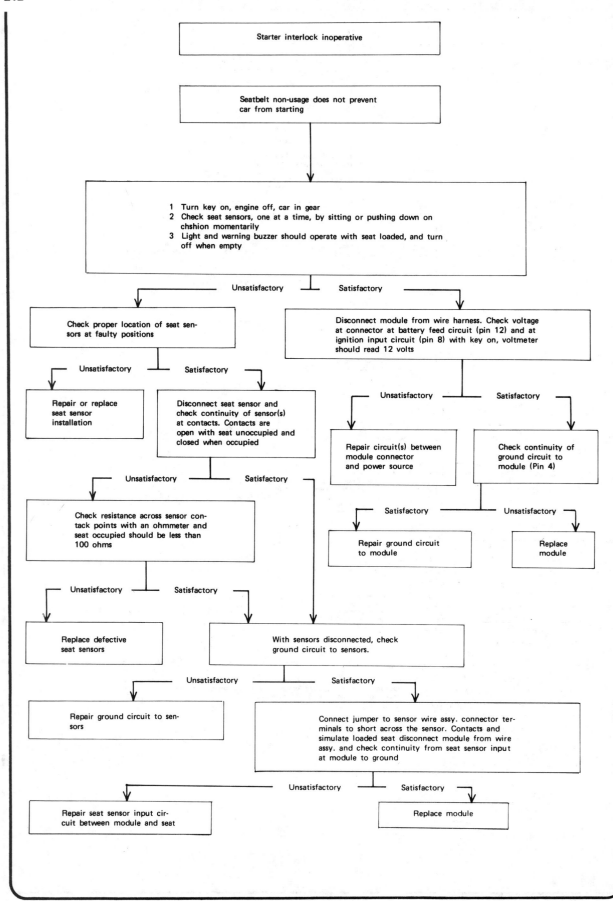

Starter interlock inoperative

Seatbelt non-usage does not prevent
car from starting

1 Turn key on, engine off, car in gear
2 Check seat sensors, one at a time, by sitting or pushing down on
  chshion momentarily
3 Light and warning buzzer should operate with seat loaded, and turn
  off when empty

Unsatisfactory   Satisfactory

Check proper location of seat sensors at faulty positions

Disconnect module from wire harness. Check voltage
at connector at battery feed circuit (pin 12) and at
ignition input circuit (pin 8) with key on, voltmeter
should read 12 volts

Unsatisfactory   Satisfactory

Repair or replace
seat sensor
installation

Disconnect seat sensor and
check continuity of sensor(s)
at contacts. Contacts are
open with seat unoccupied and
closed when occupied

Unsatisfactory   Satisfactory

Repair circuit(s) between
module connector
and power source

Check continuity of
ground circuit to
module (Pin 4)

Check resistance across sensor con-
tack points with an ohmmeter and
seat occupied should be less than
100 ohms

Satisfactory   Unsatisfactory

Repair ground circuit
to module

Replace
module

Unsatisfactory   Satisfactory

Replace defective
seat sensors

With sensors disconnected, check
ground circuit to sensors.

Unsatisfactory   Satisfactory

Repair ground circuit to sensors

Connect jumper to sensor wire assy. connector terminals to short across the sensor. Contacts and
simulate loaded seat disconnect module from wire
assy. and check continuity from seat sensor input
at module to ground

Unsatisfactory   Satisfactory

Repair seat sensor input circuit between module and seat

Replace module

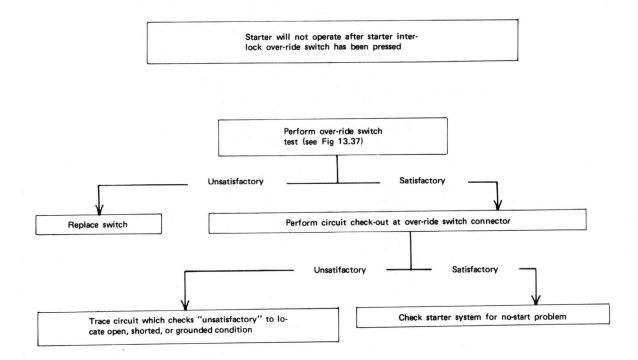

Starter will not operate after starter inter-lock over-ride switch has been pressed

Perform over-ride switch test (see Fig 13.37)

Unsatisfactory — Satisfactory

Replace switch

Perform circuit check-out at over-ride switch connector

Unsatifactory — Satisfactory

Trace circuit which checks "unsatisfactory" to locate open, shorted, or grounded condition

Check starter system for no-start problem

8 Air conditioning system - general description

Car air conditioning is the use of refrigeration principles to cool the incoming air to the car to a suitable level for the comfort of the occupants.

Liquid refrigerant is stored in a receiver under high pressure but when it is released into the evaporator by the operation of the expansion valve the result and decrease in pressure causes partial boiling. This process lowers the refrigerant temperature, then as it flows through the evaporator coils the passenger compartment air passing over the outside surface of the coils causes further boiling. The passenger compartment heat is partially absorbed by the boiling refrigerant and becomes transferred to the resultant refrigerant vapour. It is now necessary to dispose of the heat in the vapour, convert the vapour back to liquid then return the liquid to the starting point in the cycle. These functions are performed by the compressor which pumps the vapour from the evaporator under high pressure to the condenser which is situated in the outside air cooling stream at the front of the car. The increased pressure in the condenser raises the saturation (or condensation) temperature to a point higher than that of the outside air. As the refrigerant cools in the air stream, it condenses back to a liquid, still under high pressure, where it is returned to the receiver.

It may seen strange that comparatively cool passenger compartment air can be transferred to warmer air outside the car but the answer lie in the difference between the refrigerant pressure in the evaporator and the condenser. In the evaporator, the expansion valve reduced the pressure (and hence the boiling point) to a lower valve. This boiling point is lower than the passenger compartment temperature and therefore absorbs some of its heat. In the condenser, the compressor raises the condensation point above the outside air temperature and therefore heat is transferred from the heated refrigerant vapour to the outside air with the result that the refrigerant liquifies. The expansion valve and compressor therefore simply produce the conditions which will permit the laws of nature to function.

9 Air conditioning system - precautions

The refrigerant used in the air conditioning system is known as Refrigerant-12 (R-12). Although classified as a safe refrigerant because it is non-explosive, non-inflammable, non-corrosive and is practically odourless, it evaporates so quickly at normal atmospheric pressures that it freezes anything which contacts it. It is therefore imperative that any attention to the pressure system is carried out by a suitable qualified and equipped technician.

In the event of refrigerant contacting the eyes they must be immediately washed out with a few drops of sterile mineral oil then further washed with a copious supply of weak boracic acid solution.

To prevent a dangerous explosion no welding, steam cleaning, body baking processes or other operation which will heat any part of the system is permitted whilst the system is closed to atmosphere (whether filled with refrigerant or not).

10 Air conditioning system - discharging, evacuating and recharging

Whenever any item of equipment is to be removed from the air conditioning system it is essential that the refrigerant is discharged by a properly equipped specialist first of all. After any repairs etc. have been made the system must be evacuated and recharged, again by a specialist.

11 Air conditioning system - component parts

Controls

The function control lever (lower lever on control panel) actuates a vacuum selector which controls vacuum motors at the outside/recirculation door, air conditioning heat door, defrost/heat door and water valve. The compressor clutch is operated by a cam on the function control lever when air conditioning is selected.

The temperature control (upper) lever operates the temperature blend door in the evaporator case and the vacuum controlled water valve switch. A thermostat is located on the evaporator case to limit icing of the evaporator core. The blower motor resistor is located inside the blower housing next to the blower motor.

The on/off switch on the right of the panel controls the rear window defrosting.

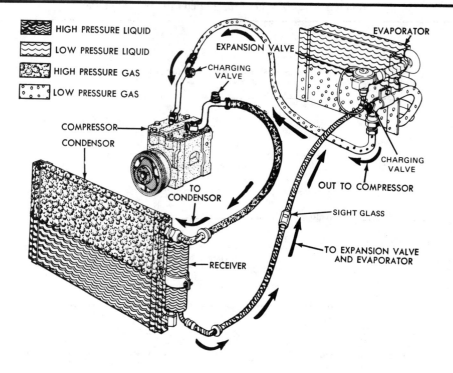

HIGH PRESSURE LIQUID
LOW PRESSURE LIQUID
HIGH PRESSURE GAS
LOW PRESSURE GAS

Fig. 13.40. Theoretical layout of the air conditioning system

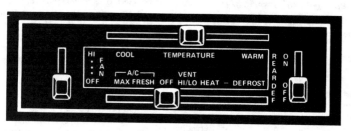

CONTROL IN "OFF" POSITION

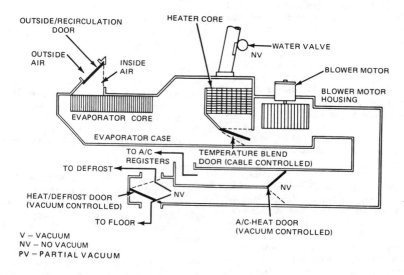

V – VACUUM
NV – NO VACUUM
PV – PARTIAL VACUUM

Fig. 13.42. Air conditioning 'off'

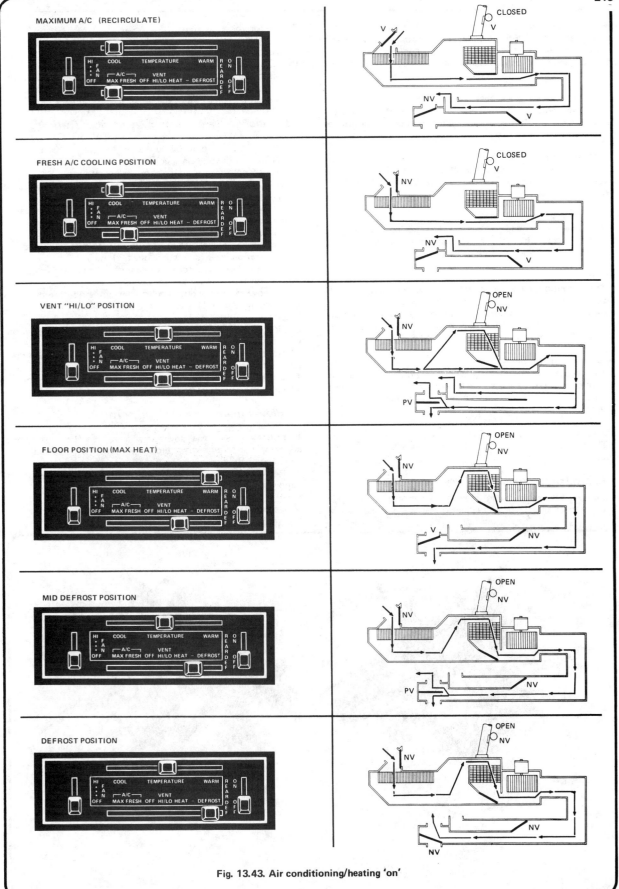

Fig. 13.43. Air conditioning/heating 'on'

Evaporator case assembly

This assembly is located beneath the instrument panel and must be removed to service the evaporator core and heater core. The case assembly also contains the outside/recirculation air door and temperature blend door.

Blower motor housing assembly

This assembly, located on the right side of the evaporator case, contains the blower motor, wheel assembly and resistor assembly.

Air conditioning heat air plenum

The plenum is attached to the rear portion of the evaporator case and contains the air conditioning heat door, the defrost/heat door and vacuum motor.

Compressor assembly

The compressor and clutch are located on the engine, mounted horizontally on the forward left-hand side. Belt tension is adjusted by repositioning an idle pulley.

Expansion valve

The expansion valve regulates the refrigerant flow into the evaporator according to the system requirements. A temperature sensor and pressure indicator are mounted in the evaporator outlet and signal the expansion valve to either open or close to regulate refrigerant flow.

Receiver/dehydrator unit

The receiver/dehydrator unit is used to store the refrigerant and is mounted on the side of the condenser support frame. The dehydrator is necessary to remove any possible moisture in the system.

Condenser

The condenser is sited ahead of the car engine cooling system radiator.

12 Control panel assembly - removal and refitting

1 Remove the two retaining screws from the face of the panel.
2 Disconnect the temperature control cable from the case of the evaporator.
3 Pull the control panel assembly away from the console.
4 Disconnect the vacuum harness from the vacuum selector and the two vacuum hoses from the water valve switch.
5 Disconnect all the wiring from the panel then remove the control head assembly.
6 Refitting is a reversal of the removal procedure.

13 Evaporator case assembly - removal and refitting

Note: This can only be done once the system has been discharged by a refrigeration specialist.
1 Disconnect the evaporator core refrigerant lines.
2 Disconnect the two heater hoses from the heater core tubes in the engine compartment.
3 Remove the glovebox, lower right-hand dash trim panel, heater control head assembly and lower instrument panel.
4 Disconnect the evaporator case vacuum hoses.
5 Disconnect the temperature control cable from the blend door operation lever (one screw, one push nut).
6 Remove the evaporator case retaining bolts located beside the outside/recirculation air control door.
7 Remove the air conditioning and heater distribution ducts.
8 Disconnect the blower lead plug from the blower motor resistors.
9 Remove the three evaporator/dash panel securing nuts in the engine compartment.
10 Rotate the assembly downwards and away from the dash panel and out from under the instrument panel.
11 Refitting is the reverse of the removal procedure, following which the system must be evacuated and recharged.

14 Blower motor - removal and refitting

1 Initially remove the glovebox then remove the three screws attaching the scroll shaped blower motor housing to the right-hand end of the evaporator case.
2 Remove the blower motor housing (three screws) then remove the motor from the front portion of the housing (three nuts).
3 Refitting is a reversal of the removal procedure.

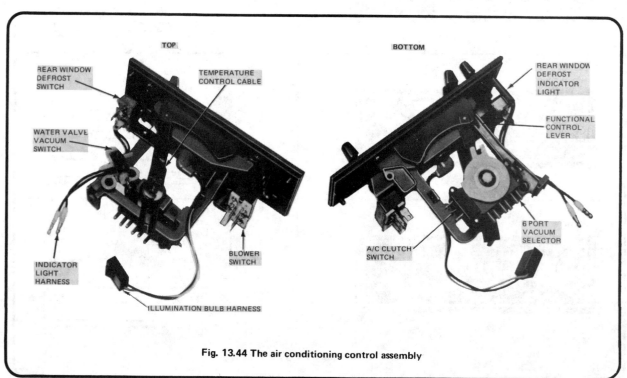

Fig. 13.44 The air conditioning control assembly

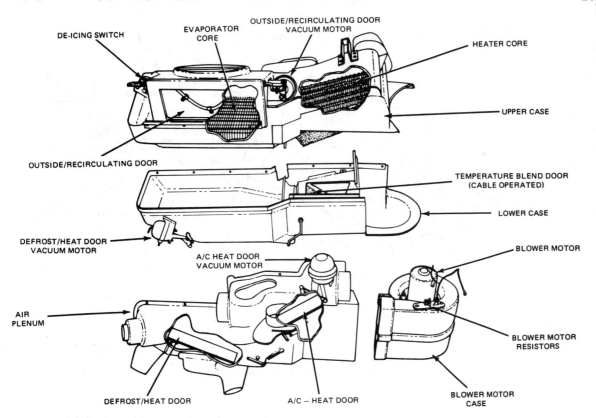

DE-ICING SWITCH

EVAPORATOR CORE

OUTSIDE/RECIRCULATING DOOR VACUUM MOTOR

HEATER CORE

UPPER CASE

OUTSIDE/RECIRCULATING DOOR

TEMPERATURE BLEND DOOR (CABLE OPERATED)

LOWER CASE

DEFROST/HEAT DOOR VACUUM MOTOR

A/C HEAT DOOR VACUUM MOTOR

BLOWER MOTOR

AIR PLENUM

BLOWER MOTOR RESISTORS

DEFROST/HEAT DOOR

A/C – HEAT DOOR

BLOWER MOTOR CASE

Fig. 13.45. Exploded view of the evaporator can assembly

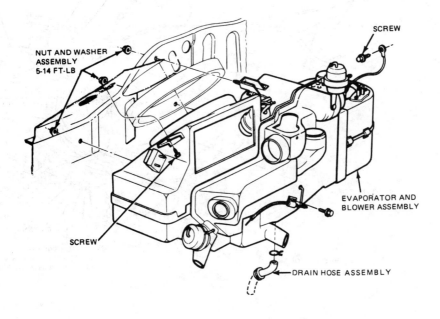

SCREW

NUT AND WASHER ASSEMBLY 5-14 FT-LB

EVAPORATOR AND BLOWER ASSEMBLY

SCREW

DRAIN HOSE ASSEMBLY

Fig. 13.46. The evaporator and blower installation

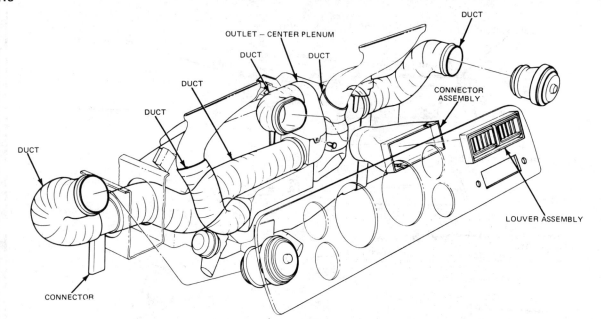

Fig. 13.47. The air ducting layout

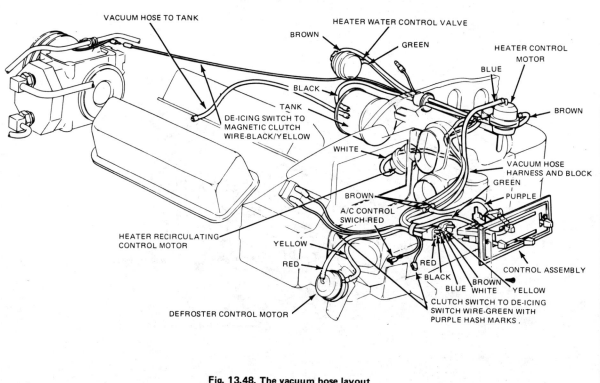

Fig. 13.48. The vacuum hose layout

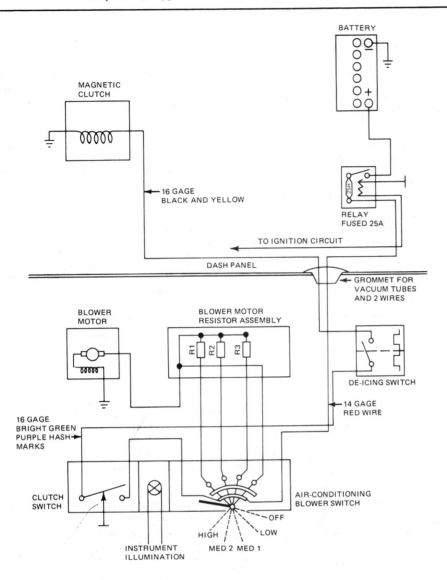

Fig. 13.49. Schematic wiring diagram of air conditioning system

15 Blower motor resistor - removal and refitting

1 Initially remove the glovebox then disconnect the plug and two resistor mounting screws.
2 Refitting is a reversal of the removal procedure.

16 Evaporator core and/or heater core - removal and refitting

1 Remove the evaporator case then disconnect the vacuum motor linkage from the air conditioning heat and defrost/heat doors.
2 Remove the foam evaporator case/dash panel pad located around the evaporator core inlet and outlet.
3 Remove the scroll shaped blower motor housing (three screws) on the right-hand end of the evaporator case.
4 Remove the twelve screws with secure the plenum to the rear of the evaporator case.
5 Dismantle the evaporator case, taking care not to damage the case moulding.
6 Carefully remove the de-icing bulb from the front of the evaporator core.

7 Remove the evaporator case/core mounting screws from the front of the case.
8 Remove the evaporator and heater core.
9 Refitting is a reversal of the removal procedure.

17 Condenser and receiver/dehydrator unit - removal and refitting

Note: This can only be done once the system has been discharged by a refrigeration specialist.
1 Remove the upper radiator air deflector.
2 Disconnect the condenser/compressor hose at the condenser.
3 Disconnect the evaporator/condenser hose at the receiver tank. Plug any open hoses and fittings to prevent the ingress of dirt.
4 Remove the upper condenser mounting brackets.
5 Remove the two condenser mountings bolts (one on each side).
6 Slide the condenser base forwards and downwards through the front body opening.
7 When refitting, first position the condenser-to-radiator support and install the two lower mounting screws.
8 Fit the two upper condenser mounting brackets.
9 Connect the hoses and install the upper radiator air deflector.

10 Arrange for the system to be evacuated and recharged.

18 Compressor - removal and refitting

Note: Initially arrange for the system to be discharged by a refrigeration specialist.

1   Check the compressor oil level for reference purposes later.
2   Disconnect the two compressor hoses.
3   Energise the compressor clutch and then remove the clutch mounting bolt.
4   Fit a 5/8 - 11 in bolt in the clutch driveshaft hole and tighten it (with the clutch still energized) to withdraw the clutch from the shaft. Disconnect the clutch feed wire at the convector.
5   Loosen the idler pulley and remove the drive belt and clutch.
6   Finally remove the compressor mounting bolts and lift away the compressor.
7   When refitting the compressor, whether it be new or used, set the oil level to that noted at paragraph 1. Also ensure that the compressor shaft is perfectly clean, free from burrs, dry and brightly polished.
8   Mount the clutch on the shaft and fit the mounting screw and washer finger-tight. Place the unit on the mounting bracket and install the four mounting bolts finger-tight.
9   Connect the clutch lead, energize the clutch and torque tighten the mounting bolt to the valve given in the Specifications.
10 Fit the belt then adjust and tighten the idler pulley.
11 Connect the compressor hoses then arrange for the system to be evacuated and recharged by a refrigeration specialist.
12 Run the compressor for about ten minutes then check the oil level and add or remove oil as necessary (see Section 8.23).
13 Finally, tighten the clutch mounting screw to the correct torque.

19 Magnetic clutch - removal and refitting

1   Loosen and remove the drivebelt then energise the clutch and remove the clutch mounting bolt.
2   Fit a 5/8 - 11 in bolt in the clutch driveshaft hole and tighten it (with the clutch still energised) to withdraw the clutch from the shaft.
3   Carefully remove any burrs or dirt from the compressor shaft; the shaft must be dry and brightly polished. Install the clutch, clutch mounting bolt and washer.
4   Energize the clutch and torque tighten the bolt to the specified valve.
5   Fit and adjust the drivebelt.

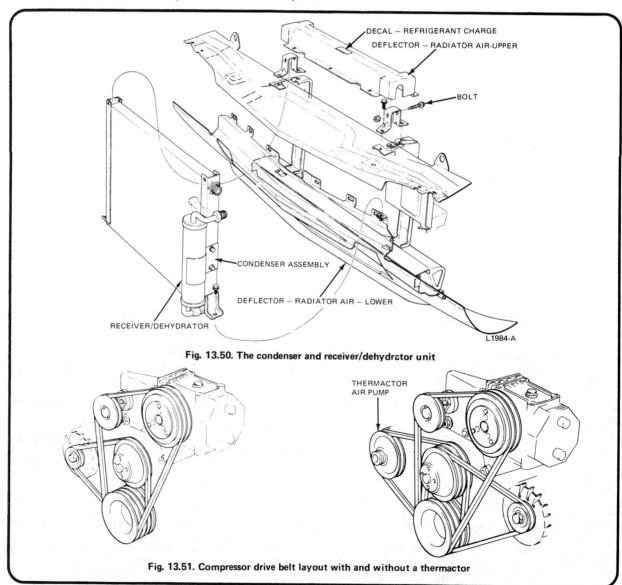

Fig. 13.50. The condenser and receiver/dehydrator unit

Fig. 13.51. Compressor drive belt layout with and without a thermactor

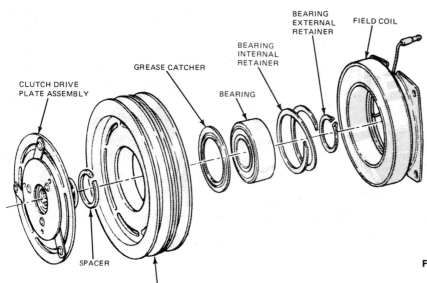

CLUTCH DRIVE PLATE ASSEMBLY · GREASE CATCHER · BEARING INTERNAL RETAINER · BEARING · BEARING EXTERNAL RETAINER · FIELD COIL · SPACER · PULLEY ASSEMBLY

Fig. 13.52 The compressor clutch assembly

20 Compressor valve plate and head gasket - removal and refitting

Note: Initially arrange for the system to be discharged by a refrigeration specialist.

1 Place a suitable drip tray beneath the compressor then remove the cylinder head bolts.
2 Using a soft faced hammer tap the valve plate and cylinder head upwards on the overhanging edge of the valve plate.
3 Using the same method, tap the valve plate off the cylinder head.
4 Remove the drip tray then carefully remove all traces of gasket from the cylinder head, valve plate and cylinder face. Take great care not to scratch the mating surfaces.
5 When refitting, apply a light film of clean refrigeration oil to each face of the valve plate gasket.
6 Position the valve pate gasket on the cylinder block face so that it is located on the dowels then apply a light film of clean refrigeration oil on each side of the cylinder head gasket.
7 Place the gasket and cylinder head on the cylinder block, then tighten the cylinder head bolts to the correct torque.
8 Arrange for the system to be evacuated and recharged by a refrigeration specialist.

21 Compressor crankshaft seals - removal and refitting

1 Oil leakage can occur from the carbon ring, bellows of the oil seal assembly or the cover plate rectangular 'O' ring. Refer to Fig. 13.55. which shows the oil leakage paths. If leakage is evident, it is essential that the system is discharged, before any repair is undertaken, by a refrigeration specialist.
2 Loosen and remove the compressor drivebelt.
3 Remove the clutch and Woodruff key.
4 Carefully remove the secondary dust shield to avoid marking the shaft.
5 Carefully clean all dirt from around the seal plate and place a small container beneath the seal plate.
6 Remove the seal plate retaining screws then carefully remove the plate and gasket taking care not to mark the sealing surfaces or the polished shaft surface.
7 Remove the carbon seal ring and seal housing.
8 Carefully clean the compressor shaft, seal plate and compressor gasket faces.
9 Check for nicks and burrs on the crankshaft front bearing journal and on the crankshaft surface.
10 When fitting a new seal assembly wash the component parts in clean refrigeration oil.
11 Position the seal over the end of the shaft, carbon ring

retainer facing outwards. Move it backwards and forwards a few times to ensure a good seal.
12 Push the seal fully home, ensuring that the seal drive ring slots engage with the drive pins on the shaft bearing journal face.
13 Locate the carbon ring in the seal ring retainer with the polished carbon surface facing outwards.
14 Apply a light film of clear refrigeration oil on the crankcase and seal cover plate mating faces, then place the rectangular 'O' ring in the groove in the crankcase.
15 Fit the seal cover plate, polished side towards the carbon ring, then fit the retaining screws.
16 Tighten the cover screws evenly whilst turning the crankshaft and at the same time ensure that the clearance between the crankshaft and the hole in the cover is even all the way round.
17 Tighten the cover securing screws diagonally to the specified torque.
18 Ensure that the compressor shaft is clean then refit the Woodruff key.
19 Replace the clutch and belt, then check the belt tension.
20 Check the compressor oil level (see Section 8.23).
21 Arrange for the system to be evacuated and recharged by a refrigeration specialist.

22 Clutch bearing - removal and refitting

1 Remove the clutch assembly as previously described. Place it face down then remove the external retainer from the drive plate shaft.
2 Support the clutch, face down, by its outer edge so as to clear the drive plate. Insert a 5/8 - 11 in bolt through the drive plate shaft and hand tighten the bolt.
3 Carefully apply enough pressure on the bolt to free the shaft from the inner race of the bearing then remove the drive plate assembly. **Note:** If any warping or damage is evident the entire clutch assembly must be renewed.
4 Remove the internal retainer from the pulley assembly.
5 Support the pulley, face up, by the bearing bore then use a suitable tool applied to the bearing **inner** race and press at the bearing. Do not remove the grease catcher.
6 When refitting the bearing, first ensure that all the bearing contact surfaces are clean.
7 Support the pulley assembly near the bearing bore then press the bearing in squarely by its **outer** race. Refit the internal retainer.
8 Support the pulley assembly, face up, by the inner race, then insert a 5/8 - 11 in bolt into the front of the drive face plate and carefully press the shaft into the bearing inner race by exerting pressure on the bolt.

9   Refit the external retainer onto the drive plate shaft and rotate the pulley relative to the drive plate to ensure that it is secure but not binding.

10 Fit the clutch assembly to the compressor shaft and adjust the belt tension.

23 Compressor - oil level check

1   Under normal running circumstances there is no need to check the compressor oil level. However, if leakage of oil or refrigerant has occurred, or if for any other reason it is suspected that the oil level is low (eg; after fitment of a replacement compressor) the level must be checked. Before any attempt is made to remove the oil filler plug it is essential that the system is discharged by a refrigeration specialist.

2   Obtain a piece of 1/8 in (3 mm) diameter rod and make up a dipstick to the dimensions shown in Fig. 13.56.

3   Remove the oil filler plug and check the oil level. If necessary revolve the compressor crankshaft to ensure that the full depth of oil is measured. Do not allow any dirt or grease to enter the compressor.

4   If the oil level is below the minimum dipstick marking top-up using oil to Ford Part Number 'C9AZ-19577-A (ESA-M2C31-A). If too much oil is present, either draw out the excess using a trap as shown in Fig. 13.57, or remove the compressor from the car and tip out the surplus. To completely fill the crankcase will require approximately 10 oz. of the oil.

5   Replace the filler plug then arrange for the system to be evacuated and recharged by a refrigeration specialist.

6   Run the system for about ten minutes to allow the oil to circulate and drain back to the sump then again arrange for the system to be discharged. Repeat the oil level check already described then arrange for the system to be evacuated and recharged.

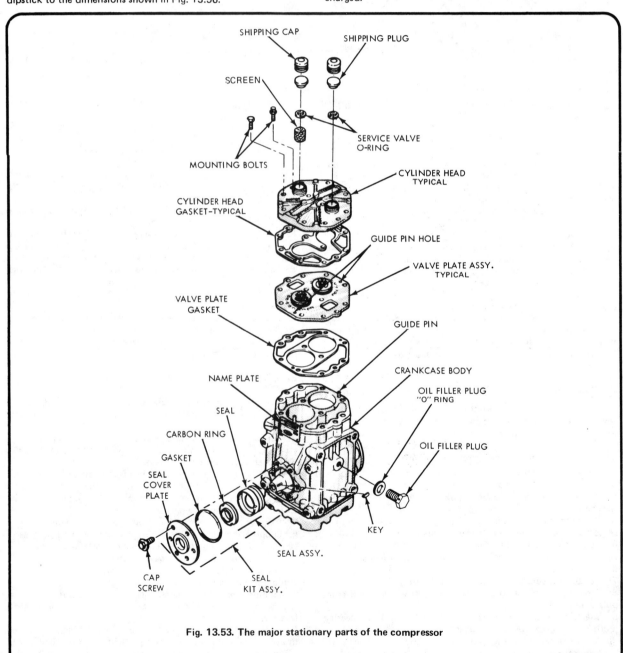

Fig. 13.53. The major stationary parts of the compressor

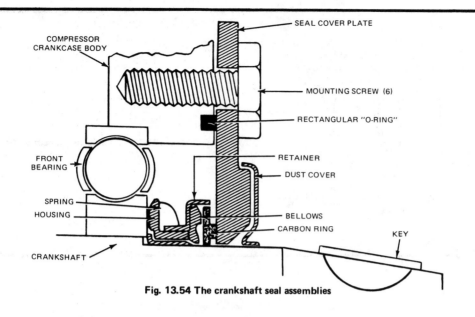

Fig. 13.54 The crankshaft seal assemblies

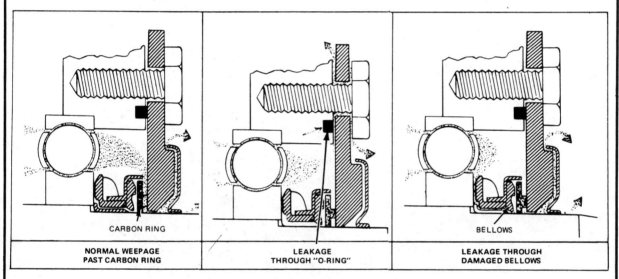

| NORMAL WEEPAGE PAST CARBON RING | LEAKAGE THROUGH "O-RING" | LEAKAGE THROUGH DAMAGED BELLOWS |

Fig. 13.55 Oil leakage paths due to defective seals

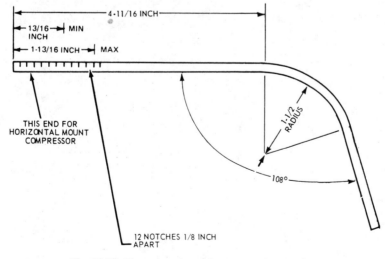

Fig. 13.56. Dimensions for making an oil level dipstick

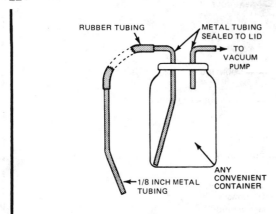

Fig. 13.57. A suitable compressor oil trap

Metric conversion tables

Inches	Decimals	Millimetres	Millimetres to Inches		Inches to Millimetres	
			mm	Inches	Inches	mm
1/64	0.015625	0.3969	0.01	0.00039	0.001	0.0254
1/32	0.03125	0.7937	0.02	0.00079	0.002	0.0508
3/64	0.046875	1.1906	0.03	0.00118	0.003	0.0762
1/16	0.0625	1.5875	0.04	0.00157	0.004	0.1016
5/64	0.078125	1.9844	0.05	0.00197	0.005	0.1270
3/32	0.09375	2.3812	0.06	0.00236	0.006	0.1524
7/64	0.109375	2.7781	0.07	0.00276	0.007	0.1778
1/8	0.125	3.1750	0.08	0.00315	0.008	0.2032
9/64	0.140625	3.5719	0.09	0.00354	0.009	0.2286
5/32	0.15625	3.9687	0.1	0.00394	0.01	0.254
11/64	0.171875	4.3656	0.2	0.00787	0.02	0.508
3/16	0.1875	4.7625	0.3	0.01181	0.03	0.762
13/64	0.203125	5.1594	0.4	0.01575	0.04	1.016
7/32	0.21875	5.5562	0.5	0.01969	0.05	1.270
15/64	0.234375	5.9531	0.6	0.02362	0.06	1.524
1/4	0.25	6.3500	0.7	0.02756	0.07	1.778
17/64	0.265625	6.7469	0.8	0.03150	0.08	2.032
9/32	0.28125	7.1437	0.9	0.03543	0.09	2.286
19/64	0.296875	7.5406	1	0.03947	0.1	2.54
5/16	0.3125	7.9375	2	0.07874	0.2	5.08
21/64	0.328125	8.3344	3	0.11811	0.3	7.62
11/32	0.34375	8.7312	4	0.15748	0.4	10.16
23/64	0.359375	9.1281	5	0.19685	0.5	12.70
3/8	0.375	9.5250	6	0.23622	0.6	15.24
25/64	0.390625	9.9219	7	0.27559	0.7	17.78
13/32	0.40625	10.3187	8	0.31496	0.8	20.32
27/64	0.421875	10.7156	9	0.35433	0.9	22.86
7/16	0.4375	11.1125	10	0.39370	1	25.4
29/64	0.453125	11.5094	11	0.43307	2	50.8
15/32	0.46875	11.9062	12	0.47244	3	76.2
31/64	0.484375	12.3031	13	0.51181	4	101.6
1/2	0.5	12.7000	14	0.55118	5	127.0
33/64	0.515625	13.0969	15	0.59055	6	152.4
17/32	0.53125	13.4937	16	0.62992	7	177.8
35/64	0.546875	13.8906	17	0.66929	8	203.2
9/16	0.5625	14.2875	18	0.70866	9	228.6
37/64	0.578125	14.6844	19	0.74803	10	254.0
19/32	0.59375	15.0812	20	0.78740	11	279.4
39/64	0.609375	15.4781	21	0.82677	12	304.8
5/8	0.625	15.8750	22	0.86614	13	330.2
41/64	0.640625	16.2719	23	0.90551	14	355.6
21/32	0.65625	16.6687	24	0.94488	15	381.0
43/64	0.671875	17.0656	25	0.98425	16	406.4
11/16	0.6875	17.4625	26	1.02362	17	431.8
45/64	0.703125	17.8594	27	1.06299	18	457.2
23/32	0.71875	18.2562	28	1.10236	19	482.6
47/64	0.734375	18.6531	29	1.14173	20	508.0
3/4	0.75	19.0500	30	1.18110	21	533.4
49/64	0.765625	19.4469	31	1.22047	22	558.8
25/32	0.78125	19.8437	32	1.25984	23	584.2
51/64	0.796875	20.2406	33	1.29921	24	609.6
13/16	0.8125	20.6375	34	1.33858	25	635.0
53/64	0.828125	21.0344	35	1.37795	26	660.4
27/32	0.84375	21.4312	36	1.41732	27	685.8
55/64	0.859375	21.8281	37	1.4567	28	711.2
7/8	0.875	22.2250	38	1.4961	29	736.6
57/64	0.890625	22.6219	39	1.5354	30	762.0
29/32	0.90625	23.0187	40	1.5748	31	787.4
59/64	0.921875	23.4156	41	1.6142	32	812.8
15/16	0.9375	23.8125	42	1.6535	33	838.2
61/64	0.953125	24.2094	43	1.6929	34	863.6
31/32	0.96875	24.6062	44	1.7323	35	889.0
63/64	0.984375	25.0031	45	1.7717	36	914.4

Safety first!

Professional motor mechanics are trained in safe working procedures. However enthusiastic you may be about getting on with the job in hand, do take the time to ensure that your safety is not put at risk. A moment's lack of attention can result in an accident, as can failure to observe certain elementary precautions.

There will always be new ways of having accidents, and the following points do not pretend to be a comprehensive list of all dangers; they are intended rather to make you aware of the risks and to encourage a safety-conscious approach to all work you carry out on your vehicle.

Essential DOs and DON'Ts

DON'T rely on a single jack when working underneath the vehicle. Always use reliable additional means of support, such as axle stands, securely placed under a part of the vehicle that you know will not give way.

DON'T attempt to loosen or tighten high-torque nuts (e.g. wheel hub nuts) while the vehicle is on a jack; it may be pulled off.

DON'T start the engine without first ascertaining that the transmission is in neutral (or 'Park' where applicable) and the parking brake applied.

DON'T suddenly remove the filler cap from a hot cooling system – cover it with a cloth and release the pressure gradually first, or you may get scalded by escaping coolant.

DON'T attempt to drain oil until you are sure it has cooled sufficiently to avoid scalding you.

DON'T grasp any part of the engine, exhaust or catalytic converter without first ascertaining that it is sufficiently cool to avoid burning you.

DON'T allow brake fluid or antifreeze to contact vehicle paintwork.

DON'T syphon toxic liquids such as fuel, brake fluid or antifreeze by mouth, or allow them to remain on your skin.

DON'T inhale dust – it may be injurious to health (see *Asbestos* below).

DON'T allow any spilt oil or grease to remain on the floor – wipe it up straight away, before someone slips on it.

DON'T use ill-fitting spanners or other tools which may slip and cause injury.

DON'T attempt to lift a heavy component which may be beyond your capability – get assistance.

DON'T rush to finish a job, or take unverified short cuts.

DON'T allow children or animals in or around an unattended vehicle.

DO wear eye protection when using power tools such as drill, sander, bench grinder etc, and when working under the vehicle.

DO use a barrier cream on your hands prior to undertaking dirty jobs – it will protect your skin from infection as well as making the dirt easier to remove afterwards; but make sure your hands aren't left slippery.

DO keep loose clothing (cuffs, tie etc) and long hair well out of the way of moving mechanical parts.

DO remove rings, wristwatch etc, before working on the vehicle – especially the electrical system.

DO ensure that any lifting tackle used has a safe working load rating adequate for the job.

DO keep your work area tidy – it is only too easy to fall over articles left lying around.

DO get someone to check periodically that all is well, when working alone on the vehicle.

DO carry out work in a logical sequence and check that everything is correctly assembled and tightened afterwards.

DO remember that your vehicle's safety affects that of yourself and others. If in doubt on any point, get specialist advice.

IF, in spite of following these precautions, you are unfortunate enough to injure yourself, seek medical attention as soon as possible.

Asbestos

Certain friction, insulating, sealing, and other products – such as brake linings, brake bands, clutch linings, torque converters, gaskets, etc – contain asbestos. *Extreme care must be taken to avoid inhalation of dust from such products since it is hazardous to health.* If in doubt, assume that they *do* contain asbestos.

Fire

Remember at all times that petrol (gasoline) is highly flammable. Never smoke, or have any kind of naked flame around, when working on the vehicle. But the risk does not end there – a spark caused by an electrical short-circuit, by two metal surfaces contacting each other, by careless use of tools, or even by static electricity built up in your body under certain conditions, can ignite petrol vapour, which in a confined space is highly explosive.

Always disconnect the battery earth (ground) terminal before working on any part of the fuel or electrical system, and never risk spilling fuel on to a hot engine or exhaust.

It is recommended that a fire extinguisher of a type suitable for fuel and electrical fires is kept handy in the garage or workplace at all times. Never try to extinguish a fuel or electrical fire with water.

Fumes

Certain fumes are highly toxic and can quickly cause unconsciousness and even death if inhaled to any extent. Petrol (gasoline) vapour comes into this category, as do the vapours from certain solvents such as trichloroethylene. Any draining or pouring of such volatile fluids should be done in a well ventilated area.

When using cleaning fluids and solvents, read the instructions carefully. Never use materials from unmarked containers – they may give off poisonous vapours.

Never run the engine of a motor vehicle in an enclosed space such as a garage. Exhaust fumes contain carbon monoxide which is extremely poisonous; if you need to run the engine, always do so in the open air or at least have the rear of the vehicle outside the workplace.

If you are fortunate enough to have the use of an inspection pit, never drain or pour petrol, and never run the engine, while the vehicle is standing over it; the fumes, being heavier than air, will concentrate in the pit with possibly lethal results.

The battery

Never cause a spark, or allow a naked light, near the vehicle's battery. It will normally be giving off a certain amount of hydrogen gas, which is highly explosive.

Always disconnect the battery earth (ground) terminal before working on the fuel or electrical systems.

If possible, loosen the filler plugs or cover when charging the battery from an external source. Do not charge at an excessive rate or the battery may burst.

Take care when topping up and when carrying the battery. The acid electrolyte, even when diluted, is very corrosive and should not be allowed to contact the eyes or skin.

If you ever need to prepare electrolyte yourself, always add the acid slowly to the water, and never the other way round. Protect against splashes by wearing rubber gloves and goggles.

When jump starting a car using a booster battery, for negative earth (ground) vehicles, connect the jump leads in the following sequence: First connect one jump lead between the positive (+) terminals of the two batteries. Then connect the other jump lead first to the negative (−) terminal of the booster battery, and then to a good earthing (ground) point on the vehicle to be started, at least 18 in (45 cm) from the battery if possible. Ensure that hands and jump leads are clear of any moving parts, and that the two vehicles do not touch. Disconnect the leads in the reverse order.

Mains electricity

When using an electric power tool, inspection light etc, which works from the mains, always ensure that the appliance is correctly connected to its plug and that, where necessary, it is properly earthed (grounded). Do not use such appliances in damp conditions and, again, beware of creating a spark or applying excessive heat in the vicinity of fuel or fuel vapour.

Ignition HT voltage

A severe electric shock can result from touching certain parts of the ignition system, such as the HT leads, when the engine is running or being cranked, particularly if components are damp or the insulation is defective. Where an electronic ignition system is fitted, the HT voltage is much higher and could prove fatal.

Index